12-4-10

To Bob

A TRUE BASEBALL FAN!

I HOPE THE BOOK BRINGS BACK

MANY HAPPY MEMORIES OF THE

HALL OF FAME.

Deanna Corcoran

Induction Day
at Cooperstown

*A History of the Baseball
Hall of Fame Ceremony*

DENNIS CORCORAN

McFarland & Company, Inc., Publishers
Jefferson, North Carolina, and London

Unless otherwise noted, all photographs come from the
National Baseball Hall of Fame Library, Cooperstown, New York.

Library of Congress Cataloguing-in-Publication Data

Corcoran, Dennis.
Induction day at Cooperstown : a history of the Baseball Hall of
Fame ceremony / Dennis Corcoran.
p.   cm.
Includes bibliographical references and index.

ISBN 978-0-7864-4416-8
softcover : 50# alkaline paper

1. National Baseball Hall of Fame and Museum — Rituals— History.
2. Baseball players— United States— Biography.   I National
Baseball Hall of Fame and Museum.   II. Title.
GV863.A1C635   2011   796.35709747'74 — dc22   2010040329

British Library cataloguing data are available

Front cover: 1947 Induction Ceremony, Ford Frick (left) and Ed Walsh
(*National Baseball Hall of Fame and Museum*).

Manufactured in the United States of America

*McFarland & Company, Inc., Publishers
Box 611, Jefferson, North Carolina 28640
www.mcfarlandpub.com*

To the memory of my younger brother Tommy,
who left this world at the tender age
of two and a half

Table of Contents

Acknowledgments

A common theme in most of the Hall of Fame speeches is that the inductees could not have reached their ultimate honor without the help of many people along the way. I feel the same way because the publication of this book could not have reached fruition without the help of many people.

I will start by thanking my family, beginning with my mother and father. My father was my friend and companion for my first baseball game at Yankee Stadium in 1953, along with many other games throughout the years. My mother wasn't a baseball fan but she supported me and my baseball card collection. We lived in a four-room apartment (Parkchester section of the Bronx), and it was my father and not my mother who eventually made the decision to throw out my baseball cards.

It was my wife, Pat, who encouraged me years later to renew my interest in collecting baseball cards, which helped revive many happy memories. Her support helped to ignite a baseball odyssey that ultimately led to the writing of this book. My daughter Brenda's future husband, Chris, was a semipro baseball player and his trips to Cooperstown to participate in several tournaments brought many happy moments to all of us, especially when he hit a home run at Doubleday Field. My daughter encouraged me to think about writing another book since I had written a local history book about our hometown of Pleasantville back in the 1990s. She has since shown her support with words of encouragement while reading all my drafts prior to the final manuscript and allowing me the time to work on my book each time we visited her and Chris in Florida. Chris has been invaluable with all his computer assistance with the only problem being that he and Brenda live 1,300 miles away. Finally, the source of all my inspiration has been my "little guys," six-year-old Tyler and four-year-old Topher, my two grandsons. My brother Bill, brothers-in-law Frank and Robert Power and Frank's son-in-law Frank Kehoe have also helped with their encouragement.

Longtime friends Bruce and Carol Thomas, along with Frank and Irene Gatto, have also been very helpful: Bruce, for his patience in listening to me early in the process, and Carol for her warm hospitality when we visited them in upstate New York; the Gattos for supporting me every step of the way, including using the publishing expertise of their good friends, Gerry and Barbara Levine. Gerry described the production end while Barbara gave me insight into book publishing.

My friend Bert Ruiz has been one of my biggest supporters with his encouragement and experience, having written a book, *The Colombian Civil War*, for McFarland.

I am grateful to the many fans I have interviewed, including Catherine Walker, Fred St. John, Homer Ousterhout, Stacy Samuels, and especially Willis Gardner.

I want to pay tribute to the Society for American Baseball Research (SABR). As a member since 2002, I've had many pleasant experiences with this group beginning with a local chapter in Westchester County. They have always been supportive, in particular Vinnie Gennaro and the coordinator, Cliff Blau. Vin has always offered encouragement and I will discuss Cliff in detail later.

I have met many new friends during the annual national SABR Convention. Father Gerry Beirne, Len Lewin, Lyle Spatz and John Dillon have all been helpful, with special thanks going to Rick Huhn, another McFarland author, for his encouragement.

Also, a note of thanks to another SABR member, Harry Higham, who was instrumental in helping me meet renowned baseball historian John Thorn. John was encouraging with his support of the book's concept.

During my years of research, the Mount Pleasant Library in Pleasantville has been invaluable in helping me find numerous books that have helped in my research, especially reference librarians Martha Mesiti, and Natasha Padzerskaia, along with Suzanne Haber. Director John Fearon was also invaluable with his computer assistance. Another local person who has helped me with all my office needs is big-time Yankees fan Bob Angiello.

Also, Wayne Wright and Amy Blechman of the New York State Historical Association helped me locate information about the weather records for most of the induction ceremonies. Jim Kelvin, the publisher of *The Freeman's Journal*, has been very gracious in supplying two photos from recent inductions.

It goes without saying that this project would never have succeeded without the Hall of Fame. Hall of Famers Bob Feller, Bobby Doerr, Robin Roberts, Monte Irvin and George Kell were all helpful with their telephone interviews. A special thanks to Feller's wife, Annie, for sharing information about the special spouses activities that take place each induction weekend. I'd like to salute Ralph Kiner for allowing me to interview him in person and Fergie Jenkins, who has always been so gracious the several times I have interviewed him in Cooperstown. Dr. Susan Dellinger helped also with a story about her grandfather, Edd Roush.

The following people from the Hall of Fame were helpful: recent retirees Peter Clarke and Ted Spencer as well as former historian Cliff Kachline and the retired Bill Guilfoile. Former director of the Hall of Fame Howard Talbot and the retired president of the Hall of Fame's board of directors, Ed Stack, went out of their way to allow me to meet with them twice for interviews. Tom Heitz, former librarian at the Hall of Fame, was always accommodating whenever I asked for his assistance.

I would also like to express my appreciation to Bill Deane, the former director of research for the Hall of Fame Library, who was the person most responsible for guiding me when I began this journey.

Everyone at the Hall of Fame has gone out of his way to assist me, beginning with Jeff Idelson, Hall of Fame president, whom I interviewed when he was vice president of communications and education. I would also like to express my appreciation to Hall officials Brad Horn and Craig Muder, along with Pat Kelly, the director of the photo archives, for her warm assistance in helping me finalize the photos for this book.

Thanks to the research staff, beginning with library director Jim Gates, and in particular the director of research, Tim Wiles, along with library associates Freddie Barowski and Gabe Schector. Tim made himself available to answer all my questions, and Freddie and Gabe always responded to my requests over the last five years.

I would like to express my gratitude to my neighbor and friend, Bob Hughes, along with his wife, Betsy. She helped me with some grammatical corrections, and most of all Bob, who helped organize my manuscript with his technological expertise.

I'm indebted to Jim and Margaret Wolff. They have made all my time and effort so much easier by not only providing me with a warm and friendly home away from home during the last five years, but also by listening and advising me as well. A big part of the wonderful atmosphere at their Bed and Breakfast Inn has been their two lovable beagles, Ruby and Molly.

Westchester SABR coordinator Cliff Blau has been my editor, baseball fact checker, and advisor during this whole process and I feel very fortunate to have had him to assist me in completing this manuscript.

Finally, I owe a special debt of gratitude to my sister Pat and her expertise as a manuscript editor. She has spent countless hours reading and editing my drafts. I don't know where the book would be without her.

Preface

What has made me travel three and a half hours from my home in Pleasantville, New York, to Cooperstown numerous times over the last five years and spend many hours and days at the National Baseball Hall of Fame and Museum's Library? The source of my inspiration to devote all this time to the history of the induction ceremony has been very simply, the fans.

Unless you have been a part of a Hall of Fame Induction Ceremony and witnessed the appearance of fans from all over the country, it's hard to comprehend the extent of their loyalty and involvement that is on display every year for this event.

I had watched several induction ceremonies on television and after seeing the ESPN cameras pan the mass of humanity that crowds into Cooperstown each year, I decided to see for myself what all the fuss was about when I attended the 2004 induction.

My wife, Pat, and I were invited to join longtime attendees Joe and Barbara D'Amato and watch the ceremony from their tent on the grounds of the Alfred Clark Gymnasium (ACG). Joe is my friend Jim Carroll's brother-in-law, so we joined them along with Jim's other brother-in-law, Mike, his wife, Cathy, and Jim's daughters Jane and Marianne along with some of their other friends. They started coming in 1992 when the ceremony was moved to the immense grounds next to the ACG. They didn't like all the congestion that they experienced being closer so another member of the group, Scot Macomber, decided to pitch a tent in 1994. Their tent is back on the hill, a formidable walk from the stage where the inductees speak. They started something because many other longtime attendees now have tents as well.

During that 2004 Induction Weekend, I participated in the Connecting Generations trivia contest that was held on Saturday afternoon inside the Alfred Clark Gymnasium with five Hall of Famers taking part. My wife and I then gathered with more than 1,000 fans Saturday night outside the steps to the entrance of the Hall of Fame to wait patiently for the Red Carpet Gala to begin. This annual event welcomes all the Hall of Famers as they arrive by trolley from the Otesaga Hotel for a reception held inside the Hall of Fame Gallery. We then attended the induction on Sunday afternoon on the grounds of the ACG along with 15,000 fans honoring inductees Dennis Eckersley and Paul Molitor. Finally, on Monday morning, we took part on the grounds outside the gymnasium with about a thousand fans as ESPN interviewed Eckersley and Molitor, along with fellow Hall of Famers Lou Brock and Johnny Bench during the Hall of Fame Roundtable discussion.

Following the weekend I realized that much has been written about the Hall of Fame but nothing about the history of Induction Weekend. Being a retired social studies teacher as well as a historian, I decided to research this annual event after seeing the enthusiasm of all these loyal fans.

I have now attended five inductions (I missed the 2007 Ripken-Gwynn gigantic induction), and the devotion and loyalty exhibited by these fans is truly phenomenal. There are the fans like the D'Amatos, who come every year from New Jersey, along with many other devotees who come from New York, the surrounding states in the east and Midwest, as well as Canada, too.

Another annual attendee I met in 2005 was Rudy Gafur, who moved to Toronto, Canada, from Guyana many years ago. He became so enamored with his adopted sport of baseball that he started coming to the Induction Ceremony in 1980 and wrote a book about it called *Cooperstown Is My Mecca*. He introduced me to many other devotees, including fans who come every year and camp outside the General Store next to the Hall of Fame on Saturday night of Induction Weekend. They're there in order

Roberto Clemente uses his video camera to record the introduction of the Hall of Famers before the Doubleday exhibition game in 1968.

to purchase bats on Sunday morning that are inscribed with the names of the inductees.

Another group that comes every year is the stamp collectors, who arrive early Sunday morning at the post office. They want to purchase the first edition cancellations of commemorative stamps issued each year on Induction Day.

Then there are the fans who attend only one induction because of a favorite player or, in some instances, the induction of an admired baseball executive, manager or umpire. Some even come because a particular baseball writer or broadcaster is being honored. These fans will spare no expense in traveling across the country, finding food and lodging, visiting the museum and taking part in other activities connected to Induction Weekend. This all started with the first induction in 1939. One of the fans attending the inaugural induction was a recent high school graduate who hitchhiked all the way from Minnesota.

Special fans that I met in 2009 will be highlighted in Chapter 10. One is a Babe Ruth impersonator who has come many times, and the other is an Oakland A's fan who has come twice.

Fans have also initiated grassroots campaigns that helped to get individuals elected. Support has also come from sportswriters and Hall of Famers who have campaigned for players through the Veterans Committee.

Television has given rise to another example of fan response. It began in the 1980s when the ceremonies were televised by ESPN, resulting in fans displaying signs, uniforms, chants, cheers, etc., that helped to bring attention to themselves but more importantly to their heroes.

Interest is also generated by fans seeking autographs, and they have been coming since the first induction. Now autographs are big business, especially for the Hall of Famers. Many fans pay a lot of money at various establishments on the streets of Cooperstown to procure signatures on different items. Yet some Hall of Famers will at times sign for charity as with Fergie Jenkins and his foundation. Occasionally Hall of Famers will sign for free depending on the situation.

Baseball players themselves are fans, too, just like the rest of us, as evidenced when back-to-back no-hit pitcher Johnny Vander Meer filmed the proceedings at the first Doubleday Field all-star game in 1939. One of the most precious moments occurred when the great Roberto Clemente was photographed videotaping the introduction of the Hall of Famers at Doubleday Field during the 1968 exhibition game.

Finally, most Hall of Famers make reference to the fans in attendance during their induction speeches as indispensible to the game of baseball. This book will not only chronicle the history of the Induction Ceremony, but will also give testimony to a small sample of those fans that have come over the last 70 years to honor their heroes.

Introduction

This book will examine the history of why Cooperstown was chosen as the birthplace of baseball and how this little village nestled between the Berkshire and Catskill mountains became the home of the National Baseball Hall of Fame and Museum. This will be detailed in the first two chapters; the first Induction Ceremony will be presented in Chapter 3.

The details of how the Baseball Writers Association of America (BBWAA) became the primary gatekeepers of the selection process and the Veterans Committee (VC) and its predecessors became the secondary source for induction will also be discussed in Chapter 3. The book will go on to describe how the VC has evolved over the years and how it has been the source of controversy for many selections throughout its history.

Also, individual and group support will be cited, including a number of different examples of grassroots campaigns that helped the individual reach Cooperstown.

The elections from the 1940s up through 2009 will be discussed in Chapters 4 through 10. All the inductions from 1936 through 2009 will follow chronologically and will most times have a three-part format for each inductee.

The first part will describe how the Hall of Famers were chosen, either by the BBWAA or the VC. The second part will give a brief biography of each inductee with a short paragraph at the end describing something interesting about them, baseball or otherwise. The final part will detail the ceremony and highlight each speech by those inductees who were alive as well their representatives if they had died or were too ill to attend.

Please note this is the first time that the induction speeches have been documented in a book.

The evolution of the National Baseball Hall of Fame and Museum from its beginning as a two-story building to its present three-story, state-of-the-art museum will be chronicled from 1939 through 2009.

The book will conclude with a brief Afterword.

Please note that all of the Hall of Fame speeches that are quoted are excerpted from the Induction Ceremonies of the National Baseball Hall of Fame and Museum, Inc.[1] Also, those Hall of Famers who share "My Favorite Cooperstown Memory" came from an article written by Jeff Idelson in the *2005 Hall of Fame Yearbook*.[2]

Several books were utilized for statistical information. They were *The ESPN Baseball Encyclopedia, Fifth Edition*, *The SABR Baseball List and Record Book*, and the statistical records as listed in the *2009 Hall of Fame Yearbook*.

A final note will be mentioned regarding those inductees who were controversial. Throughout my book I will refer to three books regarding those controversial selections. The first book is by noted baseball historian and analyst Bill James. He wrote *Whatever*

Happened to the Hall of Fame? in 1994. James examines the whole Hall of Fame voting process and gives his opinion on those choices that he considers controversial. He is a member of the Society for American Baseball Research (SABR) and is responsible for sabermetrics. James coined this term and it refers to the statistical analysis of baseball statistics. He bases his judgments on five statistical methods that he uses to determine who should be in the Hall of Fame.[3]

The second book is by the late James Vail, a member of SABR who wrote *Road to Cooperstown* in 2001. He is most critical of those Hall of Famers who had questionable career statistics and were elected by the Veterans Committee because they had former teammates or other influential friends on the VC. He calls this favoritism cronyism.[4]

The third book is by Robert Cohen, who wrote *Hall of Fame or Hall of Shame?* in 2009. He rates players on how dominant they were offensively at the position they played. Their dominance is based on eight questions that he asks regarding their Hall of Fame qualifications.[5]

As a way of reducing the number of notes, when each author and his book is quoted, the source will be cited in parentheses rather than with endnotes.

I would just like to close by quoting the late Leonard Koppett, a respected author and longtime member of the BBWAA and also a member of the VC. He applauds the fact that "voter freedom leads to disputes, and leaves room for argument." He concludes, "Argument is the lifeblood of sports interest and myth-making."[6]

CHAPTER 1

Abner Graves and
Not Abner Doubleday

Today the National Baseball Hall of Fame and Museum is located in Cooperstown, New York, because of Abner Graves and not Abner Doubleday. It was Graves and not Doubleday who was instrumental in establishing Cooperstown as the birthplace of baseball. Let me explain why the people of Cooperstown are indebted to Abner G. and not Abner D.

It all started because baseball pioneer Albert Spalding wanted to prove to another baseball pioneer, Henry Chadwick, that baseball started in America. Chadwick lived the first 12 years of his life in England before he came to America and argued that baseball evolved from the British game of rounders.

Spalding formed a commission in 1905 to resolve the dispute. Abraham Mills was the chairman of the group and suffice to say that the Mills Commission didn't do a good job in finding the answer. They concluded that baseball was invented by the Civil War general Abner Doubleday based solely on two letters that were written by an opportunist named Abner Graves. Graves claimed that Doubleday invented the game around 1839 in a quaint little village in upstate New York by the name of Cooperstown.

The commission never investigated Graves' claims that Doubleday introduced this new game to replace town ball with a more organized game called base ball. Graves' assertions were challenged right from the start. Doubleday would have been a freshman at West Point in 1839 and would not have been allowed to leave the United States Military Academy during the summer when he was supposedly teaching Graves and his companions the game of baseball. A legitimate question was raised as to how Graves could remember specific rules and details about the game that Doubleday taught him and his buddies 66 years later when he would have been only five years old in 1839.

Abner Graves' motivations for coming forth with this story were also questioned after he ended his second and final letter to Albert Spalding and the Mills Commission by stating, "I would rather have Uncle Sam declare War on England and clean her up rather than have one of her citizens beat us out of Base Ball."[1]

The question of character was also raised years after Graves wrote the letters. Graves shot and killed his much younger wife in 1924 because he thought she was going to poison him. Graves was committed to an insane asylum where he died two years later at age 92.

Additional information revealed that when Abner Doubleday wrote his memoirs near the end of his life in 1893 there was no mention made of baseball. Critics rebuked the Doubleday myth even more when they specified examples of baseball being played in many other places before 1839.

Left: Civil War hero Abner Doubleday, who became more famous for (falsely) being declared the inventor of baseball. *Right:* Opportunist Abner Graves, who is responsible for the "Doubleday Myth."

Nevertheless, the Mills Commission concluded that Abner Doubleday invented baseball and published their conclusion in Albert Spalding's *Baseball Guide of 1908*. Despite all the criticism, Spalding and the Mills Commission were able to convince the American public of the Doubleday hoax.

Much has been written about Doubleday not inventing baseball, yet there are still many examples today that perpetuate the Doubleday myth. Doubleday Field in Cooperstown had signage right up until recently that said "Birthplace of Baseball." The United States Military Academy still plays its baseball games at Doubleday Field at West Point. There is a minor league team in upstate New York that is called the Auburn Doubledays. Finally, Abner Doubleday's birthplace in Ballston Spa, New York, has signage outside his boyhood home referring to him as the "inventor of baseball."

Abner Doubleday had a distinguished career as a military officer, was an accomplished public speaker, and is credited with establishing a means of transportation in the city of San Francisco that is still a major tourist attraction today.

He graduated from the United States Military Academy in 1842, in a class that included Ulysses Grant and William Sherman. He was a captain in the army, and was in charge of firing the first cannon against the South in defense of Fort Sumter, South Carolina, thus beginning the Civil War. Doubleday was also involved in the battles of Bull Run, Fredericksburg, Chancellorsville, Antietam, and most importantly, Gettysburg. He was responsible for repelling Pickett's charge and today there is a statute of him at the battlefield. He became a major general at the end of the war, and then after the war was an assistant commissioner of the Freedmen's Bureau in Galveston, Texas. Prior to his retiring from the military in 1873, he designed and obtained a charter for the first cable car franchise in San Francisco.

Yet despite these achievements he is more famous for a myth regarding something he knew nothing about and had no control over since he had passed away.

Jeff Idelson, the president of the Hall of Fame and previously vice-president of communication and education, addressed the myth issue by stating, "We stopped laying claim to being the birthplace of baseball a long time ago. Cooperstown is one of the earliest places baseball was played. The game evolved over time, it wasn't born in one place."[2]

Cooperstown, in spite of all the controversy, has demonstrated it is an idyllic setting for the National Baseball Hall of Fame and Museum. The village has proven that it deserves to be the home of baseball, but it didn't happen until it overcame a number of obstacles, as you will see in the next chapter.

CHAPTER 2

Alexander Cleland and the People of Cooperstown Pull It Off

Cooperstown was originally noted as the home of James Fenimore Cooper, the author of *The Last of the Mohicans*, but today it is also the home of the National Baseball Hall of Fame and Museum. How was this village of fewer than 2,000 people able to do this? It took a special resolve by the people of the village to confirm the findings of the Mills Commission Report by establishing Cooperstown as the birthplace of baseball. However, it probably never would have happened if not for the vision of a man who was born in Scotland and knew very little about baseball.

Our story begins with four residents of Ilion, New York, who began the Doubleday Memorial Fund by contributing a quarter each to establish Cooperstown as the place where baseball began. They got the support of a former major league baseball player turned sportswriter, Samuel Crane.

Crane was offended that Phinney's Field, the site where Abner Graves supposedly learned about this new game of baseball from Abner Doubleday in 1839, had reverted to a cow pasture. He visited Cooperstown many times from 1917 through 1925 to drum up support for a national ball field in honor of Abner Doubleday.

A local dentist, Dr. Ernest Pitcher, and the Cooperstown Chamber of Commerce raised $3,772 in 1919 and acquired a two-year lease on the Elihu Phinney property. Crane's writings convinced former National League president John Tener and his successor, John Heydler, to visit Cooperstown. It was Tener who encouraged village officials to develop the Phinney property with a ball field as a memorial to Doubleday. Heydler was so impressed with the enthusiasm of the local people that he came back on September 6, 1920, to dedicate the Doubleday ball field. Heydler umpired the first inning of a game between Cooperstown and Milford as the townspeople raised $450 from a street fair that would go toward building a permanent ballpark.

The village taxpayers, after turning it down the first time, voted to purchase the property in 1923. The people purchased additional land in 1927 that extended the property out to Main Street. During this time a wooden grandstand that included bleachers behind home plate and down the lines was added as well. No further work was done on it until 1933.

At last they were able to apply for a Works Progress Administration grant under President Franklin D. Roosevelt's New Deal program. The work was begun as additional parcels of land were acquired to enlarge left field. Doubleday Field was formally reopened on August 3, 1934, as a crowd of 2,000 saw the Cooperstown Leatherstockings defeat the Oneonta Merchants 5–4 in 11 innings.

Edward Clark was a successful New York City lawyer who had married the boss's daughter. Clark had grown up in Athens, New York, while his wife, Caroline, had grown up in the Cooperstown area. They both liked Cooperstown and purchased a summer home there in 1854. Clark was the lawyer for Isaac Singer, the inventor who perfected the sewing machine. They eventually formed a partnership and became very wealthy although they dissolved their partnership in 1867. Despite the breakup, Clark prospered and continued to share in the company's profits. The Clarks also became more involved in Cooperstown and developed a sense of civic responsibility toward their village. This attribute was passed on to their son, Alfred, and his four sons, especially Edward Severin and Stephen.

Edward Severin built the Fenimore House in Cooperstown in 1930, which was sold to the New York State Historical Association in 1944. He constructed the Otesaga Hotel in 1909 and in memory of his father the Alfred Corning Clark Gymnasium in 1930 as well. He also built the Mary Imogene Bassett Hospital in 1922, in honor of a local physician, and the stone barn on the Fenimore Farm, which is now part of the Farmers Museum.

Stephen was a successful lawyer who served in the New York State Assembly in 1910, and was also a lieutenant colonel in World War I, where he earned the Distinguished Service Medal. Following the war, he became an avid art collector and was the chairman of both the Museum of Modern Art in New York City and the New York State Historical Society. His sense of civic responsibility made him a nationally known philanthropist, which saw him create the Clark Foundation that financed the Bassett Hospital, provided college scholarships for the local high school, and helped numerous other charities.

However, Stephen was concerned about Cooperstown's economy after a hops blight killed off the major crop in the area following World War I. Hops had been exported to Germany for the making of beer, but with Prohibition and the crop disease, hops production ceased. He thought about promoting tourism as a way of bringing people to his picturesque village but wasn't sure how to do it.

One of his employees was Alexander Cleland, a Scottish immigrant who came to the United States in 1903. He worked for various agencies as a social worker before becoming the director of the Clark House in New York City in 1931. The Clark House was there to help immigrants find housing and employment. Cleland and Clark were both cut from the same cloth in their humanitarian spirit to help others. Neither was a baseball fan, but unbeknownst to them, they were about to develop an interest in the national pastime that would help to change Cooperstown forever.

Cleland would come up to Cooperstown often to meet with his boss to discuss business matters concerning the Clark House. This was the case when Cleland was walking through the village in May 1934 after concluding his meeting with Clark. He came upon laborers as they worked on Doubleday Field and inquired as to what they were doing. One enthusiastic worker told Cleland of the upcoming centennial in 1939, celebrating 100 years of baseball. He found out that Cooperstown was the birthplace of baseball and Doubleday Field was part of the upcoming celebration.

On the train ride back to New York City, Cleland gave a lot of thought to what he had just witnessed at Doubleday Field. His boss was already involved in the museum business and thought a baseball museum that could house past, present and future memorabilia would interest a lot of people. He didn't know much about baseball, but Cleland was business savvy and knew that a museum would be a magnet for tourists from all over the country and help boost the village's economy. Cleland projected his idea to the centennial celebration and felt strongly that "nostalgia plus publicity would mean profits."[1] He presented the idea to his boss and Clark concurred wholeheartedly and recognized the possibilities in his director's plans.

Cleland knew this undertaking would require a lot of work and he would need the support of Major League Baseball (MLB) and the baseball writers to promote the idea of a museum. Eventually, if he was going to bring this idea to fruition, he would need the support of the people of Cooperstown wrapped around a grand promotional idea in order to bring visitors to the village for the centennial.

A very important local person who would be invaluable to Cleland was Walter Littell, editor of the local newspaper, *The Otsego Farmer*. Littell had been contacted by a local farmer in nearby Fly Creek who supposedly found the belongings of Abner Graves in an old trunk in the attic of his farmhouse. The farmhouse was about to be demolished, so Littell contacted Clark and told him about one of the items, an old, undersized baseball that was misshaped and stuffed with cloth. Clark paid the farmer $5 because of its historical significance.

Many people believed that this ball was used by Abner Doubleday when he was showing Graves and the others how to play baseball. This would be the missing link as described by historian James Vlasich.[2] It became known as the Doubleday baseball and it would become the first item to be displayed in a room on the second floor of the Village Club and Library Building where memorabilia would be exhibited. Ironically, it is one of the few items that the museum paid for rather than received by way of donation. Catherine Walker, a lifelong resident of Cooperstown and a longtime attendant at the Hall of Fame, said, "If you wanted to see any of the artifacts at the Village Club you would just go to the desk at the Library and ask for a key to the room where they were housed, spend as much time as you liked, and lock it up when you were done."[3]

Clark and Cleland took an important step in February 1935 and formed the Doubleday Field Association that included important members of the community, including the Cooperstown Board of Trustees, the Chamber of Commerce, and the Otsego County Historical Society. Alexander Cleland was appointed executive secretary and Stephen Clark vice president. They vowed to publicize and promote the museum idea and also convince MLB to help the association promote baseball's centennial. Eventually, it would evolve into the Cooperstown Centennial Committee.

Cleland and the association knew their plan couldn't succeed without the backing of MLB. Although baseball commissioner Kenesaw Mountain Landis never showed any interest in their project, National League president John Heydler, who always supported the village, was eventually named the baseball director of the centennial celebration. Unfortunately, he had to resign as National League president because of health reasons. Luckily his successor, Ford Frick, would be the impetus that would make the support of MLB a reality. Frick was an enthusiastic supporter of Cleland's plan and promised baseball would cooperate in the endeavor.

Cleland visited Frick at the League Office in New York City in the spring of 1935 and proposed a major league all-star game be played in Cooperstown as a way of generating publicity for the centennial celebration. The National League president listened and then presented Cleland with a much more profound idea. Frick began by telling the Scotsman that he had visited the campus of New York University up in the Bronx a few days before their meeting and saw the Hall of Fame for Great Americans there. Frick proposed a hall of fame for baseball's greatest stars that would be part of the museum complex. Ford Frick had a sense of history and believed that this hall of fame would not only honor baseball's finest, but also would help fans know the accomplishments of the greats of the game and allow them to compare the stars from one era with those of another era.

Frick achieved a lot of things during his career in baseball, but his proudest accomplishment was the Hall of Fame.[4]

Frick was anxious to spread the word about Cooperstown's centennial plans for the National Baseball Museum and the Hall of Fame so the story appeared for the first time nationwide, by way of the Associated Press, on August 16, 1935. This was right in the middle of the baseball season because Frick was so sure that the story would appeal to baseball fans everywhere. This nationwide publicity was the beginning of Stephen Clark's dream of establishing Cooperstown as a tourist destination, which would succeed far beyond his wildest dreams.

The centennial celebration had nationwide attention and then the State of New York got involved as well. The state sponsored legislation that raised $2,500 to help defray the cost of the centennial. They also tied the centennial promotion to the World's Fair in New York City, which was opening in 1939.

Ford Frick met with representatives from the Baseball Writers Association of America (BBWAA) to get their support for the Hall of Fame, which they fully endorsed. The decision was then made to have the (BBWAA) make the final determination on who would be selected for the Hall of Fame. The first election would take place in 1936 and they would have an annual election each of the following years so that by the time of the Centennial Celebration in 1939 there would have been four elections. This process would generate national publicity because it would spark the interest of fans throughout the country. The selection process and the inductees chosen will be discussed in Chapter 3.

Alexander Cleland found that his effort to get artifacts for the museum was a long, arduous, and often disappointing process. Nevertheless, some people in baseball did step forward. Clark Griffith, the owner of the Washington Senators, was helpful when he sent Cleland pictures of several presidents throwing out the first ball on Opening Day.

The widow of Christy Mathewson also contributed a mitt, uniform and later a bust of her husband. Christy's manager with the New York Giants, John McGraw, had also passed away, and his widow had his alma mater, St. Bonaventure, contribute a statuette to the museum.

On the other hand, some of the living inductees were reluctant to give anything. Cleland persisted, and finally the first to respond and the most cooperative was baseball's all-time winningest pitcher, Cy Young. Cleland visited him at his home in Ohio and received from him the 1908 ball that was used for his 500th win, his 1911 Boston Braves uniform, which was the last uniform that he wore, and three trophies. Cleland was still disappointed in the overall response, but his persistence and determination eventually got other Hall of Famers to contribute.

Then memorabilia from all over the country started to come in as baseball publications and other newspapers took up the cause in soliciting artifacts for the museum. The result was the museum received so many items that Cleland and the committee realized the Village Club was too small.

Plans were announced in July 1937 that a fireproof museum building would be specifically designed to house the numerous donations. It was decided to construct the museum at 25 Main Street, right next to the Alfred Corning Clark Gymnasium. This was a smart, economical move because the gym was equipped with a heating plant that could serve both buildings and help cut the cost of fuel, a major consideration due to Cooperstown's harsh winters. The museum building would be connected to the gymnasium building and would be only two blocks from Doubleday Field.

The two-story colonial brick building would be similar in appearance to the buildings of Colonial Williamsburg. The brick would be integrated with stone and would have a slate roof. There would be five even-sized, square-shaped windows stretched across the front of the second floor of the building. The entrance would have two majestic pillars featuring four white marble steps flanked by a wrought iron railing and a white granite keystone designed in the shape of a baseball. It was impressive looking but much smaller than the three-story, state-of-the-art building that greets visitors today.

Once inside the building, visitors would see 1,200 square feet of space on the first floor that would serve as a plaque gallery for all the baseball greats, as well as a museum, library, ticket office, retail shop and the director's office. The second floor would be used to store library materials. The museum would be completed in July 1938 and for the rest of the year would attract thousands of visitors from all over the world. It would be dedicated during the centennial year on June 12, 1939.

It was now time to upgrade Doubleday Field in order to accommodate major leaguers for an eventual all-star game as Alexander Cleland had originally proposed. Major League Baseball wanted to get it ready for 1939 so they sent the New York Giants' veteran head groundskeeper, Henry Fabian, to Cooperstown. Fabian was recognized as the leading groundskeeper in baseball and had taken care of the Polo Grounds for 25 years. He inspected Doubleday Field during the summer of 1938 and was impressed with its beautiful setting. His recommendations were eventually carried out and a sodded infield was installed, with outfield dimensions extended in order to get it ready for 1939. His expertise would help to transform Doubleday Field into a suitable ballpark that would accommodate major and minor league baseball well into the future.

The project would be carried out by the Works Progress Administration (WPA). The WPA would use 28 workers who would construct a steel-covered grandstand, seed the entire field, develop a drainage system, and install new wooden bleachers, a new board fence for the outfield and a stone masonry wall for the rest of the facility. The WPA would pay $23,401.90 for labor costs, and the village would pick up the tab of $17,300 for materials and equipment.[5]

Cleland and his committee remained steadfast as they moved toward the target date of 1939, but the plan almost blew up in their faces because of Bruce Cartwright, Jr.

Bruce was the grandson of Alexander Joy Cartwright and wrote Cleland that his grandfather was the one who had written the first rules of baseball while he was a member of the Knickerbocker Baseball Club in 1845. His grandfather then traveled west in 1849 to pursue the gold rush in California and soon after moved to Hawaii where he became a successful businessman. Bruce lived in Hawaii and had the city manager of Honolulu send a follow up letter to Cleland supporting his position.

During this time Frank G. Menke had published an article in *Ken* magazine stating that the claims Doubleday invented baseball were false and that Alexander Cartwright was the inventor of baseball. Menke declared that Doubleday was a student at West Point in 1839, and he criticized the Mills Commission report for a faulty investigation.[6]

Alexander Cleland and the Cooperstown organizers decided that they would give recognition to Bruce's grandfather with an Alexander Cartwright Day during the summer of 1839. They would still recognize Doubleday but also pay tribute to Cartwright, thus avoiding a controversy that could have derailed their plans.

Cooperstown officials confer with Alexander Cleland and Henry Fabian on the renovation of Doubleday Field in the summer of 1938. *Left to right:* Professor Ralph Perry, Henry Fabian, Mayor Theodore Lettis, Alexander Cleland, Carter Burnett and Rowan Spraker (courtesy of the New York State Historical Association, Cooperstown, New York).

It was now 1938 and although there were many who doubted the legitimacy of Doubleday, there was no turning back. The museum was finished and two elections had been conducted by the Baseball Writers and a Veterans Committee with 13 inductees selected for the Hall of Fame. Stephen Clark had invested his time and money in the museum complex and Major League Baseball had pledged $100,000 to help promote the centennial in 1939.

Cartwright was finally given the ultimate recognition when the Centennial Committee on Old Timers elected Alexander Cartwright and Henry Chadwick to the Hall of Fame in 1938. Cartwright's plaque read:

> "Father of Modern Baseball."
> Set Bases 90 Feet apart
> Established 9 innings as Game
> And 9 Players as Team. Organized
> the Knickerbocker Baseball Club
> of N.Y. in 1845

Thus, the biggest controversy that threatened to derail the Cooperstown celebration was averted, but historian James Vlasich reveals the reasoning behind Cartwright's election. Stephen Clark had initiated an investigation into Doubleday's background following all the controversy over Cartwright or Doubleday being the legitimate inventor of baseball. Clark had supported the premise that Doubleday was the inventor of baseball, especially when he purchased the Doubleday baseball, supposedly the missing link to the inventor of baseball. Nonetheless, he was disturbed by the Cartwright information and six weeks after he found out that Doubleday couldn't have been in Cooperstown in 1839, Alexander Cartwright was elected to the Hall of Fame in 1938. As a result of the 1938 Centennial Committee election, many of the Doubleday backers began to withdraw their support.

If Clark had known this in the beginning he would never have financed the museum complex. Nevertheless, he had already committed to it so the plans continued. Just before he died in 1960, Clark admitted "that the evidence against Doubleday was too overwhelming." Clark went on to say, "Nobody invented baseball. It grew out of rounders and town ball and things of that sort."[7]

However, controversy has surrounded Cartwright as well. In 2009, Monica Nucciarone wrote *Alexander Cartwright: The Life Behind the Legend*, the definitive biography of his life. She calls into question the rules that are attributed to him as listed on his plaque. It seems that there is no primary source verifying that he wrote these rules. He also had several prominent Knickerbocker teammates who possibly were responsible for them, but again there is no definitive source.[8]

The person who was the source for this information on Cartwright was his grandson Bruce. He maintained that his grandfather told him stories about his baseball background with the Knickerbockers, but again there is no verifiable source. Thus, Bruce became the first example of an individual who helped to get someone into the Hall of Fame because of a grassroots campaign. The major difference between this and future grassroots campaigns are that there is no factual evidence to support its legitimacy.

MLB was now ready to give all its support to promote baseball's centennial. The National Baseball Centennial Commission was formed in 1938 with Commissioner Landis serving as the chairman. Alexander Cleland would be asked to join later after its first meeting in October 1938.

Alexander Cleland had been publicizing and promoting Cooperstown ever since he had that idea on the train back in 1934, but now the centennial celebration required a well-known public relations firm that would have the resources to spread the word about the centennial throughout the country. They chose the flamboyant Steve Hannigan, president of a New York City public relations firm, and he began by calling the celebration the Cavalcade of Baseball. A centennial insignia was designed that would be worn on all baseball uniforms by major and minor league teams during the season.

Hannigan and the commission wanted to emphasize how baseball taught the lessons of democracy, contrasting it with what was happening across the Atlantic where Hitler and Nazi Germany were running roughshod over the European continent. The development of the national pastime paralleled the growth and greatness of America. The cavalcade wanted to show how baseball reached across all levels from elementary school, American Legion, high school, semi-pro, and professional.

The commission would get the message across by using all available media and would produce a National Centennial Handbook that would explain how communities could participate in the celebration at the local level. Separate promotional films were developed by both the American and National leagues.

This national baseball centennial could not have come along at a more opportune time as baseball, like everything else, had suffered from the Great Depression. Attendance was down for most of the 16 major league teams. Ford Frick, as president of the National League, helped rescue the Brooklyn Dodgers, Philadelphia Phillies, and the Boston Braves financially with the help of an infusion of cash and encouragement of new investors for each club. Frick then developed strategies for these clubs to become financially responsible.

The Cavalcade of Baseball wouldn't really begin until March 1939 around the time of spring training. Nevertheless, at the Cooperstown Chamber of Commerce Dinner in January the plans were revealed to the village leaders first, because they would be in the forefront of the celebration.

A month later, the Baseball Writers Dinner was held in New York City where the commission's promotional plans were formally announced. The Cavalcade of Baseball would be celebrated with a number of events throughout the baseball season with most of them centered in Cooperstown. President Roosevelt sent a proclamation expressing his gratitude toward Abner Doubleday and finishing it with the following: "General Doubleday was a distinguished soldier in the Civil War, but his part in giving us baseball shows again that peace has her victories no less renowned than war."[9]

Postmaster James Farley also announced at the dinner a commemorative stamp would be issued that would celebrate baseball. Farley avoided controversy by stating the stamp would depict a scene of boys playing baseball on a sandlot without any picture of either Doubleday or Cartwright. The stamp "typified the heritage of American youth."[10]

Congress and President Roosevelt declared June 12 to be the date that they would commemorate the centennial of baseball. Roosevelt wrote to the museum on April 19, and recognizing the effort put forth by Cooperstown he stated it was "most fitting that the history of our perennial popular sport should be immortalized ... where the game originated and where the first diamond was devised 100 years ago."[11] The museum was so proud of the letter that they framed it and placed it on a wall where every visitor could read it.

The first event in Cooperstown took place on May 6 as Doubleday Field was finally finished with WPA workers completing the job at 4:00 A.M. The Manilius School defeated Albany Academy 9–2 as Doubleday Field officially opened the centennial celebration in Cooperstown. The two military schools brought their entire student bodies as the WPA formally turned Doubleday Field over to Cooperstown. The mayor, Roland Spraker, received a duplicate copy of a plaque that was placed on the outside wall commemorating Doubleday Field as the birthplace of baseball.

The Doubleday family had 24 family members present on May 30, Memorial Day, as the United States Military Academy fittingly played Colgate. A portrait of Abner Doubleday was presented to the museum where it would be hung over the fireplace on the first floor.

The big event of the whole summer took place on June 12, when 25 Hall of Famers were inducted, and the National Baseball Hall of Fame and Museum was officially dedicated. This day will be the subject of Chapter 3.

American Legion Day was held on July 15 with a statewide participation by legionnaires from New York as well as Connecticut. This was an example that the Cavalcade of Baseball wasn't just about professional baseball but, as the promoters had promised, a celebration of all levels of amateur baseball as well.

Finally, the last major event of the summer was the event that honored Alexander Cartwright on August 26. The Knickerbocker rules were used as teams from Cooperstown and Fort Plain, New York, played each other. The pitching distance was 45 feet, with 11 players to a side, and the first team to score 21 runs won the game. Members of the Cartwright family were there with many of them coming all the way from Hawaii. Unfortunately, Alexander Cartwright's grandson, Bruce, died three months before his grandfather

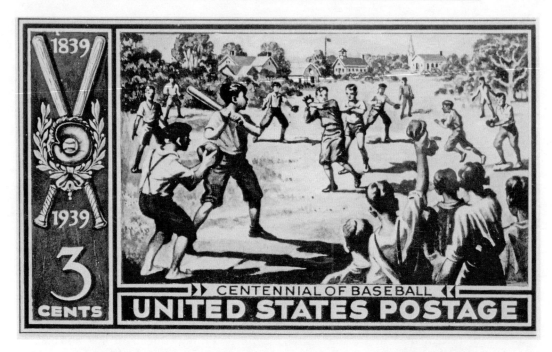

The postage stamp that commemorated the "Centennial" of baseball in 1939.

was officially honored with a plaque on June 12. Also, it had to seem somewhat strange and paradoxical that Cartwright's plaque was actually placed just to the right of the Abner Doubleday portrait in the first floor of the museum. A ceremony was also held in Hawaii, where a duplicate plaque was placed on a wall at a park that was now dedicated to Alexander Cartwright. Thus, this event brought an end to the four-month gala celebration of the Cavalcade of Baseball.

Today, looking back 70 years later at Cooperstown and baseball's centennial, it is a tribute to Alexander Cleland and the people of Cooperstown that despite all the controversy surrounding Abner Doubleday, they were able to have a memorable celebration of baseball. It was "a triumph of public relations, organization, and old fashioned persistence," according to Jim Reisler in his book *A Great Day in Cooperstown*.[12] Sportswriter Dan Daniel stated, "The village has spent a great deal of time in preparation and doubted that any other town of its size could have done itself so proud. It was the village's finest hour."[13]

A big reason why so many fans believed the Doubleday myth was because of Major League Baseball. Critic Frank Menke brought them to task as he points out, "Major League officials adopted the Mills thesis without checking for inaccuracies."[14] A perfect example is that the most important baseball fan in the country, President Franklin Delano Roosevelt, believed it and showed wholehearted support for it with his statements.

The Cavalcade of Baseball and the centennial celebration were a fitting tribute to the village of Cooperstown, but especially to Alexander Cleland. He retired from the Hall of Fame as its executive secretary in 1941 and died in Whippany, New Jersey, in 1954 at the age of 77. Cleland overcame controversy, resistance, delays, and a lot of other obstacles but never wavered as he helped make the National Baseball Museum and Hall of Fame a worldwide tourist attraction.

Talmage Boston, in his book, *1939: Baseball's Tipping Point*, states, "The celebration

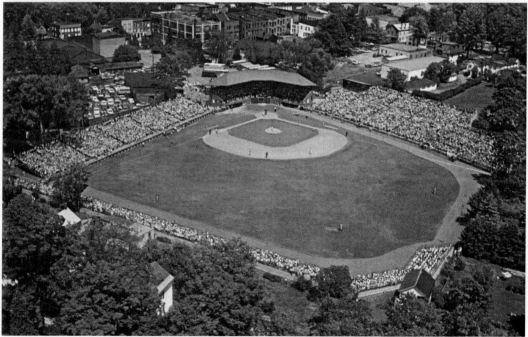

Top: Baseball being played on the Phinney cow pasture before it became Doubleday Field. *Above:* An aerial view of Doubleday Field today.

of baseball history would not be equaled again on a national level until a PBS viewing audience in the tens of millions watched Ken Burns' documentary, *Baseball*, in September of 1994." Boston adds, "Regardless of the Doubleday historical inaccuracy, the Hall of Fame has seen history preserved, honored excellence, and connected with older and younger generations. Mission Statement accomplished."[15]

CHAPTER 3

June 12, 1939 —
Where Is Ty Cobb?

Ford Frick and Alexander Cleland weren't sure how they were going to elect the baseball greats to the Hall of Fame after Frick came up with his grand idea. The two men first thought they would have fans across the country vote, but they realized that this could become very subjective and result in a popularity contest. Instead, a six-man board of baseball officials determined that the Baseball Writers Association of America (BBWAA) would select players from the twentieth century while a special Committee of Old Timers would select nineteenth century individuals.

The goal of the Hall of Fame was to have ten inductees from the twentieth century and five inductees from the nineteenth century by the 1939 opening of the museum.

The BBWAA elections continue to this day and the other constant that has never changed is that a nominee must receive 75 percent of the vote in order to gain admittance, whether it is by the writers or the veterans committee. Just about everything else has undergone change over the years although one other intangible has also continued ever since the first election in 1936 and that is controversy.

1936

The results of the first BBWAA vote were announced on January 29, 1936, with five great players achieving immortality. There were 226 ballots cast as center fielder Ty Cobb finished first with 98.2 percent (222 votes). Shortstop Honus Wagner and right fielder Babe Ruth tied for second with 95.1 percent (215 votes). Pitcher Christy Mathewson finished fourth with 90.7 percent (205 votes) and fellow pitcher Walter Johnson fifth with 87.6 percent (189 votes).

The first controversy arose because the two groups couldn't make up their minds where Cy Young belonged. He was baseball's winningest pitcher, but half of his career was in the nineteenth century and half was in the twentieth century. As a result he finished eighth in the BBWAA election with 49 percent and fourth in the Old Timers committee vote with 41 percent.

Each elector could vote for ten individuals but there were no guidelines as to eligibility. As a result active players such as Rogers Hornsby (46 percent), Mickey Cochrane (35 percent) and Lou Gehrig (23 percent) received strong support. "Shoeless" Joe Jackson, who was banned from baseball, along with players with fewer than 10 years in the majors received votes. Meanwhile, no one achieved the 75 percent in the veterans vote; 78 ballots were cast by players, writers, managers, and other baseball officials who had familiarity with nine-teenth-century baseball. The results weren't released until early February because the com-mittee changed some of the requirements during the course of the vote. Since the goal was to have only five inductees from the nineteenth century, the electors were told to vote for only five after originally being allowed to vote for ten people. Since most had already voted for ten people it was decided that each vote would only count as ½ thus making it very difficult to achieve the 75 percent.

Inductees

Ty Cobb of the Detroit Tigers is considered by most to be the greatest hitter of all time. He was controversial because of his antagonistic personality and combative style of play. Yet, he had the highest lifetime batting average ever at .366 and won 12 batting titles while hitting more than .400 three times. He had 897 stolen bases, including the most of home (54). He appeared in three World Series and also managed the Tigers from 1920 through 1926. The left-handed hitting Cobb held his hands apart on the bat while playing during the Deadball Era but was frustrated when he saw Babe Ruth and the home run take over in the 1920s. He proved he could hit for power in 1925 when he hit three home runs, a double and two singles in a game and then hit two more homers in the next game.

When Cobb was 18 and away playing baseball, he found out his mother had killed his father, thinking that he was a prowler trying to break into their home. He spent the rest of his life fighting to be the best because his father said, "Don't come home a failure."[1]

Honus Wagner began his career with the Louisville Colonels of the National League in 1897. When the team dissolved after the 1899 season, he became a member of his favorite team, the Pittsburgh Pirates. The versatile Wagner played several positions until he became their shortstop at the age of 29. He was an outstanding fielder with his big hands and strong arm. He was also a great hitter, winning eight batting titles while batting .327 lifetime. Wagner helped to defeat Cobb's Tigers in the 1909 World Series.

Wagner chewed tobacco but never smoked cigarettes and objected when the Piedmont Cigarette Company put his picture on one of their cards. He had them pulled because he didn't want young boys to smoke. Today one of his cards is worth more than $1 million.

George Herman "Babe" Ruth began his career as a pitcher and became the ace left-hander of the Boston Red Sox, helping lead them to World Series titles in 1915, 1916 and 1918. Ruth was converted into an outfielder because of his potent bat and later was traded to the Yankees before the 1920 season. There he would become the "Sultan of Swat," because of all his home runs as he helped baseball recover from the Black Sox scandal of 1919. He helped lead the Yankees to four World Series championships and retired with 714 home runs, including 60 in 1927, and a batting average of .342.

The most famous and controversial home run Ruth ever hit was against the Chicago Cubs in the third game of the 1932 World Series. It happened at Wrigley Field when the Babe supposedly pointed his bat toward the outfield. He then hit a homer into the center field bleachers. It is still debated to this day whether he called his shot.

Christy Mathewson was a right-handed pitcher whose best pitch was the fadeaway, which would be called the screwball today. His best season was in 1908 when he won 37 games while striking out 259 and walking only 42. "Matty" helped lead the New York Giants to four pennants and two World Series triumphs. His greatest achievement was when he pitched three complete game shutouts in six days as the Giants defeated the Philadelphia Athletics during the 1905 World Series. He won 373 games lifetime.

Matty was a captain in the army during World War I and was accidentally gassed while taking part in training exercises in France. Later, he developed tuberculosis and died in 1925 at the age of 46 while a patient at Saranac Lake, New York.

Walter Johnson pitched 21 years for the Washington Senators and was second all time in victories with 417. "Big Train" was a gentleman who never argued with umpires or brushed back hitters. His best year was 1913 when he had a record of 36–7, 1.09 ERA,11 shutouts, and struck out 243 while walking only 38. He threw a no-hitter, and due to lack of run support holds the major league record for winning 1–0 games (38) and losing 1–0 games (26). He helped lead them to two pennants in 1924 and 1925 and their only World Series title in 1924. Johnson pinch-hit 110 times and batted .433 in 1925, a major league record for pitchers. Big Train threw mainly fastballs with an easy sidearm motion.

Johnson was called Big Train because of the way his fastball "came roaring down the tracks." "Ping" Bodie described Johnson's fastball by saying, "You can't hit what you can't see."[2]

1937

The BBWAA changed the process in 1937 as the voters were discouraged from voting for active players, although player-managers such as Rogers Hornsby still received votes. The BBWAA cast 201 ballots with three candidates being elected.

Outstanding second baseman Nap Lajoie finished first with 83.6 percent (168 votes). Lajoie had finished sixth in 1936 with 64.6 percent (146 votes). The great center fielder Tris Speaker finished second with 82.09 percent (165 votes). He had finished seventh in 1936 with 58.8 percent (133 votes). Fortune smiled on Cy Young as he made it with 76.12 percent (153 votes). Cy had 49.1 percent (111 votes) in the 1936 election.

The Hall of Fame, after all the confusion with no nineteenth-century player receiving the necessary 75 percent, decided instead to choose a Centennial Commission that would select inductees for outstanding service to baseball apart from playing the game. This group would be made up of six men including Landis, Frick, American League President Will Harridge, Judge William Bramham, president of the minor leagues, George Trautman, president of the American Association (minor league), and former National League president John Heydler.

Five pioneers were elected: two long serving and highly successful managers, Connie Mack of the Philadelphia Athletics and John McGraw of the New York Giants, along with the first president of the National League, Morgan Bulkeley, and the first president of the American League, Ban Johnson. Finally, George Wright, the star shortstop of baseball's first professional team, the Cincinnati Red Stockings, was also selected.

The Bulkeley selection would be the first of many selections by a veterans committee that would be criticized as questionable. This was because he was president for less than a year and was more a figurehead than an executive who did anything significant.

George Wright was a contradiction to the Hall's desire to pick people for their outstanding service rather than their playing ability. He primarily was a star player but three weeks after the results were released, Richard Vidmer of the New York *Herald Tribune* wrote that the committee may have confused him with his brother Harry. Harry managed his brother on some highly successful teams and was referred to by many as "The Father of Professional Baseball."[3] Also, George had died three months earlier in 1937, and as you will see with some later inductees, death would often be a factor when it occurred close to the election date. Harry Wright was eventually elected in 1953. All of the pioneer inductees had passed away except Mack.

Controversy would continue to be a major factor with many of the selections made by future veterans committees. Although Ford Frick fashioned the Hall of Fame to honor greatness and not create controversy, the interest these selections sparked would add to the hall's appeal, and thus controversy would continue right up to the present day.

Inductees

Napoleon "Nap" Lajoie began with the Philadelphia Phillies in 1896 where he eventually went on to play second base. He jumped to the new American League in 1901 when he joined the Philadelphia Athletics. Nap won the American League's first Triple Crown in 1901, including the highest-ever batting average in the American League at .422. He was traded in 1902 to Cleveland where he became their player-manager and the team's nickname was changed to the Naps. He was a graceful fielder and batted .338 lifetime.

Lajoie battled Ty Cobb down to the wire for the 1910 batting title. Cobb sat out his last game while Lajoie played the St. Louis Browns. Browns' manager Jack O'Connor hated Cobb and had his third baseman play back so Lajoie got seven bunt hits. Lajoie received many congratulatory telegrams including seven from Cobb's teammates. Cobb was declared the winner however, after an error was changed to a hit from a previous game. League president Ban Johnson then had the Browns' manager fired for what he did.

Tris Speaker helped lead the Boston Red Sox to two World Series titles, in 1912 and 1915. He was traded to the Cleveland Indians, became their player-manager in 1919, and led them to their first World Series victory in 1920. Speaker was the premier center fielder of his time and has the most assists lifetime at 449. He was also a great hitter who led the league in hitting in 1916 with a .386 average and finished with a lifetime batting average of .345 while compiling the most doubles with 793.

Tris Speaker told respected sportswriter and author Fred Lieb that he was once a member of the Ku Klux Klan (KKK).[4] He eventually left them and later was instrumental in helping convert Larry Doby, the first black player in the American League, into a center fielder after he was a second baseman in the Negro Leagues. Doby became a proficient outfielder and helped the Indians win the 1948 World Series.

Legend has it that Denton Young became Cy by throwing at a wooden fence, making it look like a cyclone hit it. He began his career with the Cleveland Spiders of the National League and pitched in the National League for 11 years before being recruited in 1901 by the Boston Americans (now the Red Sox) of the American League. He led them to back-to-back pennants and the first World Series title against the Pittsburgh Pirates in 1903. He pitched three no-hitters including the American League's first perfect game. He won more than 30 games five times and had the most wins with a record of 511–316 (.619).

Commissioner Ford Frick decided to honor Cy Young with a pitching award after he died in 1955. Originally, it was for the best pitcher in baseball, but now it is for the best pitcher in each league.

Morgan Bulkeley is the only Hall of Famer who fought in the Civil War. Later he was the owner of the Hartford Dark Blues of the National Association. When Chicago White Stockings owner William Hulbert drew up the constitution that formed the National League in 1876 he surprised everyone by nominating Bulkeley, who was elected the National League's first president. He stayed only ten months and went on to become president of the Aetna Insurance Company. He also had a significant political career in Connecticut where he was a mayor, then governor, and later a United States senator.

One reason Bulkeley was chosen the first president of the National League was because he gave the new league credibility because he was an easterner.

Ban Johnson was president of a minor league called the Western League in 1894 that became the American League in 1901. His American League battled it out with the National League for two years before an agreement was reached in 1903. Johnson was one of three men who formed a National Commission to oversee baseball. The commission was replaced by a commissioner in 1920 after the Black Sox scandal during the 1919 World Series.

Despite an abrasive personality, Ban Johnson, during his tenure as president of the American League (1900 to 1927), helped clean up baseball by clamping down on violence and establishing a World Series championship between the two leagues. Branch Rickey said, "His contribution to the game is not closely equaled by any other single person."[5]

Connie Mack was manager of the Philadelphia Athletics for 50 years and led them to nine pennants and five World Series titles. Mack won more games than any other manager, but he also lost more games than anyone else (3,731–3,948). Baseball analyst and historian Bill James thought he was a great manager who stayed too long.

Did you ever hear of Cornelius McGillicuddy? This was Connie Mack's actual name, but he changed it when he was a player because his name was too long for the box score.

John McGraw was a fiery third baseman for Ned Hanlon's successful Baltimore Orioles teams of the 1890s. McGraw batted .334 for his 16-year career, including .399 in 1899. However, it was as a manager that McGraw made his mark. He was the New York Giants manager for 31 years when they won 10 pennants and three World Series. He was a tough taskmaster whose managing style was the opposite of Connie Mack, whom he lost to in two out of three World Series. McGraw's lifetime record was 2,763–1,948 (.548).

Umpire Bill Klem, a frequent nemesis of McGraw, said, "John McGraw off the field helped friends and his charity knew no restraint."[6] Evidence of this is shown in McGraw's hiring of numerous ex-ballplayers for jobs around the Polo Grounds and in his being known as a soft touch.

George Wright played for the Cincinnati Red Stockings when his brother Harry was the manager and they won 84 straight games before losing during the 1870 season. Later he played for Harry and the Boston Red Stockings in the first professional league, the National Association. They won four pennants in five seasons before Boston became one of the original teams in the National League that was formed in 1876. Nothing else changed as Boston won pennants in 1877 and 1878. George then became the player-manager of the Providence Grays in 1879 and beat out his brother's Boston team to win his seventh pennant in nine years.

Wright designed the first golf course in the Boston area and also developed tennis players like Dwight Davis, the founder of the Davis Cup. This is the prestigious award that countries compete to win. His son, Beals, played on a U.S. Davis Cup team.

1938

The 1938 BBWAA election was more consistent than the two previous elections as only retired twentieth-century players received votes, including Rogers Hornsby, who was now retired as a player after the 1937 season.

The results were announced with 262 ballots cast and the only player elected was pitcher Grover Cleveland Alexander, who had 80.9 percent (212 votes). Alexander had finished only fourteenth in the 1936 BBWAA election with 24 percent (55 votes) but had more than doubled his vote total to 125 votes in 1937 as he finished fourth with 62 percent.

The Centennial Commission was composed of the same six members and they again chose people for their service and not for their playing. The committee chose, as mentioned previously, Alexander Cartwright, who was credited with the game's first playing rules, and Henry Chadwick, who helped create the baseball box score and promoted the game through his writings. Both men had passed away.

Inductees

Grover Cleveland Alexander had an outstanding rookie season with the Phillies in 1911 when he led the league in victories (28). He went on to lead the league in victories and strikeouts six times each and ERA four times. He served in World War I as an artillery commander and came home shell-shocked and partially deaf in his left ear. He helped the St. Louis Cardinals win their first world title in 1926 when he struck out Tony Lazzeri of the Yankees with the bases loaded in Game 7. He retired with 373 victories.

Although an alcoholic, he suffered from epilepsy, which he developed after being hit in the temple while trying to break up a double play in the minors. Many believe his drinking covered up his epilepsy, since the former was more socially accepted. His death was listed as cardiac failure, but his wife, Aimee, believed he died from an epileptic seizure. He nevertheless was given full military honors at his burial in Minnesota.

Alexander Cartwright, Jr., a.k.a. "Alick," was a bank clerk and a volunteer fireman with the Knickerbocker Fire Company in New York City. He helped organize the Knickerbocker Baseball Club in 1845. The Knickerbockers are credited with playing the first organized game at Elysian Fields in Hoboken, New Jersey, on June 19, 1846.

As a prominent citizen in Hawaii he was part of the annexation movement, and also was the first chief of the Honolulu Fire Department.

Henry Chadwick was born in England and came to Brooklyn when he was 13. He started out as a cricket correspondent then switched to baseball. He was baseball's first reporter and helped to compile rules for baseball, came up with a scoring method for the sport, and adapted the box score, first used in cricket, to baseball. Chadwick also wrote instructional and reference books about baseball before becoming the editor for Albert Spalding's annual *Official Baseball Guide*.

Despite their differences over the origin of baseball Albert Spalding and Henry Chadwick had a long friendship. Chadwick willed his extensive baseball library to Spalding, while Spalding had a monument erected at Chadwick's gravesite.

1939

Two hundred seventy-four ballots were cast in the 1939 BBWAA election as first baseman George Sisler finished first with 85.8 percent (235 votes). Sisler had 597 votes in four BBWAA elections. Cerebral second baseman Eddie Collins finished second with 77.74 percent (213 votes). Collins had 563 votes in four elections. Right fielder Willie Keeler finished third, with 75.6 percent (207 votes). Keeler had 537 votes in four BBWAA elections. He passed away in 1923.

The six-member Centennial Committee, which had selected the previous nineteenth century pioneers in the 1937 and 1938 elections, never met the original goal of the Hall of Fame and that was to select five players from the nineteenth century. The committee never had a chance to meet so a new, smaller committee was formed, the Old-Timers Committee, consisting of the major league's triumvirate: Commissioner Landis and the two league presidents, Frick and Harridge. This committee finally met the original goal when they selected six nineteenth century players. Their selections, all of whom had passed away, were announced on May 2, 1939, less than six weeks before the opening of the Hall of Fame.

All six men chosen appeared on the controversial 1936 veterans' ballot. The first two picks were Cap Anson, a star first baseman and successful manager for the Chicago White Stockings, and Buck Ewing, the game's premier catcher in the 1880s and early 1890s. Both men had finished first with the most votes (39½ votes each) from the original old timer's group that cast 78 ballots in 1936.

The next selection was Charles Radbourn, an 1880s pitcher who had finished seventh in the 1936 balloting (16 votes). Also selected was Charles Comiskey, an outstanding defensive first baseman in the 1880s, a successful manager and eventual longtime owner of the Chicago White Sox. He received six votes from the 1936 committee. Multifaceted Albert Spalding was also chosen although he received only four votes in 1936. Spalding was already discussed regarding the controversial Mills Commission Report that gave us Abner Doubleday as the inventor of baseball.

The final selection was "Candy" Cummings, the most likely inventor of the curveball. His selection was controversial because his major league career was short (six years), and like several other members of the Hall of Fame he was selected because of a single contribution. Adding to his controversy is that he was suggested as a candidate by the committee like all the other candidates on the 1936 ballot, but he finished tied for last place with two other individuals. None of them received any votes!

On December 7, 1939, the BBWAA made the decision to allow the immortal Yankees first baseman Lou Gehrig to bypass the election process and admitted him to the Hall of Fame. This was done after Gehrig had announced his retirement in July 1939, following the diagnosis of his incurable disease, amyotrophic lateral sclerosis. He died from the disease in 1941 at the age of 37.

Also, the BBWAA decided to have the next election in 1942 because by electing twelve twentieth-century players they had met their quota of ten players.

Inductees

George Sisler broke in as a first baseman and pitcher with the Browns in 1915. His most memorable moment in baseball was when he beat the great Walter Johnson 2–1 in his rookie season. He became a full-time first baseman in 1917 where he excelled defensively. Sisler batted .407 and set the major league record for hits with 257 in 1920 (Ichiro Suzuki broke it in 2004). He was the MVP when he batted .420 and had a 41-game hitting streak in 1922.

Sisler batted .340 lifetime, but he could have been better. He developed the flu that affected his sinuses and caused him to have double vision, which prevented him from playing in 1923. He played seven more seasons, but he was never as good, as Yankee pitcher Bob Shawkey explained: "He was never the same because when he was batting he could watch you for so long and when he looked down to refocus we would pitch."[7]

The Hall of Fame's first induction (class of 1939): *Left to right, standing:* Honus Wagner, Grover Cleveland Alexander, Tris Speaker, Nap Lajoie, George Sisler and Walter Johnson. *Seated:* Eddie Collins, Babe Ruth, Connie Mack and Cy Young.

Eddie Collins became the regular second baseman for the Philadelphia A's in 1909. He was an excellent defensive second baseman and holds the career records for most games played at second base (2,650), most assists (7,630), and most total chances (14,591). He helped lead the A's to four pennants and three world titles from 1910 through 1914. He was sold to the Chicago White Sox in 1914 in a cost-cutting move. There he led the Sox to two more pennants and a world title in 1917. Collins batted more than .400 for three different World Series champions. A great bunter, he finished his 25-year career by batting .333 lifetime, with 3,315 hits, 741 stolen bases and an on-base percentage of .424. Collins was considered by many to be one of the smartest to ever play baseball.

He and Herb Pennock, star pitcher for the Yankees, are the answers to an interesting trivia question. Collins' son married Pennock's daughter, making them the only two Hall of Famers whose offspring married each other.

"Wee" Willie Keeler was given that nickname because of his diminutive size (5'5", 140 pounds). He came into his own with the Baltimore Orioles in 1894 where manager Ned Hanlon made him into a right fielder because of his strong arm and good speed. There he became one of the greatest slap hitters of all time. He used a short but heavy bat (30 inches, 46 ounces) while choking up on it. His best season was 1897 when he batted .424, including a 44-game hitting streak. He played on three pennant winners with the Orioles and then two more with the Brooklyn Superbas. He was the first to play for all three New York teams and batted .341 with 495 stolen bases for 19 seasons.

When a reporter asked the affable Keeler how someone his size could hit so well he responded with his classic line, "Keep a clear eye and hit 'em where they ain't."[8]

Adrian "Cap" Anson was recruited by William Hulbert from the National Association to play first base for his Chicago White Stockings and the National League in 1876. He became player-manager in 1879 and also earned his nickname for being their captain as well. He committed the most lifetime errors (583) due in large part to the fact that he was the last first baseman to wear a glove (1892). Despite this shortcoming, Anson became baseball's first superstar, winning four batting titles and becoming the first player to amass 3,000 hits, although the final total has been disputed by researchers. Anson was tough as he marched his players onto the field in military fashion before games, but he was also an innovator who was one of the first managers to bring his team to spring training and have a pitching rotation. Chicago won six pennants during his 22 years with them.

Cap Anson was the poster boy for segregated baseball when he refused to play an exhibition game in 1883 because the other team had a black player, and he helped to bar several black players from playing in the major leagues in 1885.

William Ewing was given the nickname "Buck" after he had a successful hunting trip as a teenager. He spent more than half of his career with the New York Giants. Ewing was an outstanding defensive catcher who had a muscular forearm that helped him snap the ball and produced a legendary throwing arm. Offensively, he seldom struck out and batted more than .300 (.303 or .311 depending on the source). Although not fast, he studied opposing pitchers and finished with 354 stolen bases. He helped lead the Giants to pennants in 1888 and 1889.

Ewing was the first catcher to use a pillow-style padded mitt, have pre-game strategy meetings and, some historians believe, the first catcher to crouch when catching.

Charles Radbourn was a 5'9" right-handed pitcher during the nineteenth century, who after warming up would say, "Old Hoss is ready."[9] He won 25 games as a rookie for the Providence Grays, and would go on to win 20 or more games nine of the eleven seasons he pitched. Hoss was truly a workhorse because he pitched more than 600 innings twice, more than 500 innings once, and six consecutive seasons with more than 400 innings. His best season was in 1884 when he struck out 441 batters and finished with a record of 59–12. He won 308 games in his short career and quit because his arm was so sore that he couldn't lift it to comb his hair.

Two major differences when Radbourn played were he pitched underhanded and the pitching distance was 55'6" inches not 60'6" as it is today.

Charles Comiskey, a.k.a. "Commie," was a first baseman for the St. Louis Browns in the American Association in 1882 where he was the player-manager on four straight pennant winners. Commie became the owner of the St. Paul team in the Western League and then the team moved to Chicago where the league became the American League in 1901. He built the league's most lavish ballpark in Comiskey Park in 1910 as the White Sox went on to win five pennants and two World Series titles during their first 20 years. His world unraveled after the Black Sox scandal following the World Series in 1919.

Charles Comiskey is considered to have caused his players to throw the series because he was a penny-pincher. He had players play in dirty uniforms to save on laundering, and gave $3 for meal money each day rather than the $4 other teams gave. This was a paradox because he gave free grandstand tickets to schoolchildren and servicemen, and gave 10 percent of the gate receipts ($17,000) to the American Red Cross in 1917.

Albert Spalding achieved unparalleled success as a baseball pitcher, pioneer, entrepreneur, and business magnate. He retired as a player at the age of 27 because of a sore arm. Spalding compiled a pitching record of 252–65 while leading the Boston Red Stockings to four pennants in the National Association. He then led the Chicago White Stockings to a pennant in their inaugural season in the National League in 1876. He helped draw up the constitution for the National League and succeeded William Hulbert as Chicago's owner when Hulbert died in 1882. During this time Spalding started a successful sporting goods business that was the chief supplier of baseballs for major league baseball for more than a century. Spalding took his Chicago team and a group of all-stars on a six-month worldwide tour in 1888 and 1889. As we know, Spalding is also responsible for giving us the Doubleday myth.

Small wonder that Spalding's motto was "Everything is possible to him who dares."[10]

Arthur Cummings, a.k.a. "Candy," was walking along a beach in Brooklyn with friends as a kid and started tossing clamshells. He watched as they skimmed the water and darted to the left and at other times darted to the right. He then decided to try it on a baseball in 1863 and after years of frustration and ridicule from others, he was finally able to master it. He went on to pitch in the National Association and compiled a record of 124–72. He did this while pitching underhanded from a pitcher's box when the distance to home plate was only 45 feet. Cummings then pitched in the National League for two years but had a record of only 21–22 before quitting at the end of the 1877 season from a sore arm.

Most historians believe Cummings invented the curveball, but he had his doubters such as Fred Goldsmith, who claimed he invented it in 1866. Cummings wrote an article for a baseball magazine in 1908 when he was almost 60 years of age to support his claim.[11]

Lou Gehrig replaced Wally Pipp at first base for the Yankees on June 2, 1925, and went on to play in 2,130 straight games. During the streak he had concussions, broken fingers, back spasms, and other injuries but still kept going. Cal Ripken, Jr., broke Gehrig's record in 1995, but the "Iron Horse" was much more than his streak. He won the Triple Crown in 1934 as well as two MVP awards. He holds the league record for RBIs (184) and is third on the career list (1,995). He's also third in slugging average (.632) and fifth in on base percentage (.447). He helped lead the Yanks to six of seven World Series titles while batting .361. Gehrig finished with 493 home runs and batted .340 lifetime.

He was honored at Yankee Stadium on July 4, 1939, as 62,000 people attended. The reserved Gehrig didn't want to talk but manager Joe McCarthy insisted and he gave a fine speech and spoke the immortal line, "Today I consider myself the luckiest man on the face of the earth."[12] Following the speech, Babe Ruth, who hadn't spoken to Gehrig in five years after a falling out, came up to him and gave him a big hug.

Baseball Centennial Ceremony

The pivotal day in the Cavalcade of Baseball was June 12, 1939. This was a Monday and was the day set aside by Congress to help Cooperstown and the nation celebrate baseball's centennial. The dedication was slated to begin at noon but it was pushed back to 12:15 because President Roosevelt was scheduled to give a speech at West Point.

Major League Baseball gave itself a two-day holiday to commemorate the centennial. Schools in Cooperstown closed at 10:00 A.M. and most businesses closed at noon as everyone in the village prepared for the arrival of baseball's VIPs, including all the living inductees.

Cooperstown had only two full-time policemen so for security they had to bring in extra policemen from nearby Oneonta and Utica and also state police while hiring Pinkerton plainclothesmen as well.

One of the events that everyone in Cooperstown looked forward to was the arrival of the Centennial Special train that was coming from Grand Central Terminal in New York City. It was a specially designated train, containing 13 Pullman cars that left the city Sunday around 11:00 P.M. and arrived in Cooperstown at 9:00 A.M. Monday. This was the first train that had come to Cooperstown in more than five years.

John Tener, the former National League president, had become interested in Cooperstown through the writings of Sam Crane, the former baseball player and now a sports writer for the New York *Journal.* Crane was supportive of Cooperstown's claim as the birthplace of baseball and had convinced Tener, who had made several visits to the village. Tener helped bring the railroad to Cooperstown because he thought it would eventually bring baseball fans to the village. Unfortunately, due to the Great Depression and the advent of the automobile as the new way of travel, the railroad ceased operation in 1934. Nevertheless, workers and many local people were so excited about the arrival of the special train that they got out their hoes and cleared the tracks of the weeds that had accumulated over the tracks during the last five years. Ken Smith, former sportswriter and later director of the Hall of Fame, rode the train with all the famous dignitaries.

Many of the pictures taken that day were by Homer Ousterhoudt, a 21-year-old Cooperstown inhabitant. He was one of three natives present at the first induction that I was fortunate enough to interview in 2005. He took photos of people departing from the Centennial Special, then during the parade to Doubleday Field, and later for the all-star game at Doubleday. Homer proudly shared with us how he had worked as a cement mixer when they were building the museum in 1937 and later as a mason's helper who carried bricks that became part of the museum's red brick façade.

Following their departure from the train, many converged on the Cooper Inn to have something to eat. Some future Hall of Famers were there to participate in the Doubleday game or came to see what all the fuss was about on this special day. People like the great Pirates third baseman Pie Traynor, now managing his old team, and Casey Stengel, manager of the Boston Bees of the National League. Bill McKechnie, manager of the Cincinnati Reds, and Joe McCarthy, manager of the great Yankees teams of the 1930s and 1940s, were all there.

The great New York Giants left-hander Carl Hubbell, another future Hall of Famer, while standing outside the inn and watching all the people mill about uttered a memorable line when he said, "So this is where all the grief started."[13] All of these baseball notables then walked along Main Street and mingled with fans, regaling them with tales from their baseball careers.

Jim Farley, the postmaster general of the United States, had come to Cooperstown on the Centennial Special but skipped breakfast so that he could get to the post office, opposite the museum building. There he would begin selling the special centennial stamp for three cents; it would be affixed to the special-issue postcards with the Cooperstown postmark. This first-day cover would start a tradition. Just like today, many fans lined up to purchase these first-day covers, with Commissioner Landis purchasing the first one from Postmaster Farley. This transaction was preserved for posterity with a photograph as Ford Frick stood smiling behind Landis. They sold 450,000 first-day covers that day, far exceeding what they expected to sell.

The dedication ceremony began right on time as baseball dignitaries found their seats on the raised stage that had been assembled in front of the museum. Baseball executives were joined by prominent Cooperstown people, all of whom played major roles in the Cavalcade of Baseball. A huge crowd gathered, jamming Main Street all the way to the traffic light on Pioneer Street. Many fans perched on parked cars, leaned out windows, or found other vantage points, such as rooftops, in order to see the proceedings.

Catherine Walker, the Hall of Fame employee who shared her memories about viewing the Doubleday Ball at the Village Club, was also present. She was eight years old as she sat on her father's shoulders while they stood on the steps of the post office, opposite the stage where she was an eyewitness to baseball history. There was national media coverage with NBC radio announcer Tom Manning and NBC Blue newsreel coverage with the premier sportscaster of the day, Bill Stern, doing the honors.

It was a beautiful, cloudless day as Charles J. Doyle, from the Pittsburgh *Sun-Telegraph* and president of the Baseball Writers Association of America (BBWAA), served as master of ceremonies. Doyle paid tribute to baseball's immortals and Abner Doubleday, the inventor of baseball, before introducing Cooperstown's mayor, Roland Spraker, who welcomed everyone to Cooperstown. John Tener and John Heydler, former National League presidents and two of Cooperstown's earliest supporters, were there. Heydler, who helped conceive the idea of the Cavalcade of Baseball as a year-long celebration for the Centennial Celebration, introduced Commissioner Landis.

Landis officially dedicated the museum by declaring, "Since baseball had spread all across the country and around the world, it was fitting that it should have a national museum" and be located where baseball began. Landis went on and paid tribute to the thirteen pioneers and twelve players who had been nominated to the Hall of Fame, but felt that the museum should be dedicated "to all America, to lovers of good sportsmanship, healthy bodies, and clean minds."

Theodore Lettis, chairman of the Cooperstown Centennial Committee, handed a pair of shears to National League president Ford Frick, who cut a red ribbon. Then the American League president, Will Harridge, cut a white ribbon and then the shears were passed to William Bramham, president of the minor leagues, who cut a blue ribbon. Landis then opened the door with the key that Chairman Lettis had given him. Doyle next read the names of the twelve pioneers elected to the hall who had passed away. The reading of each name was followed by a roll of drums. It should be noted that unlike today no one representing the families spoke. The organizers had a full day planned and didn't want to spend too much time having speakers since the 11 living inductees would be speaking.

The band then played "Take Me Out to the Ballgame" as out stepped the only living pioneer, 76-year-old Connie Mack, who was handed a miniature replica of his plaque, just like the others would also receive. The lean, longtime manager of the Philadelphia Athletics wore his customary suit as he thanked the people of Cooperstown for "having the game of baseball start here." He then expressed his gratitude for being selected and paid tribute to the three executives who had cut the ribbons, as well as to the commissioner. Mack, who was accustomed to speaking in public, later said that he was so overwhelmed by the moment that he found it difficult to speak. He came back two more times and passed away in 1956 at the age of 93.

Doyle then read the names of the two players who were elected by the BBWAA and had passed away, New York Giants pitching great Christy Mathewson and the singles-hitting outfielder, Wee Willie Keeler, as taps was played after each name was read.

The next inductee to emerge from behind the door was the "Flying Dutchman," Honus Wagner, 65. The outstanding shortstop and then coach of the Pittsburgh Pirates in 1939 looked disheveled in a rumpled suit and a tie that had the back longer then the front. He spoke briefly and reminisced as he talked about traveling 14 miles by walking, hitch-hiking or riding on a buggy in order to see Connie Mack play when he was with Pittsburgh. He then referred to Cooperstown "as a wonderful little town that puts me in mind of being in Sleepy Hollow." He closed by telling the crowd that "I want to thank you for coming today." Although Wagner never came back and died in 1955 at the age of 81, his widow came back at least once.

The next inductee was the renowned Tris Speaker, 51. Speaker, nicknamed "The Gray Eagle," was dressed in gray with his gray hair, which had turned prematurely gray when he was a young man. Speaker made the briefest speech, saying that Connie Mack expressed how all the inductees felt as he thanked the sportswriters for his selection. It should be noted that many of today's Hall of Famers would be very pleased with the brevity of each individual's remarks. Today, some of the induction speeches are longer than 25 minutes. Speaker came back two more times before passing away in 1958 at the age of 70.

Larry Lajoie, 64, was the next one up. Lajoie, pronounced "Lazhoway," told the crowd that he was glad to be honored with all these greats, and shared his joy by telling everyone how much he was enjoying this day. Lajoie never came back because he was more content to do other things with his life. He died in 1959 at the age of 84.

Cy Young, 72, was the next great to appear. He was upbeat as he paid tribute to the other inductees and sounded an optimistic tone during his speech by stating, "Nothing pleases me better than to see that the younger generation is following our footsteps. I do hope that a hundred years from now, the game will be greater."

Although some people were upset that it took two ballots to get Young inducted, he was the most cooperative inductee right from the start and he came back to Cooperstown five times, including 1955, four months before he died at the age of 88.

Walter Johnson, 51, the great pitcher for the Washington Senators, was the next Hall of Famer to speak. "The Big Train" said, "I'm very proud to have my name enrolled in the Hall of Fame, and I'm very happy to have my name enrolled with these men." He never had a chance to come back and died suddenly from a cerebral hemorrhage in 1946 at the age of 59.

Another quiet and modest inductee like Johnson was the former St. Louis Browns first baseman George Sisler, 46, who said proudly, "I think I'm one of the youngest here, but it is certainly nice to be here and greet all of you gentlemen. I think this is a great thing for baseball to commemorate the fine records of all these great men who had played baseball. I'm certainly glad to do my little part in helping this great day."

This humble inductee never told the crowd that he had to make the decision to come to this ceremony while his wife went to his oldest son's college graduation from Colgate University. He came back three more times and died in 1973, having just turned 80.

Another outstanding second baseman was the next speaker, Eddie Collins, 52, who was dressed in a double-breasted suit with two-toned shoes. Eddie was self-effacing when he uttered the most memorable line of the day: "This is about the proudest day of my life, and to be able to rub elbows with the players here today, why I feel that I'd be happy to be the batboy for such a team as this." Collins never made it back for another induction and died in 1951 at the age of 63. However, his widow did attend several inductions.

The next inductee proved to be one of the more popular with the fans because of his circumstances and that was Grover Cleveland "Pete" Alexander, 62, who had battled alcoholism, so the crowd felt for him as he made his very gracious speech. He said, "I had many a thrill in my baseball career and many a treat, but I consider this the greatest treat, one of the greatest thrills I have had in my long career in baseball." It should be noted that he acquired his nickname from the term "sneaky pete," the name given to alcohol after it was declared illegal because of Prohibition. Pete continued, "I'm proud to be a member with these gentlemen here. In my dreams I often think what I could do with a team like this. I do wish to say it's a mighty proud moment in my life to be here." When he finished, the crowd roared their approval. As he made his way back to his seat, Walter Johnson stood up and wrapped his arms around his fellow pitcher.

His battle with the bottle caused him to struggle to make ends meet after his playing career was over. Officials of the hall did try to help him by offering him a job as a night watchman, but he declined. He never came back and died in 1950 at the age of 62.

The greatest and most famous baseball player of all time, Babe Ruth, was the last speaker and the crowd roared as he approached the podium. He was the only inductee to appear without a tie as he spoke about the future just like Cy Young before him. The Babe said, "I hope that some day some of the young fellas coming into the game will know how it feels to be picked for the Hall of Fame." Ruth continued, "And I hope the coming generation — the young boys today — that they'll work hard and also will be in it." He then echoed Young when he said, "I hope it goes another one hundred years and the next one hundred years is the greatest." He concluded, "So it's a pleasure for me to come up here and to be in the Hall of Fame."

Ruth never made it back and died in 1948 at the age of 53. However, his family has continued to come back, beginning with his widow, then his daughters, and now his grandchildren.

The third fan I interviewed who witnessed the 1939 induction was Fred St. John. He was a fifteen-year-old boy when he followed the Babe to the Otesaga Hotel before he left to go back to New York City. Fred had his one dollar Brownie camera with him and nervously asked the Sultan of Swat if he could take his picture. Ruth nodded, but then said, "Wait a minute, I think you've got your finger on the lens." Ruth then went over to the nervous teenager and moved his finger. Ruth then said, "Now point it and take a deep breath and hold still and then shoot it." After he had taken the picture the baseball great said to him, "There, I don't want you to take a bad picture of me." St. John, a retired post office supervisor, was happy to give me a print of his photo, some 66 years later.

However, if they ever gave out an award for the fan who went above and beyond, then Frank McCusky would have won it hands down. He had graduated from a high school in Minneapolis and had decided that he wanted to be a part of this historic day. He left his home and hitchhiked approximately 1,200 miles, arriving in Cooperstown at 10:00 P.M. Saturday. Thanks to the hospitality of Mr. and Mrs. Albert Coleman at 14 Delaware Street, he had a place to stay for the next two nights. He then became one of the 15,000 fans to witness the festivities on June 12.[14]

Thus, the dedication of the museum and the first induction were now over and Landis officially opened the museum to the public. During this time as everyone mingled on the stage, umpire Tom Connolly congratulated Collins, Lajoie, and Speaker on their speeches and then quipped, "Your language has improved a lot since I was umpiring behind you."[15] Connolly was the premier American League ump and was there along with the premier National League ump, Bill Klem, to officiate the all-star game later at Doubleday Field. Both umpires would be inducted into the Hall of Fame in 1953.

People gather on the platform in front of the Hall of Fame after the ceremony.

A group photo was taken of the ten living Hall of Famers; it would appear in newspapers across the country the next day. There was one conspicuous absentee, and that was "The Georgia Peach," Ty Cobb. Cobb, 52, arrived soon after the picture was taken. Howard Talbot, director of the Hall of Fame for 25 years, was another eyewitness to the event. He was 14 at the time and came with his family from nearby Edmeston. His most vivid memory was Ty Cobb getting there late and climbing over the railing of the stage during the Induction Ceremony. Cobb later said that he was delayed in Utica because one of his children became sick after having driven across country from his home in Menlo Park, California, with two of his five children. He would not admit the truth until years later when he said he didn't want to be photographed with the commissioner because he felt Landis had not cleared his name sufficiently for an alleged game-throwing plot in 1926.

Nevertheless, Ty Cobb came back five times just like Cy Young, and contrary to his personality, he was always gracious and enjoyed going back to Cooperstown very much. Cobb died in 1961 at the age of 74. His son Jimmy came back often after his father died.

The next activity would be a parade of less than three blocks from the museum to Doubleday Field that kicked off at 2:30. Since there would be two old-time games before the all-star game, many of the assembled dressed in nineteenth-century garb as they watched and mingled with the baseball stars of yesterday and today. Most of the immortals remained in street clothes, but Eddie Collins, Honus Wagner, Walter Johnson, and Babe Ruth changed into their old uniforms at the Knox Girls' School gymnasium. The parade included several local bands and soldiers from nearby Fort Jay, many of whom grew handlebar moustaches.

Doubleday Field was packed with 10,000 people as they watched the first game, a recreation of a game of town ball played by a group of boys from Cooperstown High School. Baseball's elder statesman, Connie Mack, remembered playing it as a boy growing up in

Top: Ty Cobb (holding baseball) is about to sign an autograph after arriving late for the ceremony. *Bottom:* The Hall of Famers march along Main Street from the Hall of Fame to Doubleday Field. They are followed by the American and National League all-stars.

Massachusetts as he watched from the grandstand. The umpire was dressed in a stovepipe hat, long tight pants, and a flowered waistcoat.

The next game was a version of 1850s baseball as played by two of the first organized baseball teams, the Knickerbockers of New York and the Excelsiors of Brooklyn. The John Jay soldiers played the two-inning game that included another distinctive outfit worn by the umpire, who wore a top hat with a frock coat and carried a cane and a red umbrella. NBC also broadcast these two games as well as the featured next game from a table behind home plate. The announcers were Arch McDonald and New York Yankees broadcaster Mel Allen.

The final game is the one everyone had come to see and this was the all-star game that would be made up of two players from all sixteen major league teams. Originally it was supposed to be two stars from each team but many teams didn't send their best players. The Yankees, for instance, sent George Selkirk and their backup catcher, Arndt Jorgens, but no Joe DiMaggio or Red Ruffing. Even so, nine future Hall of Famers played, including Arky Vaughan, Lloyd Waner, Lefty Grove, Dizzy Dean, Joe Medwick, Hank Greenberg, Charlie Gehringer, Mel Ott, and Billy Herman.

What made it most enjoyable for the fans was the participation of four of the immortals in the contest. Honus Wagner and Eddie Collins were designated honorary captains. They chose their teams by gripping a bat and then putting hand over hand just like kids have done for ages in schoolyards and sandlots across America. Wagner, known for his huge hands, easily grabbed the knob of the bat to get first pick. He chose Lefty Grove while Collins chose Dizzy Dean, emphasizing the importance of pitching. Ironically, neither Collins nor Wagner had ever met before this day. Walter Johnson, a good-hitting pitcher in his day, hit grounders to the infielders before the game started. The biggest thrill for the fans, however, was when Babe Ruth came up to pinch-hit for the Wagners in the bottom of the fifth inning. Unfortunately, he popped out to the catcher, his former teammate Jorgens.

Honus Wagner and Eddie Collins use a bat to see who will pick first.

Babe Ruth pinch hitting in the game.

As Jorgens went after the ball, the fans yelled, "Drop it! Drop it!" Later the opposing pitcher, Syl Johnson, said he tried to give "The Bambino" a pitch he could hit. Ruth agreed, but admitted with a grin, "I can't hit the floor with my hat."[16] The game ended after six and a half innings in favor of the Wagners 4–2, because the participants had to make train connections.

This whole experience for the major leaguers turned out to be a lot better than they had expected. When they first heard about the game in the beginning of the season they joked about it by referring to the two pioneers as Abner "Doubleplay" and Alexander "Cartwheel." Many of them had traveled to the game at their own expense and they came away from it with a deeper sense of appreciation for the history of baseball, especially after seeing the greats of the game. Dan Daniel, of the New York *World Telegram*, wrote, "To keep Cooperstown, the Museum, and the Hall of Fame alive, the pickup game might be made an annual affair. Or, the two leagues might get together, and each year, assign two clubs to play a game at Cooperstown."[17] Daniel's latter suggestion came to pass, starting a tradition with the first game in 1940 and the last one in 2008, when major league scheduling made it impossible to continue.

Everyone connected to the planning and execution of the Cavalcade of Baseball had to feel a tremendous amount of satisfaction, but no one could have felt more joy and fulfillment at what had been accomplished then Stephen Clark and especially Alexander Cleland.

Chapter 4

Where Is Everybody?
1940–1949

The BBWAA had decided in 1939 to have the election every three years because they had met their goal of electing ten twentieth-century players; thus, it wasn't necessary to have the next election until 1942. This decision was widely criticized because the BBWAA had averaged three players per year from 1936 through 1939, an ideal number for an annual induction. The BBWAA was instructed to select players active in the twentieth century with a new requirement that they had to be retired at least one year.

1942

The BBWAA cast 233 ballots in 1942 as National League second baseman and all-time great hitter Rogers Hornsby was selected as the only inductee, receiving 78.1 percent of the vote (182 votes). It should be pointed out that the BBWAA had to choose from a pool of players who were active from 1901 through 1940. The voters gave a priority to players from the 1900s and 1910s since they finished in the next seven spots. Hornsby received votes when he was still active (1936 and 1937) so it took him five elections (562 total votes) to achieve immortality.

Hornsby is one of the greatest hitters of all time so he should have gone in the year after he retired (1938), but he had such an obnoxious personality he undoubtedly rubbed many writers the wrong way.

A dramatic difference between Hall of Fame elections then and today was illustrated with Hornsby's response to the news of his induction. He heard about it while sitting in a barber's chair in Fort Worth, Texas, on January 20, 1942. Hornsby was the manager of a minor league team, the Fort Worth Cats, at the time and responded with typical bluntness by stating, "It's quite a distinction but right now there's a couple of more important things like winning the war and baseball."[1]

There was no induction in 1942 due to World War II and restrictions on travel because of gas rationing resulting in very few visitors to the Hall of Fame. Hornsby never was formally inducted and showed no interest as evidenced by the fact that he came once in 1953 only because he was the Cincinnati Reds' manager in the annual Doubleday Field exhibition game. Hornsby died at the age of 66 in 1963.

Commissioner Landis completely revised the Old Timers' Committee, renamed it the Hall of Fame Committee, and removed himself and the two league presidents. He made it a permanent governing body from 1939 through 1944 and replaced the triumvirate with A's owner and manager Connie Mack, Yankees' president Ed Barrow, Boston Braves' president Bob Quinn and sportswriter Sid Mercer. Regrettably nothing really changed because they never convened since the baseball people were too busy with their jobs and were too old to take the time to research and do what was needed.

Inductee

Rogers Hornsby was born in Texas in 1896 and his first name was his mother's maiden name. The National League second baseman trailed only Ty Cobb with the second highest lifetime batting average at .358. He batted more than .400 three times, including .424 in 1924. The "Rajah" won seven batting titles, two Triple Crowns, and played in two World Series, winning his only one in 1926 with the St. Louis Cardinals as their player-manager. One reason he had a keen batting eye was he supposedly never attended movies or read newspapers. His life revolved around baseball and horse racing. He once said, "One provided income while the other took it away."[2]

He could be crude and nasty toward people and it cost him his managing job with the Chicago Cubs in mid-season in 1932 when they went on to win the pennant. He was so despised by the players that they didn't vote him any share of the World Series money.

1944

There were no elections in 1943 or 1944, creating more complaints that the stars of the 1880s and 1890s were continuing to be ignored. On August 4, 1944, Landis named three new members to the committee including Hall of Fame president Stephen C. Clark and treasurer Paul Kerr along with Boston sportswriter Mel Webb. Clark became chairman and Kerr secretary, giving the committee the impetus to carry out Landis's instructions. Landis wanted at least 10 people who played between 1876 and 1900 elected.

Sadly, on November 25, 1944, Commissioner Landis died; the Hall of Fame Committee met at baseball's winter meetings two weeks later in New York City and unanimously moved to elect Landis. He was not formally inducted until 1946.

Inductee

Kenesaw Mountain Landis was born in Ohio in 1866 and was named after the battle in the Civil War in which his father, a Union surgeon, lost his leg. As a federal district judge, he helped uphold baseball's reserve clause and preserve Major League Baseball when he had the Federal League lawsuit settled out of court in 1916. Landis was chosen baseball's first commissioner in 1920 after the Black Sox scandal of the 1919 World Series. Eight Chicago White Sox players were acquitted in court in 1921 of throwing the World Series. Landis ignored the acquittal and went on to ban them from baseball for life as he helped to clean up the sport and rid it of gambling. Despite being arbitrary and dictatorial in this case he had another side as well. During the seventh game of the 1934 World Series between the Cards and the Tigers being played at Tiger Stadium, the Detroit fans started showering debris on the Cards left fielder, Joe Medwick. Landis had the Cards take him out of the game for his own safety as St. Louis went on to win the game and the series.

As a small gesture during the Depression, Landis took a pay cut of $10,000 to $55,000.

1945

The next BBWAA election was in 1945. The BBWAA again had to choose from players who were active from 1901 through 1943. The BBWAA cast 247 ballots and for the first time in six elections no one received the necessary 75 percent needed for induction. One reason is that they had too wide a range (43 years) resulting in votes for 94 candidates. Following much criticism, the Hall of Fame Committee resumed annual elections.

The Hall of Fame Committee at that time also had the responsibility of overseeing the BBWAA elections so they fine-tuned the criteria for voters to observe when considering a candidate. The criteria were playing ability, integrity, sportsmanship, character and contribution to the team on which they played and to baseball in general.

The Old-Timers Committee (still called that but actually the Hall of Fame Committee), as instructed by Commissioner Landis, selected ten members from the nineteenth century, including seven whose careers extended into the early twentieth century.

There were several reasons why the committee chose players whose careers went beyond the nineteenth century. The committee was trying to help out the BBWAA after they failed to elect anyone by selecting those players who had all received significant support from the BBWAA. Three of them played positions that had no representation in the hall prior to their selection. They were Jimmy Collins at third along with Ed Delahanty and Fred Clarke in left field. Also, there was a strong emphasis on picking players from pennant winners. Eight of the ten chosen had started on at least four championship teams. Fred Clarke and Hugh Duffy were the only living inductees at the time of the vote.

Jimmy Collins collected 464 votes in six BBWAA elections and was a unanimous selection.

Fred Clarke had 256 votes in six elections and was also a unanimous selection, due in large part to his success as a manager. It should be noted that Fred's grandson lobbied the Hall of Fame Committee in 1945, helping to get his grandfather elected. This was another example of a grassroots campaign just like Cartwright's grandson helped to get his grandfather elected in 1938.

Catcher and manager Wilbert Robinson had 238 votes in six BBWAA elections and was also a unanimous selection.

Catcher Roger Bresnahan received the third highest amount of votes with 414 in six BBWAA elections. Nevertheless, Bresnahan was controversial because he had ordinary offensive numbers. Baseball analyst Bill James in *Politics of Glory* calls his election "a clear, unmistakable error" (p. 41). James Vail in *The Road to Cooperstown* calls him "statistically, one of worst selections ever" (p. 96). Robert Cohen in *Baseball Hall of Fame or Hall of Shame?* rates him and Ray Schalk last for Hall of Fame catchers, calling them "completely unwarranted" (p. 117). Also, he died just before the December 1944 election, which gave a boost to his selection.

David Fleitz in *Ghosts in the Gallery at Cooperstown* admits that Bresnahan's selection was very controversial but also states he was important to John McGraw's Giants pennant winning teams of 1904 and 1905 with his handling of the pitching staff.[3]

Ed Delahanty easily had the most impressive offensive stats of the ten inductees and had the most votes at 579.

Outfielder Hugh Duffy received 206 votes in the six elections.

Shortstop and manager Hughie Jennings received 216 votes in six elections. Yet Bill James felt his selection was also "an unmistakable error" because he had a short career and wasn't a dominant shortstop (p. 42). Robert Cohen felt he "wasn't a legitimate Hall of Famer, because he didn't play long enough and only had six good seasons" (p. 95). James Vail believes his membership might be more justifiable if Jennings was cited for managing as well as playing (p. 235).

Versatile position player Michael "King" Kelly played his entire career in the nineteenth century. He received 15 votes in the 1936 special veterans' committee vote. Kelly was a catcher and played on nine pennant winners.

Pioneer Jim O'Rourke was another versatile outfielder who also played in the nineteenth century except for one game in 1904. O'Rourke didn't receive any votes in the 1936 special veterans' committee vote, but being on six pennant winners helped his cause.

Slugging first baseman Dan Brouthers also played all but one year in the nineteenth century (two games in 1904). He received two votes in the 1936 special committee election. Brouthers was also helped by playing on six pennant winners.

Inductees

Jimmy Collins helped lead the Boston Beaneaters to two pennants in 1897 and 1898. Collins jumped to the American League in 1901 as the player-manager of the Boston Americans (later the Red Sox) and helped lead them to two pennants. Boston beat the Pirates in the first World Series between the American and National Leagues in 1903 but didn't play in 1904 because the New York Giants refused to play them.

Jimmy Collins became a third baseman in 1895 when his Louisville manager brought him in from the outfield after the Baltimore Orioles bunted on the regular third baseman for seven straight hits. When the next batter tried to bunt, Collins ran in, grabbed the ball barehanded, and threw underhanded to first base for the out. He was the first to do this, and he also revolutionized third-base play by playing off third base and moving in or out on each play. Honus Wagner named him his all-time third baseman.

Fred Clarke broke in as a rookie left fielder with the Louisville Colonels in 1894 by going five for five. He became owner Barney Dreyfuss's player-manager at the age of 24 and went with him to Pittsburgh where he helped move his longtime teammate, Honus Wagner, to shortstop. They helped the Pirates win four pennants and one World Series. Clarke used his speed to steal 509 bases while batting .390 in 1897 and .312 lifetime.

Fred Clarke was an innovator who introduced flip-down sunglasses and a mechanical way of handling the tarpaulin that covers the infield.

He also became a millionaire in retirement when oil was discovered on his Kansas farm.

Wilbert Robinson was the catcher and captain of the old Baltimore Orioles that won three pennants in the 1890s. He had seven hits and 11 RBIs in a game in 1892. During his career he had every finger on both hands broken at least once. He managed Brooklyn, which was called the Robins after him. He led them to two pennants and more than 1000 victories in his 18 years as their manager.

"Uncle Robbie," as he was affectionately called by the Brooklyn fans, was one of baseball's most colorful characters. He started a Bonehead Club to fine players for stupid plays and he became its first member for turning in a laundry list to the ump instead of the starting lineup before the game started. He once caught a baseball that dropped from an airplane and exploded on his chest as he caught it, making him think he was mortally wounded. It turned out to be a grapefruit and not a baseball!

Roger Bresnahan was known as the "Duke of Tralee" because of his Irish brogue, but he was actually born in Toledo, Ohio, in 1879 to Irish immigrant parents. He came up to the majors and played all nine positions before settling in as a catcher. He had good speed and stole 34 bases and finished second in the National League with an on base average of .443 as the leadoff hitter for John McGraw's 1903 Giants. He has the most lifetime stolen bases of any catcher with 212. He was also an innovative catcher and was the first to wear shin guards and have padding around the catcher's mask.

The great New York Giants pitcher Christy Mathewson convinced Bresnahan to become a full-time catcher and he went on to catch his three complete game shutouts in the 1905 World Series championship over the Philadelphia A's, while batting .313.

Ed Delahanty made his debut with the Philadelphia Phillies in 1888 and was an infielder before finding his natural position as a left fielder. He became the dominant player of the 1890s as he went on to bat more than .400 three times and was the only player ever to lead both the American and National leagues in hitting. He finished with a lifetime batting average of .346 and was a five-tool player long before the term was ever used. He had a very good arm with 243 outfield assists and led the league in home runs twice, slugging percentage five times, and had 455 stolen bases for his career.

However, all of these accomplishments were diminished by a gambling addiction and a serious drinking problem. His life would end tragically in 1903 at the age of 35 when he was put off a train in Canada near Niagara Falls at the International Bridge for drunk and disorderly conduct. He either fell or slipped off the bridge into the Niagara River and the authorities found his body a week later below the Horseshoe Falls in Canada. What makes this story more bizarre is that money and jewelry he had on him were never found.

Hugh Duffy had the distinction of playing in four major leagues: the National, Players, and American leagues as well as the American Association. He became a star center fielder with the Boston Beaneaters of the National League and helped lead them to five pennants. He teamed with Tommy McCarthy to form the best defensive outfield that became known as "The Heavenly Twins." He later became a manager, coach, and scout and was second to Connie Mack with 68 years in baseball.

He had the highest batting average ever at .440 in 1894, but he didn't know it until after the season was over. He later said, "No one thought much of averages in those days. I didn't realize I hit that much until months later."[4]

Hughie Jennings batted .401 for the 1896 pennant-winning Orioles and was such a good fielder that Honus Wagner modeled himself after Jennings as a shortstop. Jennings played 13 years and batted .312. He went on to win pennants during his first three seasons (1907 to 1909) managing the Detroit Tigers. Jennings also coached for close friend John McGraw's New York Giants when they won four straight pennants (1921 through 1924.)

He was called "Ee-yah" because that is what he would yell at his players to give them encouragement when he was managing. Jennings fulfilled a lifelong ambition when he became a lawyer by getting his law degree at Cornell University in exchange for coaching the school's baseball team.

Michael Kelly acquired the nickname "King" as one of baseball's first superstars. He helped the Chicago White Stockings win five pennants while leading the league in batting in 1886 with a .388 average. He was a catcher and also a good defensive outfielder who became an exceptional base stealer. The King developed the hook slide to evade tags and inspired the popular song "Slide Kelly Slide." Kelly had the matinee idol's good looks and performed on the stage as well. He would often arrive for games in a horse-driven carriage dressed in a silk hat and an ascot.

Sadly, alcohol took its toll on him. The "King" was almost destitute when he was on his way to perform at a theater in Boston and was stricken with pneumonia in 1894. He was accidentally dropped from a stretcher while being brought into the hospital. As he rolled on the floor, he maintained his flair for the dramatic right to the end by saying, "That's my last slide."[5] He died a few days later at the age of 36.

Jim O'Rourke was the main breadwinner in his family since his father had died. When he signed his first contract in 1872, his mother wouldn't consent until the team agreed to provide a farm laborer to take over Jim's farm duties. He had the distinction of getting the National League's first hit in 1876 when he singled for the Boston Red Stockings. He played all nine positions with left field being his main position. He was the catcher for six Hall of Fame pitchers and batted .310 lifetime.

O'Rourke was called "Orator Jim" because of his command of the English language.

He was player-manager of the Buffalo Bisons in 1881 when one of his players asked for a raise. Orator Jim replied, "I'm sorry but the condition of our exchequer will not permit anything of the sort." The player, being totally confused, dropped his request.[6]

Dan Brouthers was an adequate fielding first baseman, but he was one of baseball's first power hitters. He was also a five-time batting champ who played for 11 teams in three leagues over his 19-year career. He batted .342 lifetime, the ninth highest in history. He appeared in two games for the New York Giants in 1904 at the age of 46. John McGraw then gave him various jobs at the Polo Grounds, where he worked for over 20 years.

Brouthers joined John Montgomery Ward's Brotherhood of Professional Baseball Players in 1885 and went on to become a vice-president of the organization. They sat down with the owners in order to do away with the reserve clause, which bound a player for life to a team. When the owners refused to budge, the Players League was formed in 1890 but collapsed after one year. The Brotherhood folded the following year.

1946

Since a high number of candidates (94) had received votes in the 1945 BBWAA election, a two-step ballot process would be instituted to narrow the field for a final vote in the 1946 BBWAA election. The top 20 candidates would proceed to a final ballot. During the first ballot there was a tie for 20th place so a total of 21 candidates were put on the final ballot. A voter could vote for only five finalists, but the results were the same with no one reaching the required 75 percent.

The 1946 Old Timers Committee chose at its April meeting 11 new members, several of whom were controversial. These selections would be formally recognized during the 1947 Induction Ceremony.

Rube Waddell, an eccentric left-handed pitcher, garnered the most votes of the 11 new members in seven BBWAA elections with 839.

Cubs first baseman and player-manager Frank Chance received 804 BBWAA votes and finished first in both the 1945 and 1946 elections.

Ed Walsh was the most successful spitball pitcher of all time and received the third most votes with 683.

Johnny Evers was the second baseman on the same successful Cubs' teams with Chance and received the fourth highest BBWAA vote tally with 603 votes.

There was a significant drop-off for fifth place as former successful pitcher and manager Clark Griffith, who was best known as the Washington Senators owner, had 286 votes in the BBWAA elections.

Pitcher Joe "Iron Man" McGinnity received 236 votes in six BBWAA elections.

Eddie Plank was a left-handed pitcher who won 326 games and received only 219 votes in six BBWAA elections. It seems strange that with his record the best he could do was 27 percent of the vote in 1942 when he finished 18th.

Joe Tinker was the shortstop on those same Cubs teams as Chance and Evers and received 183 votes.

The three Cubs infielders (Chance, Evers and Tinker) were made famous by the Franklin Adams poem, *Baseball's Sad Lexicon*. Adams wrote the poem in 1910 for the New York *Evening Mail*, and even though he was a New York sportswriter, he was a die-hard Cubs fan. Adams wrote the poem after witnessing a double play the Cubs made against the Giants at the Polo Grounds. It turns out that as a unit (1903 to 1910), they never once led the league in double plays. Despite the high vote totals for Chance and Evers, their many critics believe the main reason they all went in together was because of the poem. All three had only ordinary offensive numbers, but what also influenced voters was that they were a part of the most successful Cubs teams ever, and Chance was also their player-manager.

Jesse Burkett received only 11 votes on six BBWAA ballots, but a lot of that can be attributed to the fact that he played a good portion of his career in the nineteenth century and also his irascible personality. Nevertheless, the outfielder was a bona fide hitting star.

Pitcher Jack Chesbro received only 10 votes and pitched all but two of his 11 seasons in the twentieth century. He was controversial because his major claim to fame is winning 41 games in 1904, the most wins in a season by a pitcher since the pitching distance was moved to its present distance of 60'6" in 1893.

Tommy McCarthy, an outfielder, played his entire career before 1900 so he wasn't eligible on the BBWAA ballot. He received only one vote from the 1936 Veterans Committee (VC). McCarthy was a good outfielder but nothing else stands out so that is why he is one of the most controversial selections ever by the VC. James has him the lowest rated right fielder in the Hall of Fame (p. 178). Vail calls him "statistically, one of the worst selections ever" (p. 96). Finally, Cohen states his selection "is indefensible" (p. 202). David Fleitz, who always "sees the glass half full rather than half empty," states: "It appears that McCarthy was elected not for his statistical achievements but for his contributions to baseball strategy. He was directly responsible for several rule changes, most notably the infield fly rule."[7]

Waddell, Chance, McGinnity, Plank, Chesbro and McCarthy had already passed away at the time of the vote (April 1946).

A reason given for the committee's selections, especially in 1946, was they were trying to make up for the failure of the BBWAA to elect anyone in 1945 or 1946. The Hall of Fame Committee (VC), however, violated their own rules by electing four players (Evers, Plank, Tinker, and Walsh) who had begun their careers after 1900, which was supposed to be the sole domain of the BBWAA.

The problem was really twofold. First, both groups (BBWAA and the Hall of Fame Committee) were so intent in getting players in from the 1900s and 1910s that they bypassed more legitimate candidates such as Lefty Grove and Mickey Cochrane. Secondly, they didn't do enough research so that they picked, as an example, Tommy McCarthy over more deserving nineteenth century candidates such as Billy Hamilton and Sam Thompson.

Inductees

George Edward Waddell was born on a Friday the 13th and died on an April Fool's Day. During the intervening 37 years he struck out more batters, frustrated more managers, and attracted more fans than any pitcher of his era. The lefthander was nicknamed "Rube" while pitching for a semipro team, due in part to his being uneducated and from a poor rural background. Yet he enjoyed tremendous success with Connie Mack and the A's when he led the league in strikeouts six straight years, including 349 in 1904. Waddell led the league in wins, strikeouts, and ERA (pitching's Triple Crown) in 1905.

Off the field, he got into trouble because of his drinking, but he was a caring man who once carried a teammate off the field after he had been knocked unconscious, brought him to a hospital, and stayed with him all night. He also helped to save a town when the Mississippi River overflowed its banks and he stood in water up to his neck while putting up sandbags. He developed pneumonia and later died in 1914 of TB at the age of 37.

Frank Chance was selected to the Hall of Fame as a first baseman but his record as a player-manager for the Chicago Cubs helped get him elected. Many would say that fate played a part throughout his life starting in college when he planned to be a dentist but instead signed with Chicago after the Cubs' owner heard about him while Chance was playing amateur baseball. He came up as a catcher but he had teammate Johnny Kling ahead of him so manager Frank Selee moved him to first base. He was reluctant to make the switch and almost quit but went on to be a fine defensive player. Finally, when Selee had to step down because of illness, the players voted for the new manager and Chance won in a close vote over Kling. Chance went on to become "The Peerless Leader" as he led his team to four pennants in five years and two World Series titles.

Ed Walsh broke in with the Chicago White Sox in 1904 and learned to throw the spitball from a teammate. He went on to win two games against the heavily favored Cubs during the 1906 World Series as the Hitless Wonders defeated their crosstown rivals. Walsh had a phenomenal season in 1908 as he won 40 games and pitched 464 innings. He has the lowest career ERA at 1.82.

"Big Ed" explained how he threw the spitball by putting spit on the ball between the seams and then gripping it and throwing it like a fastball. It had the speed of a fastball but no rotation so it broke like a knuckleball. The spitball has been called the Deadball Era's equivalent to the split-fingered fastball. It was declared illegal in 1920.

Johnny Evers had his best season in 1914 when he was traded to the Boston Braves from the Cubs, winning the Chalmers Award as the league's MVP. The Miracle Braves won the pennant and World Series as Evers batted .438 to defeat the Philadelphia A's. Evers had a terrible disposition toward everyone, including his double play partner with the Cubs, Joe Tinker. They didn't speak for years but finally made up after they retired.

Evers was so intense that he supposedly went home and studied the rule book every night. It paid off during the 1908 season when he made ump Hank O'Day aware of a runner who missed second base during a game and nothing was done about it. O'Day didn't miss the call when the same thing happened again and he called Fred Merkle out in a crucial game between the Cubs and Giants. The result was a 1–1 tie, forcing a replay that the Cubs won to clinch the pennant and then went on to win the World Series.

Clark Griffith won 20 or more games six straight years with the Chicago Cubs and earned the nickname of the "Old Fox." Griffith became the player-manager of the Chicago White Sox in 1901 to help launch the American League. They won the league's first pennant with the Old Fox winning 24 games. Griffith finished with 237 victories. He became manager of the Washington Senators in 1912 and their owner in 1919. During his 36 years as the Senators' owner they won three pennants and one World Series in 1924.

Griffith's long tenure as Washington's owner helped him cultivate friendships with eight presidents. He started the tradition of the president throwing out the first ball to start the season. He was also responsible for speaking to President Franklin Roosevelt (FDR) before FDR gave the green light that kept baseball going through World War II.

Joe "Iron Man" McGinnity had an auspicious rookie season, winning 28 games for the Baltimore Orioles in 1899. He led the majors in victories five times and won 246 games in his short 10-year career. He was called "Iron Man" since he worked in an iron foundry during the off-season. However, the nickname was apt since he led the league in innings pitched four times, pitched both ends of a double header five times, and had 314 complete games. Also, he won another 200 games in the minors after he retired from the majors and pitched well into his 50s. He claimed he never had a sore arm because he changed his arm angle when it got tired.

His career almost ended in 1901 when he spat tobacco juice in umpire Tom Connolly's face. The American League was ready to permanently ban him, but he was sincerely penitent when he apologized to Connolly and was instead given a 12-game suspension.

Eddie Plank was a sidearm pitcher who won 20 or more games seven times during his 14 years with the Philadelphia A's. Plank also won 21 games in the Federal League. He was a part of six pennant winning teams and three World Series champions. He also collected 331 hits to put him in the top 20 for pitchers and once stole home in a 1909 game.

When Plank pitched, he irritated everyone, including the fans. He was constantly fidgeting between pitches and talking to himself as he rattled the hitters with all his distractions. His games took so long that the hometown fans hated to attend because they were afraid they would miss their trains or be late for supper.

He retired to his hometown of Gettysburg and served as a tour guide of the Gettysburg Battlefield where he was affectionately called "Gettysburg Eddie."

Joe Tinker started as a third baseman in 1902, but Cubs manager Frank Selee switched him to shortstop where he led the league in fielding four times and two times each in assists, putouts, and double plays. Tinker was a very good hit and run man who stole 336 bases lifetime. He was the first big name player to jump to the Federal League in 1914 and became the player-manager of the Chicago Whales when they won the 1915 pennant.

Tinker would not have been a controversial choice if the immortal pitcher Christy Mathewson had anything to say about it. Tinker batted .350 against him in 1902 and .400 in 1906. He continued his success against Mathewson when he hit a homer in the Merkle Boner tie game in 1908 and then a key triple in the 4–2 Cub victory to clinch the pennant over the Giants.

Jesse Burkett had limited range and a weak arm as an outfielder. Hitting was another story, however, as he twice batted more than .400 and led the National League in batting three times. He was an excellent leadoff hitter who drew a lot of walks, stole bases, and was considered the league's best bunter. Burkett retired with a .338 batting average and a .415 on base percentage.

Burkett was called "The Crab" because of his nasty disposition on the field. He once threw a ball at an unruly crowd and had to be removed from a game by six policemen after being thrown out of both games of a double header. Yet there was another side to him as evidenced by the fact that he jumped into the Ohio River as a 12 year old to rescue a girl who had fallen out of a boat. She died and he never got over it.

Jack Chesbro is the only Hall of Famer who played in the Cooperstown area when he pitched for a semi-pro team in 1896. He helped the Pittsburgh Pirates win the pennant in 1902 when he won 28 games. He jumped to the New York Highlanders (Yankees) in 1903 and went on to have his best season ever in 1904, developing an effective spitball while winning 41 games and leading the league in six other categories.

However, he is most remembered for one pitch. He threw a wild pitch that sailed over the head of his catcher and let in the winning run as Boston won the pennant at the Highlanders' Hilltop Park on the last day of the season. The press never let him forget it right up until he died in 1931. His widow even tried to change the official score for the game, from a wild pitch to a passed ball on the part of the catcher, but her effort failed.

Tommy McCarthy, as an outfielder, was very adept at trapping the ball as he let it land just in front of him and then he would throw out the base runner coming into second. He had a good throwing arm and while playing for the St. Louis Browns of the American Association he had 44 assists in the 1888 season, the fourth highest of all time by an outfielder. He was a good leadoff hitter for the Boston Beaneaters when he and Hugh Duffy helped lead Boston to pennants in 1892 and 1893.

Duffy in center field and McCarthy in right field were known as "The Heavenly Twins," as mentioned previously. They were friends off the field as well, opening a bowling alley and a saloon, which they called Duffy and McCarthy.

Induction

World War II was now over so the first induction ceremony was held since 1939. Commissioner Kenesaw Mountain Landis was honored at the 1946 Induction Ceremony. The ceremony was held in Cooperstown on June 13 with about 2,000 people in attendance on a day when the weather was in the 70s. Commissioner Happy Chandler spoke briefly in honoring his predecessor and then introduced New York governor Thomas Dewey who talked about the history of baseball and then spoke of the "iron will and uncompromising honesty" of Landis in helping baseball recover from the 1919 Black Sox scandal. Dewey said Landis "brought back to the great American game the confidence of the public," and concluded: "He will go down as a man whose high character saved the symbol of American life."

At the entrance to the Doubleday Field parking lot there is a statue called "The Sandlot Kid." This statue of a small farm boy with a bat in his hand was designed by Victor Salvatore and was erected as a memorial to Commissioner Landis.

The 1945 and 1946 inductees would be honored at the 1947 ceremony.

1947

The Hall of Fame Committee (Old Timers Committee) met in December 1946 and made the proper decision to clear up the confusion. Any player retired in the last 25 years would be the responsibility of the BBWAA and anyone retired before would come under the jurisdiction of the Old Timers Committee. They also clarified the final, or runoff, ballot by making it necessary only if no one received 75 percent on the first ballot.

Another important change was instituted in the eligibility of the BBWAA voters. They now would be allowed to cast a ballot only if they had been BBWAA members for ten years, which is still the requirement today. As a result there would be a 39 percent reduction in the number of ballots cast in the 1947 election.

The Hall of Fame Committee (VC) didn't meet in 1947 to consider players who retired before 1922, as required by this new arrangement. Since they had elected 21 inductees in two years, and given their controversial selections, it probably was a wise move.

This new system worked as the committee and the BBWAA got it right when 161 ballots were cast in the 1947 BBWAA election and four worthy candidates received the necessary 75 percent for induction. All four were still alive so this was the biggest class of inductees elected by the BBWAA since the first one in 1936 (five).

Carl Hubbell, New York Giants ace left-handed pitcher, finished first with 87 percent (140 votes) in his third year of eligibility. This total was more than Hubbell garnered (125 votes) in two prior elections.

Frankie Frisch, the feisty second baseman, finished second with 84.5 percent (136 votes) in his sixth year of eligibility. He received 329 votes in five previous elections, including 14 votes in 1936 when he was a player-manager.

Mickey Cochrane, premier catcher and successful player-manager, finished third with 79.5 percent (128 votes) in his sixth year of eligibility. He received 401 votes in five previous elections.

Robert "Lefty" Grove, one of the all-time power pitchers, finished fourth with 76.4 percent (123 votes) in his fourth year of eligibility. Granted there was a lot of confusion as the BBWAA focused on players during the prior three elections who retired before 1920, but it was an injustice that it took him four elections and he barely made it in 1947. He totaled 111 votes in three previous elections. Grove had an explosive temperament, which undoubtedly didn't endear him to most sportswriters.

Inductees

Carl Hubbell started out as a pitcher by trying to throw the sinker but learned an entirely new pitch, the screwball. This pitch would make the left-hander the bane of all National League hitters. He went on to win 20 or more games for the Giants five straight seasons (1933 through '37), and was also the league's MVP in 1933 and 1936. He became known as the "Meal Ticket" as he helped lead the Giants to three pennants and a world championship in 1933. He finished with a record of 253–154 (.622).

Hubbell had one of the most memorable All-Star pitching performances in the 1934 game. The first two batters for the American League got on, but then he struck out in a row Babe Ruth, Lou Gehrig, and Jimmie Foxx and the next inning Al Simmons and Joe Cronin. All five were future Hall of Famers, as was his catcher, the Cubs' Gabby Hartnett, who sighed and said, "We got to look at that all season."[8]

Frankie Frisch went to Fordham University, where he was a second team All-American halfback on the football team as well as a star on the baseball team. "The Fordham Flash" was signed by the New York Giants and the second baseman helped lead them to two World Series titles before being traded in 1927 to the St. Louis Cardinals for Rogers Hornsby. He was the 1931 MVP as he helped the Cards win a pennant and the World Series. He became their player-manager and won another championship in 1934 with "The Gashouse Gang." Frisch batted .316 lifetime and played on the most pennant winners (8) in the National League.

Frisch was the captain of the Giants under John McGraw, who turned him into a switch-hitter and was grooming Frisch to succeed him as manager. However, they often clashed and had a falling out that led to the Hornsby trade. Years later Frisch admitted that he made it because he had McGraw as a teacher.

Mickey Cochrane was also a multiple sports star, like Frisch, while at Boston University and broke in as a catcher with the A's in 1925. He helped lead them to two world titles and three pennants along with fellow inductee Lefty Grove. He was traded to the Detroit Tigers and became the player-manager in 1934. He won his second MVP in 1934 (his first MVP award came in 1928) and led the Tigers to two pennants and their first world championship in 1935. He had a career batting average of .320 and an on base percentage of .419.

Cochrane suffered a nervous breakdown in 1936 because ownership gave him general manager duties while he was also managing and playing. He overcame this by being only a player-manager when he came back. Sadly, he was hit in the head by a pitch in 1937 that fractured his skull in three places. In a coma for ten days, he eventually recovered, but Mickey's playing career was over and he stopped managing in 1938.

Lefty Grove was a late bloomer who began his major league career with the A's in 1925 at the age of 25. The fireballing left-hander made up for lost time by winning 20 or more games seven straight times in the nine years he was with the A's. He was 4–2 in three World Series for the A's (1929 through 1931) with an ERA of 1.75 as he helped them win in 1929 and 1930. He won the 1931 MVP Award in 1931 as he went 31–4 and became the only left-handed pitcher to win 30 games since 1896. He then pitched eight seasons with the Red Sox and retired after the 1941 season as he notched his 300th win. The high-strung pitcher with the terrible temper is the only pitcher to win nine ERA titles.

Grove pitched with the Baltimore Orioles in the International League and was so valuable that owner Jack Dunn finally sold him to Connie Mack and the A's for $100,600. He won 111 games in the minors, so his combined record was 411–177 (.696).

Induction

The 1947 Induction Ceremony on July 21 was witnessed by about 2,000 people on a warm day with the temperature in the 80s. Unfortunately, the only inductee present was Ed Walsh, 66, from the class of 1946, who spoke briefly. Walsh came two more times and died in 1959 at the age of 78.

Inductees Jesse Burkett and Hugh Duffy never came to any inductions. Burkett died in 1953 at the age of 84 and Duffy died in 1954 at the age of 87.

Clark Griffith was there for the first induction in 1939 but there is no record of him attending any other inductions. He died in 1955 at the age of 85.

Johnny Evers died four months before the ceremony (age 65) while teammate Joe Tinker had health problems and died on his 68th birthday in 1948.

The four inductees from 1947 were all alive but none made it to the ceremony. Hubbell came in 1950 and only two more times after that and died in 1988 at the age of 85. Cochrane, like Hubbell, made it to the dedication of the new wing in 1950 but never came again and died in 1962 at the age of 59.

Frisch didn't make it until 1955 but attended 10 more ceremonies before dying from injuries in a car accident in 1973 at the age of 74. As you will read he was an influential member of the Veterans Committee (VC) from 1967 through 1972 and helped to get several of his teammates elected, all of whom were controversial.

Grove didn't make his first induction until 1963 but came back nine more times. He died in 1975 at the age of 75.

Today it would be unimaginable for the four inductees not to show up for their induction as happened in 1947.

1948

The 1948 BBWAA election had 121 ballots cast, the lowest total for any BBWAA election, due mainly to the 10 year requirement as two candidates were selected.

Herb Pennock finished first in the 1948 election with 77.7 percent (94 votes). He received a total of 336 votes for seven previous elections. The stellar lefthander was a part of many Yankees championships but never heard the good news. He died a month before the announcement on January 30 at the age of 53 of a cerebral hemorrhage.

Pie Traynor, the all-time third baseman for the Pittsburgh Pirates, finished second with 76.9 percent (93 votes). He had a total of 339 votes for seven previous elections so it was only fitting that Traynor and Pennock achieve induction the same year since their vote totals were separated by only three votes. Traynor actually missed induction by only two votes in 1947. He wasn't formally inducted until 1949 since there wasn't a ceremony in 1948.

The Hall of Fame committee (VC) didn't meet again in 1948.

Inductees

Herb Pennock was signed by the A's right out of high school. He was let go by Connie Mack, who later admitted that it was the biggest mistake he ever made in more than 50 years in baseball. He wound up with the Red Sox before being traded to the Yankees in 1923, where he became their ace and helped them win three titles that decade by going 5–0 in three World Series with an ERA of 1.95. He wound up his 22-year career with a record of 241–162 (.598).

Pennock was "The Squire of Kennett Square" (Pennsylvania) because of his demeanor and the fact that he had fox hunts on his estate in the place where he was born and bred. Yet when he developed a sore arm near the end of his career, he uncharacteristically went against conventional wisdom and tried unsuccessfully to treat it by sting therapy, allowing a swarm of bees to sting his arm.

Harold Traynor was called "Pie" as a young boy when he played baseball for his local parish team and his favorite treat was a piece of pie. He was converted from shortstop to third base by Pirates manager Bill McKechnie in 1922. He became a premier defensive player and led third basemen in different defensive categories each year. Renowned sports columnist Red Smith said, "Watching Pie Traynor play third base was like looking over Da Vinci's shoulder."[9] He helped the Pirates win the 1925 World Series against the Senators as he led all fielders with 24 assists, batted .346, and hit a home run off Walter Johnson. He hit .320 lifetime and never struck out more than 28 times in a season.

Pie Traynor never learned to drive because he enjoyed walking. Once while going to a World Series in New York in the 1950s he walked 100 blocks from his hotel in Manhattan to Yankee Stadium in the Bronx.

1949

The 1949 BBWAA election had 153 ballots cast, but since no one received 75 percent, the new runoff procedure (1947) was necessary. Charlie Gehringer won the runoff with 85 percent (159 votes). What was odd about the runoff was there were 187 ballots cast, some 34 more than the original election. Gehringer also won the first ballot with 67 percent of the vote. The steady second baseman for the Detroit Tigers had received 216 votes in four previous elections. The runoff procedure was eliminated after 1949 but returned again in 1960.

The Old Timers Committee didn't meet formally in 1949 but cast ballots by mail on candidates from the pre–1924 era. The results were announced on May 9 and two well-qualified pitchers were selected.

Mordecai "Three Finger" Brown was the ace of the Chicago Cubs during the time they won four pennants between 1906 and 1910. He received 310 votes in seven previous BBWAA elections. Brown died the year before (1948) at the age of 71.

"Kid" Nichols was a 361-game winner, but because more than half of his career was spent in the nineteenth century, he didn't receive much support from the BBWAA, with only 21 votes in five elections.

Inductees

Charlie Gehringer broke in with the Detroit Tigers in 1924, played second base with them for 19 years and had a record of consistency unmatched by most Hall of Famers. He had a lifetime batting average of .320, batted .321 in three World Series, and hit .500 in the first six All-Star Games. Gehringer won a batting title and was the MVP in 1937, and also led the league in fielding percentage nine times. He was known as the "Mechanical Man" because of his consistency. Teammate Doc Cramer said, "You wind him up on opening day and forget about him."[10]

Once, Gehringer stepped completely out of character in a game against the St. Louis Browns. He thought he had made the third out and went out to second base and stood next to the Browns' second baseman, Oscar Melillo, who said, "Charlie, thanks all the same, but I don't need any help."[11]

Charles Nichols broke in with the Boston Beaneaters in 1890 where he became the ace of the staff at the age of 20. He was called "Kid" because of his youthful appearance and it became his moniker for the rest of his life. He won more games in the 1890s than anyone else, including Cy Young. He helped lead his team to five pennants in eight years by winning 30 or more games seven times. Nichols had 531 complete games along with 361 victories during his 15-year career. He was a switch hitter who had 16 home runs and was also a good fielding pitcher who once had no errors during a season.

His hometown was Kansas City, Missouri, where one of his players on the amateur baseball team that he coached was Casey Stengel. When he retired, Nichols and his wife became very active bowlers and organized the first men and women's bowling league. He won a bowling championship in his hometown at the age of 64.

Mordecai Brown earned the nickname "Three Finger" because he had an accident on his uncle's farm when he was seven. It happened after he put his right hand in his uncle's corn chopper and lost half of his index finger with permanent impairment to his thumb and forefinger. The disability was a blessing in disguise because it made his curveball dip like a knuckleball. He won 20 games six straight seasons for the Chicago Cubs and helped them win four pennants and two World Series. He finished with a record of 239–130 and the third lowest ERA ever at 2.06. The thing he was most proud of was that he defeated the great Christy Mathewson of the New York Giants nine straight times, including the final game of the season in 1908 that clinched the pennant by one game over the Giants.

Brown's uncle kept the corn chopper on his farm for many years where it served as a tourist attraction.

Induction

The 1949 Induction Ceremony was held on June 13 with more than 1,000 fans in attendance on a day when the temperature reached 90 degrees. It was only the third induction of the 1940s, yet it was not without controversy because Charlie Gehringer wasn't there just as the four inductees hadn't been there in 1947. He probably had the most legitimate reason of any absentee because the longtime bachelor got married. Nevertheless, renowned sports columnist Shirley Povich wrote a scathing article in the *Washington Post*, basically condemning him for being a no-show.[12] Gehringer, always conscientious, made amends by coming for the building dedication in 1950 and became one of the most consistent attendees ever as he went on to make 30 more appearances before he died in 1993 at the age of 89. He also was the first former player to be appointed to the VC (1953) and served with distinction for many years.

Pie Traynor (1948) and Kid Nichols (1949) were honored and received their plaques from the legendary Branch Rickey. The "Kid," 79, never made it back as he died in 1953 at the age of 83. Traynor, 49, came to Cooperstown for three more inductions, including one each decade (1959, 1968, 1971), before passing away in 1972 at the age of 72.

Finally, a surprise for the crowd was the appearance of Fred Clarke (1945), 76, who spoke briefly, as did Nichols and Traynor. This was his only appearance and he passed away in 1960 at the age of 87.

CHAPTER 5

Joe DiMaggio Isn't a First Ballot Hall of Famer? 1950–1959

1950

Nineteen fifty marked the first expansion of the National Baseball Hall of Fame and Museum. There were more than 1,000 fans present July 24 on a cool day with the temperature never rising above 70 as the new wing was dedicated, doubling the size of the museum. The cost of this new addition was $175,000. This new wing would now be the main entrance to the building. Cy Young spoke for the five other Hall of Famers who were there, including Ed Walsh, Tris Speaker, and first time attendees Charlie Gehringer, Mickey Cochrane and Carl Hubbell.

The BBWAA voted on players who had been retired 25 years as they did in 1949. This meant that they could vote for anyone who played from 1925 or later provided they hadn't been active in 1949. No one received the 75 percent needed for election as 168 ballots were cast, and since the Hall of Fame Committee (VC) didn't have an election, the induction ceremony was cancelled for the first time.

1951

The 1951 BBWAA election had 226 ballots cast as two candidates reached 75 percent. Longtime New York Giants' right fielder Mel Ott finished first with 87.17 percent (197 votes). Ott retired after the 1947 season and was selected in his third year on the ballot. He had a total of 406 votes and finished first in 1950 with 69.5 percent.

American League slugging first baseman Jimmie Foxx finished second with 79.20 percent (179 votes). Foxx retired in 1946 and made it his sixth year on the ballot (474 total votes). The fact that it took him this long is another example of an injustice because he had the credentials (member of the 500 home run club) to have been a first ballot inductee.

Inductees

Mel Ott came to the New York Giants as a 17-year-old catcher in 1926. Ott batted left-handed and had an unorthodox batting style — he lifted his front foot before swinging his

The crowd listens during the 1953 Induction Ceremony. Notice the new wing that was added in 1950.

hands to produce a level swing with terrific power. Giants' manager John McGraw made him into a right fielder as Ott helped lead the Giants to three pennants and one World Series title. He hit 511 home runs, batted .304, and was a player-manager for six years.

He was very popular with the Giants fans because of his attitude, which was obvious when he said, "I could watch the fans and I'd think what an ungrateful fellow a ballplayer would be who just didn't give everything he had every moment of every game."[1]

Jimmie Foxx was from Maryland where "Home Run" Baker discovered the muscular six-footer and helped him sign with Connie Mack's Philadelphia Athletics (A's.) He started out as a catcher in 1925, but Foxx later switched to first base. He helped lead the A's to three World Series and two championships while batting .344 for the World Series lifetime. He went on to win two MVPs with the A's along with a Triple Crown in 1933. Due to economic restraints, Mack was forced to trade him to the Boston Red Sox in 1936, where he would win his third MVP. He had an impressive 20-year career and retired in 1945 with 534 home runs and a batting average of .325.

"Double XX" was a manager in the All-American Girls Professional Baseball League (AAGPBL) in 1952. In the movie *A League of Their Own*, the Tom Hanks character (Jimmy Dugan) is loosely based on Foxx.[2]

Induction

The 1951 Induction Ceremony was held on Monday, July 23, with a crowd of about 2,000 on rather a cool day as the temperature never reached 80 degrees. Mel Ott didn't make it because he was in the midst of a pennant race in the Pacific Coast League as the manager of the Oakland team. He did make it eventually to two inductions but was killed in an auto accident in 1958 at the age of 49.

Jimmie Foxx, 43, was there and spoke only a few words as he told the audience how proud he was to be a member of the Hall of Fame and also that his old manager and friend Connie Mack was there. (Reportedly, they were the only Hall of Famers there.) He also commented, "Sorry Mel Ott couldn't be here to take his place in the sun." He came back two more times and was planning on coming again in 1967 but died after choking on a piece of food. He was 59.

1952

The 1952 election saw 234 ballots cast as the Detroit Tigers' premier hitting outfielder Harry Heilmann finished first with 86.8 percent (203 votes). The Pittsburgh Pirates' all-around right fielder Paul Waner finished second with 83.3 percent (195 votes).

It took Heilmann, who retired after the 1932 season, 12 elections (668 votes) to achieve immortality as he received minimal support until 1947 and then progressed each year. He finished fourth in 1951 behind Waner, and then jumped ahead of him the next election. One reason for Heilmann's improvement was that his former teammate and manager Ty Cobb lobbied the writers on his behalf.

Waner retired after the 1945 season and accomplished immortality in seven elections (580 votes). It took Waner this long despite being a member of the 3000-hit club. Today reaching that milestone would mean almost a certain first ballot induction. James Vail points out that being a member of the 3000-hit club didn't gain widespread media attention until later (p. 183).

Inductees

Harry Heilmann broke in with the Detroit Tigers in 1914 and played mostly right field and some first base, but it was as a hitter where he excelled. He won four batting titles and was the last right-handed hitter to hit more than .400 in the American League, hitting .403 in 1923. He finished his 17-year career with a lifetime batting average of .342. When Ty Cobb became the manager of the Tigers in 1920, he transformed his former teammate from a good hitter into an outstanding hitter.

He became one of the first ballplayers to become a broadcaster (Tigers), and was chosen by Commissioner Chandler to do the All-Star Game from Detroit in 1951. Unfortunately, he died the day before the game at the age of 56.

Paul Waner played right field for 15 years with the Pittsburgh Pirates while his younger brother, Lloyd, played center field. He hit 22 triples and batted .336 as a rookie in 1926, and then won the MVP in 1927. He led his team to the pennant and won the first of three batting titles. He finished his career batting .333 and 3,152 hits. Waner went on to write a successful book on hitting and became a successful hitting coach, too.

He was an alcoholic but a lovable one; as one writer said, "He hit doubles and triples and then drank them later."[3] Columnist Mike Royko told the story that Paul always sipped from a Coke bottle in the dugout. Once a new batboy took a long swig from it, passed out, and woke up with a crushing hangover.[4] Paul gave up drinking once, but his batting average plummeted so he went back to imbibing, and his average went back up.

Induction

The 1952 Induction Ceremony was held on July 21 before a small crowd of less than a 1,000 as the temperature reached the mid–80s. Harry Heilmann was represented by his grown daughter and his widow, who spoke and said how happy her husband would have been to receive this honor.

Paul Waner, 49, was only 5' 8" tall and was inspirational in his speech as he gave encouragement to all the Little Leaguers in the audience by saying, "Don't worry about being a six-footer; it doesn't make a difference." He came back once for the 1965 induction and then died a month later at the age of 62.

Only Hall of Famers Cy Young and Charlie Gehringer were present for the ceremony.

1953

The BBWAA held the 1953 election with a new provision. It was now stipulated that a player had to be retired five years to be on the ballot. Players such as Joe DiMaggio, already retired less than five years, would remain on the ballot.

The 1953 BBWAA election cast 264 ballots and selected the colorful pitcher Dizzy Dean first with 79.2 percent (209 votes). Dean, who retired after the 1947 season, took nine elections (847 votes) to achieve the honor including three elections (1945 through 1947) when he was still playing. One reason it took him so long was because he won only 150 games in a short but spectacular career that was cut short by injury.

The good-hitting outfielder Al Simmons finished second, just making it with 75.4 percent (199 votes). Simmons, who retired after the 1944 season, didn't make it until his ninth try also (706 total votes). This included four votes in 1936 while he was still playing.

A newly established Veterans Committee (VC) was given the power for the first time to also elect umpires. The Veterans Committee would consist of 11 people, with A.G. Spink, the publisher of *The Sporting News*, serving as chairman. Charles Segar from the commissioner's office joined the committee and went on to have the longest tenure of any member, serving more than 40 years.

Inductees

Dizzy Dean acquired his nickname while in the army. In 1934 he became the leader of a boisterous bunch of players for the St. Louis Cardinals that became known as the Gashouse Gang. They went on to win the pennant and World Series as Dean compiled a record of 30–7, becoming the last National League pitcher to win 30 games. During the 1937 All-Star Game, Earl Averill hit a ball off Dean's left foot and fractured his toe. He came back from the injury too soon, which altered his pitching motion, and eventually hurt his shoulder.

Dean was never the same again and retired with a record of 150–83 (.644). He went on to become a successful baseball broadcaster.

"Ol' Diz" was like Muhammad Ali, boldly predicting victory just as Ali would do with his championship fights. He predicted that he and his brother, Paul, would win 45 games and the pennant in 1934. They won 49 games, the pennant, and the World Series.

Al Simmons was born Aloysius Syzmanski (Polish descent) and later changed his name to Simmons. He broke in with the A's in 1924 and proceeded to bat more than .300 and drive in 100 runs for 11 straight seasons while playing the outfield. He won two batting titles during that time and was *The Sporting News* MVP in 1929. He helped lead the A's to three straight pennants and two World Series titles from 1929 through 1931. Simmons played for a number of other teams during his 20-year career and batted .334 lifetime.

Like Mel Ott, Simmons had an unorthodox batting stance. A right-handed batter, his left foot pointed down toward third base and then strode toward third base as he swung, which was called "stepping into the bucket." Nevertheless, "Bucketfoot Al" did well causing Connie Mack to comment, "I wish I had nine players named Al Simmons."[5]

Induction

Both men were alive when they were honored at the 1953 Induction Ceremony on July 27. A crowd of 3,000 and seven Hall of Famers joined the inductees for the ceremony on a hot day as the temperature reached 85. Dizzy Dean, 43, was a crowd favorite according to the local papers and the crowd gave him a "tremendous ovation." He spoke first in his distinctive back-home Arkansas twang. Dean thanked everyone for the honor and then uttered the funniest line of any induction speech up until that time when he said, "I want to thank the good Lord for giving me a strong right arm, a strong back and a weak mind."

Al Simmons, 51, gave the most passionate speech up to that time as he paid tribute to his former manager, Connie Mack. He said, "I want to pay my respect for the man who is responsible for me being here today. I was a great ballplayer under Mr. Mack's guidance." He finished his accolade to Mack by stating, "Mr. Mack was the greatest man I ever met."

Later Ty Cobb spoke for the five Hall of Famers by giving a short, humble speech stating that he was proud of the Hall of Fame and thanked the fans for coming.

Dean came back twice in the 1960s and died in 1974 at the age of 64. Simmons never made it back as he died three years later from a heart attack at the age of 54.

The newly formed VC selected six men who were inducted at the 1954 ceremony.

Ed Barrow was the longtime executive and chief architect of the Yankees' dynasty. He had served on the previous old-timers committee, but unfortunately, he died three months after he was elected in December 1953 at the age of 85.

Chief Bender, pitching ace of the Philadelphia Athletics, was chosen while he was still alive, but he, too, died before he could be honored (in 1954 at age 70). He received votes in each of the 14 BBWAA elections and collected a total of 520 votes.

Tom Connolly, premier umpire of the American League, was also alive but never made it to an induction before he died in 1961 at the age of 90.

Bill Klem, the National League's premier umpire, died in 1951 at the age of 77.

Bobby Wallace, premier defensive shortstop of the 1890s right up through 1918, received very little consideration by the BBWAA, garnering only 18 votes in four elections. Yet, he was a unanimous choice of the VC, which means that committee chairman A.G. Spink and

Hall of Famers gather at Doubleday Field in 1953 before the major league exhibition game. *Left to right:* Ty Cobb, Al Simmons, Dizzy Dean, Cy Young, Connie Mack, Ed Walsh and Rogers Hornsby.

committee member Branch Rickey undoubtedly played significant roles in his election. Wallace played 20 years in St. Louis for both the Browns and the Cards. Spink's *Sporting News* was based in St. Louis and Rickey had been Wallace's teammate on the Browns. Rickey also hired him as a scout for the Cards. Another reason Wallace was given this honor by the VC was that he became the first American League shortstop to be inducted. Bill James refers to Wallace's selection as one of the game's "little mysteries" (p. 109). James Vail cites this as an example of "cronyism" (p. 103), a common thread throughout VC elections for the rest of the century. Robert Cohen believes Wallace doesn't belong in the Hall of Fame when compared to his contemporary at shortstop, George Davis (inducted in 1998) (p. 96). He never made it to Cooperstown and died in 1960, one day shy of his 87th birthday.

Harry Wright was called by Henry Chadwick "The Father of Professional Baseball" because he was involved in all aspects of the game as an organizer, manager, and player.[6] Yet it took him 16 more years to be inducted after his star player and brother, George Wright, was honored. Ken Smith, author of the first major book about the Hall of Fame, felt that "Harry Wright was one of the most prominent people left out of the Hall of Fame."[7] Smith mentions that renowned sports broadcaster Ernie Harwell fought to get him in as well.

Inductees

Ed Barrow made his mark by learning all aspects of the baseball business. He became a manager, minor league owner, and eventually president of the International League. He helped start the careers of future Hall of Famers Fred Clarke and Honus Wagner. His most significant move, however, came in 1918 when he was the manager of the Boston Red Sox and helped turn Babe Ruth from a star pitcher into a superstar outfielder. He followed Ruth to the Yankees in 1921 where he helped to build the Yankees' dynasty that won 14 pennants and 10 World Series under his watch. He was the Yankees' business manager and then president while twice being named Executive of the Year.

Barrow was innovative and responsible for painting the distances on the outfield walls (1923) and putting numbers on players' backs (1929). Branch Rickey said, "I think Ed Barrow was the greatest baseball man in my time. He knew baseball from all angles."[8]

Chief Bender was born on an Indian reservation to a mother who was a Chippewa Indian and a father who was of German descent. He graduated from the Carlisle Indian School in Pennsylvania that later would become known for the outstanding all-around athlete Jim Thorpe. Bender was a semi-pro pitcher who became another future Hall of Famer signed by Connie Mack for his Philadelphia A's in 1903. He was an immediate success for the A's as he, along with Eddie Plank, helped lead Mack's A's to five pennants in ten seasons. The A's won three championships with Bender winning five games. He had a no-hitter in 1910 and finished with a record of 208–112 (.625).

Bender was a champion skeet shooter who read English literature. He didn't like being called Chief but preferred to be called by his first name of Charley.

Tom Connolly became an umpire despite never having played the game. He was born in England and knew nothing about baseball until his family moved to Natick, Massachusetts, when he was a teenager. Nevertheless, he had a fascination for the game and its rules and eventually became an umpire. He umpired in the minors, got called up to the National League, and switched to Ban Johnson's American League in 1901 when he worked their first game due to all the other games being rained out. He then went on to work the first World Series between the American and National leagues in 1903. He was the home plate umpire in the game when pitcher Carl Mays fatally beaned Ray Chapman.

Although only five feet, seven inches, he commanded respect because of his calm demeanor and thorough knowledge of the rules. He never threw a player out of a game for six straight years. He was the exact opposite of fellow inductee Bill Klem.

Klem was a loud, demonstrative umpire who reached the National League in 1905. He went on to work the most World Series (18) and helped to gain respect for umpires with his innovations and as a spokesman for umpires' rights. He was the first umpire to wear a chest protector under his coat and the first to use hand signals for called strikes. Klem also fought to have changing facilities for umpires.

Many consider him the greatest umpire, but he could be thin-skinned, especially if called "Catfish," a nickname he detested. Despite a tough demeanor, he had a sense of humor. Once a woman fan screamed at him, "If you were my husband, I'd put poison in your coffee," and he responded, "If I were your husband I'd drink it."[9]

Bobby Wallace started out as a pitcher and third baseman before becoming a shortstop for the St. Louis Cards in 1899. This turned out to be his niche as he later became the best defensive shortstop in the American League after jumping to the St. Louis Browns. One reason was because he was one of the first to develop the technique of scooping up the ball with one hand and tossing it underhanded with one fluid motion. He set an American League record in 1902 of handling 17 chances in a game that still stands today. He finished his 25-year career in 1918 with a lifetime batting average of .268.

An example of his defensive worth was when the Browns persuaded him to play with them in 1902, they signed him to a five-year contract for $32,000. It included a no-trade clause and the team even took out a life insurance policy on him.

Harry Wright, like Connolly, was from England where his father was a star cricket player. His family also immigrated to the United States where he learned about baseball in New York City. He later went to Cincinnati and recruited the best players in 1869 to form the professional team known as the Cincinnati Red Stockings. Wright was the organizer, manager, and center fielder when the team went on a national tour and won an unheard-of 60 games in a row. He then won four championships with the Boston Red Stockings in the National Association and then two more titles in the newly-formed National League.

The Society for American Baseball Research (SABR) conducted a poll in 1999 that found Harry Wright to be the third greatest contributor to nineteenth-century baseball behind Henry Chadwick and Albert Spalding.[10]

1954

The BBWAA election of 1954 had 252 ballots cast and three players made it to the hall with shortstop Rabbit Maranville finishing first at 82.9 percent (209 votes). Maranville, noted for his defense rather than his offense, nevertheless was deemed a worthy candidate by the BBWAA, receiving 1,216 votes over 14 elections after retiring in 1936. He finished in the top ten his last five elections and actually bypassed Bill Dickey (second) and Bill Terry (third) as he jumped from fifth to first in 1954. One reason is he died a few days before the election, possibly increasing his vote total because of the death factor.

New York Yankees catcher Bill Dickey came in second with 80.2 percent (202 votes). Dickey was a good all-around catcher who received 877 votes in nine elections although he received votes in 1945 and 1946 while he was still playing.

Bill Terry, New York Giants all-around first baseman, finished third with 77.4 percent (195 votes). Terry, another worthy candidate who didn't have a lot of friends in the press, still had 1,104 votes in 15 elections, including nine votes when he was still active (1936).

Inductees

Rabbit Maranville's first name was Walter but he changed it when a young fan called him "Rabbit" because he hopped around so much while playing shortstop. He broke in with the Boston Braves and went on to lead the league in putouts six times and fielding average and assists four times each. He teamed with Hall of Fame second baseman Johnny Evers to help the "Miracle Braves" of 1914 upset the heavily-favored Philadelphia A's in the World Series. He batted .308 in the series and then hit .308 again in the 1928 Series for the Cardinals, which was an unlikely bonus since he batted only .258 lifetime.

Rabbit was a prankster who did anything for a laugh. Sometimes he would wear a rain outfit on the field when it was raining, and one time when he watched a brawl on the field, he started shadow boxing in the third base coach's box and knocked himself out.

Bill Dickey helped the Yankees win seven of eight World Series. He set a single-season record for catchers when he batted .362 in 1936, and finished his career with an average of .313. Defensively, he had an accurate arm and was an excellent handler of pitchers. He served his country as a naval flier in World War II. Later as a Yankees coach, he tutored his successor, Yogi Berra. They both had their number 8 retired by the Yankees.

Dickey was quiet and calm but behaved completely out of character in a game with the Washington Senators. He threw a punch when the runner Carl Reynolds crashed into Dickey at home plate and then got up to make sure he crossed the plate. Dickey knocked Reynolds out and was fined $1,000 and suspended for 30 games.

Bill Terry overcame a poor and humble background to become a successful player and manager with the New York Giants. He became their regular first baseman in 1925 and had a fine career as an exceptional fielding first baseman, but it was as a hitter that he would really shine. He was the last National Leaguer to hit more than .400 (1930) and retired after 14 seasons with a batting average of .341. Despite having a stormy relationship with manager John McGraw, Terry was chosen to succeed him in 1932. Terry was the player-manager for two pennants and one World Series championship, and then the manager only for one more pennant.

Terry was successful in baseball and business, but it seemed he never enjoyed it. Teammate Carl Hubbell summed him up best by declaring, "Bill managed liked he played. It was not any fun, but strictly business to him."[11]

Induction

On a day when the temperature reached only 77 degrees, there were 1,000 people for the 1954 Induction Ceremony on August 9. The only Hall of Famer outside of Dickey and Terry who was there was Cy Young. The six members chosen by the VC in 1953 were either dead or too ill to come. The first to receive his plaque was Ed Barrow, who was represented by George Weiss of the Yankees and the president of the American League, Will Harridge. Bobby Wallace was unable to come because of illness so National League president Warren Giles accepted for him. Harridge also accepted for Tom Connolly, who was also too ill to attend. The widows of Bill Klem and Chief Bender accepted for them, while 1954 BBWAA inductee Rabbit Maranville was also represented by his widow. Commissioner Ford Frick, as he presented the plaque to Rabbit's widow, referred to her late husband as the "Peter Pan of Baseball." Harry Wright had passed away many years before, so his son was scheduled to accept for him, but he was too ill to come, leaving Wright without a representative.

Columbia University gave a citation to the hall honoring two of its former students, Hall of Famers Eddie Collins and Lou Gehrig. The citation was presented by Andy Coakley, a former major leaguer and later the baseball coach at Columbia.

The highlight of the day was presentation of plaques to the BBWAA inductees, Bill Dickey and Bill Terry. Dickey, who actually didn't want to speak, did speak briefly and said, "This was the nicest thing that has happened to me as a ballplayer."

Bill Terry was introduced by Commissioner Ford Frick, who said, "He is a great manager. He should have been elected long ago." Terry choked up as he received his award, and then lightened things up by stating, "I never thought I'd feel this way," as he smiled and continued, "maybe because I've been playing the sun field over there," as he pointed to his vacant seat, on the sunny side of the platform. He then turned serious and said, "I don't know what kept me out ... maybe it was the baseball writers. Anyway, I finally made it and I thank God for it." He went on to make mention of his fellow honorees by giving a little anecdote about each one.

Dickey came back 12 times before passing away in 1993 at the age of 86.

Terry, despite his long wait to finally be honored, showed his appreciation by serving on the VC and came back 19 more times before he died in 1989 at the age of 90.

1955

The BBWAA cast 251 ballots in the 1955 election and four men were elected. Finishing first with 88.8 percent (223 votes) was the great Yankees' center fielder Joe DiMaggio. Several questions are raised beginning with how could 28 writers leave the Yankees' superstar off their ballot in 1955? Also, why did it take him three elections after he retired (1952) before he won enshrinement? It's possible that writers back then had a hard time choosing someone on the first ballot because superstars like Pete Alexander, Rogers Hornsby, Lefty Grove, and Jimmie Foxx also took several ballots before being elected.

Also, DiMaggio, along with teammate Joe Gordon, each received a vote in 1945 when they didn't play because they were involved in World War II. Nevertheless, it is still puzzling that he only finished eighth and fourth in 1953 and 1954, respectively, before his 1955 induction. DiMaggio had a total of 516 votes.

Finishing second was Chicago White Sox pitching ace Ted Lyons with 86.5 percent (217 votes). Lyons received 787 votes in 10 elections, including votes during his last two seasons in 1945 and 1946.

Brooklyn Dodgers pitching star Dazzy Vance came in third with 81.7 percent (205 votes). Vance, who retired in 1936, received 968 votes spread over 16 elections.

Finishing fourth was Chicago Cubs all-around catcher Gabby Hartnett with 77.7 percent (195 votes). He received 712 votes in 12 elections including a vote when he was still playing.

The two other 1955 inductees were third baseman Frank "Home Run" Baker and Chicago White Sox catcher Ray Schalk, both of whom were chosen by the VC.

Baker didn't have a lot of support, receiving only 245 votes in 11 previous BBWAA elections, but he wasn't controversial.

Schalk received 529 votes extended over 16 elections, including 1955, when he was voted in by the VC while still receiving BBWAA votes during the same year, which was a repeat of what happened to Chief Bender in 1953. Schalk retired 25 years before in 1930, making this his last year of eligibility with the BBWAA. Schalk's best showing, in fact, was 1955, when he finished eighth with 45 percent of the vote.

Schalk was considered a controversial selection, however, due mainly to his lifetime batting average of .253, the lowest of any position player in the Hall of Fame. Yet in BBWAA elections from 1936 through 1951, Schalk received 134 more votes than Baker.

One of Schalk's critics was Bill James, who thought he was a poor choice. James believes one reason he got in was because Warren Brown, a Chicago sportswriter, was a member of the VC in 1955 and in a book he wrote about the Chicago White Sox praised Schalk as "one of the game's great catchers" (pp. 51, 111). Robert Cohen believes his selection was "unwarranted" (p. 117).

Yet it appears that defense was an important consideration during the 1950 elections since the BBWAA chose Maranville and the VC chose Wallace and Schalk. Also Ty Cobb, Honus Wagner, and Babe Ruth all picked Schalk on their personal all-star team.

Baker meanwhile, when informed of his selection by the VC, said, "I could see myself in a big league uniform, and playing before big crowds and even being a hero. But never, never, never did I dream that I would ever be in the Hall of Fame."[12]

Fortunately for him a fan in Cambridge, Massachusetts, Sherwood Yates, didn't see it that way. He contacted many newspapers locally and in Baker's home state of Maryland as well. Eventually, the governor of Maryland, Clark G. Taylor, got involved, so all this support helped to convince the VC, resulting in Baker's induction.

Today if there is a strong possibility a player will be voted into the Hall of Fame, he anxiously awaits a phone call from the BBWAA's secretary. Contrast that with how Dazzy Vance and Joe DiMaggio found out about their honor. Vance was driving along a highway near his home in Florida when a motorcycle cop pulled up alongside him. He thought he was getting a ticket but instead the policeman told him to go home because a lot of photographers were there looking for him.

Joe D. was driving back to New York from Boston when he stopped for a light and a truck pulled up next to him. The driver recognized him and told him the news he just heard on the radio—Joe had been elected to the Hall of Fame.

Inductees

Joe DiMaggio grew up in California and played baseball on the sandlots of San Francisco with his brothers Vince and Dom, also future major leaguers. The Yankees sent the San Francisco Seals five players plus $25,000 for him, despite a bad knee, and he exceeded all their expectations by becoming one of the greatest Yankees ever. He acquired a nickname, "The Yankee Clipper," because of a certain grace that he showed whether it was playing center field, hitting a home run, or running the bases. He missed three years due to World War II, yet he led the Yankees to 10 World Series, of which they won nine, including four straight (1936 through 1939). "Jolting Joe" was chosen as an all-star all 13 seasons he played, won three MVPs, averaged 118 RBIs a season while striking out only 369 times, and had a career batting average of .325.

The crown jewel of his career was his 56-game hitting streak in 1941. He then had one right after it for 16 more games. Joe had a 61-game hitting streak with the Seals in 1933.

Ted Lyons started his career as a relief pitcher with the White Sox in 1923 and then became the ace of a perennial second-division team. He was a 20-game winner three times before he hurt his shoulder in 1931. Lyons then developed a knuckleball and an assortment of other junk pitches and went on to pitch another 12 years. During the last four years of his career, he pitched mainly at home on Sundays, which due to his popularity meant big crowds at Comiskey Park. He threw a no-hitter and led the league in ERA in 1942 at the age of 41. He won 260 games, but manager Joe McCarthy said he could have won 400 games with the Yankees.

Like all pitchers, Lyons liked to talk about his hitting. He was a good hitting pitcher and joked that during an exhibition game at Joliet Prison his line drives tore such enormous holes in the walls "that the warden stopped the game, fearful of a prison break."[13]

Dazzy Vance was the leader of the Daffiness Boys with the Dodgers. It took him a long time, however, to become a successful pitcher with Brooklyn because of control problems. He developed a curve and changeup to go with his fastball, but the biggest reason for his reversal was manager Wilbert Robinson, who specialized in helping pitchers. Vance led the league in wins, strikeouts, and ERA in 1924 and won the MVP over Rogers Hornsby when the latter had the highest batting average in the twentieth century (.424). He also pitched a no-hitter and was a relief pitcher for the world champion Cardinals in 1934. He led the league in ERA three times, strikeouts seven straight years and won 197 games.

Vance lied to the Dodgers about his age in order to get an opportunity and went on to win his first major league game at the age of 31.

Gabby Hartnett had a 20-year career as a catcher, 19 of them with the Chicago Cubs. He had a tremendous throwing arm, handled pitchers well, and led the league in fielding percentage and assists six times each. He batted .297 lifetime with 236 home runs. He was the 1935 MVP and played in four World Series. His walk-off home run beat the Pittsburgh Pirates in 1938, propelling the Cubs to the pennant. It became known as the "Homer in the Gloamin'" because the game was due to be called because of darkness. He was the catcher for Babe Ruth's "called shot" and when Carl Hubbell fanned the five Hall of Famers in a row, as mentioned previously.

His most infamous memory was when he signed an autograph for gangster Al Capone's nephew at Wrigley Field, and the next day all the newspapers carried a photo of it. He was ordered by Commissioner Landis not to see Capone again, and Hartnett responded, "I'm not explaining it to him. The next time you see him you can explain it to him."[14]

Frank Baker was born on a farm in Trappe, Maryland, where he lived his whole life. He started his career with the A's and set an American League rookie record for triples with 19. He had good hands and led the league's third basemen in putouts seven times. He helped lead the A's to four World Series in five years, resulting in three championships. His two home runs in the 1912 Series earned him the nickname "Home Run." He used a 52-ounce bat and actually led the league in home runs for four years with the most coming in 1913 when he hit 12. He was later traded to the Yankees and played in two more World Series. He batted .363 for six World Series and .307 lifetime.

Baker sat out the 1915 season after a contract dispute with Connie Mack and again in 1920. His wife had died of scarlet fever and he had to care for his two young daughters.

Ray Schalk was short (5'7"), but he had an aggressive style that made him outstanding defensively. He caught four 20-game winners in 1920 and also caught four no-hitters during his career. He was so enthusiastic about no-hitters that for many years after he retired, he would either call or write to congratulate catchers of no-hitters. Schalk holds the record for the most assists by a catcher (since 1901), and the record for most double plays. He stole 177 bases lifetime and finished third in the 1922 MVP voting. He helped to start Baseball Anonymous in order to assist indigent players.

He was devastated when eight teammates were barred for life by Commissioner Landis for throwing the 1919 World Series. He maintained if future Hall of Fame pitcher Red Faber had been available (injured), that the White Sox would have won despite the fix.

Induction

The 1955 Induction Ceremony took place on July 25 and was described by the local paper, *The Freeman's Journal*, as a day "of brilliant sunshine." Reportedly, more than 10,000 fans showed up mainly to honor Yankees great Joe DiMaggio; 11 Hall of Famers were there as well.

Frank Baker, 69, was so touched by the honor that he said on hearing of his election, "It's better to get a rosebud while you're alive then a whole bouquet when you're dead." He continued with the flowery theme during his induction speech, when after thanking the Veterans Committee he said, "Flowers you have bestowed on me will never fade." He was

The 1955 induction class. *Left to right:* Joe DiMaggio, Gabby Hartnett, Frank Baker, Ted Lyons, Ray Schalk and Dazzy Vance.

so appreciative of the honor that he came back for every induction through 1961. He died two years later at the age of 77.

Ray Schalk, 62, during his speech paid tribute to his wife when he said, "It's a dream come true," and then told the audience that he owed his career to his wife, who always kept a watchful eye on his health. Mrs. Schalk was so caught up emotionally that she cried throughout the ceremony.

Schalk came back seven more times before passing away in 1970 at the age of 77.

Dazzy Vance, 64, praised the sportswriters for electing him and "for keeping the old-timers before the fans of today."

Vance never came back and died in 1961 at the age of 69.

Ted Lyons, 54, paid tribute to his fellow inductee Ray Schalk, his first catcher and mentor with the White Sox, and called the award "the greatest thing that could happen to me." Lyons met Schalk for the first time when Lyons was pitching for Baylor University in Waco, Texas, while the Chicago White Sox were there for spring training in 1923. Schalk caught him as part of a publicity shoot, but he came away so impressed that he recommended Lyons to the team and they promptly signed him.

Lyons came back for six more inductions and died in 1986 at the age of 85.

Gabby Hartnett, 54, called the honor "the biggest day of my life." He came back for only one induction, ten years later. He died on his birthday in 1972 at the age of 72.

Joe DiMaggio, 40, befitting the superstar that he was, arrived at the ceremony with Yankees general manager George Weiss. They landed on Lake Otsego in owner Dan Topping's amphibious plane.

Finally, the crowd's patience was rewarded when the dapper DiMaggio walked to the podium, dressed in a black alpaca suit with a breast pocket handkerchief.

During his speech he told an amusing anecdote of traveling from San Francisco to his first spring training in 1936, with his two Yankees teammates Tony Lazzeri and Frankie Crosetti. DiMaggio, the 21-year-old rookie, thought he might not make it to Yankees camp because when they asked him to share the driving, as they were about to embark on the last part of the trip, he replied, "I don't drive."

He paid tribute to his longtime manager with the Yankees, Joe McCarthy, and closed by referring to his induction saying, "The last chapter has been written and now I can close the book." As he left the podium to go back to his seat, baseball commissioner Ford Frick, who had introduced him, went back to the podium. He said, "No, this is the last chapter of today's book, and this is the first chapter of the new edition."

"Jolting Joe" came back only three more times and usually didn't stay the whole weekend. His good friend and business advisor, Morris Engelberg, explained after he died in 1999, "Joe wasn't a big booster of the Hall of Fame because he thought it was too much of a commercial venture."[15] Engelberg also said, "Having a children's hospital named after him in Hollywood, Florida, meant more to him than being in the Hall."[16]

DiMaggio died in 1999 at the age of 84.

1956

In 1956 the BBWAA, as mentioned previously, now required a player to be retired five years before he would be eligible for the Hall of Fame. They also eliminated the rule which required writers to vote for 10 candidates. Thereafter, they would be advised only to vote for up to 10. Finally, the BBWAA decided to have elections in alternating years with the Veterans Committee. Thus, the BBWAA would have an election in 1956, and again in 1958 while the VC would have their next election in 1957.

The BBWAA cast 193 ballots in 1956 with slugger Hank Greenberg receiving 85 percent (164 votes) to finish first. Greenberg received a total of 938 votes in nine elections, including three votes in 1945 when he was still playing.

Former shortstop Joe Cronin finished second with 78.8 percent (152 votes). Cronin received 630 votes in 10 elections.

Inductees

Hank Greenberg became the Detroit Tigers' regular first baseman in 1933. He was 6' 4", but he was not a natural athlete and had to work hard to play first base and later the outfield. Even so, he had an amazing 13-year career that was cut short by four years for World War II. He won two MVPs and helped lead the Tigers to four pennants and two world championships. He hit a grand slam on the last day of the 1945 season to win the pennant. He batted .318 for four World Series and finished his career with 331 home runs and a .313 batting average.

Playing for the Pirates in 1947, he collided with Jackie Robinson at first base. When both were okay, Greenberg encouraged Robinson, telling him how he had been taunted because he was Jewish. Robinson later said Greenberg's support helped tremendously.

Joe Cronin's parents lost just about everything in the 1906 San Francisco earthquake. He overcame this hardship and established himself as the shortstop for the Washington Senators in 1929. The next year he was *The Sporting News* MVP as he led the league in putouts, assists, and double plays while batting .346. He was the player-manager when the Senators won their last pennant in Washington in 1933 and batted .318 in the World Series. Joe was traded to the Red Sox and spent 11 seasons as their player-manager. He hit five pinch-hit home runs in 1943, including two grand slams, and retired in 1945 with a batting average of .301. He was their bench manager when they won a pennant in 1946.

When he was with the Senators, Cronin married Clark Griffith's daughter. Griffith called his son-in-law into his office in 1934 to ask him if he should trade him to the Red Sox for $250,000. Cronin responded to Griffith, "Make the deal, you can't afford not to."[17]

Induction

The 1956 Induction Ceremony was held the morning of July 23 with a crowd estimate of over 3,000, including six Hall of Famers. The day was a mixture of clouds and rain with the temperature in the low 80s.

Joe Cronin, 49, spoke briefly, calling the honor "his greatest thrill" as he paid tribute to his fellow honoree and closed with, "I've been associated with two of the greatest men in the history of baseball, Clark Griffith and Tom Yawkey." Cronin was a player-manager for both owners and was now Yawkey's general-manager.

Cronin came back some 25 times, mostly in his official capacity as the president of the American League, beginning in 1959. He died in 1984 at the age of 77.

Hank Greenberg, 45, also called this his greatest thrill. Greenberg was selected to play in the 1939 game at Doubleday Field when the first induction class was honored. He humbly said, "I never dreamed that someday I'd be on the same platform." In closing, he paid tribute to his fellow honoree by saying, "It is a wonderful country that it is possible for this to happen to a boy from the Bronx [Greenberg] and a boy from San Francisco [Cronin]." Greenberg, like Cronin, was also a general manager (Tigers).

Greenberg made it back for three more inductions and died in 1986 at the age of 75.

1957

As had been agreed upon the year before, there was no BBWAA election but just the Veterans Committee election in 1957.

Also, the BBWAA rules were changed so that a player, to be a candidate, had to be in the major leagues for at least 10 years. His career could not have begun more than 30 years before the BBWAA election and he had to be retired at least five years. This 30-year window would be changed in 1963 back to the 20-year window (career began 20 years before the BBWAA election and player had to be retired 5 years). This is still the current practice in 2009.

All players to be considered by the VC had to be retired more than 30 years. Managers and umpires to be considered by the VC had to be retired at least five years.

Successful Yankees manager Joe McCarthy was chosen unanimously. Joe McCarthy received seven votes as a manager in four BBWAA elections. Two of the voters in the 1958 BBWAA election must have really liked the Yankees' skipper because he is the only inductee to receive votes (2) after he was elected!

McCarthy loved Cooperstown since he started coming to the inductions after he retired in 1950. So when he got the word at his home in Buffalo, his reaction was one of complete joy as he expressed a similar sentiment to Frank Baker in that he was alive "to smell the roses."

Detroit Tigers outfielder Sam Crawford was also chosen for induction. Crawford, who retired as a player in 1917, received only 38 votes in seven BBWAA elections. Crawford had a good career and remained active in baseball as the coach at USC. It's hard to explain why he didn't receive more votes, but his candidacy was helped by the great Ty Cobb, who campaigned for him and was there for his teammate's induction.

Sam Crawford was a rugged individualist who became a recluse in retirement, as he led a very isolated life in a place called Pearblossom, California, near the Mojave Desert. It should then come as no surprise that his induction notification was in perfect harmony with his lifestyle. He was living in a beach cabin that had an outdoor shower, no telephone, and a television that he never watched. It was mid–February with the ground covered in snow when the place was surrounded by many representatives from the media to inform him of the wonderful news. His neighbors were shocked because he had never told them he was a baseball player.

Inductees

Joe McCarthy, raised in poverty without a father, overcame that to become the greatest manager ever, according to baseball analyst and historian Bill James.[18] He was a successful minor league manager who managed the Chicago Cubs to a pennant in 1929. McCarthy then achieved outstanding success with the New York Yankees from 1931 through 1945, where his teams won eight pennants and seven World Series. He finished up with the Boston Red Sox as his team became the first in history to lose two consecutive pennants on the last day of the season. He finished with a winning percentage of .615 and never had a losing record in 24 years.

Joe DiMaggio said, "I never saw Joe show up a ballplayer. Never a day went by that you didn't learn from him. He was like a father to us."[19]

Sam Crawford was also known as "Wahoo Sam" for his hometown of Wahoo, Nebraska. The speedy right fielder with the strong arm started off with the Cincinnati Reds in 1899 and moved over to the Detroit Tigers in 1903, where he spent the rest of his career. Although Crawford led the National League (1901 with 16) and the American League (1908 with 7) in home runs, his real specialty was triples. He led the league six times and had the most lifetime with 309. He and Cobb led the Tigers to three straight pennants (1907 through 1909). He retired with a lifetime average of .309 and later helped to establish USC as a baseball power. They won their fifth national championship on June 16, 1968, the day Crawford died. One reason he didn't watch TV was because he liked to read. Despite having only a fifth-grade education, Crawford read authors such as Balzac, Dickens, and Santayana.

Induction

The 1957 Induction Ceremony took place on a very muggy Monday morning (July 27) in its usual place right outside the front entrance to the Hall of Fame. Some 2,000 people attended, including seven Hall of Famers and the ceremony was over in 45 minutes. A tradition was started at this ceremony when gold lapel pins were given out for the first time to all of the Hall of Famers present.

The 77-year-old non-conformist, Sam Crawford, began by visibly indicating how emotional this moment can be when he exclaimed, "When I walked up to this mike, I had a speech all ready for delivery, but the words have escaped me. All I can say over and over again is thank you." He couldn't continue as tears streamed down his face as he sat down next to his sobbing wife.

He never made it back and died in 1968 at the age of 88.

Crawford did have one request honored as "Wahoo Sam" was added to his plaque.

Joe McCarthy, 70, known as "Marse Joe," talked about his 43 years in baseball and thanked everyone who made his career with the Yankees so successful. He summed up his good fortune by stating, "A player makes the Hall of Fame on his own ... but a man who makes the Hall of Fame because of success as a manager owes big debts to those without whose help he could not possibly have achieved this honor."

What made this day even more memorable for McCarthy, who never made it to the majors as a player, was a man who was sitting on the platform as his guest. Tom Breslin was a sportswriter who wrote a story for the Wilkes-Barre *Times* in 1912 proposing McCarthy as the local team's manager. McCarthy, who was playing second base for them at the time, got the job and as the old saying goes, "the rest is history."

McCarthy came back for eight more inductions and died in 1978 at the age of 90.

1958

There were 266 ballots cast in the 1958 BBWAA election with no one receiving the necessary 75 percent for election. Outfielder Max Carey finished first with only 51 percent (136 votes). Since the VC wouldn't vote until the next year, this marked the second time that there wouldn't be an Induction Ceremony.

However, there was the dedication of the new Plaque Gallery on August 4, 1958. The new wing was to house all 83 plaques with room for many more in the future. The wing contained marble columns that supported a lofty ceiling. Along either side were raised aisles with alcoves designed to display the plaques of the immortals. Each alcove was lighted by sky domes and special lights to bring out the details of the individual plaques. The other end of the gallery had an impressive marble shaft containing the names of all the Hall of Famers who served in the Armed Services.

There were six Hall of Famers in attendance including Baker, Cobb, Cronin, Frisch, Gehringer, and McCarthy. The widows of McGraw, Mathewson, and Wagner were there along with the daughters of Nichols and Maranville.

1959

The last election of the decade was conducted in 1959 by the VC, and all 11 members unanimously chose the Brooklyn Dodgers outfielder Zack Wheat, who had retired in 1927. Wheat received 276 votes in 16 BBWAA elections from 1937 through 1955.

Opposite, top: The Hall of Fame Plaque Gallery as pictured in 1960 two years after it was dedicated in 1958. *Bottom:* A gracious Ty Cobb embraces John McGraw's widow Blanche and Christy Mathewson's widow Jane before the Doubleday Field's major league exhibition game in 1959.

Inductee

Zack Wheat was part Cherokee Indian who started his career as a left fielder with the Brooklyn Dodgers in 1909 and played 18 of 19 years with them. Wheat helped lead them to two pennants in 1916 and 1920, and was declared the winner (.335) in a three-way race for the 1918 batting title. He was able to make a successful transition from the Dead Ball Era to the Live Ball Era of the 1920s by having his three highest batting averages from 1923 through 1925. His lifetime average was .317, and he holds the all-time Brooklyn Dodgers records for hits, doubles, triples, RBIs, and total bases.

Wheat was a Kansas City policeman after retiring and was almost killed when his police car crashed while chasing a fugitive. He recovered from his injuries and found peace of mind by opening a hunting and fishing resort in Sunrise Beach, Missouri.

Induction

Despite a rainy day, some 2,500 fans were there along with eight Hall of Famers for the 1959 Induction Ceremony on July 20. Zack Wheat, 71, gave a short speech that was described as emotional but sincere. As the 84th member of the Hall of Fame, he thanked everyone who made it possible and called it "one of the greatest days of my life," and continued, "Here on my first visit, I saw a lot of things that brought back memories."

He came back five more times before passing away in 1972 at the age of 83.

CHAPTER 6

Ted Williams' Historic Speech: 1960–1969

1960

The BBWAA held the only election in 1960 because the Veterans Committee didn't meet until 1961. There were 269 ballots cast and no one received the 75 percent needed for induction. The result was that the Induction Ceremony had to be cancelled for the third time. The decision was then made to have the VC election every year beginning in 1961.

1961

The Veterans Committee in 1961 chose two fleet center fielders for the ultimate honor, Max Carey and Billy Hamilton.

Carey, who retired in 1929, received 550 votes from the BBWAA spread out over 18 elections. His best showing was the first-place finish in 1958 as mentioned previously.

Hamilton, who played all but his last year in the nineteenth century, received three votes in two BBWAA elections. Bill James, baseball analyst, credits Hall of Fame historian Lee Allen for bringing to the attention of the VC important information on Hamilton and four other nineteenth-century players who were all elected during the 1960s.[1]

Inductees

Max Carnarius changed his Prussian last name to Carey when he started out in baseball. Carey became the Pittsburgh Pirates regular center fielder in 1911. The former high school track star used his speed to make himself an outstanding outfielder and speed merchant on the bases. He led the league in putouts nine times and is ranked fourth all-time. He led the league in stolen bases 10 times and stole home 33 times, second to Ty Cobb all-time. Carey had his best season in 1925 when he batted .343 and helped lead the Pirates to a World Series title as he led everyone with a .458 batting average.

He became a manager and then president of the All-American Girls Professional League in the 1940s. Later he helped Cuban refugees who came to Florida in 1959 after the Cuban Revolution by setting up baseball leagues for their children.

Billy Hamilton, like Carey, was a high school track star (sprinter), centerfielder and a speedster on the base paths. He was so good with his headfirst slide that he was called

"Sliding Billy." He teamed with fellow Hall of Famers Ed Delahanty and Sam Thompson in the outfield for the Philadelphia Phillies in 1894 as all three batted more than .400, and Hamilton scored the most runs for a single season with 198. He retired having scored more runs (1,690) than games played (1,578).

Baseball was a lot different in the 1890s than today. First, a frustrated third baseman once grabbed Hamilton after he stole third base and then picked him up and set him down in the grandstand. Another time a ball was hit over his head and rolled to the fence, and he couldn't get it out of a tin can so he relayed the ball inside the can to the shortstop. He threw it to the catcher, who then tagged out the runner with the canned baseball.

Induction

There were more than 1,000 people who sat through a mid-morning light shower to witness the 1961 Induction Ceremony on July 24. Six Hall of Famers were present as Billy Hamilton, having died in 1940 at the age of 74, was represented by his three daughters.

Max Carey, 71, did something during his speech that had never been done before or since — he made proposals that he thought could improve baseball. First, he called for the return of the spitball, but to call it something else like a "saliva pitch." He thought this would help to cut down on the number of home runs that were being hit. Next, he proposed a brand-new statistic that would be called total advanced bases. He wanted to give credit to the runner who is able to go from first to third on a base hit, and who then scores on a sacrifice fly. Nothing ever came of his proposals. He came back two more times before passing away in 1976 at the age of 86.

Stephen Clark had passed away in September 1960 and Paul Kerr succeeded him as president of the Hall of Fame. Major League Baseball had commissioned an artist, William F. Draper, to paint a portrait of Mr. Clark. The painting was presented to the Hall of Fame the night before the induction at a ceremony in the museum, with Baseball Commissioner Ford Frick presiding. Frick spoke of Clark's foresight and financial support that helped the Hall of Fame gain national stature. It was appropriate that Frick would be speaking because it was through the efforts of Clark, Frick, and Alexander Cleland that the hall became a reality back in the 1930s. Today, both Clark's and Frick's portraits are found next to each other at the entrance to the Hall of Fame Plaque Gallery.

1962

The writers cast 160 ballots in the 1962 BBWAA election and, for the first time since the first election in 1936, two inductees were chosen on their first ballots. The Cleveland Indians' flame thrower, Bob Feller, finished first with 93.8 percent (150 votes), and the first black to integrate major league baseball, Jackie Robinson, was second with 77.5 percent (124 votes).

This was also the first time since 1953 that the Veterans Committee and the BBWAA held their elections in the same year. National League center fielder Edd Roush and successful National League manager Bill McKechnie were both selected.

Roush, who last played in 1931, was selected two years after his eligibility with the BBWAA was up. He had received 692 votes in 18 BBWAA elections and had his best showing in 1960 when he finished first with 54 percent of the vote.

McKechnie, who last managed with the Cincinnati Reds in 1946, received only 13 votes in four elections because he achieved his success as a manager and not as a player.

Inductees

Bob Feller was signed by the Cleveland Indians while still in high school and made his major league debut in 1936 at the age of 17. "Rapid Robert" had a high kick delivery with a unique pivot that gave him tremendous speed. However, it was a devastating curve that made him so difficult to hit. He averaged 25 wins a season from 1939 through 1941. He had his best season in 1946 when he won 26 games and had 348 strikeouts. He was part of two pennant winners and a World Series championship in 1948 and finished with three no-hitters, 12 one-hitters, and 44 shutouts. He had a barnstorming tour against Negro Leagues stars and Monte Irvin credits him for helping to integrate baseball.[2]

Feller was a gunnery captain on the USS *Alabama* during World War II. He was the first major leaguer to sign up after Pearl Harbor and received eight battle stars. He didn't consider himself a hero because, he said, "Heroes are the ones who don't come home."[3]

Jackie Robinson was a four-sport star at UCLA, and his brother Mack was second to Jesse Owens in the 200-meter dash during the 1936 Olympics. He was signed by Branch Rickey and made his debut with the Brooklyn Dodgers in 1947. Rickey chose Robinson to be the first to integrate baseball because he was intelligent and college-educated but most of all because he had the strength of character to withstand all the abuse that Rickey knew he would face. He was the Rookie of the Year and the award would eventually be named in his honor in 1987. Robinson won the MVP in 1949 and helped lead Brooklyn to six pennants and their only World Series title in 1955, and batted .311 lifetime.

He fought racial discrimination in the army and in the Negro Leagues, which is why Martin Luther King, Jr., said Jackie Robinson was a civil rights advocate long before sit-ins and freedom rides.

Bill McKechnie was called "Deacon" because of his strict religious upbringing. He was a utility infielder, and as a manager he helped lead the Pittsburgh Pirates to a pennant and a World Series victory in 1925. He won his second pennant in four years in 1928 with the St. Louis Cardinals and his final two pennants with the Cincinnati Reds in 1939 and 1940 when he won the World Series. McKechnie became the first manager to win pennants with three different teams, but his best managing job was done with the Boston Braves, where he inherited a perennially bad team and made them respectable. He was National League Manager of the Year in 1937 when the Braves were 79–73.

He was a master tactician who always had a calming influence on players. Johnny Vander Meer, who pitched two consecutive no-hitters for the Reds while playing for McKechnie, said, "Ballplayers never feared McKechnie, they respected him."[4]

Edd Roush was a center fielder who played 12 years with the Cincinnati Reds with whom he won two batting titles while swinging a 48-ounce bat. He also helped lead them to a World Series title in 1919 over the infamous Chicago White Sox. Roush had annual battles over salary, and one reason was he didn't like spring training because he kept himself in good shape during the off-season and was afraid that he could get hurt because many of the fields weren't in good shape. He batted .325 lifetime.

Roush was a good citizen who gave back to the community. He served eight years on the school board, another four years on the town board, and was president of the board of directors of the local bank in his hometown of Oakland City, Indiana.

The 1962 inductees pose with their plaques. *Left to right:* Edd Roush, Jackie Robinson, Bob Feller and Bill McKechnie.

Induction

The 1962 Induction Ceremony was held July 23 on a mild day with the temperature around 75. There was a crowd of more than 4,000 with Frankie Frisch, Joe Cronin, and Joe McCarthy being the only other Hall of Famers present. The ceremony took only 30 minutes as Edd Roush, 69, spoke briefly and thanked those on the VC who voted for him.

His granddaughter, Dr. Susan Dellinger, an author and a member of SABR, was at his induction and came to several others as well. She said that he always stood out with his bowtie and related the following vignette about her grandfather. During one of the inductions that Edd Roush attended in the 1970s, it was then customary for youngsters to go to the Otesaga Hotel after all the activities had concluded to get autographs. Several Hall of Famers were near the front steps of the hotel when a little boy approached the group, looking to get Susan's grandfather's autograph. The boy asked a very recognizable Hall of Famer if he was Edd Roush, and the gentleman responded, "I'm only Mr. Coffee," and then Joe DiMaggio smiled and pointed to the boy's hero.[5]

Roush came back six times and passed away in 1988 at the age of 94.

Bill McKechnie, 76, also made a brief speech as he humbly stated, "Anything that I have contributed to baseball I have been repaid seven times seven." His wife had recently died and that made it an extremely emotional time for him. He came back the next three years before dying in 1965 at the age of 79.

Probably no two closer friends have ever been inducted together than Edd Roush and Bill McKechnie. They both were teammates in the Federal League on the Newark Club, both were signed by John McGraw and the New York Giants and were traded to the Cincinnati Reds along with Christy Mathewson. They both retired to Bradenton, Florida, where the spring training ballpark was named for Bill McKechnie after he died. Edd Roush was there attending a game over 20 years later when he suffered a stroke and died.

Jackie Robinson, 43, paid tribute to three people during his induction speech. He thanked his mother, his wife, Rachel, and the man most responsible for his historic breakthrough. "I hope you don't mind if I just say a word of thanks and a tribute to my advisor and wonderful friend, Mr. Branch Rickey," he said. He finished by thanking the writers for electing him on the first ballot and said, "We have been on cloud nine since the election."

He later told his 12-year-old daughter, Sharon, "It was like a lawyer being appointed to the Supreme Court."[6] He made it back only in 1967 for Branch Rickey's induction and passed away from a heart attack in 1972 at the age of 52.

Here are two accolades of the many that Robinson received as a result of his induction. A black man saw him on the street in New York City the day before the announcement was to be made about the BBWAA selections. The man stuck out his hand and said, "I know you are going to be elected into the Baseball Hall of Fame and when you are it will be the happiest day of my life."[7] A testimonial dinner was held for him before the induction at the Waldorf Astoria in New York City where more than 900 people attended. He received a telegram from former vice-president (and future president) Richard Nixon stating, "There are days when I feel a special pride in being an American and Tuesday, January 23 [the day of the induction announcement] was one of them."[8]

The ultimate tribute was paid to Jackie Robinson in 1997 when Commissioner Bud Selig, in an unprecedented move, had every major league team retire his number 42 on the 50th anniversary of his integration of Major League Baseball.

His Hall of Fame plaque was changed in 2008 at the urging of his family to include the cultural impact of his breaking of baseball's color barrier. The last sentence on the plaque now reads, "Displayed tremendous courage and poise in 1947 when he integrated the modern major leagues in the face of intense adversity." It should be noted that Jackie insisted in 1962 his plaque make no mention of this but just represent his playing career.

Bob Feller, 43, was the last inductee to speak and he made light of the fact that his plaque didn't contain some of his other records such as most walks in a season and the lifetime walks record. He said he enjoyed playing baseball but then revealed, "You have more fun as an amateur than you do as a professional because you don't have the headaches." He talked about having a two-day honeymoon and then not seeing his wife for three years because he was off fighting in World War II.

Feller closed by stating "the big enjoyment I now get out of baseball is working out with the Little League and the American Legion in Cleveland. That's the way I stay in condition." He then thanked everyone.

He is now in 2009 the longest tenured member of the Hall of Fame ever (47 years) and has attended 38 out of 48 inductions, including the last 21.

I had the pleasure of briefly speaking with him in a phone interview and he said that Jane Clark, president of the Hall of Fame's Board of Directors, and everyone else connected to the hall have improved everything about the Induction Weekend, including security, making it a pleasure to come back every year. His one complaint is a universal one among veteran Hall of Famers, and that is the induction speeches are too long. He looks forward each year to walking around Cooperstown, meeting people and talking about baseball and World War II, or as he puts it, "teaching American history to our youth."

His wife, Annie, also was very helpful with information about how the Hall of Fame during every induction weekend now has a series of activities for the spouses.

1963

The Veterans Committee selected four inductees on January 27, 1963. This was the first time that they picked this many since the VC had been established in its present format in 1953. The reason for this is Commissioner Ford Frick empowered the committee to select up to four new members, two whose careers ended before 1931 and two whose careers ended between 1931 and 1943. The honorees before 1931 were nineteenth-century pitcher John Clarkson and right fielder Elmer Flick. The honorees after 1931 were right fielder Sam Rice and National League pitcher Eppa Rixey.

Flick, who retired in 1910, was a controversial pick because he had received only one vote from the BBWAA. Vail refers to Flick as "one of the most dubious choices" (p. 20). Cohen states Flick didn't put up the numbers in his short career to merit induction (p. 200).

David Fleitz states the main reason he got in was because of the influence of Branch Rickey on the VC. Rickey was the only member who had seen Flick play. Rickey was the person who actually called Flick, who at first he didn't believe him, but later members of his family convinced him it was true.[9] Fleitz points out Flick's qualifications weren't bad because he led the league in triples three times, stolen bases twice, and RBIs and batting once each. Flick had a career average of .315.

Sam Rice received 406 votes in 12 BBWAA elections after retiring from baseball following the 1934 season. Rice's best showing came in his next-to-last election in 1960 when he finished second with 53 percent of the vote. Ty Cobb, like he had done for so many other contemporaries, campaigned for his induction, along with sportswriter Shirley Povich. Rice was humble when he heard because he felt that the Hall of Fame was really for the greats of the game like Cobb, Ruth, and Walter Johnson.

Eppa Rixey, the greatest left-handed pitcher in Reds' history, received 290 votes in 15 BBWAA elections. Rixey didn't get much support from the BBWAA until Warren Spahn broke his record for most wins by a left-handed pitcher in the National League in 1959. People heard about him because of the record so he received his highest vote total in 1960 as he finished third, one vote behind Rice. The news that he had been inducted was met with complete modesty just as with Rice, except with self-deprecating humor. "I guess they're scraping the bottom of the barrel," was his comment.[10] Unfortunately, Eppa passed away a month after receiving the news at the age of 71.

John Clarkson was the first of four nineteenth-century pitchers who had won 300 games to gain induction. He was only 47 when he passed away in 1909. The Hall of Fame's historian, Lee Allen, assisted the committee as he had with Billy Hamilton in 1961. Attention was brought to all of the 300-game winners from the nineteenth century who had not yet been inducted as a result of Early Wynn's quest to join that group, which he did in 1963. Clarkson received five votes from the veterans vote of 1936, but only one vote (1946) from the BBWAA.

Inductees

Elmer Flick was signed by the Philadelphia Phillies in 1898 and he showed up in spring training carrying his homemade bat in a canvas bag, which he had made on his father's lathe. The farm boy from Ohio was teased unmercifully until they saw him bang the ball all over the field with his thick-handled bat. He hit .302 his rookie season and then two years later he had his best season when he batted .367 and led the league in RBIs. The fleet right fielder jumped to the American League in 1902 and spent nine years with Cleveland, but a mysterious stomach ailment ended his career in 1910.

The Detroit Tigers thought Ty Cobb had burned himself out and offered to trade him to Cleveland for Flick in 1907, but the Indians nixed it. Cobb went on to have a great career while Flick was forced to retire three years later because of his ailment.

Sam Rice was born Edgar Charles Rice and started his career as a pitcher with the Washington Senators in 1915. Clark Griffith, the manager (later the owner) couldn't remember his first name when asked by reporters so he called him Sam. Rice didn't mind so the name stuck as Griffith converted him into an outfielder because he was a good hitter. He played 19 seasons with Washington and was on the team's three pennant winners including the 1924 world champions. Rice batted .302 in the three World Series and had a lifetime batting average of .322. He holds six lifetime records for the Senators.

Tragically, he lost his wife, two children, and parents during a tornado while he was trying out for a minor league team. Rice rarely spoke about it until much later in his life. David Fleitz states, "Perhaps no member of the Hall of Fame overcame as much personal sorrow or earned as much respect from teammates and opponents alike."[11]

Eppa Rixey never planned to be a baseball pitcher, but major league umpire Cy Rigler, his basketball coach at the University of Virginia, convinced the 6'5" left-hander to try it. He was so successful that he signed with the Philadelphia Phillies in 1912 without any time in the minors. He was a twenty-game winner four times with his best season coming in 1922. He won 25 games for the Cincinnati Reds to lead the league in wins along with innings pitched while walking only 45 batters. He was a good-fielding pitcher who once handled 108 chances without an error and pitched in one World Series with the Phillies in 1915. He finished with a record of 266–251.

Rixey had an insurance agency in Cincinnati which his grandson now operates. The Eppa Rixey Insurance Agency's motto is "Hall of Fame Performance for your Insurance Needs."[12]

John Clarkson was from a wealthy Cambridge, Massachusetts, family. He had two younger brothers, and all three graduated from Harvard and played in the major leagues. The right-handed pitcher helped lead Cap Anson's Chicago White Stockings to two consecutive pennants in 1885 and 1886. During 1885 he won 53 games, the second highest of all time while leading the league in innings pitched, shutouts, and complete games. He went on to win 328 games but left after 1894 because he had a hard time making the adjustment from the old pitching distance of 55'6" to 60'6" in 1893.

Clarkson had deep psychological problems that led to alcoholism and his eventually dying in a mental institution at the age of 47. Cap Anson said after his death, "Scold him and he would not pitch; praise him and he was unbeatable."[13]

Induction

There was a light rain falling during the 1963 Induction Ceremony on August 5 as 3,000 people came, including a record 13 Hall of Famers. The four presentations were

The Hall of Famers gather for a group photograph before the Doubleday major league exhibition game in 1963. *Left to right:* **Joe Cronin, Bill Dickey, Jimmie Foxx, Frankie Frisch, Charlie Gehringer, Dizzy Dean, Lefty Grove, Ted Lyons, Joe McCarthy, Bill McKechnie, George Sisler, Elmer Flick and Sam Rice.**

finished in around 40 minutes. John Clarkson was represented by his nephew, Frederick Clarkson, while Eppa Rixey's widow accepted for him.

Elmer Flick was 87 years old when he spoke to the crowd, making him the oldest living inductee ever. He was deeply touched when he said, "This is a bigger day than I've ever had before. I'm not going to find the words to explain how I feel." He made it back for only one more induction and died in 1971, two days shy of his 95th birthday.

Sam Rice, 73, spoke briefly by sharing Flick's sentiment when he said, "This is the biggest thing any of us can have." His induction philosophy was ahead of its time when he said, "It is a tremendous honor and I think I ought to come back every year and welcome the new men coming in."

He followed through by coming to 10 of the next 12 inductions including his last one in 1974 when he was dying of cancer. He was 84.

A final postscript was added to his Cooperstown legacy when a letter that he had written to the Hall of Fame in 1965 was opened after his death. He wrote this letter at the urging of historian Lee Allen in regards to an outstanding catch he made for the Washington Senators in the 1925 World Series against the Pittsburgh Pirates. As he made this catch, running full speed during Game 3 at Griffith Stadium, he fell into the stands and disappeared for several seconds. He reappeared with the ball and the umpire declared the batter out. The

Pirates protested but the ruling was upheld and the controversy persisted long after the Pirates had won the World Series. Finally, three weeks after his death, hall director Paul Kerr opened the letter and Rice revealed that he had indeed caught the ball although he had hit his head on something in the stands and lost consciousness for several seconds before emerging from the stands with the ball firmly in his glove.

A tradition was started in 1963 that continues to this day. The Hall of Fame directors instituted an award to honor a baseball writer for lifelong service to the game and the award was named in memory of J.G. Taylor Spink, the late editor and publisher of *The Sporting News*. Appropriately, by a vote of his fellow newspapermen, Mr. Spink became the first recipient of the award. Each year's winner would be added to the plaque that would be on display in the museum area devoted to sportswriters and broadcasters.

1964

The 1964 BBWAA election had 201 ballots cast but no one reached the necessary 75 percent, so as prescribed by the rules, a run-off election was held among the top 30 vote-getters. Longtime shortstop for the Chicago White Sox Luke Appling finished on top in the run-off just as he had in the first election. He received 84 percent (189 votes), and as the rules stipulated was the only one selected, even though Yankees pitcher Red Ruffing had also achieved higher than the 75 percent with 81.74 percent in the run-off election. Appling received a total of 358 votes in seven BBWAA elections, but his candidacy was helped tremendously following the 1962 election when Bob Feller wrote an article for the *Saturday Evening Post* entitled "Trouble with the Hall of Fame." Feller said that Appling was the best all-around shortstop in the history of the American League.[14] This helped Appling tremendously as he got almost 100 more votes in the 1964 election, helping him to finish first with 71 percent before winning the run-off election.

Six others were voted into the Hall of Fame by the Veterans Committee, including two nineteenth-century stars, pitcher Tim Keefe and shortstop John Montgomery Ward. Coincidentally, they were former teammates and at one time were married to sisters until Ward divorced his wife and later married someone else. Ward had passed away in 1925 at the age of 65 and Keefe in 1933 at age 76.

Ward was a multi-faceted baseball man, and Lee Allen proclaimed, "So there he is, a perfect game pitcher, hard-hitting shortstop, manager, organizer, and owner. And now he is a Hall of Famer. He is a welcome addition to the pantheon."[15]

The first manager of the Yankees' dynasty, Miller Huggins, was also honored. Huggins received the most votes of any manager in eight BBWAA elections (527 votes), coming closest in 1946 when he received 64 percent of the vote. Later that decade, it was ruled only the VC could elect managers.

The final three inductees were Chicago White Sox pitching ace Red Faber, spitballer Burleigh Grimes, and good-hitting outfielder Heinie Manush.

Faber retired in 1934 and received 306 votes in 16 BBWAA elections. Grimes retired in 1935, and received 281 votes in 14 elections.

Heinie Manush retired in 1940, and despite a lifetime batting average of .330, received only 72 votes in six BBWAA elections. James Vail believes his batting credentials weren't exceptional for that era, and having two former teammates on the VC (Joe Cronin and Charlie Gehringer) helped as well (p. 104). Robert Cohen looks on him with ambivalence stating "he wasn't a bad choice," but he is skeptical because he was a good hitter but he wasn't a dominant player (p. 147).

Inductees

Luke Appling made his debut with the White Sox in the 1930 season, and the next year he was their regular shortstop. He was error prone during his first two years, but he had a good arm and good range and went on to lead the league in assists seven times and putouts twice. However, his forte was hitting as he won two batting titles and went on to post a career batting average of .310 and hit .444 for seven All-Star Games. He played 20 years for the Sox and in 1969 he was voted their greatest living player. Appling was called "Old Aches and Pains" because he complained so much about his maladies, yet it didn't stop him from leading the league four times in games played.

Possibly his most memorable hit was a home run he hit off Warren Spahn in an old-timers game at the age of 75.

Urban "Red" Faber broke in with the White Sox in 1914 and would go on to pitch 20 years for them. His signature pitch was the spitball, which helped make him a 20-game winner four times, including 1915 when he won 24 games. The highlight of his career was during the 1917 World Series when he won three games as the Sox defeated the New York Giants for the championship. He hurt his ankle before the 1919 World Series and was unable to participate, as mentioned previously. He won 254 games in spite of being on teams that finished in the second division 15 times.

Faber was forced to learn how to pitch the spitball in the minors after hurting his arm in a distance-throwing contest, but after perfecting the spitter it was his ticket to the majors.

Burleigh Grimes also learned to throw the spitball in the minors. He chewed slippery elm that he used to produce a very good spitball although the elm irritated his face earning him the nickname "Ol' Stubblebeard." He pitched with seven different teams, including nine years with the Brooklyn Dodgers. He was a 20-game winner five times with his best season coming with the Pirates in 1928 when he led the league with 25 wins. He pitched in four World Series with three different teams, including 1931 when he won two games as the St. Louis Cardinals clinched the title. He threw the last legal spitter in 1934 and finished with 270 wins for his 19-year career.

Grimes was a stubborn competitor who developed this toughness as a young boy when he escaped injury in a lumber camp accident after seven tiers of logs fell on him.

Heinie Manush broke in with the Detroit Tigers in 1923 as an outfielder and gave a preview of his hitting prowess when he batted .334. He won the batting crown in 1926 with a .378 batting average, but his best year was two years later when he again hit .378 and also led the league in hits and doubles. He had a 33-game hitting streak for the Washington Senators and helped them win their last pennant in 1933.

Goose Goslin and Heinie Manush had a similarity saga going throughout their careers. Goslin beat out Manush for the 1928 batting title on the last day of the season. They were actually playing each other as Goslin won it on his last at-bat. They were traded for each other in 1930 and were teammates on the pennant-winning Senators. Finally, they went into the Hall of Fame four years apart and Manush died three days before Goslin in 1971.

Miller Huggins had to choose between baseball and becoming a lawyer. His professor and future United States president, William Howard Taft, advised him to pursue baseball which he did by becoming a major league second baseman for 13 years. The diminutive

Huggins (5' 4") became the Yankees' bench manager in 1918 and led them to six pennants and three World Series. Tragically, at the age of 50, he died of blood poisoning late in the 1929 season after compiling a record of 1413–1134. He was the first to be honored by the Yankees in 1932 with a monument at Yankee Stadium.

Superstar Babe Ruth was undisciplined and constantly challenged Huggins' authority. Finally, Huggins fined him $5,000 and suspended him in 1925 after he came late for batting practice. Later, Ruth apologized to the team as Huggins gained the respect of the team and the Yankees won three straight American League titles (1926 through 1928).

Tim Keefe teamed with Mickey Welch (future Hall of Famer) for nine years, first with the Troy Trojans and then with the New York Giants to form the dominant one-two pitching duo of the nineteenth century. Keefe won 30 or more games six straight seasons, including a 19-game winning streak in 1888. Tim pitched on three pennant winners and helped Giants teammate John Ward form the first players union that led to the creation of the Players League in 1890. Keefe developed a change of pace, and it helped make him the premier strikeout pitcher of his era. His lifetime record was 342–225.

Keefe was called "Sir Timothy" because of his style of dress, but he was an extremely sensitive person who suffered a nervous breakdown and almost left baseball after he beaned a batter. Fortunately both players recovered to resume their careers.

John Montgomery Ward, a.k.a. "Monte," started his major league career as a pitcher in 1878 with the Providence Grays. Later, he won 86 games in two years, including a perfect game and an 18-inning shutout. But he hurt his arm and was forced to give up pitching in 1884. Ward reinvented himself by becoming one of the better-fielding shortstops in the National League and demonstrated his speed by stealing 111 bases in 1887 to lead the league. Along with five other Hall of Famers, Ward helped to lead the New York Giants to two straight pennants in 1888 and 1889. He finished his career as the only player to win more than 150 games and collect more than 2,000 hits.

Ward went on to become a manager, get a law degree, form a union and the Players League, own the Boston Braves for one year, author several baseball books while learning five languages, and become an outstanding amateur golfer.

Induction

Nineteen sixty-four was the twenty-fifth anniversary of the first induction ceremony and in recognition of the Hall of Fame's silver anniversary, a citation with 25 silver dollars on a cushion of red velvet was presented to the Hall of Fame president, Paul Kerr, by *The Sporting News.* The Hall of Fame also received a telegram from President Lyndon Johnson congratulating them. George Sisler, the only living member from the original class of eleven, was present and was given thunderous applause when he was introduced.

The 1964 Induction Ceremony on July 27 had an estimated crowd of 1,500, including 14 Hall of Famers, who came despite a temperature of 90. The three inductees who had passed away were the first to be honored as John Montgomery Ward's grandniece, Ruth Koenig, came up first. Tim Keefe's niece, Paula Brodbine, accepted for her uncle and since there were no surviving relatives of Miller Huggins, owner Dan Topping, Jr., of the New York Yankees accepted for him.

Red Faber, 76, spoke briefly and said, "It's hard for me to imagine that I would be elected to it, but now that I am about to join all those celebrities, I hardly know what to say." He never made it back and died 12 years later at the age of 88.

Burleigh Grimes, 71, also spoke briefly and concluded his remarks with the words, "I'm happy that it came soon enough so that I could receive this plaque."

He came back 11 more times, including 10 straight years from 1975 through 1984. He also served on the Veterans Committee from 1977 to 1985. Grimes was one of only a few inductees to make it into his nineties, dying at 92 in 1985.

Heinie Manush, 63, spoke longer than his predecessors, and told the story of how he was one of the few ballplayers to get thrown out a World Series game. It was the fourth game of the 1933 World Series and on a close play at first base he was called out, causing him to become so incensed with the umpire that he grabbed his bowtie and pulled it back as far as he could and let go. The umpire gulped a couple of times as the tie came back and hit him in the throat, and then threw Manush out. Fortunately for him there wasn't instant replay or television back then, so when Commissioner Landis walked into the locker room the next day Manush told him that he brushed into the umpire; he was afraid if he told the truth he would be suspended. Landis accepted his explanation and just said, "When you know plays are going to be close, just keep your hands to yourself."

Manush came back three times and died at age 69 in 1971.

Luke Appling, 57, was the last speaker and was succinct as he told of all the thrills he had in baseball. "Standing here at this platform is the greatest thing that could happen to a ballplayer," he said. He then thanked everyone who helped him along the way as well as the press before concluding, "I accept this with pride and humbleness."

He came back six times and died in 1991 at the age of 83.

1965

The BBWAA continued to hold their elections in even-numbered years as they had done since 1956. However, when the VC produced only one inductee in 1965, there was much criticism, resulting in the BBWAA going back to annual elections beginning in 1966.

The VC chose pitcher Jim "Pud" Galvin, who last pitched in 1892, and had died in 1902 at the age of 45. He was the last of the five nineteenth-century selections that Hall of Fame historian Lee Allen had helped get inducted during the 1960s.

Inductee

James Galvin was called "Pud" because the short, squat, right-handed pitcher made pudding of batters that he faced. He had a blazing fastball and an outstanding pickoff move. He once walked three straight batters and then picked off each one. Twice he won 46 games for the Buffalo Bisons of the National League, and during his career he also pitched in the American Association and the Players League. He was the first to win 300 games and finished with the most wins of any nineteenth century pitcher (361). Galvin had the second most innings pitched (5,941) and the most complete games (639).

During the seven years he pitched in Buffalo he became friendly with the mayor of Buffalo, Grover Cleveland, who later became president of the United States.

Induction

The 1965 Induction Ceremony was held on July 26 as a crowd of 3,000 appeared on a mild day even though the only honoree was deceased. One possible reason was because

The 1965 American Legion Player of the Year was Rollie Fingers. Here he receives his award from Joe McGuff of the BBWAA prior to the major league exhibition game. Fingers was inducted into the Hall of Fame in 1992.

they knew many Hall of Famers would be there, and if so, they were right because 22 came. Until that time, this was the largest group ever for an induction which was significant, since there were only 31 living members.

Pud Galvin was represented by a daughter, Marie Wentzer, and a son, Walter. It is coincidental that Galvin was 5'8" just like future Hall of Famer Kirby Puckett and both men gained a lot of weight after they retired, and each passed away at the age of 45.

Ford Frick, who would retire as commissioner at the end of the year, announced plans for the building of a Hall of Fame Library at a groundbreaking exercise that took place in the back of the building after the ceremony.

A portrait of the commissioner was also presented to the Hall of Fame by Joe Cronin and Warren Giles, the presidents of the American and National Leagues respectively. This was done because of all Frick had done for baseball, including coming up with the idea of a Hall of Fame. As mentioned previously, this painting adjoins a portrait of Stephen Clark at the entrance to the Hall of Fame Plaque Gallery.

Finally, during the annual Doubleday Field game, the winner of the American Legion Baseball Player of the Year was 18-year-old Rollie Fingers, a future Hall of Famer.

1966

The BBWAA election of 1966 produced 302 ballots and "The Splendid Splinter" of the Boston Red Sox, Ted Williams, was elected in his first year of eligibility with 93.4 percent (282 votes). It seems unfathomable how he could be left off 20 ballots, but given Williams' adversarial relationship with the press, it wasn't shocking.

The VC selected the "Ol' Perfessor," manager Casey Stengel. Stengel won seven World Series as manager of the New York Yankees, and also played for 14 seasons. He received most of his 113 votes as a manager and not as a player. The election of managers was made the exclusive domain of the Veterans Committee in 1968. When he retired as the New York Mets' manager in 1965, the normal five-year waiting period was waived and the VC elected him to the Hall of Fame because there was concern for his health. He was completely surprised when he was informed at the Mets spring training facility in St. Petersburg, Florida.

Inductees

Ted Williams came to the Red Sox in 1939, batted .327, and arguably the left fielder went on to become baseball's greatest hitter. He won two Triple Crowns and was the last major leaguer to hit .400 when he hit .406 in 1941. He won the MVP award twice, was chosen for 17 All-Star Games and hit a three-run home run in the 1941 game to win it for the American League. He made it to one World Series and capped off his 19 years with Boston by winning the Comeback Player of the Year in 1960 and hitting a home run on his last at-bat. He finished with the sixth highest batting average of all-time (.344), the highest on base percentage ever (.482) and 521 home runs.

He accomplished all of this while missing almost five years due to military service in both World War II and the Korean War. He trained pilots for the Navy in World War II, and flew 39 combat missions for the Marines in the Korean War, including a crash landing.

Charles Stengel being from Kansas City, Missouri, was called "KC," and this eventually became "Casey." He batted .284 as an outfielder in the National League and had an undistinguished nine-year career as a manager with the Dodgers and the Braves before becoming the Yankees' manager in 1949. There he won ten pennants and seven World Series in 12 years, including an unprecedented five straight championships. He ended his career with the woeful Mets (1962 through 1965).

The classic example of Casey's odd speech pattern (Stengelese) came at the Congressional Anti-Trust Hearings in 1958. Casey had them baffled and confused after 45 minutes of answering their questions. His star, Mickey Mantle, was the next witness and answered their first question by saying, "My views are just about the same as Casey's," and with that the Senate went wild with laughter.[16]

Induction

The 1966 Induction Ceremony was held for the first time on July 25 in Cooper Park, directly behind the Hall of Fame, on a day when the temperature got into the high 80s. It was held here instead of in front of the building because a big crowd was expected, especially since Williams from Boston and Stengel from New York were being honored. They were right because some 7,500 people attended; huge loudspeakers were set up so that everyone could hear the speeches. Surprisingly, the only Hall of Famers there were Joe Cronin, Joe McCarthy, Bill Terry and Bill Dickey.

Ted Williams, 48, spoke first and had to wait to speak as the crowd gave him a standing ovation. He didn't disappoint them as he gave a most memorable speech. Williams always had a stormy relationship with baseball writers, especially those in Boston. So he addressed it right in the beginning of his ten-minute speech. "I know I didn't have 280 close friends amongst the writers." He went on to tell them, "I want ... to say thank you from the bottom of my heart and this is the greatest thrill of my life." He concluded his speech with the most significant words that have ever been uttered in a Hall of Fame speech. "Inside this building there are plaques dedicated to baseball men of all generations and I'm privileged to join them." He went on, "Baseball gives every boy a chance to excel and I hope someday the

Ted Williams gives his historic speech at the 1966 Induction Ceremony.

names of Satchel Paige and Josh Gibson in some way can be added as a symbol of the great Negro players that are not here only because they were not given a chance."

The speech was handwritten the day before by Williams and is now a part of the Hall of Fame. Due in large part to what he said, the Negro Leaguers would be given their rightful place in the Hall of Fame, beginning with Satchel Paige in 1971.

No one ever said that Ted Williams didn't have an enormous ego. He didn't like his image of him on the original plaque and asked the hall to recast it and they did. Despite the Hall of Fame's considerate gesture, Williams didn't come back for another induction until Tom Yawkey's in 1980. He came back to the Hall of Fame in 1985 for the unveiling of noted artist Armand LaMontagne's wooden statue of Williams, a year after the artist had made one of Babe Ruth. He came back for 11 more inductions, admitting that he had made a mistake in not coming back sooner. He became the chief advocate for encouraging others to make the annual trip as he became a dominant figure at Induction Weekend. During the Sunday night dinner, which is attended only by the Hall of Famers, former commissioner Fay Vincent commented, "Ted Williams is clearly the pope amongst his cardinals."[17] His devotion to the hall was illustrated when Williams, a world class fisherman, passed up a chance to go salmon fishing with some of the best fishermen in the world because it conflicted with Induction Weekend. He died in 2002 at the age of 83.

Casey Stengel, a few days shy of his seventy-sixth birthday, gave a 21-minute induction speech (the longest ever up until that time) rambling on about his career. It was delivered in classic Stengelese. He thanked many people including George Weiss, whom he first met in the minors when Weiss was the opposing general manager. Stengel said, "He proved a very great acquaintanceship because whenever I was discharged, Mr. Weiss found it out and would re-employ me." He concluded by stating, "I want to thank everyone who did something for me as well as the tremendous fans."

Published reports of the speech at the time called it, "An assault on rhetoric as he brought gales of laughter from the fans by conducting a nonstop, ungrammatical reminiscence of baseball going back a half a century."[18]

He loved coming back with his wife, Edna, and came the next seven out of eight years. Colleen Tallman, a reservations representative at the Otesaga Hotel, started her career at the hotel as a waitress and that's when she first met Casey. She said he would get there a couple of days early before the Induction Weekend so that he could walk into town, sit on a bench and regale the people with his stories as he signed autographs. One day she told Stengel about her son and how playing baseball helped get him through school. She told him that he had joined the Navy so Stengel, an old Navy veteran himself, asked her for his address and then wrote her son, something she never forgot.

Stengel died in 1975 at the age of 85.

1967

The 1967 BBWAA election had two players tie for first, Yankees pitching ace Red Ruffing and St. Louis Cardinals stalwart left fielder Joe Medwick. There were 292 ballots cast and both players received 72.6 percent (212 votes). There was a run-off election with more ballots cast (306) than were cast for the initial election. Red Ruffing finished first with 86.93 percent (266 votes). Medwick finished second with 81.05 percent, but just as in 1964 when both Luke Appling and Ruffing received more than the 75 percent needed, only the top vote getter was inducted. These controversial decisions led to the elimination of run-off elections in the future. Also, annual elections were permanently reestablished. Thus, Red Ruffing was elected by the BBWAA in his last year of eligibility. He had 1,085 votes in 15 elections. His candidacy, like Luke Appling's, was boosted by the 1962 *Saturday Evening Post* article by Bob Feller.

The Veterans Committee elected Pittsburgh Pirates center fielder Lloyd Waner and renowned baseball executive Branch Rickey, posthumously.

Waner, who retired after the 1945 season, followed his brother Paul (1952) into the Hall of Fame, making them the second set of brothers (joining George and Harry Wright) enshrined in Cooperstown. He was considered a marginal Hall of Fame selection, having received 138 votes over nine BBWAA elections. James Vail calls his selection "dubious" (p. 133). Robert Cohen rates him the last of the 22 centerfielders and states, "He clearly doesn't belong in the Hall of Fame" (p. 177).

Branch Rickey played briefly in the major leagues before beginning his brilliant executive career. He received a total of five votes in two different BBWAA elections.

Inductees

Red Ruffing broke in with the Boston Red Sox in 1924 as a right-handed pitcher and over the next six years he compiled a record of 39–96 on some terrible teams. He was transformed after being traded to the highly successful Yankees in 1930. He improved his control and added an effective changeup and had 20 or more wins four straight years. He helped lead them to seven pennants and five World Series championships. Ruffing was one of the best hitting pitchers of all time. He pinch-hit 250 times, had 273 RBIs, and a batting average of .269. He finished with a record of 273–225.

Ruffing worked with his father in the coal mines and played first base on the company's team. Tragically, at the age of 16, he lost four toes after his left foot got caught between two coal cars. When he went back to baseball, he became a pitcher because running was too difficult for him. Despite this handicap, he went on to a Hall of Fame career.

Branch Rickey was a former player and manager, but it was as an executive that he made his most significant impact. His most important contribution was the integration of baseball by Jackie Robinson in 1947. He also started the first farm system with the Cardinals and it helped them win pennants. Then with Brooklyn his farm system also produced pennants, and finally, with the Pirates, his farm system led to the 1960 title.

While coaching a college baseball team, Rickey was able to convince a hotel to allow a black player on his team to stay with him after he was turned down for a room. Later, in the room, the player rubbed his hands together and cried to his coach, "Black skin, black skin, if only if I could make it white."[19] This story was the impetus behind his determination to integrate baseball.

Lloyd Waner joined the Pittsburgh Pirates in 1927, and had a phenomenal year as he set a rookie record for hits (223) while batting .355. He helped propel the Pirates into the World Series where they were swept by the Yankees despite Lloyd's .400 batting average. He was a model leadoff hitter with good speed who always got a piece of the ball and rarely struck out. He once went 77 games without striking out. His led the league in putouts four times and finished his 18-year career with a .316 batting average.

The story goes that a New York Giants fan with a Brooklyn accent called Lloyd "Little Poison" and brother Paul "Big Poison" instead of "Little Person" and "Big Person." The newspapers picked up on it and the nicknames stuck.[20]

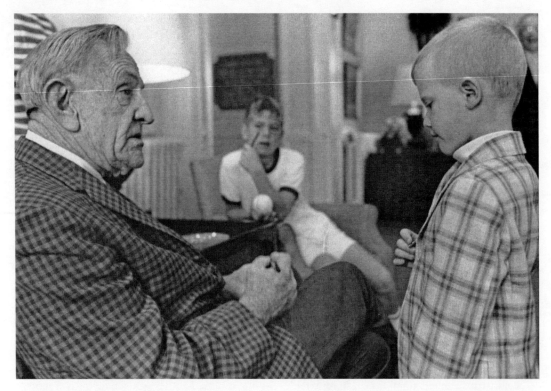

Casey Stengel entertains a young fan waiting for his autograph during the Induction Weekend in 1968.

Induction

The 1967 Induction Ceremony took place at Cooper Park on July 24 with some 2,000 people there despite an intermittent light rain. Eight Hall of Famers joined them for the 35-minute ceremony. The first inductee presented by Commissioner William Eckert was Branch Rickey, who died in 1965 at the age of 83. He was represented by his oldest son-in-law, John Eckler. He spoke for 24 family members who were there, including Rickey's widow. Mr. Eckler thanked the Veterans Committee and told the audience that his father-in-law was a very capable man and could have been a minister, public official, or held a high political office but instead gave his life to baseball. So he and all the family were proud that Branch Rickey's accomplishments were now acknowledged and permanently preserved in the Hall of Fame. Rickey was a member of the VC from 1953 until 1965.

Lloyd Waner, 61, spoke briefly and called this honor "the biggest thrill I ever had." He showed his appreciation by coming back 11 times in the next 12 years. He died in 1982 at the age of 76.

Red Ruffing, 62, was the last inductee to speak and he paid special tribute to his wife as his biggest fan and also gave her credit for helping him win most of his 273 victories. She was such a demonstrative fan when he pitched that "no one would sit within twenty feet of her." He capped off the tribute to her by saying that "this is one of the greatest moments in my life, just like the day I married my wife."

Ruffing came back on a regular basis for a total of nine times, even after suffering a stroke and being confined to a wheelchair. He died in 1986 at the age of 80.

1968

A major change was instituted by the BBWAA in 1968 and that was any candidate who was on the ballot in 1967 had to receive at least 5 percent of the vote in order to remain on the ballot. A screening committee was also instituted to choose players who had retired in 1962. The reason this was done was to reduce the number of candidates on the ballot. There were now 20 teams in the major leagues making a lot more players eligible who had played 10 years. It was controversial because if it had been applied previously many Hall of Famers who were elected by the BBWAA would have become ineligible.

The BBWAA cast 283 ballots in the 1968 election. Joe Medwick, star National League left fielder, achieved induction on his last BBWAA ballot by receiving 84.8 percent (240 votes). He did well in nine previous elections by garnering 901 votes. Naturally, he was happy to get in but commented, "This was the longest slump of my career. I had gone 0 for 20 before, but never 0 for 20 years."[21] Medwick didn't receive any votes for the first seven years after he retired in 1948, which many attribute to his stormy relationship with the press and his teammates.

Two other outfielders were selected by the Veterans Committee in 1968, and they were Kiki Cuyler and Goose Goslin. Cuyler didn't receive a vote for ten years after he retired in 1938. Then he slowly picked up support from the BBWAA, receiving 357 votes in 12 elections.

Goslin's last season was also 1938, but Goslin didn't fare as well with the BBWAA as Cuyler, He received only 111 votes over nine elections.

Despite this low vote total, author Lawrence Ritter's *Glory of Their Times* was instrumental in his selection. Ritter's book came out in 1966 and made the case for Goslin being in the Hall of Fame and sure enough, sixteen months after the book came out, the VC unanimously selected him for immortality. Ritter was one of Goslin's guests at his induction.

Inductees

Joe Medwick broke in with the Cardinals late in the 1932 season, and batted .349. He had his best season in 1937 when he was the MVP and became the last National Leaguer to win the Triple Crown. He set a National League record with 64 doubles in 1936, batted .326 in two World Series, and for his 17-year career hit .324.

He got into fights for different reasons, one being that he didn't like to be called "Ducky Wucky," a nickname that stood for the way he walked. Medwick became the only player ever taken out of a World Series game for his own safety. His St. Louis Cardinals were winning the 1934 World Series against the Detroit Tigers 9–0 during the seventh game at Tiger Stadium when he got into a fight with their third baseman after he hit a triple. The fans pelted him with debris after he went out to play left field in the sixth inning. Later Commissioner Landis took him out, and the Cards won the game (9–0) and the series.

Goose Goslin was born Leon but acquired his nickname because of his long neck, prominent nose, and how he flapped his arms before catching a ball in left field. He wasn't a proficient fielder, but hitting was another matter. He won the batting title in 1928 with a .379 average, and during his 18-year career he played for three teams, including the Senators three times, and batted .316. He was the only player to play every inning of every game for

Washington during their three World Series. He hit .344, and slugged three home runs when they won it in 1924. He also played for the Detroit Tigers on two pennant winners, including their first world championship team in 1935.

Goslin was discovered while playing for a New Jersey team by umpire Bill McGowan, who recommended him to the Sally League. When Goslin broke in with the Senators, he repaid the favor by telling owner Clark Griffith about McGowan, and he was soon in the major leagues. They both capped off their careers by being named to the Hall of Fame.

Kiki Cuyler's real first name was Hazen but he was called "Cuy" as a youngster and eventually it became "Cuy, Cuy," with the newspapers spelling it "Kiki." The swift right fielder led the league in stolen bases four times, and had his best year in 1925 when he hit .357, led the league in triples with 26, and helped lead the Pirates to a World Series championship. He had a controversial falling out with new manager Donie Bush in 1927 and never played a game in the 1927 World Series. He was traded to the Cubs and helped lead them to two pennants, finishing his career with a .321 average.

Cuyler's son wanted to play pro baseball, but Cuyler knew he wasn't good enough so he proposed they settle it with a 100-yard dash, with the winner having his wishes granted. Cuyler, retired because of his legs, still won the race so his son went into the army.

Induction

Some 3,500 fans and 16 Hall of Famers withstood an early scorching sun on July 22 to witness the 1968 Induction Ceremony and also the dedication of the new library. The ceremony was held on the front porch of the new building overlooking Cooper Park, where it was first held in 1966. It was a separate two-story building in the back of the Hall of Fame and it would become the first facility that would be devoted exclusively to the sport of baseball. Warren Giles and Joe Cronin, presidents of the National and American Leagues, respectively, officially cut the ribbon that opened the building. Former commissioner Ford Frick was there and this must have brought back fond memories of when he cut the ribbon to open the museum in 1939. He then gave the symbolic key to Commissioner Eckert who spoke briefly and acknowledged the architect, Robert Hutchins, and the builder, Neil Neilson.

Kiki Cuyler's widow was there to represent her husband, who had passed away of a heart attack at the age of 51 in 1950. She spoke briefly and showed awareness by saying how proud her husband would have been to be one of the 110 members of the Hall of Fame.

Goose Goslin, 68, was very emotional and said briefly, "I want to thank all who selected me for this great honor. I will take it with me to my grave."

An interesting backdrop to Goslin's induction was when he and his family and friends made plans to stay an additional night at the Otesaga Hotel. He was told they couldn't because there were no more rooms. A convention had booked whatever rooms were left. It seems the hotel had asked him several weeks before if he wanted the rooms for another night but he never responded. Goslin was furious but nothing could be done to change it. Larry Ritter, his friend who was part of his party that was turned away, wrote about the whole incident years later for *Baseball Quarterly*. Ritter took a lighthearted approach in his article saying, "Goslin was honored, acclaimed, and applauded in the morning, and unceremoniously ejected from his hotel room that afternoon." The article was titled, *The Day They Kicked Goose Out of Cooperstown.*[22] Undoubtedly, this experience bothered Goslin, because he never came back to Cooperstown and died in 1971 at the age of 70.

The 1968 Induction Ceremony is held on the steps of the new library.

No doubt this incident led to a positive change for the future by the Hall of Fame. The Otesaga would be closed to the public on Induction Weekend, except for Hall of Famers, their families, and the press.

Joe Medwick, 57, also was brief in his remarks as he said, "It's been a long time coming, but I'm very, very proud to be among the great Hall of Famers." He showed no bitterness at having to wait so long by coming to six of the next seven inductions. He suffered a fatal heart attack while serving as the Cardinals' minor league batting instructor in 1975 and died at the age of 63.

1969

There were 340 ballots cast in the 1969 BBWAA election, and two players were selected. The great St. Louis Cardinal Stan Musial received 93.2 percent (317 votes) in his first year of eligibility, and the outstanding Brooklyn Dodgers catcher Roy Campanella ("Campy") received 79.4 percent (270 votes) to finish second in his fifth year of eligibility.

As a kid growing up in the Bronx in the 1950s, I enjoyed reading Allan Roth's annual *Who's Who in Baseball* and in just about every lifetime offensive category Musial was the leader. This, plus the fact that he was popular with everyone from fans and players to the press, makes it difficult to understand how 23 writers could leave him off their ballots. Campy did well in his previous BBWAA elections, receiving a total of 991 votes for five elections while always finishing in the top three.

The VC unanimously selected two pitchers, Stan Coveleski and Waite Hoyt, for the hall in 1969. Coveleski received only 41 votes from the BBWAA while Hoyt received 235. Both are considered marginal Hall of Famers. Coveleski was also interviewed by Larry Ritter for his book and Bill James thinks this helped him reach the Hall of Fame (p. 170).

Inductees

Stan Musial began his fabulous career with the Cardinals as an outfielder at the end of the 1941 season by hitting .426, a small preview of what was to come. He would lead the Cards to four pennants and three world titles in the next five years. He became the first player in the National League to win three MVPs with his best season coming in 1948 as he led the league in batting average (.376) and RBIs (131) and missed by one home run (39) copping the Triple Crown. Despite hitting 475 home runs lifetime, he never struck out more than 46 times in a season. He was a durable player who played in 895 straight games. Musial played in 24 All-Star Games and has the most home runs (6), including the game winner in 1960. He finished with 3,630 hits while batting .331.

Musial started as a pitcher but injured his shoulder in the minors, forcing him to give up pitching, making this injury the most fortuitous in baseball history. He was so beloved that Dodgers fans at Ebbets Field gave him the affectionate moniker, "Stan the Man."

Roy Campanella played nine years in the Negro Leagues before being signed by the Brooklyn Dodgers for whom he made his debut in 1948. He was an outstanding defensive catcher and led the National League in fielding percentage four times. He helped lead the Dodgers to five pennants and Brooklyn's only world championship in 1955. He was a three-time winner of the MVP award and never got to go with the Dodgers to Los Angeles because an auto accident ended his 10-year career in 1958.

Campy was honored by the Dodgers on May 7, 1959, at the Los Angeles Coliseum in an exhibition game against the Yankees with the largest crowd ever (93,103) for a major league baseball game. During the night game all the lights were turned out and every person lit a match to honor him on his 38th birthday. More than $50,000 was raised to help with his medical costs.

Stan Coveleski spent a total of eight years in the minors and didn't stick in the majors until 1916 after he learned to throw the spitter. He became one of the best spitballers because he could make it break in three directions. He had his best season in 1920 when he won 24 games and led the league in strikeouts. He helped the Cleveland Indians win their first pennant and then pitched three complete-game victories and finished with an ERA of 0.67 in the World Series as they defeated the Brooklyn Dodgers. He was 20–5 in 1925 and led the league in winning percentage as he helped lead the Senators to a pennant. He finished his career with a record of 215–142 (.602).

His brother Harry pitched nine seasons in the majors and won 20 games three times, but unlike other pitching brothers, they refused to pitch against each other. Harry's rationale for it was that whoever didn't win, people would say he wasn't trying.

Waite Hoyt was pitching for the Red Sox when he was traded to the Yankees in 1921. Like so many others who went from Boston to New York during this time he thrived. During his nine plus years there, he helped lead them to six pennants and three world titles. His best year was with the great Yankees team of 1927 when he won 22 games and then won a game in the World Series when they swept the Pirates. Hoyt had a record of 6–4 in seven World Series, including 27 straight scoreless innings. He finished with a World Series ERA of 1.83. His overall record for 21 seasons was 237–182.

Hoyt was a Cincinnati Reds' broadcaster for more than 20 years and became known as a great storyteller. He told one about when he worked as a mortician for his father-in-law and picked up a corpse near Yankee Stadium. He put it in his car's trunk while he went and pitched a shutout, then got back in his car after the game and delivered the body.

Induction

The 1969 Induction Ceremony was held on July 28 and it marked the thirtieth anniversary of the Hall of Fame. Some 5,000 people and 20 Hall of Famers witnessed an early rain that stopped and cleared up for the rest of the ceremony.

Appropriately, there was a special presentation as the first complete encyclopedia of major league baseball was donated to the Baseball Hall of Fame Library on behalf of the Macmillan Publishing Company. It was presented in honor of recently deceased Hall of Fame historian Lee Allen.

Dick Young, president of the BBWAA, began the proceedings with a follow up to Ted Williams' historic 1966 speech by sharing with the audience a motion that had been approved by the BBWAA. The motion said that the stars of the Negro Leagues should be honored by the Hall of Fame.

Roy Campanella, 48, a paraplegic since the auto accident in 1958, was the first speaker, and spoke from his wheelchair. It was fitting that this former Negro Leaguer led off the proceedings. Campy uttered a line that he had said before and that was something every major league baseball player could relate to: "I always believed that any professional athlete to be good you have to have a little boy in you." He then mentioned an example — when you see players jump up and down after getting a big double in a game or hugging everyone at home plate after a home run. He also said, "Regardless of being in this wheelchair, I consider today as one of the greatest moments in my life. Words cannot express everything that I'd like to say. Today means so much to me. Thank you and may my fellow members accept me for what I have done."

He enjoyed his Cooperstown experience very much and came back 17 times. He was a member of the Negro League Committee as well as the Veterans Committee from 1978 until 1993, when he died at the age of 71.

Stan Coveleski, 79, started his speech by saying, "I'm no speaker, I'm a coal miner." He thanked the VC for voting for him and then told the audience that he worked in the coal mines when he was 12, working from 7:00 A.M. until 6:00 P.M., six days a week, earning $3.75 for 66 hours of work. He got emotional and the new commissioner, Bowie Kuhn had to help him get through it. He told how he learned to throw the spitball in the minors from Hall of Fame pitcher Joe McGinnity. He talked about his major league career up through the 1920 World Series and then abruptly brought his speech to an end by saying, "So I think that's about all I have to say."

He was so appreciative of the honor that he came back every year for the next ten years. He died in 1984 at the age of 94. It should be noted that Covey's real name was Stanislaus Kowalewski, which was later changed to Stan Coveleskie. The e on the end of his name was dropped by sportswriters.

Waite Hoyt, 70, an experienced broadcaster, started by saying, "I have started the first game of three World Series, and I can tell you they were much easier than this." Despite his nervousness, he used a phrase that was as succinct as any other speech in describing all the people who were helpful to an honoree. He said, "I would like to express my gratitude for the contributions that everyone has made to the life of one individual." He called this honor "the pinnacle of our dreams" and told the audience that he had played with or against all 16 of the Hall of Famers that were at the induction as well as his fellow inductee, Stan Coveleski. He wondered what it would have been like to play against fellow inductees Stan Musial and Roy Campanella.

Hoyt told how he found out about his induction while playing golf in Florida. He went home to inform his wife about his good news and when she wasn't home, he left word to tell her that he was in the Hall of Fame. His wife wasn't that aware of baseball so when she heard she told all her girlfriends, "What do you think, what do you think, Waite's in the House of Fame."

He came back to the Hall of Fame five more times, served on the VC from 1971 through 1976, and died in 1984 at the age 84.

Peter Clarke, recently retired curator of collections at the Hall of Fame, related that back in 1969 when the staff was much smaller, Waite Hoyt, so appreciative of his induction, took Clark and several members of the Hall of Fame staff and their spouses to dinner at the Otesaga.

Stan Musial, 48, was the last inductee to speak and was especially gracious toward his fellow honorees. He said how proud his Polish immigrant father would have been not only of him but his fellow Polish inductee, Stan Coveleski. He then spoke of his National League rival, Roy Campanella, by saying how his constant conversation while he was catching and Stan was batting was more of a distraction than what the Dodgers' pitchers were throwing. Finally, he admitted that he didn't have Waite Hoyt's speaking ability, so that he needed to write down his remarks because it wouldn't be enough to speak from the heart alone. He said this was the greatest honor of all the honors he has received and he closed by thanking everyone for listening to him.

Consistency was a constant throughout Musial's career and life, and it has continued in his support of Induction Weekend. He has come back more than 30 times and was a member of the Veterans Committee from 1973 through 2001, before it was changed to a new format. He has endeared himself to new and old fans alike during many induction ceremonies with his harmonica rendition of "Take Me Out to the Ball Game."

CHAPTER 7

The Negro Leagues
Are Given Full Recognition:
1970–1979

1970

The BBWAA cast 300 ballots in 1970 and chose Cleveland shortstop and player-manager Lou Boudreau in his tenth year of eligibility with 77.3 percent (232 votes). He received a total of 1,035 votes in ten elections.

The Veterans Committee chose Yankees' center fielder Earle Combs, who retired in 1935. He received only 132 votes in 14 BBWAA elections. Bill James didn't support Phil Rizzuto for the Hall of Fame but thought Rizzuto was a better selection (1994) than Combs (p. 433). Robert Cohen states Combs had a short career that wasn't dominant and his selection "probably shouldn't have been made" (p. 176). Combs himself was surprised when he heard the news. The mild-mannered and modest Kentuckian, in keeping with his personality, after hearing of his election, said, "I thought the Hall of Fame was for superstars, not just average players like me."[1]

Cardinals pitcher Jesse Haines and former commissioner Ford Frick were also chosen. Haines received only 96 votes during 12 BBWAA elections and was one of the most controversial choices ever made by the VC. Bill James, James Vail and Robert Cohen are all very critical of his selection. James and Vail both attribute his selection to Frankie Frisch's influence on the Veterans Committee. Frisch was Haines's Cardinals manager and according to James, Fred Lieb and Roy Stockton, writers on the committee, also helped in his selection. Both Lieb and Stockton wrote books about the Cardinals and Stockton covered the Cardinals for a St. Louis newspaper (p. 163). Cohen rates Haines a good pitcher but states there were many other pitchers who were just as good who aren't in the Hall of Fame. Cohen calls his selection "a mistake" (p. 284).

Inductees

Lou Boudreau, an outstanding basketball player at the University of Illinois, switched to baseball and eventually signed with the Indians. He became their regular shortstop in 1940, and then at 24 became the Indians' player-manager in 1942. He brought it all together in 1948 with a magical season, winning the MVP and helping defeat the Red Sox after they tied in the regular season with two home runs in a one-game playoff. Boudreau and the

Indians capped it off with a World Series victory over the Boston Braves. Yet this almost didn't happen because owner Bill Veeck was ready to trade him after the 1947 season but backed off when he received more than 4,000 letters of protest. Boudreau batted .295 lifetime and also had the best shortstop fielding average (.973).

Boudreau devised the Ted Williams shift during the 1946 season. He moved all the players on the left side of the infield to the right side of second base because Williams was a tremendous pull hitter. Shifts against pull hitters are common practice today.

Earle Combs was a fleet center fielder and an excellent leadoff hitter for the great Yankees teams of the 1920s and the early 1930s. He drew a lot of walks, batted .325 lifetime, didn't strike out much, and had an on base percentage of .397. He led the league in triples three times, including 23 in 1927 when he had his best season, and he also led the league in hits (231) while batting .356 for arguably one of the greatest teams of all time. He was a part of three championship teams with a World Series batting average of .350. Combs missed almost three full seasons because of injuries. His most significant injury occurred when he crashed into an outfield wall in 1934. He fractured his skull and was in a coma while spending two months in a hospital. He recovered but retired the next year.

Combs had a distinguished career outside of baseball where he was a member of the Kentucky Banking Commission and the chairman of the Kentucky Board of Regents.

Jesse Haines was in the minors for seven years and didn't start pitching with the Cards until he was almost 27. He had three 20-win seasons and pitched a no-hitter in 1924. His best season was in 1927 when he went 24–10 while leading the league in complete games (25) and shutouts (6). He helped lead the Cards to four World Series while compiling a record of 3–1 and an ERA of 1.67. He won two games against the Yankees in 1926 when St. Louis won its first World Series. In 1937, he finally retired at the age of 44, having tied a National League record by pitching for the same team for 18 years. He was affectionately called "Pops" by teammates and finished with a record of 210–158 (.571). Haines is in the hall because of the knuckleball. Unlike most knuckleballers, he threw it with his knuckles rather than with his fingertips yet maintained good control of it.

Haines also had a distinguished career outside of baseball as a county auditor in Ohio.

Ford Frick was a college baseball player, a New York City baseball writer, and a radio sports broadcaster before becoming the National League president in 1934. His defining moment came in 1947. He threatened to banish the St. Louis Cardinals' players for life after they were going to strike because of Jackie Robinson, forcing them to back down. He became the baseball commissioner in 1951 and his 14-year tenure was defined mainly by movement of major league franchises as well as expansion to the West Coast. In 1956, he also recognized pitchers with a separate award in honor of Cy Young.

Frick was the person responsible for starting the Hall of Fame and there are now more than 100 other halls of fame. The Ford Frick Award, instituted in 1978, honors broadcasters' contributions to baseball.

Opposite: **The Hall of Famers attend the 1970 major league exhibition game at Doubleday Field. *Left to right:* Bob Feller, Bill Terry, Waite Hoyt, Luke Appling, Casey Stengel, Ted Lyons, Sam Rice, Bill Dickey, Frankie Frisch, Commissioner Bowie Kuhn, Lefty Grove, Joe Cronin, Zach Wheat, Max Carey, Ford Frick, Edd Roush, Red Ruffing, Lou Boudreau and Lloyd Waner.**

Induction

Some 5,000 fans, along with 22 Hall of Famers, attended the 1970 Induction Ceremony on July 27 in 90-degree heat. Jesse Haines, 77, spoke first and said that was probably because he had just gotten out of a hospital four weeks before (having had a kidney removed). He related a story of when he was young his mother had him bring food to a little old lady who was a neighbor and she would tell him to tell his mother, "I'm much obliged, many times obliged to her." Jesse closed by uttering similar sentiments when he said, "I say to the old timers committee, you got me here today, and I want to say to you fellows, I'm a thousand times obliged."

Haines came back the next four years and died in 1975 at the age of 85.

Earle Combs, 71, spoke next and kept it short because Lefty Grove told him "if I went over 10 minutes, he was going to come up and pull me down." He told of "this being the greatest thrill of his lifetime," and then he spoke of playing with Babe Ruth and Lou Gehrig. Combs said he was the only person in baseball who was with Gehrig for his whole consecutive game streak from the beginning to the end. (Combs played with Gehrig and then was a coach during his streak.)

He came back the next two years and passed away in 1976 at the age of 77.

Ford Frick, 75, spoke next, and began, "I have appeared on this rostrum many times and I never seemed to be at a loss for words and now I find that words fail me." Contrary to what he said, Frick's speech was poignant as he spoke of being humbled by the other Hall of Famers with all their physical achievements, but he also spoke of the pride he felt on what Cooperstown had become. He spoke of the continuity that Cooperstown brings to the game of baseball. "Children still have the right to dream, they have the right to idolize and the God-given privilege of having their heroes and appreciating them because of their continuity." He concluded his remarks by stating, "A lot of people question past generations but I leave this thought with you, that without the memories of the past there could be no dreams of greatness in the future, without those passing yesterdays, there could possibly be no bright tomorrows."

Frick was the chairman of the board of directors for the Hall of Fame beginning in 1966 and served on the VC from 1966 through 1969. After having attended every induction from the first one in 1939 through 1965 as either the president of the National League or commissioner of baseball, he now came back to the next three as an honoree.

He died in Bronxville, New York, in 1978 at the age of 83.

The last speaker was Lou Boudreau, 53, and he began with, "My prayers have been answered. There are no words to describe the feelings I have today." He thanked the political representatives who came from his home state of Illinois, and finished by giving praise to the Hall of Famers gathered with him as a part of baseball's rich heritage.

Like most inductees, Lou had a group that came to honor him. "Boudreau's Buddies" consisted of more than 100 people from his hometown of Harvey, Illinois. It included his daughter and her husband, 30-game winner for the Detroit Tigers Denny McLain.

Boudreau came back only three times before his death in 2001 at the age of 84.

1971

The 1971 BBWAA election had 360 ballots cast with no one achieving the necessary 75 percent for induction.

The hall authorized the Veterans Committee to choose four old-time players for enshrinement. They were also asked to pick two players from the post–1925 period and one executive or umpire. Thus, the VC amended their rules to allow them to choose seven new inductees and the eighth inductee was chosen by the newly formed Negro League Committee.

This special committee consisted of former Negro League players, including Roy Campanella, Monte Irvin, Judy Johnson, Eppie Barnes, and Bill Yancey; three former executives, Frank Forbes, Ed Gottlieb, and Alex Pompez; and two writers, Sam Lacy and Wendell Smith. This was the largest class chosen by the VC since 11 were chosen in 1946. The first selection made by the newly formed committee was all-time great Negro Leagues pitcher Satchel Paige. However, there was controversy because the Hall of Fame's board of directors originally wanted to have the Negro League Committee's selections put in a separate display area of the Hall of Fame. There were protests from Jackie Robinson, the NAACP, and the BBWAA because these Negro League greats were being given second class status. Satchel Paige told a reporter, "I was just as good as the white boys, and I ain't going in the back door of the Hall of Fame."[2] The final result was that the Hall of Fame's board of directors reconsidered and, beginning with Paige, all Negro League selections would be given equal status with all other inductees. Paige actually received one vote from the BBWAA in 1951.

Four of the six players chosen by the VC in 1971 were as controversial as the VC picks from 1946. Also chosen was executive George Weiss.

Shortstop Dave Bancroft was chosen 41 years after he retired. He received 172 votes from the BBWAA over 15 elections. Bill James called his selection a "mistake" (p. 110), and James Vail called it "one of the more dubious choices" (p. 20). Robert Cohen states Bancroft's "statistics should not have been good enough to get him into the Hall of Fame" (p. 95). They all attribute his selection as another example of the Frankie Frisch and Bill Terry influence on the VC. Frisch, Terry and Bancroft had been teammates with the Giants. Robert Cohen said Bancroft was an outstanding defensive shortstop, but his offensive statistics weren't good enough for the Hall of Fame (p. 95). Bancroft's reaction was one of complete shock and surprise when he found out.

Jake Beckley, first baseman, was chosen 64 years after he retired. Jake played in the nineteenth century and the first decade of the twentieth century and received only one vote from the 1936 old-timers poll and one vote from the BBWAA election in 1942. He never played on a pennant winner and was virtually forgotten after he retired. David Fleitz called him "perhaps the most obscure member of the Hall of Fame."[3] Yet his stats were impressive, and that's why the VC elected him.

Chick Hafey, a good-hitting left fielder for the Cardinals and the Reds, was chosen 34 years after he retired. Hafey received minimal support from the BBWAA on 12 ballots with a total of 81 votes. James was very critical and felt that Hafey didn't play enough games because of health problems (p. 166). Vail calls his selection "one of the worst choices ever" (p. 20). Cohen states Hafey was a good hitter but "his career numbers pale compared to other Hall of Famers" (p. 146).

However, Hafey also received unqualified support from the respected sports columnist Bob Broeg of the St. Louis *Post Dispatch*. Broeg felt that Hafey could run faster, field better, and hit as well as Hall of Famer Joe Medwick, the man who succeeded him in left field for the Cards and who had been selected by the BBWAA in 1968.[4]

Harry Hooper was an outfielder who was chosen 46 years after he retired. He had only 22 votes from the BBWAA in six elections. Bill James thinks the main reason Hooper got in was because of Larry Ritter's book, *The Glory of Their Times* (p. 170). James Vail believes that his Red Sox teammate, Hall of Famer Waite Hoyt, a member of the VC, also helped Hooper's cause (p. 105). Robert Cohen rates him last of all the right fielders in the Hall of Fame and feels that "he never should have been voted in" (p. 204).

Joe Kelley, an outfielder and one of many stars for the old Baltimore Orioles, was chosen 65 years after he retired. He received only two votes from the BBWAA, which can be attributed to Kelley, having played more than half of his career in the nineteenth century.

Rube Marquard was a pitcher for the Giants and Dodgers and was chosen 46 years after he retired. He received 143 votes from the BBWAA in 13 elections. Bill James pulled no punches in his criticism when he called Marquard, "The worst starting pitcher in the Hall of Fame" (p. 170). James Vail considered him another "dubious choice" (p. 20), and Robert Cohen rates Marquard last of all the pitchers in the Hall of Fame, calling him "one of the poorest choices ever made by the VC" (p. 285).

Marquard also benefitted from *The Glory of their Times*, and New York sportswriter Dan Daniel, a member of the VC, stated that he received more letters of support for Rube than any other player.[5]

Each inductee's notification is unique, but one of the most unusual stories has to be how Rube Marquard received his notice. He and his wife were aboard the luxury liner *Queen Elizabeth II* when he was informed by his friend and *Glory* author Larry Ritter. Later, when the captain of the ship heard about the honor a special reception was held for Marquard as the band played "Take Me Out to the Ball Game."

George Weiss, the very successful Yankees' general manager, was voted into the Hall of Fame five years after he retired in 1966 as the chief executive of the New York Mets.

Inductees

Satchel Paige, whose real name was Leroy, acquired his nickname because of all the suitcases that he had to carry while working at a railroad station. He pitched 25 years for many teams in the Negro Leagues, including the Pittsburgh Crawfords and Kansas City Monarchs. He was a colorful showman who drew the largest crowds wherever he pitched. He had pinpoint control and Joe DiMaggio, who faced him on a barnstorming tour, praised him, saying, "He was the best and fastest pitcher I ever faced."[6] He signed with the Indians in 1948 as the oldest rookie (age 42) ever. As a relief pitcher, he helped them win a pennant and later the World Series. He also pitched with the St. Louis Browns and later came out of retirement to pitch three innings of relief for the Kansas City A's in 1965 at the age of 59.

Paige was arguably the Negro League's greatest star just like Babe Ruth was his counterpart in Major League Baseball. They both were also incorrigible youths who went to reform schools where they matured, learned to play baseball, and became men.

Dave Bancroft helped the Philadelphia Phillies win a pennant during his rookie season as their regular shortstop in 1915. He was called "Bany" and also "Beauty" because that's what he called good pitches and good plays by teammates. Bany was an outstanding defensive shortstop who set a major league record for total chances with 984 in 1922. He once hit six singles in a game in 1920. He batted .279 lifetime.

Manager John McGraw thought so highly of him that he traded a pitcher, shortstop, and $100,000 for him in 1920, the largest amount of cash ever made in a trade up until that time. Bancroft didn't disappoint. He became their captain and helped lead the Giants to three pennants and two championships in three years.

Jake Beckley was a left-handed first baseman who could field but was put there because he had a weak arm. He was called "Eagle Eye" because he always got a piece of the ball and didn't strike out much. Eagle Eye finished with a .308 batting average while collecting 2,934 hits. He had the most triples lifetime (244) when he retired and also the most games at first base (2,380). Those records have since been broken, but he still holds the major league record for most putouts by a first baseman (23,731).

Beckley was a character who liked to try the hidden ball trick on unsuspecting young ballplayers like Honus Wagner. Once Beckley hid the ball under first base but couldn't find it as Wagner went to second base chuckling all the way. Finally, he would often flip the bat and bunt the ball with the handle of the bat. He did this until it became illegal.

Chick Hafey signed with the Cards as a pitcher, but Branch Rickey switched him to the outfield after he saw how he could hit. He batted .329 or better for six straight seasons and won the batting title (.349) in 1931 in the closest race in National League history. He played on four pennant winners and two championship teams while with the Cards. He had significant sinus and eyesight problems that were alleviated somewhat when he finally started wearing glasses in 1929. He batted .317 lifetime, and Rogers Hornsby felt he might have been one of the all-time hitters if it weren't for his health problems.

Chick Hafey was mild-mannered but when the penny-pinching Branch Rickey refused to meet his reasonable demands for a raise, Hafey stormed out of spring training and was traded to the Reds, who were more than willing to give him what he wanted.

Harry Hooper was studying engineering in college when the Red Sox offered him a contract that included the opportunity to help design their new home field, Fenway Park. He never got to work on Fenway, but he did break in with the Red Sox where he became their regular right fielder and played for six years with Tris Speaker in center and Duffy Lewis in left to form the best defensive outfield of the Dead Ball Era. Hooper had good range and a strong and accurate arm that produced 344 assists during his career. He was a good leadoff hitter who taught himself to bat left-handed and stole 375 bases, including 40 in 1910. He helped lead Boston to four world titles and batted .281 lifetime.

Hooper and shortstop Everett Scott helped convince Red Sox manager Ed Barrow to make their star pitcher an everyday player, and that player was Babe Ruth.

Joe Kelley became the regular left fielder with the Baltimore Orioles and helped lead them to three straight pennants from 1894 through 1896. They competed against the second-place team for the Temple Cup and lost in 1894 and 1895 before winning it in 1896 and again in 1897 when they finished second. He went to Brooklyn in 1899 and was a part of two more pennants. He had 443 lifetime stolen bases and became a player-manager for the Cincinnati Reds, finishing his career with a .317 average.

Kelley married the daughter of the Orioles' owner, and Hall of Famer Wee Willie Keeler was his best man. He is buried in a cemetery in Baltimore with three other Orioles.

Rube Marquard's father wanted his son to get an education, and once he signed a pro contract, he and his father didn't speak to each other for 10 years. Richard Marquard, as a left-handed minor league pitcher, acquired the nickname, "Rube" because of his resemblance to the Hall of Fame pitcher Rube Waddell. He broke in with the Giants but didn't realize his potential until Wilbert Robinson, the old Oriole, became his coach. He helped Rube have his best three seasons (1911 through 1913) and team with Christy Mathewson to lead the Giants to three pennants as he won 73 games, including the major league record of 19 straight in 1912. He was reunited with now Brooklyn manager Robinson and pitched on two more pennant winners. He finished with a record of 201–177 (.532).

Marquard off the field shared the stage with actress Blossom Seely, whom he married and divorced, and was friendly with theatrical greats Al Jolson and George M. Cohan.

George Weiss, executive with the New York Yankees for three decades, started the Yankees' farm system in 1932 that produced nine pennants and eight championships in 16 years. He helped to convince business manager Ed Barrow to buy Joe DiMaggio from the Pacific Coast League after Joe had hurt his knee. As Barrow's successor, he hired Casey Stengel and, during Weiss's 13-year reign, the Yankees won 10 pennants and eight World Series. He finished his career as president of the expansion New York Mets.

In 1923, Weiss, as the owner of a New Haven team, was on a train headed to Chicago for baseball's winter meetings with his manager, Bill Donovan. When they went to bed, Weiss took the upper berth while the older Donovan took the lower berth. Later, the train hit a stalled car on the tracks and Donovan was killed while Weiss survived unhurt.

Induction

The 1971 Induction Ceremony was held on August 9, a warm day (85 degrees), with 4,000 spectators in attendance, along with 24 Hall of Famers. The honorees received from the Hillerich and Bradsby Bat Company a full-sized autograph bat on a plaque that bore an engraving of the Hall of Fame building.

Prior to the induction speeches the recording device used to play "The Star-Spangled Banner" broke down. Hall of Fame director Ken Smith filled the void and sang the national anthem, which he would continue to do for several more inductions.

The first inductee to receive his plaque was Dave "Beauty" Bancroft, who was unable to attend due to illness. Lo and behold, former teammate, Hall of Famer, and his biggest supporter on the VC, Frankie Frisch, was his representative. Frisch spoke briefly and called Bancroft "the best shortstop in the National League between 1915 and 1925." He continued, "He was the main cog in the Giants' three pennants from 1921 through 1923." Bancroft died a year later at the age of 81.

Jake Beckley had died in 1918 at the age of 50 so another Pirates Hall of Famer, Pie Traynor, accepted in his place. Beckley was no longer obscure because the people of his hometown of Hannibal, Missouri (home of Mark Twain), had a Jake Beckley Day in his honor and dedicated a monument to him.

Chick Hafey, 67, was next and spoke briefly, thanking the VC and calling it "the greatest thing that ever happened to me."

He promised to come back and did in 1972 but died the next year at the age of 70.

Harry Hooper, 83, spoke longer than the previous speakers, and paid tribute to several people who were a part of his grassroots campaign. This was commendable because most times others who were inducted because of similar efforts never acknowledged important contributors without whom they would have never made it to Cooperstown. Hooper thanked his old college coach who tried unsuccessfully to get him in, the Chicago White Sox fans who voted for him as their all-time right fielder, along with a special mention of one old-time Red Sox fan, Ed Daly, who attended the ceremony. He also thanked his son John, who checked record books, and helped make his father's case to the VC.

Hooper attended the next three inductions and died at age 87 in 1974.

Joe Kelley, who had died in 1943 at 71, was represented by his son, Joe Kelley, Jr., who was 72 at the time. He thanked everyone from the VC on behalf of his family, but regretted his mother couldn't be there, having died two years before at the age of 93.

Rube Marquard, 84, told the audience how his father wouldn't let him come back home after he signed a professional contract because he felt "all ballplayers were no good," and that he needed an education to get a job. Marquard succeeded despite his father and went on to praise his manager with the New York Giants, John McGraw. "He was the greatest manager in baseball. He loved his players and they loved him."

Marquard came back for the next eight inductions and died in 1980 at the age of 93.

Satchel Paige, 65, received the most applause from the crowd when it was his turn to speak. He framed his speech around the classic phrase that he coined, "Don't look back, something might be gaining on you." Always remembering those words helped keep him going as he finally made the majors in 1948. He acknowledged Bob Feller and Bill Veeck during his speech. Feller was his teammate on the Indians in 1948, and Veeck was the owner who brought him to the majors and then signed him again for the St. Louis Browns. Paige had pitched against Feller's All-Stars during a barnstorming tour. He finished his speech by saying, "I am the proudest man in the place today."

He came back three times and died in 1982 at the age of 75.

Old Satchel was again recognized during the 2006 Induction Weekend as part of the ceremony honoring 17 inductees associated with Negro baseball. A statue of him pitching with his high kick was unveiled outside, next to the steps of the Hall of Fame Library.

George Weiss was ill so his friend Ford Frick represented him. Frick said George Weiss "contributed as much to baseball as any man the game could ever know." He read a message that Weiss had dictated to him. "Being inducted today is the pinnacle of my dreams, particularly for one who never possessed the ability on the field." He closed with, "It is probably the greatest disappointment of my life that I cannot be with you today." George Weiss died a year later at the age of 77.

1972

The 1972 BBWAA election had 396 ballots cast and three players were chosen, including the phenomenal Dodgers left-hander Sandy Koufax, the one and only Yankees catcher Yogi Berra, and 300-game winner Early Wynn.

Sandy Koufax was first and received 86.9 percent (344 votes) and was selected in his first year of eligibility. Yogi Berra was second and received 85.6 percent (339 votes). He was selected in his second year of eligibility after having finished first in the 1971 ballot, but fell below the 75 percent requirement as he received 67 percent (242 votes). Early Wynn just made it with 76 percent (301 votes). He was selected in his fourth year of eligibility, having received a total of 474 votes previously.

The Negro League Committee chose the great catcher Josh Gibson as their second selection and the slugging first baseman Buck Leonard as their third selection.

Gibson had died in 1947, but Leonard was alive and well when he attended Satchel Paige's induction in 1971. He was so excited about his fellow Negro Leaguer's achievement that he compared it to "men walking on the moon."[7]

The next year in February he was asked by Monte Irvin to come to New York from his home in Rocky Mount, North Carolina, "to help pick a Negro League all-star team." He had no idea what was happening when he walked into the Americana Hotel until he saw all the media people and baseball commissioner Bowie Kuhn. Leonard still didn't know until Kuhn announced that he was chosen for the Hall of Fame. He called it "the greatest moment of his life."[8]

The VC chose Yankees left-hander pitcher Lefty Gomez, Giants' right fielder Ross Youngs, and former American League president Will Harridge.

Gomez was selected 29 years after he retired and is probably best remembered more for his funny quips than any significant pitching statistic. Yet he was a star pitcher and did receive 495 votes in 15 BBWAA elections. He loved to joke about his own hitting saying that "I was the worst hitter I ever saw and that the only time I ever broke a bat was when I broke one while backing out of the garage."[9] He even quipped about his own health after undergoing triple bypass surgery in 1979. "That's the first triple I ever got."[10]

Ross Youngs, Giants' right fielder, retired prematurely at the age of 29 because of a kidney disorder. He didn't do badly in 17 BBWAA elections with 474 votes, yet he is considered controversial by Bill James and James Vail because they feel his selection was due to the influence that his two former Giants teammates, good old Frankie Frisch again and Bill Terry, had as members of the Veterans Committee. Robert Cohen calls his selection "a big mistake" (p. 201).

However, Youngs' manager, John McGraw, called him "the best outfielder he ever saw."[11] Also, Ford Frick, the former commissioner and Hall of Famer, was asked to pick his personal all-star team and had the obvious choices in the outfield of Ruth, Cobb, and Tris Speaker. He then said, "I've got to find a place for Pep Youngs [Ross], I've just got to put him in there somewhere."[12]

Will Harridge was selected 14 years after he retired as president of the American League, and one year after he died at the age of 87. He had been involved with the Hall of Fame when he helped open it in 1939 then served on the original Centennial Committee and the Old Timers Committee and then the VC from 1953 until his death in 1971.

Inductees

Sandy Koufax was signed by the Brooklyn Dodgers in 1955 because of a blazing fastball. He had control issues and didn't pitch in the 1955 and 1956 World Series. He improved significantly when the Dodgers moved to Los Angeles in 1958, mainly because of pitching coach Joe Becker and backup catcher Norm Sherry. Koufax won the first of five straight ERA titles in 1962 and then had three phenomenal years in 1963, 1965 and 1966. He won the MVP in 1963 and three unanimous Cy Young Awards while throwing four no-hitters, including a perfect game. He also helped the Dodgers win two out of three World Series as he won four games with an ERA of 0.95. Due to an arthritic elbow, he had to retire after 1966 with a lifetime record of 165–87 (.655).

Koufax was a man of principle. He was Jewish and refused to pitch a World Series game because it fell on Yom Kippur, the most important holy day in the Jewish calendar.

Yogi Berra was born Lawrence but got his name because his buddies saw an Indian snake charmer with that name in a movie. Berra signed with the Yankees as a catcher and then spent two years in the Navy during World War II where he saw action during the D-Day invasion in 1944. He made the Yankees in 1946 and became a good defensive catcher who went on to win three MVPs and become the most successful player in World Series history. He played on 14 pennant winners and 10 World Series champions. He batted .285 lifetime and was also a successful manager who won pennants in both leagues.

Berra is the master of the malaprop (ridiculous misuse of a word.) One of the memorable lines that is attributed to him was when his 1973 Mets won the pennant after coming from last place to first place the last month of the season: "It ain't over 'til it's over."[13]

Early Wynn's career improved significantly when he came under the influence of Cleveland pitching coach Mel Harder, who helped turn him into a consistent winner. "Gus," as he was nicknamed, had four 20-win seasons with the Indians. He helped lead the Indians to 111 wins and a pennant in 1954. Wynn was traded to the Chicago White Sox in 1959, went on to win the Cy Young Award for both leagues that year at the age of 39 with 22 wins, and helped lead the "Go Go" Sox to the pennant. It took him five tries to notch his 300th win, which he did in 1963. He finished with a record of 300–244.

Wynn would not hesitate to move batters off the plate. Reportedly, it is told that he would throw at his own mother if she crowded the plate.

Josh Gibson had an extraordinary 17-year career that established him as the Negro Leagues' greatest all-time hitter as well as a very good defensive catcher. He teamed with Satchel Paige for five years with the Pittsburgh Crawfords to form the Negro Leagues' best battery. He then teamed with fellow inductee Buck Leonard on the Homestead Grays team in 1937 to form the Negro Leagues' most powerful duo, winning nine consecutive pennants. He became known for his prodigious home runs and led the league in homers six times. He also won two batting titles and hit .424 against major league all-stars.

As legend has it, Gibson was discovered while a spectator at a Homestead Grays game that was played at Pittsburgh's Forbes Field. The Grays' regular catcher got hurt and Josh volunteered at the age of 18 to take his place, thus beginning his illustrious career.

Buck Leonard was born Walter but his parents called him "Buddy," which one of his brothers pronounced "Buck," and that became his name. Buck teamed with Josh Gibson and together the Grays' duo became known as the Ruth (Gibson) and Gehrig (Leonard) of black baseball. Leonard was good defensively because of his agility and ability to dig out throws in the dirt. He played in 12 East-West all-star games. He also hit at least .382 against major league all-stars. Available records have him hitting between .320 and .355.

He played 17 years with the Homestead Grays while every other Negro Leagues' star jumped to different teams in order to make more money. Little wonder Negro Leagues' historian Jim Riley called Leonard "the best-liked player in the Negro Leagues."[14]

Lefty Gomez was a four-time, 20-game winner for the Yanks in the 1930s and led the league in more than 15 categories over his 14-year career. He won pitching's Triple Crowns (wins, strikeouts and ERA) in 1934 and 1937. He was the starting pitcher in five All-Star Games and was 6–0 for the Yankees in five World Series championships. He finished with a record of 189–102 (.649).

Lefty Gomez was known as "El Goofy" because he was able to find humor in baseball. He tried to ease the tension in the dugout after Gehrig's streak ended by putting his arm around him and saying, "It took them 15 years to get you out of the lineup. They got me out of there in 15 minutes."[15] He was a goodwill ambassador for the Wilson Sporting Goods Company. Once, when filling out a job application for them, he answered the question why he left his last job by stating, "I couldn't get anyone out."[16]

Ross Youngs was given the nickname "Pep" (short for peppy) because of his enthusiasm and spirited play by Giants' manager John McGraw. Youngs was fast, hit for average, and played good defense as he led the league's outfielders in assists three times. He helped lead the Giants to four straight pennants and two world championships. Youngs ignited a rally during the 1921 Series when he hit a double and triple in the same inning to help the Giants defeat the Yankees. He hit .375 in the 1922 Series when the Giants defeated the Yanks again. He finished his 10-year career with a batting average of .322.

Youngs contracted Bright's disease, a severe kidney disorder, during the 1926 season, yet returned to the lineup and managed to finish the season with a .306 average. He never played again, and died in October 1927 at the age of 30.

Will Harridge was a railroad agent who was involved in the travel arrangements for the teams of the American League. He impressed American League president Ban Johnson, who hired him as his personal secretary. Harridge eventually became the league president in 1931. While Johnson was controversial and combative, Harridge was calm and dignified. Harridge helped launch the All-Star Game in 1933, became a proponent of night baseball, and helped to make batting helmets mandatory. He retired in 1958, and was the chairman of the board for the American League until he died in 1971.

Harridge was decisive when he suspended Yankees catcher Bill Dickey for 30 days and fined him $1,000 for breaking Carl Reynolds' jaw in a collision at home plate. Yankees owner Jacob Ruppert was so upset he didn't speak to Harridge for a year.

Induction

The 1972 Induction Ceremony took place on a mild day, August 7, with a record turnout of 15,000 fans to honor all the inductees, especially the incomparable Yogi Berra. There was also a record 28 Hall of Famers present. The first inductee to speak was the inimitable Yogi Berra, 47. His speech was brief but did contain some Yogisms, contrived or otherwise. He started off with, "I guess the first thing I should do is thank everybody who made this day necessary." He then paid tribute to Bill Dickey, Casey Stengel, George Weiss, and his wife, Carmen, whom he called the perfect baseball wife because she planned his family's entire lives around the game. He thanked the fans for their support and baseball because "it has given me more than I could ever hope for." He closed with, "I hope when I am through with this game I will put something back."

He got back only one time in the '70s and one time in the '80s because of managing and coaching responsibilities, but once they ended he has come to every induction since 1991. His favorite Cooperstown memory was summed up with a typical Yogism, "I love coming up and if I'm still living, I'll be coming up." He served on the VC from 1994 through 2001.

Josh Gibson, Jr., represented his father, who died of a cerebral hemorrhage in 1947 at the age of 35. He spoke briefly as he said not only his family was proud of this award but also the city of Pittsburgh. He closed by saying, "Wake up, Dad, you just made it in."

Lefty Gomez spoke next and despite his humorous reputation spoke briefly and in a serious manner. He called his induction "the greatest pleasure I have had in my life." He did have one quip: "I want to thank Joe DiMaggio for running down all my mistakes." He came back three times in the 1980s and died in 1989 at the age of 80.

Will Harridge's grandson, Will Harridge III, represented him and was very brief, saying he was sure that his grandfather would have liked to have been there for the honor.

Sandy Koufax spoke next as he became, with Lou Gehrig, the youngest inductee at the age of 36. He said that he didn't really have a speech but wanted to thank the people who helped him. He began by thanking the people who had faith in him during the first six years of his career because he was "ready to look for a job somewhere else." He then thanked specific people such as pitching coach Joe Becker, his two main catchers, Roy Campanella and Johnny Roseboro, owner Walter O'Malley, and manager Walter Alston. He closed with a nice tribute to the fans by thanking "the people inside the fence and the people outside the fence for how good you've been to me and tell you just how much I appreciate being here in such distinguished company."

It should be noted that the people inside the fence have special tickets that allow them to sit in folding chairs and be closer to the proceedings. Everyone else without a ticket is outside the fence. This includes thousands of people who come for a particular inductee to those who come back year after year, no matter who the inductee is.

Buck Leonard, 64, delivered one of the most heartfelt induction speeches that was ever given. He shared with his audience how making the Hall of Fame wasn't in his dreams because he wasn't allowed to play in the major leagues. He then went into detail about his meeting with Monte Irvin at the Americana Hotel in New York City where he was asked to join others on the platform as they asked him about Josh Gibson, who was being honored. Leonard describes how he really began to sweat, and "the sweat was falling down on his brand-new suit," as they said, "The Committee has also seen fit to select Buck Leonard to the Hall of Fame." He was speechless and when someone asked him a question, he said, "It was the greatest moment of my life being at that time selected for the Hall of Fame." Later he said, "My greatest thrill doesn't come from something I did on the field, but what somebody did for me, and that was to select me for the Hall of Fame." He finished with an acknowledgment of his Christian faith when he said, "It is nice to receive praise and honor from men, but the greatest praise and honor comes from our lord and savior Jesus Christ." He later showed his gratitude by writing a letter to each member of the Committee.

Further showing his appreciation, he came back 16 more times, even when he was in a wheelchair. He died in 1977 at the age of 90 in the place where he lived his whole life, Rocky Mount, North Carolina.

Early Wynn spoke next and was brief as he shared with the audience how fortunate he was to be an all-star, play in the World Series and be elected to the Hall of Fame.

Wynn came back seven more times before he died in 1999 at the age of 79.

The last speaker was the daughter of Pep Youngs, Mrs. Caroline Thompson. She spoke briefly and thanked everyone on behalf of her mother for this honor to her father.

1973

The 1973 BBWAA election had 380 ballots cast and all-time-great lefty pitcher Warren Spahn was voted in during his first year of eligibility. He was the only candidate to earn induction after he received 83.2 percent (316 votes).

There was a special election held by the BBWAA in March after Pittsburgh Pirates outstanding right fielder Roberto Clemente was killed on New Year's Eve at the age of 38 in a plane crash while on a humanitarian mission. The Hall of Fame directors unanimously waived the five-year retirement rule and Clemente received 93 percent of the BBWAA vote in this special election.

The Negro League Committee selected Monte Irvin as their fourth inductee in three years. Since he was a member of the committee, he removed himself from the voting and the rest of the committee selected him. Irvin remained on the Negro Committee until it dissolved in 1977 and then was a member of the VC from 1983 through 1998.

The VC selected their third umpire, Billy Evans of the American League, who also achieved success as an executive following his retirement.

The VC also selected nineteenth-century 300 game winner Mickey Welch. The inductions of Early Wynn in 1972 and Warren Spahn in 1973 as 300-game winners helped influence the VC to remember Welch because he was the only 300-game winner who hadn't been inducted.

The final VC selection was National League first baseman George Kelly, who also became one of the more controversial selections they ever made. He received only 14 votes in 20 BBWAA elections. Bill James called him "one of the least qualified players in the Hall of Fame" (p. 178). James Vail called him "one of the worse choices ever" (p. 108). Both attribute his selection to Bill Terry and Waite Hoyt (former teammates), Dan Daniel and Fred Lieb (New York Giants sportswriters) and Bill DeWitt (General Manager with the Reds, one of his former teams), all being on the VC. Robert Cohen rates Kelly (with Frank Chance) last of the Hall of Fame first basemen and definitely not deserving of the honor (pp. 43–44).

Inductees

Warren Spahn saw limited time with the Boston Braves before serving three years in World War II. He came back in 1946 to become the most successful left-handed pitcher of all time. He had thirteen 20-win seasons during his 21 seasons. He and pitcher Johnny Sain helped lead the Braves to the 1948 pennant with the team mantra, "Spahn and Sain and pray for rain." He won the Cy Young Award in 1957 as the now–Milwaukee Braves went on to win the World Series over the Yankees. "Spahnie" was a good all-around athlete who fielded his position well and had the most home runs by a National League pitcher (35). He finished with the most wins (363) and shutouts (63) by a left-hander. His final record was 363–245 (.597) with a lifetime ERA of 3.09.

Spahn saw action at the Battle of the Bulge, where he was decorated for bravery with a Bronze Star and a Purple Heart after being hit by shrapnel.

Roberto Clemente spent his entire 18-year career with the Pirates and set a record for the most games played in right field. Clemente had an outstanding arm and won 12 Gold Gloves while leading the league in assists five times. Offensively, he won four batting titles and was the league's MVP in 1966. He led the Pirates to two world titles in 1960 and 1971 when he hit safely in all 14 World Series games that he played. He recorded his 3,000th hit on his final at-bat during the 1972 season and batted .317 lifetime.

He was killed in a plane crash while trying to deliver supplies to Nicaragua following an earthquake on December 31, 1972. Later the major league humanitarian award was renamed after him. Clemente's philosophy was, "If you have an opportunity to make things better and you don't, then you are wasting your time on earth."[17]

Monte Irvin started with the Newark Eagles of the Negro National League and teamed with future Hall of Famer Larry Doby to help Newark win the Negro League World Series in 1946. Although statistics are sketchy, he batted close to .400 during most of his career with them. He broke in with the New York Giants as a 30-year-old rookie outfielder in 1949. He finished third in the MVP voting in 1951 by batting .312 and leading the league in RBIs with 121. He capped off the season by hitting .458 in the World Series that included stealing home as they lost to the Yanks in six games. He was a part of their championship in 1954 and batted .293 lifetime.

Irvin worked for Commissioner Bowie Kuhn and Kuhn paid this tribute to him at his induction: "And never do I feel has baseball produced a kinder, more decent, more beloved man, or one who has meant more to me personally than Monte Irvin."

Billy Evans was the youngest umpire at 22 when he began in 1906. He umpired six World Series, Walter Johnson's first game, and also six no-hitters. Honus Wagner picked him as his all-time umpire because he avoided disputes and had an even disposition.

There were some down moments, too; he was almost killed after being hit by a bottle from an irate teenage fan. He refused to press charges because the boy apologized and his parents stayed with him in the hospital while he recovered. Once Evans and Ty Cobb got into a fight after a game near the umpire's dressing room, and despite Evans being a college boxer, it was like a street fight and Cobb won. Cobb regretted it, but gained the upmost respect for Evans because he never said anything about it.

Mickey Welch started his major league career with the Troy Trojans in 1880, winning 34 games when the pitching distance was 45'. He was still successful when the distance was moved to 50' in 1881. The Trojans folded and Welch joined the New York Gothams in 1883. There he had phenomenal success: he consistently won 22 or more games with his best season coming in 1885 when he won 44 games for the team now called the Giants. Welch was the second part of a two-man rotation that included ace Tim Keefe. The two led the Giants to the pennant in 1888 and 1889. Pitching almost 5,000 innings took a toll on his arm — he pitched only 12 seasons, compiling a record of 307–210 (.593).

Welch and Keefe pitched almost nine years together and they remained friends for the rest of their lives. Keefe was quiet and studious and was called "Sir Timothy" while the 5'9" Welch was outgoing and jovial and was called "Smiling Mickey."

George Kelly, called "High Pockets" because of his height (6'4"), enjoyed his greatest success from 1921 through 1924 when he helped lead the New York Giants to four pennants and two world championships. He led the league in RBIs twice and home runs once. His forte was defense where he had a powerful arm and was the cutoff man for all three outfield positions. He hit .300 or better seven times and batted .297 lifetime.

John McGraw was his manager when the Giants won four straight pennants and High Pockets was one of seven Hall of Famers who played for McGraw during that period, including Bill Terry and Frankie Frisch. McGraw said, "Kelly got more important hits for us during this period than any other player."[18]

Induction

The 1973 Induction Ceremony on August 6 was on a hot, steamy day as 24 Hall of Famers were in attendance. The first person being honored was umpire Billy Evans. He died in 1956 at the age of 71 so his grandson, William C. Evans, was there to represent him. The grandson spoke briefly, thanking the VC and regretting that his grandfather wasn't alive to accept the award. During Commissioner Kuhn's introduction of Evans, Kuhn gave a very succinct description of umpires when he said, "Our umpires are the least appreciated men of baseball yet they are the everyday guardians of integrity."

He also listed the many accomplishments of Billy Evans after he retired from umpiring: general manager of the Cleveland Indians (Evans was the first to be called by that name), general manager of the Detroit Tigers, farm director of the Boston Red Sox, and president of the Southern Association. Furthermore, Evans was an executive with the Cleveland Rams of the National Football League.

Monte Irvin, 54, spoke after Commissioner Kuhn's heartwarming introduction. He began by saying that he would rather face Warren Spahn than make a speech. He spoke graciously of three of his fellow inductees saying that Spahn was the toughest left-hander he ever faced, that George Kelly was a very versatile player, and that Roberto Clemente, a close friend and a great player, could do everything well. He spoke of how his playing in the Negro Leagues now "doesn't seem to have been in vain." He closed by mentioning some of his greatest experiences in baseball including all the honors he received while playing in Puerto Rico, Mexico, Venezuela, and Cuba while a member of the Negro Leagues, but "none could equal the great feeling that I have right now."

Irvin has come back to 28 inductions.

George Kelly, 77, spoke briefly of the "double honor of going in with a man, Warren Spahn, that I helped coach." He gave thanks to God for this honor and he thanked fellow members of the San Francisco Old Timers Hall of Fame who came to honor him. He closed with, "The finest thing that life can send is a gift of one who you can call a friend." High Pockets came back the next five years and passed away in 1984 at the age of 88.

Warren Spahn, 52, was introduced by Commissioner Kuhn who informed the audience that Spahn didn't win a game until he was 25 and went on from there to have the most victories by a lefty, and to also pitch a no-hitter when he was 40. During Spahn's speech his brother-in-law, Leo Curran, seated near the stage, suffered a heart attack and had to be taken to a hospital. Spahn was visibly upset but was eventually persuaded to continue. He was very proud to introduce his father, who taught him the fundamentals of pitching.

Spahnie returned on a consistent basis for 24 more induction ceremonies before he passed away in 2004 at the age of 83.

Roberto Clemente was represented by his widow, Vera, and his three sons as well as his mother, Luisa Walker. Vera spoke briefly as she called the honor "a momentous last triumph, and if he were here, he would dedicate it to the people of Puerto Rico, the people of Pittsburgh, and to all his fans throughout the United States." The ceremony was broadcast to Puerto Rico as Clemente became the first Latin American player to be inducted into the Hall of Fame. It was also fitting that he went in with his boyhood hero, Monte Irvin. Something good that came out of his tragic death was his dream of a sports complex became a reality when it was built in Puerto Rico. Also, the right field wall at the PNC Park in Pittsburgh is 21 feet high in honor of the number 21 that he wore during his career. Recently, his plaque was changed due to an error in the placement of his three names. The plaque now has his correct name, Roberto Clemente Walker.

The last inductee was Mickey Welch and his daughter, Mrs. Julia Weiss, thanked "those who made it possible for him to get this honor." Welch died in 1941 at the age of 82.

1974

The 1974 BBWAA elections saw 365 ballots cast. Superstar Mickey Mantle was chosen in his first year of eligibility as he finished first with 88.2 percent (322 votes). Whitey Ford, outstanding left-handed pitcher for the Yankees, finished second behind his teammate and friend. Ford had 77.8 percent (284 votes) in his second year of eligibility. He had 67 percent (255 votes) to finish second also in the 1973 BBWAA election.

The Negro League Committee chose the fleet center fielder Cool Papa Bell as their fifth selection. There were some similarities between him and fellow inductee Mickey Mantle. They played the same position, were switch hitters, and were both very fast although some consider Cool Papa Bell the fastest player of all time.

The Veterans Committee selected National League umpire Jocko Conlan, who became the fourth umpire selected. The VC also selected first baseman Jim Bottomley, who received 293 votes in 12 BBWAA elections and wasn't considered controversial, although some called him a borderline Hall of Famer. Also selected was nineteenth-century right fielder Sam Thompson, who ended his career in 1898 except for 8 games he played in 1906. The statistic for runs batted in (RBI) didn't become an official baseball statistic until 1920, long after Sam Thompson's career was over. It was not until much later that researchers realized how good Sam Thompson was at driving in runs. He knocked in .923 runs per game, which is higher than anyone else, including Lou Gehrig, Hank Greenberg, Joe DiMaggio, and Babe Ruth, who are ranked second through fifth, respectively. Batters who hit for power and drove in runs weren't considered important during the nineteenth century and this was why Thompson became a forgotten man when he died in 1922 at age 62. He never received one vote from the BBWAA, but fortunately, because of the research that was done by historians, Sam Thompson was duly recognized in 1974 by the Hall of Fame for what he had accomplished.

Inductees

Mickey Mantle was taught to be a switch-hitter when he was five. He broke in as a right fielder for the Yankees in 1951. He hurt his knee in the 1951 World Series, which would be a continuation of leg problems that started in high school and would plague him the rest of his career and take away his legendary speed. He succeeded Joe DiMaggio in center field in 1952, and from there he won three MVPs and a Triple Crown. "The Mick" helped lead the Yanks to 12 pennants and 7 World Series championships. He holds four World Series records, including most home runs (18). He finished his career with 536 home runs, a .298 batting average, and an on-base percentage of .421.

Mantle was a well-known carouser, who as a recovering alcoholic in 1993 lectured youth groups on the dangers of alcohol. He received a liver transplant just before he died, and he and his family helped to establish the Mickey Mantle Foundation for organ donation.

Whitey Ford won nine straight games in his rookie season of 1950, then spent the next two years in the army and resumed his career in 1954. Ford compiled a record of 25–4 and won the Cy Young Award in 1961. He set 15 World Series records, including 33⅔ consecutive scoreless innings as he helped the Yankees win six championships. He finished with a record of 236–106, for a winning percentage of .690. Teammate Elston Howard dubbed Ford "Chairman of the Board."

Ford and Mantle were so close that Mantle considered Ford to be "like a brother." Once, when in San Francisco for the 1961 All-Star Game, the two played golf at Giants owner Horace Stoneham's country club and ran up a debt of $400. Stoneham said he would cancel it if Ford struck out Giants superstar Willie Mays. When Ford did it, Mantle was so excited that he came running in from center to pound Ford on the back.

Cool Papa Bell was born James Bell and he supposedly acquired his nickname when a teammate with the St. Louis Stars commented, "He's a cool one," and his manager responded, "A cool papa." As a center fielder he played shallow to capitalize on his tremendous speed. Bill Veeck, the legendary owner, saw him play and said, "Defensively, he was the equal of Speaker, Joe DiMaggio, and Willie Mays."[19] He won a championship with the Stars and also with the Pittsburgh Crawfords. Bell played from 1922 through 1946, and according to the latest available statistics, Bell batted .317 and stole 144 bases.

There are many stories of his legendary speed such as running the bases in 13.1 seconds, compared to the major league record of 13.5 seconds. Bell said the field was wet and he actually ran it in 12 seconds. According to Monte Irvin, the great Olympic sprinter Jesse Owens was challenged by Bell to race several times but Owens always declined.[20]

Jocko Conlan was born John, but while a minor league outfielder a sportswriter called him "Jocko." He was a career minor leaguer before spending two years with the Chicago White Sox, where he replaced an umpire overcome by the heat. He spent five years in the minors before becoming a National League umpire in 1941. His 24-year career included five World Series and six All-Star Games. Conlan, although only 5'7", was tough and had many classic confrontations with manager Leo Durocher. Nevertheless, he was a colorful and enthusiastic umpire who wore a polka-dot bow tie, liked to smile, and talked to all the players. He was so popular that he received a standing ovation in every National League ballpark during his last season in 1964.

Jim Bottomley was called "Sunny Jim" because of his pleasant disposition. His other trademark was the rakish angle at which he always wore his cap. He played 11 seasons with the Cards and helped lead them to four World Series in six years and two championships. He batted .345 in 1926 when the Cards won their first title, and then made a tremendous catch in foul territory for the final out in their win over the A's in 1931. His best season was 1928 when he won the MVP by leading the league in four categories. He finished third in the closest batting race ever in 1931, and batted .310 for his 16-year career.

"Sunny Jim" had some outstanding days during his career — hitting for the cycle, hitting three triples in a game, and having three five-hit games— but they all pale to his six-hit game at Ebbets Field in 1924. His Cards were playing Wilbert Robinson's Dodgers when he had three singles, a double, and two home runs, including a grand slam, to set a record of 12 RBIs, breaking Robinson's old record.

Sam Thompson broke in with the Detroit Wolverines in 1885 when he was 25. They won a pennant in 1887 and then defeated the St. Louis Browns of the American Association in the post-season when Thompson hit .362 and had two home runs. When they disbanded after the 1888 season, he was sold to the Philadelphia Quakers (Phillies). He was teamed with Ed Delahanty and Billy Hamilton to form a Hall of Fame outfield as they all hit more than .400 in 1894. Thompson was an all-around player who hit the second most home runs (126) of any nineteenth century player and also had 203 hits in 1887. He hit .331 for his 15-year career.

He actually came back in 1906 at the age of 46 and played eight games for the Detroit Tigers because their outfield was depleted by injuries.

Induction

The 1974 Induction Ceremony was held on August 12 with temperatures in the low 80s as 8,000 fans came mainly to honor Mantle and Ford. There were 25 Hall of Famers and the first inductee to be honored was Sam Thompson with his nephew, Lawrence Thompson, representing him. His nephew spoke briefly, expressing his appreciation on behalf of the family and calling attention to Victor Meyer, whose effort on behalf of his uncle had helped gain recognition for Sam Thompson.

Jim Bottomley was the next to be honored and having passed away in 1959 at the age of 59, was represented by his widow, Mrs. James Bottomley Tucker. She thanked all the people who made it possible for her husband to be inducted.

Jocko Conlan, 74, then spoke and praised former National League president Warren Giles for improving the lot of the league's umpires by increasing their pay and pension benefits. Conlan also introduced his family including his son, a congressman from Arizona.

He came back for the next 13 inductions and passed away in 1989 at the age of 89. George Grande, the masterful MC for more than 25 ceremonies, would always introduce Conlon, who would then come on stage and indicate the "safe sign" before sitting down.

Cool Papa Bell, 71, was the next inductee and he began by saying, "I'm standing here to receive the greatest honor that a ballplayer can receive and I thank God for enabling me to smell the rose while I'm still living." He was very gracious in giving thanks to everyone who helped him reach the Hall of Fame.

Bell came back for 13 more inductions before passing away in 1991 at the age of 87. When he was into his 80s, it was very difficult for him to sign autographs because of severe arthritis in his hands so he would have his daughter help him by putting them on pieces of paper beforehand in order to give them to his fans.

Whitey Ford, 45, began his short speech by keeping it light. He told the audience how nervous he was escorting his daughter down the aisle when she got married three weeks before, but he thought he was more nervous today. He then commented on the fact that it was a "pretty good week for the Fords." (It was the week President Richard Nixon had resigned and Vice President Gerald Ford became the president.) He thanked his teammates for scoring runs and then humorously made reference to Mickey Mantle, when he said, "Mickey said if I didn't throw so many long balls to center field he probably could have played another five years."

Ford returned only once that decade, once in the 1980s, seven times in the 1990s, and then on a regular basis.

His favorite Cooperstown memory relates to his induction. He said, "I went to bed early the night before the ceremony while Mickey took his four boys and my two boys and found a locked room in the Otesaga with a pool table. Mickey pushed one of the kids through a window in the room to open the door. They then shot pool all night as Mickey only got about two hours of sleep and here I was in my room sweating what I was going to say. His speech was great and mine was terrible. Mickey didn't use any notes."

Mickey Mantle gave a longer speech but tried to keep it light as well. He began with some self-deprecating humor when he thanked the commissioner in reading from his plaque for "leaving out all those strikeouts." He then told everyone to be patient with him because "I'm not in the Hall of Fame for my speaking." He continued by saying he thought this was the first time that someone was in the Hall of Fame who was named after a Hall of Famer. He was named after Mickey Cochrane, and he apologized beforehand to anyone in the audience named Gordon (Cochrane's actual first name), "but I'm glad he [his father] didn't name me Gordon." He made reference to the scout, Tom Greenwade, who signed him out of high school. (Greenwade later said after signing him, "Now I know how Paul Kritchell felt after signing Lou Gehrig.") He also made reference to some of his teammates, but he singled out Whitey Ford. "He's been a great friend all the way through for me," Mantle said. He had special praise for his father, "the most influential person in my life," and manager Casey Stengel, of whom he said, "Outside of my dad, Casey is the man most responsible for me being here today." He closed with Bill Terry's request that both he and Ford come back for future inductions. Mantle said, "I just hope that Whitey and I can live up to the expectations what these guys stand for, and I'm sure we're going to try."

Unfortunately, he never did return, due mainly to security issues, but even after security got much better, he still stayed away. He died in 1995 at the age of 63.

The four inductees listen during the 1974 Induction Ceremony. *Left to right:* Mickey Mantle, Whitey Ford, Cool Papa Bell and Jocko Conlan.

1975

The 1975 BBWAA election saw 362 ballots cast. Only slugging outfielder Ralph Kiner reached the 75 percent plateau, barely, as he received 75.4 percent (273 votes). This was one vote more than was needed on his 15th and final try. He received 1,824 votes in 13 elections.

Judy Johnson, Negro League third baseman, became the sixth man chosen by the Negro League Committee. Since he was a member of the committee, he was excused while they selected him. According to *Total Baseball Biographical Encyclopedia* there might have been other Negro League third basemen with better overall stats, but he was selected for his "professionalism and his intelligent dedicated style."[21]

The VC selected Cleveland Indians' center fielder Earl Averill. Averill was a unanimous selection by the VC, but during his speech he said that it would have had no meaning if he wasn't alive to enjoy it, He felt so strongly about this that previously he had said that if he had been elected posthumously, he didn't want his family to accept it. Despite receiving only 34 votes in six BBWAA elections, Averill wasn't considered a controversial selection. His cause was also helped by a grassroots effort, which he mentioned during his induction speech.

Second baseman Billy Herman was also chosen by the VC. He received only 127 votes from the BBWAA in seven elections. Despite this modest amount of votes, Herman wasn't considered controversial either. Also, playing on four pennant winners and then being a coach on five more pennant winners, including a World Series champion, kept his name in the public eye and undoubtedly didn't hurt his cause.

Former player and manager Bucky Harris was the final VC selection. He received 97 votes from the BBWAA in seven elections, which was mainly for managing, although he played 12 years as well.

Inductees

Ralph Kiner played left field for the Pirates and went on to become the only player to lead the league in home runs his first seven seasons. The Pirates acquired Hank Greenberg in 1947 and moved the left field stands in 30 feet to accommodate Hank's power. They called it Greenberg Gardens. Greenberg hit 25 home runs, but Kiner hit 51 so Greenberg Gardens became Kiner's Korner. Kiner led the league in home runs (54), RBIs (127), and walks (117) while batting .310 in 1949. He played for two more teams but had back problems and retired after 10 seasons at the age of 32 with 369 homers while batting .279 lifetime with an on-base percentage of .398.

Kiner and Greenberg were roommates and lifelong friends, even though Hank was 11 years older. They negotiated the first pension plan for players (Greenberg represented management). Kiner called Greenberg "the biggest influence on my life."[22]

Judy Johnson was born William but became "Judy" after he started his career because of his resemblance to a former player named Judy Gans. He was a superb fielding third baseman who helped lead the Hilldale Daisies to three straight pennants and the championship against the Kansas City Monarchs in 1925. Later in his career he was the captain of the star-studded Pittsburgh Crawfords that defeated the New York Cubans for the title in 1935.

Johnson was mentored by the great Negro Leaguer and future Hall of Famer Pop Lloyd. Later, as player-manager of the Homestead Grays in 1930, he lost his starting catcher and pulled someone out of the stands to do the catching. He developed a special relationship with this player just as Lloyd had with him. The player was the great Josh Gibson.

Earl Averill, called the "Rock" because of his sturdy build, homered in his first at-bat and batted .332 as the Indians rookie center fielder in 1929. His best season was 1936 when he batted .378, had 28 homers, 126 RBIs, and led the league in hits with 232. He played in 673 straight games, hit for the cycle, and was in five All-Star Games. He made it to one World Series with the Tigers and finished with 238 home runs and a lifetime batting average of .318. His son Earl Averill, Jr., was a major leaguer as well.

Averill is most known for smashing a ball off Dizzy Dean's foot and breaking his big toe in the 1937 All-Star Game. Later that season, Averill was diagnosed with a congenital spinal problem after temporarily becoming paralyzed from the waist down while coming out of the dugout. Coincidentally, he recovered but had back problems and was never the same, just as Dean was never the same pitcher after Averill broke his toe.

Billy Herman, during his ten years with the Chicago Cubs, helped lead them to three pennants. He was one of the best hit-and-run batters of all time and had his best season in 1935 when he led the league in hits (227) and set a record for second basemen with 57 doubles while batting .341, and then .333 in the World Series. He was also a very adept second baseman where he led the league in putouts a record seven times while setting a major league record for handling 900 or more chances five times. In 1941, he won his fourth pennant in ten years with the Dodgers. He batted .304 lifetime.

Herman, because of his size, barely made his high school team, but grew and overcame his deficiencies to become a ten-time All-Star while batting .433.

Bucky Harris was a good defensive second baseman who batted .274, and became a player-manager for the Washington Senators in 1924. The "boy wonder" went on to lead them to their first two pennants and only title in 1924. He tasted success one more time when he led the Yankees to a pennant and World Series championship in 1947. He ended his career with 2,157 victories. Hall of Famers Goose Goslin and Charlie Gehringer said he was the best manager they ever played for.

Harris was born Stanley but acquired his nickname while playing basketball as a kid when his coach said he shook off defenders like a "bucking bronco." Only 5'9", he played professional basketball in Pennsylvania in the 1920s during the off season.

Induction

The 1975 Induction Ceremony was held on August 18 on a day that the temperature never made it out of the 70s. Some 7,500 people attended, along with 25 Hall of Famers. The mayor of Cooperstown, Walter Taylor, as was customary, addressed the crowd to welcome them on what he called "our annual population explosion day."

Earl Averill, 73, spoke first and told of some of the honors that he had received from the Indians after his Hall of Fame announcement, including being chosen the "greatest Indians player." However, the greatest honor for him was being inducted into the Hall of Fame. He gave special praise to John Eichman from a sports scoop magazine for writing a number of articles about him that helped him make it to Cooperstown. He also thanked the VC for selecting him with a unanimous vote. Bill James wrote that Averill paid out of his own pocket to bring a number of the people who had campaigned for him to the induction ceremony.[23]

He came back for seven of the next eight inductions, including the 1983 induction, when he died two weeks later at the age of 81.

The next inductee introduced was Bucky Harris. Commissioner Kuhn, having grown up in Washington, D.C., felt a "special emotion and love" for this particular inductee. Unfortunately, Harris, 78, was unable to be there because of health reasons so his son, Judge Stanley Harris, represented him. A special two-way amplified phone was hooked up so that he could listen and also speak. The judge shared with the audience that his father suffered from Parkinson's disease, which affected his physical abilities, but that his mental capabilities were good. The disease was under control but an emotional event like this would put a lot of stress on him so that is why he didn't attend.

His son explained how his father was a fair and firm manager and gave an example of how he forced the big, lumbering pitcher Bobo Newsom to run out a ground ball by calmly threatening to fine him $100, which produced the desired result. The son said his father had three things he wanted him to say. "Congratulate the other inductees, thank the Veterans Committee, and thank his many friends who were there." Bucky Harris then spoke to Commissioner Kuhn on the phone and said, "Tell my son that he did well, I thank him." He died two years later on his birthday at the age of 81.

Billy Herman, 66, spoke next and readily admitted to the audience that he was a utility player in high school and that baseball "was always a struggle for him," so the honor was probably a little more special for him. "This is without a doubt the greatest honor I have ever had, and my wife and I plan to come back every year for this wonderful day," he told the audience.

A man of his word, Herman made it back for 17 of the next 19 inductions and also served on the VC from 1991 through 1992. He died like Averill, a month after his last induction in 1992, at the age of 83.

Judy Johnson, 75, was next, and like Billy Herman before him, he made sure to mention his wife right away. This was because Cool Papa Bell had forgotten to mention his wife during his induction speech the year before so he made sure to ask Commissioner Kuhn before he began the Induction Ceremony to introduce his wife.

Early on in his speech Johnson became very emotional and was comforted by his son-in-law, ex-major leaguer Billy Bruton, when he dried his eyes with a handkerchief. That helped Johnson regain his composure. Johnson then told a very funny story about him and his sister. His father, who had boxed and wanted his son to box as well, had him train with his older sister. They practiced two rounds after school each day and he was not allowed to hit her in the face, stomach or breasts. The gloves were made of horse hair and were "hard as bricks" so he spent most of his time not punching but dodging her punches. Johnson went on to say, "She would come around with a haymaker right across the face and tears would follow." He continued, "One day her glove flew off and just as she stopped to pick it up, I don't have to tell you what happened." That ended his father's dream of his son becoming a boxer and allowed him to focus on baseball.

Bowie Kuhn, obviously touched by the speech, said after it was over, "I think now you see a little more clearly why this is such a wonderful event." Johnson had hoped he would be able to come back, and that he did as he returned for the next 13 inductions before dying of a stroke in 1989 at the age of 89. His home in Marshallton, Delaware, was placed on the National Register of Homes after he died.

Ralph Kiner, 52, a great storyteller as a New York Mets announcer, didn't disappoint during his humorous speech. Kiner began his speech by going out of his way to thank Jack Lang, the secretary of the BBWAA, for doing a good job of counting the votes during his 15th and final try because Kiner made it by only one vote. He told the story of the Pirates' general manager Branch Rickey cutting his salary 25 percent after he led the league in home runs for the seventh straight season in 1952. Kiner asked, "How could you cut me?" Rickey answered, "We finished last with you, and we could finish last without you." Sure enough he was traded to the Cubs during the 1953 season.

I had the pleasure of interviewing Ralph Kiner and he shared this anecdote from his induction ceremony. He missed the bus back to the Otesaga after the Induction Ceremony was over so as he was walking back to the hotel a nice Oriental gentleman, who had trouble pronouncing the letter "l," approached him and said, "Congratulations on your erection." Kiner didn't know how to reply so he said nothing.

His favorite Cooperstown memory was Judy Johnson's induction speech. Kiner felt for Johnson when he broke down and couldn't continue and then recovered to tell that very funny story about boxing with his sister.

Kiner has been one of the most consistent attendees, having returned for more than 30 inductions, even after he had a stroke in 2004. Being a broadcaster himself, he has often introduced the winners of the Ford Frick Award.

1976

The 1976 BBWAA election produced 388 ballots as pitcher Robin Roberts finished first with 86.9 percent (337 votes), and pitcher Bob Lemon finished second with 78.6 percent (305 votes).

Roberts, the ace of the Philadelphia Phillies' staff during the 1950s, was selected in his fourth year on the ballot after receiving 1,037 votes. When he didn't win induction in 1973, the prolific American author James Michener, a good friend of Roberts, was so upset that he personally wrote many members of the BBWAA lobbying for his friend's election. Michener never told Roberts what he did and despite the support it still took him another three elections to achieve induction.

Bob Lemon, a star right-hander for the Cleveland Indians in the 1950s, didn't make the Hall of Fame until his 12th year on the ballot, receiving 1,370 votes.

Oscar Charleston was a center fielder and the seventh inductee selected by the Negro League Committee. He was considered by some to be the greatest baseball player ever.

The VC selected National League third baseman Freddie Lindstrom, nineteenth-century slugging first baseman Roger Connor, and American League umpire Cal Hubbard.

Fred Lindstrom was a controversial selection because in 21 years of eligibility he received only 22 votes that came on only five ballots during the BBWAA elections. Both Bill James and James Vail state Lindstrom shouldn't be in the Hall of Fame and that he got in mainly due to his teammate Bill Terry being on the VC in 1975 (p. 166 and p. 105). On the other hand, Robert Cohen isn't as critical, stating that Lindstrom was elected because there were only four third basemen in the Hall of Fame in 1975 (p. 75). Also, Cohen said even though there were other third basemen "who would have been better selections, Lindstrom wasn't a bad choice" (p. 77).

Roger Connor was one of eight nineteenth-century players elected to the hall by the VC who never received one vote in any BBWAA election. His friend, Hall of Fame umpire Bill Klem, campaigned for him, but according to David Fleitz, Connor was long forgotten until Hank Aaron broke Babe Ruth's all-time home run record in 1974. Fans and sportswriters discovered that Ruth had broken Connor's lifetime home run record and then he was elected by the VC two years later.[24]

Cal Hubbard became the fifth umpire selected to the Hall of Fame, some seven years after he had retired as a supervisor of umpires and twenty-five years after he retired as an American League umpire. He has the distinction of being in the College and Pro Football Halls of Fame as well as the Baseball Hall of Fame.

Inductees

Robin Roberts had a basketball scholarship to Michigan State but he also played baseball there and, after pitching two no-hitters, was signed by the Phillies and made his debut in 1948. He won his 20th game in 1950 on the last day of the season to clinch the pennant for the team called the Whiz Kids because of all their young players. This was the beginning of six straight 20-win seasons, including leading the league in victories four straight times as well as twice being chosen *The Sporting News* Pitcher of the Year. His best year was 1952 when he was 28–7 and had his best ERA at 2.59. He was the Phils' Opening Day starter 12 straight seasons, an all-star seven times, and finished with a record of 286–245.

Roberts was very active in the Players Association and was instrumental in convincing the union to select Marvin Miller as their president in 1966. Miller went on to lead baseball into the era of free agency.

Bob Lemon was a third baseman and an outfielder with the Indians before he became a pitcher in 1946. Indians coach Bill McKechnie helped him develop an assortment of pitches and in 1948 he won 20 games for the first of seven 20-win seasons. He pitched a no-hitter in 1948 when the Indians won the pennant and the World Series. He helped the Tribe win another pennant in 1954, was Pitcher of the Year three times, and was an all-star seven times. Lem was also a good fielder and hit 37 home runs and batted .284 lifetime as a pinch hitter. He finished with a record of 207–128 (.618).

His low key approach helped him become a manager of the year with the White Sox in 1977. However, he had the most success with the Yankees when he took over for Billy Martin in 1978 when they were 10½ games out, and went on to win the pennant and the World Series. He did it again with the Yanks in 1981 when they again won the pennant. Oscar Charleston began with the Indianapolis ABCs in 1915 and went on to play for more than 10 teams in his long career. Charlie covered so much ground in center field that the left and right fielders only had to play near the foul lines. Based on available statistics, Charleston batted .348 lifetime with 128 home runs. He also hit 11 home runs and batted .326 against major leaguers. He played first base and managed the 1932 Pittsburgh Crawfords that included Satchel Paige, Josh Gibson, and Judy Johnson. This squad is considered the greatest team to play in the Negro Leagues.

Oscar Charleston got into a lot of scraps during his career. Once during a game in 1915, Charlie punched an umpire and went to jail. Supposedly, at another game in 1935, he got into it with a mouthy Klansman and quieted him after he ripped his hood off.

Freddie Lindstrom, in 1924, became the youngest player ever at 18 to play in a World Series. He batted .333 for the Giants, but they lost to the Senators in the seventh game when two ground balls bounced over his head at third base after hitting pebbles in the ninth and then in extra innings. He had his best two seasons in 1928 and 1930 when he had 231 hits twice, batted .358 and .379 respectively, and drove in 100-plus runs each season. He played for three more teams, including the 1935 pennant winning Cubs. He retired in 1936 with a .311 average at the young age of 31 due to back problems.

When Lindstrom broke his leg in 1931, John McGraw came to see him in the hospital. McGraw got mad at him for something so Lindstrom said, "I hope you break your leg." Sure enough, McGraw was hit by a cab leaving the hospital. Both of them recovered and laughed about it later.[25]

Roger Connor came up as a left-handed third baseman with the Troy Trojans in 1880, but after 60 errors in 83 games was switched to first base. Connor became an adept first baseman and the first player to hit a grand slam and three home runs in one game. The Trojans folded after the 1882 season and he joined the New York Gothams in 1883, where he helped them win pennants in 1888 and 1889. Connor not only hit 138 home runs lifetime, but also had 233 triples. He jumped to the Players League in 1890 and returned to the National League where he retired with a lifetime batting average of .316.

Connor at 6'3" was one of several tall players on the Gothams in 1885. Manager Jim Mutrie called them "my big fellows, my Giants!"[26] Thus, their new name was born.

Cal Hubbard was an All-American defensive end in college and All-Pro in the NFL where he was an offensive and defensive tackle and was on four championship teams. He always had an interest in baseball rules and after umpiring in the minors became an American League umpire in 1936. He umpired three All-Star Games and four World Series. He retired in 1951 when a hunting accident damaged his eye. The physically-imposing Hubbard was called "His Majesty" and had three assets: an even temper, a strong sense of fairness, and a superior knowledge of the rules.

One time, Yogi Berra was catching and disagreeing with his calls so Cal declared, "No

The only Induction Ceremony to be held at the Otesaga Hotel took place in 1976. *Left to right:* Francis Cowell, grandson of Roger Connor, Freddie Lindstrom, Cal Hubbard, Robin Roberts, Bob Lemon and Mrs. Katherine Horsley, sister of Oscar Charleston.

sense in both of us umpiring this game, but I'm being paid for this and you're not. It breaks my heart but the guy who has to go is you."[27] Berra never said another word.

Induction

The 1976 Induction Ceremony was on August 9, but because of the rainy weather it was held for the first and only time in the ballroom of the Otesaga Hotel with 23 Hall of Famers sharing in this one-time event. Some 500 people were crammed into the Otesaga ballroom and seating was arranged for hundreds more on the Otesaga veranda.

The first inductee honored was Oscar Charleston, who died in 1954 at the age of 57. Representing him was his sister, Mrs. Katherine Horsley. She was very brief in her remarks calling it "the greatest delight of my life and I appreciate the privilege of accepting this plaque in honor of my brother's name." She thanked everyone who helped to bring this about, including the Hall of Fame historian, Cliff Kachline, and the Otesaga Hotel for everything they did for her.

Roger Connor was honored next, and accepting for him was his grandson, Francis Colwell. Connor had died in 1931 at the age of 73. Colwell said his mother and his family had spent many hours to "achieve this goal."

The next recipient was Cal Hubbard, 75, and Commissioner Bowie Kuhn deferred to Hall of Fame president Paul Kerr to introduce him; Kerr had presented Hubbard for induction into the Pro Football Hall of Fame in Canton, Ohio, in 1963. Hubbard began by "thanking the good Lord for letting me live long enough to be here to receive this honor." He then gave an honest assessment of his own election, saying it must be difficult for the VC to choose an umpire because they don't have stats like they have for ballplayers. He paused during his speech saying, "I'm out of breath because I smoked cigars and cigarettes too long." He finished by echoing something Mickey Mantle had said, "If I had known that I was going to live this long, I'd have tried to take better care of myself." He came back for the next induction and died in 1977 at the age of 76.

Freddie Lindstrom, 70, talked about coming to Cooperstown and Doubleday Field when they honored his son Chuck as the American Legion Player of the Year in 1953. He made reference to a book about God and was thankful that "the handiwork of the Supreme Being" allowed him to be alive for "the greatest thing that ever happened to me."

He made it to five more inductions before passing away in 1981 at the age of 75.

Bob Lemon, 55, began by saying, "It goes without saying that this is the whole thing. Where do you go from here?" He was magnanimous in thanking the BBWAA, even those writers who didn't vote for him, as he exclaimed, "I love everybody today." He made reference to his teammate, pitcher Early Wynn, as being so mean that he would hit his own mother with a pitch. Lemon then told how he actually hit his mother when he was a kid in junior high. It happened while he was demonstrating to her how to throw a curve in front of their home in California. Fortunately, she recovered and was now at her son's induction. He closed with, "I owe baseball, baseball owes me nothing."

He came back 14 more times and passed away in 2000 at the age of 79.

Robin Roberts, 49, was the last speaker and he kept it light as he asked Hall of Fame director Kenny Smith "if he didn't think it would be appropriate if I would invite everyone who ever hit a home run off me to be here today." Smith's response was

"Cooperstown wasn't big enough." Robin was thrilled to be honored and said he would be back every year.

No one has ever been more faithful to his word — he has come back every year and has not missed an induction in 34 years. His favorite Cooperstown memory was meeting the Hall's old-timers. I actually asked him and he said that he especially enjoyed Bill Terry, Charlie Gehringer, and Jocko Conlan. Roberts has been a member of the board of directors since the mid–1990s.

1977

Three hundred eighty-three ballots were cast in the 1977 BBWAA election with only slugging shortstop Ernie Banks reaching the Promised Land. He received 83.8 percent (321 votes) in his first year of eligibility.

The Negro League Committee selected as their eighth and ninth choices the great all-around player Martin Dihigo and the great shortstop of yesteryear, Pop Lloyd.

The VC selected former catcher and manager Al Lopez, former American League shortstop Joe Sewell, and nineteenth-century pitcher Amos Rusie.

Lopez received 357 votes in nine BBWAA elections with the barest of support for him as a player. It picked up after his success as a manager.

Sewell didn't get much support in seven BBWAA elections — he received only 31 votes. Yet no criticism of his election could be found.

Rusie, the fireballing right-hander, received even less support from the BBWAA with only 17 votes in five elections. However, since he played nine out of his ten seasons in the nineteenth century, this result was not surprising. What helped his candidacy was an article written by Rick Johnson for the *Indianapolis Star* magazine in 1973 that resulted in the Indiana state legislature introducing a bill honoring him.[28]

Inductees

Ernie Banks was the shortstop for the Kansas City Monarchs of the Negro American League when the Chicago Cubs signed him and brought him to the majors in 1953. He went on to have a stellar career first as a shortstop and then as a first baseman. He was the first player in the National League to win back-to-back MVPs, and the first to win them while playing for teams that finished under .500. He hit more than 40 home runs five times and had consecutive game streaks of 424 games and 717 games and also won a Gold Glove as a shortstop. He finished with 512 home runs while batting .274.

Banks was called "Mr. Cub" because of his loyalty and enthusiasm for the Cubs. Teammate Ron Santo played with him for 11 years and said, "He hasn't changed since the day I met him. He never said a bad word about anybody."[29]

Martin Dihigo was a dark-skinned Cuban who pitched and played the infield and the outfield. He started out in Cuba and was brought to the U.S. and played for the Cuban Stars in New York, where he hit .369 in 1926 and .336 in 1927. He also pitched no-hitters in Mexico, Venezuela, and Puerto Rico, and in the Mexican League he was 18–2 in 1938 with an ERA of 0.90 while batting .387. Dihigo was called "El Maestro" in Mexico because of his versatility. He was the player-manager of the New York Cubans in 1935 when they lost in the League Championship Series to the Pittsburgh Crawfords. He is the only player to be honored by the baseball halls of fame in Mexico and Cuba as well. During retirement, he was Cuba's minister of sports.

Johnny Mize played for Dihigo in the Dominican Republic in 1943. Mize said, "He could play all nine positions, run, manage and hit. He was the greatest player I ever saw."[30]

John Henry Lloyd was called "Pop" because he played well into his 40s. He played for many teams from 1905 through 1932 because he went where he could make the most money. Negro baseball pioneer Sol White helped to make him a shortstop in 1907. Lloyd also played for another Hall of Fame pioneer, Rube Foster and his Chicago American Giants from 1914 through 1917, where he batted cleanup. He played year round and in Cuba he was known as "El Cuchara" or the "Tablespoon" because of his ability to scoop up balls hit to him. He played against Ty Cobb and the Tigers in Cuba and batted .500 while Cobb batted .370.

Lloyd was called the "Black Honus Wagner" and when Wagner heard it, he turned it around and said, "It's a privilege to be compared to him."[31]

Al Lopez was an outstanding defensive catcher who led the league in fielding four times and caught the most games until his record was later broken. He started his managerial career in the majors with the Cleveland Indians in 1951. They set an American League record in 1954 when the Tribe won 111 games, only to be swept by the New York Giants in the World Series. He moved on to the Chicago White Sox in 1957 and won another pennant with the "Go-Go Sox" in 1959 only to lose again to the Los Angeles Dodgers.

Lopez beat his former mentor, Casey Stengel, the only two years the Yankees didn't win the pennant from 1949 through 1960. Lopez, known as "El Senor," finished second seven times in eight years to the Yankees. He had a record of 1,410–1,004 (.584).

Lopez caught spring training as a teenager for the Washington Senators in his hometown of Tampa, Florida. He caught batting practice for the pitchers, including Walter Johnson.

Joe Sewell began his career as the Indians' shortstop under tragic circumstances. He was called up in September 1920 after the regular shortstop, Ray Chapman, had been killed by a pitch thrown by Yankees pitcher Carl Mays. He held up by hitting .329 for 22 games, as Cleveland won the pennant and their first World Series. He led the league in fielding three times and putouts and assists four times each. Although he was small (5'6½"), he was durable, having consecutive game streaks of 460 and 1,103 games. He finished up his career at third base for the Yankees and batted .333 in the 1932 World Series victory. He finished with a batting average of .312 for 14 seasons.

Joe Sewell set the single season record in 1932 when he struck out three times in 503 at-bats. Sewell struck out 114 times in 7,132 at-bats, making him the most difficult batter to strike out in major league history. The key to his success was using a 40-ounce bat.

Amos Rusie grew up in Indiana and was known as the "Hoosier Thunderbolt" because of his outstanding fastball. He won 28 or more games six times for the New York Giants, making him a sports celebrity, which would later lead to drinking and marital problems. He had additional problems with one of the worst owners in baseball, Andrew Freedman, who fined Rusie and tried to get out of paying him part of his contract. As a result of these problems and arm woes, Rusie didn't pitch for three years. He retired in 1901 due to chronic arm problems and ended up at 246–174 (.592).

Amos Rusie was the main reason that the pitching distance was moved back from 55'6" to its present distance of 60'6" in 1893. The owners wanted to instill more offense and reduce the dominance of fastball pitchers like Rusie. So he went out and won 140 games from 1893 through 1898, including 36 in 1894, despite sitting out 1896.

Induction

The 1977 Induction Ceremony was held on August 8 on a day when the sun eventually came out as 27 Hall of Famers were present. A crowd of 10,000 people came, indicating a lot of Cubs fans were there for Ernie Banks.

The first person to be honored was Martin Dihigo. Commissioner Kuhn told the crowd that the mayor of Miami, Florida, had proclaimed August 8 "Martin Dihigo Day" and that a municipal park would be named after him as well. Dihigo was also the first Cuban to be inducted into the Hall of Fame. He died in Cuba in 1971 at the age of 66. Representing him was his second cousin, former major league player Jose Valdivielso. He told the audience that a large delegation had come to Cooperstown from Miami and New York City to salute his cousin and how proud the people of Cuba and Latin America were of Dihigo's induction. He thanked Monte Irvin and the committee for the honor.

John Henry "Pop" Lloyd, who had died in 1965 at the age of 80, was the next to be honored. He was represented by the assistant superintendent of schools in Atlantic City, James L. Usry, who worked with Pop for more than 20 years in Little League baseball. He thanked several sportswriters and state politicians for helping to "bring this dream to fruition." Usry called the honor "the ultimate award in sportdom."

Amos Rusie had died in 1942 at the age of 61, and was represented by his nephew, John Amos Rusie. He spoke briefly and said, "On behalf of the Rusie family we will treasure this day the rest of our lives."

Next up was Joe Sewell, 79, who felt happy that he was still alive to receive this honor as he gave credence to the myth when he said, "Baseball has been a great game from the day that Abner Doubleday originated our game." He went on to tell his audience that he would take three things away from his Cooperstown experience. He said, "This is my first trip here, I hope it won't be my last. I'm taking away a ring that they gave me and will prize it the rest of my life and a plaque today and a lot of pleasant memories."

He promised to be back and he did indeed come back for 11 more inductions before passing away at the age of 91 in 1991.

It should be noted that Sewell was president of the student body his senior year at the University of Alabama and went back to his alma mater to coach the baseball team. His two brothers followed him there and both played in the major leagues. He had intended to be a doctor like his father until baseball took over. His offspring helped to rectify the situation because his two sons became doctors and his daughter married a doctor.

Al Lopez, 68, was the next honoree to speak and he was magnanimous in his praise of the media that covered him when he managed in the minors, as well as the majors, along with the six managers for whom he played. He singled out his long-term coaches Don Gutteridge and Ray Berres as "working with him and not for him." He finished with, "I want to thank you for the proudest and happiest moment of my life."

Lopez served on the VC from 1978 through 1994. He said his proudest Cooperstown moment was when Juan Marichal spoke at one of the Saturday night dinners because he was probably the only one who understood what he said since he gave the speech in Spanish. He came back 17 more times before he died in 2005 at the age of 97, making him the oldest living Hall of Famer at the time of his death.

The final speaker was Ernie Banks and, before he spoke, Commissioner Kuhn gave an example of his good-hearted nature. Kuhn said Banks called several people when he got the news of his induction, including Eddie Mathews, to express his concern that Mathews didn't get enough votes for induction. (Mathews was voted in a year later.)

Banks started off by telling everyone his familiar refrain, "We have sunshine so let's play two." He spoke briefly saying, "I once read that a person's success is dependent not only on the talent that God gave him but also on the people who believed in him." He then went on to thank a number of people, including Cubs owner Phil Wrigley, whom he called "one of the finest gentlemen that I ever met." Commissioner Kuhn closed the ceremony, pointing out a sign in the audience that read, "America Loves Ernie Banks."

Banks has returned more than 11 times although he has been absent more often than not recently. When he has returned, he has many fans, including Peter Clarke and Catherine Walker. Clarke, former assistant hall curator of collections, said Banks has "an infectious personality." Walker, witness to the first induction, and now an attendant at the hall said that Banks often sang at the Museum Reception and "sounded like Lou Rawls."[32]

1978

The BBWAA in 1978 cast 379 ballots and slugging Braves third baseman Eddie Mathews was the only one selected, receiving 79.4 percent (301 votes). He was selected in his fifth year of eligibility, receiving 995 votes in five elections.

The Negro League Committee disbanded after 1977, and the VC was expanded to 18 members in 1978. It was felt by the board of directors that the VC was putting in too many people so it was decided that no more than two people a year would be selected. They would choose from three categories. The first category was players who retired from baseball before 1946 or players who retired after 1945 and who received 100 or more votes in one or more BBWAA elections. The second category consisted of executives, managers, or umpires. The final category was the Negro Leagues.

The result was the VC selected outstanding Cleveland Indians' pitcher Addie Joss and innovative executive Larry MacPhail.

Joss had died tragically in 1911 at the age of 31 from spinal meningitis after a nine-year career, which made him ineligible since he had not played the minimum ten years. However, Jerry Nason, a sports editor for the *Boston Globe*, started a campaign for him in the 1950s. He then got support from revered sports columnist Red Smith and hall historian Lee Allen, who amassed a huge file on him. Outspoken sports columnist Leonard Koppett argued in a 1971 column for the rules to be amended. Fred Lieb, veteran baseball writer, and a member of the VC, had seen Joss pitch and said he was the best pitcher of the first quarter of the twentieth century. Joe Reichler, from the commissioner's office, was in favor of the Joss induction. He finally got things moving when he became a member of the VC in 1978. He and Lieb were able to persuade the other members of the committee to amend the rules and Joss was elected.

Inductees

Eddie Mathews signed a baseball contract with the Boston Braves right after his senior prom while still dressed in his tuxedo. He broke in with Boston in 1952 and became the only rookie to hit three home runs in a game. He and Hank Aaron became the most prolific home run duo ever with 863 homers. Together they helped lead the Braves to two pennants and Milwaukee's only World Series title in 1957. Mathews clinched it with a backhand stab for the last out in the victory over the Yankees. He finished his career with 512 lifetime home runs, a nine-time all-star, and a .271 average.

He is the only Brave to play in all three cities including Boston, Milwaukee, and Atlanta. He was the captain with the Braves in 1965, a coach with them after he retired, and the manager when Aaron broke Ruth's home run record in 1974.

Addie Joss gave a preview of things to come when he pitched a one-hit shutout in his first game for Cleveland in 1902. He led the league with 27 wins in 1907, one of four seasons where he won more than 20 games. He also pitched two no-hitters, including a perfect game against Ed Walsh and the Chicago White Sox in 1908. This game is considered by many to be the greatest pitching duel in major league history because Walsh gave up only four hits with the winning run coming on a passed ball. Joss has the second lowest career ERA at 1.88 behind Walsh at 1.82. He finished his career at 160–97 (.623).

When his teammates wanted to go to his funeral as a team, the league refused because they had a game scheduled on April 17, 1911. They threatened to strike and the league relented. The team attended one of the biggest funerals ever held in Toledo, Ohio. Later that season, a special all-star game was held and $13,000 was raised for the family.

Larry MacPhail, as the general manager of the Cincinnati Reds, laid the foundation for the Reds winning pennants in 1939 and 1940. He moved over to the Brooklyn Dodgers as their owner in 1938 and saw them win the pennant in 1941. He became a partner in the purchase of the Yankees in 1945. He left baseball after the Yankees' championship in 1947. MacPhail fought in World War I and was in the War Department in World War II. He retired to raise horses and run Bowie Race Track.

MacPhail was known as the "Flaming Redhead" because of his flamboyant way of doing things. He helped to introduce Old Timers Day, airplane travel for teams, radio and TV broadcasts of games, and batting helmets. His biggest contribution was night baseball, which he introduced in 1935 at Crosley Field in Cincinnati.

Induction

The 1978 Induction Ceremony was held on August 7 on an overcast day with 23 Hall of Famers present. It was decided as a way of honoring former Commissioner Ford Frick, who had passed away in 1978, that an award for broadcasters who made a special contribution to baseball would be instituted. Frick conceived the idea for the Baseball Hall of Fame and was also a former broadcaster. Longtime Yankees broadcaster Mel Allen and former Dodgers and Yankees broadcaster Red Barber were the first recipients.

The first inductee to be honored was Addie Joss, and accepting for him was a relative, Dr. William Swartz. He said, "It is with humble gratitude that I accept this plaque on behalf of the remaining relatives of Addie Joss."

The next recipient was Larry MacPhail, who had died in 1975 at the age of 85. MacPhail was responsible for many firsts in baseball, and he also became the first inductee to have two people speak for him, sons Lee and Bill MacPhail. Bill introduced other members of the family and also made mention of a close family friend who was in the audience, National Football League commissioner Pete Rozelle. Lee, the president of the American League, and a future Hall of Famer himself, said that his father would have never accepted membership in the Hall of Fame because he thought it should be for the people on the field. He said his father made a tremendous impact on major league baseball even though he was in it for only 13 years. He added, "I can attest to it personally because I've been in baseball 36 years and I still am called Larry on occasion." He then listed some of his father's accomplishments but said the thing his father was proudest of was helping to build contending teams with the Reds, Dodgers and Yankees.

MacPhail's son then told a funny story of how his father wanted to join the train that was coming in from Boston after the Dodgers clinched the pennant in 1941. He wanted to come in with the team so he waited at 125th Street Station before it arrived at Grand Central Station (GCS). Manager Leo Durocher, with whom he had many battles, decided to have the train skip 125th Street so when everyone celebrated at GCS, MacPhail was left fuming as he waited on the 125th Street Station platform.

Lee told the audience how everyone laughed at his father when he predicted in the late 1940s that there would be four leagues and 24 teams, and today (1978) there are four divisions and 26 teams. He closed with, "Our family thanks you for the honor that you have accorded him."

Eddie Mathews, 46, was the final inductee and he began, "If I had been this nervous when I played, I wouldn't be standing here right now." He went on to pay tribute to his elementary and high school coaches as well as his American Legion coach because they "didn't make a lot of money, but were dedicated to helping young athletes." He closed by saying it would take about a week to sink in, and thanked the fans "because without you there wouldn't be much baseball."

He came back for seven more inductions before passing away in 2001 at the age of 69. His widow has returned for a number of inductions since his death.

1979

The 1979 BBWAA election saw 432 ballots cast but only one candidate received the necessary 75 percent, and that was the incomparable Giants' center fielder Willie Mays. He received 94.7 percent (409 votes) in his first year of eligibility. My only question — which I have posed before and will pose again — is how could 23 voters leave Mays off their ballots?

The VC selected former National League president Warren Giles and single-season RBI record holder Hack Wilson. Giles, like most baseball executives elected to the hall, wasn't controversial. Wilson, despite receiving 545 votes in 15 elections, is considered controversial. Bill James states he shouldn't be in Cooperstown but got in because he had similar statistics to players who were already in (pp. 72, 94). James Vail felt a major factor for his getting in was because of his one outstanding year in 1930 when he set the record for RBIs with 191 (p. 76). Robert Cohen is ambivalent about his selection, stating that he wasn't a particularly bad selection but nevertheless one that probably shouldn't have been made (p. 171).

Inductees

Willie Mays played two years with the Birmingham Black Barons of the Negro Leagues. He signed with the Giants, took part in their 1951 win over the Dodgers in a three-game playoff for the pennant, and won the Rookie of the Year award. He was the MVP in 1954, and then led the Giants to a sweep of the Indians in the World Series. He helped lead the transplanted San Francisco Giants to another World Series in 1962 and won his second MVP in 1965 when he hit more than 50 home runs (52) for the second time. Mays won 12 Gold Gloves and appeared in 24 All-Star Games before playing in one more World Series with the Mets in 1973. Lifetime he batted .302 and hit 660 home runs.

Vic Wertz hit the ball to the deepest part of center field in the Polo Grounds during the first game of the 1954 World Series. Mays sprinted with his back to the plate and turned at the last second to snag the ball over his shoulder. He then spun in one motion and threw to second to hold the runner at first. Joe DiMaggio said, "Ballplayers strive for perfection on the field and while that is impossible, Willie Mays comes the closest."[33]

Warren Giles was general manager of the Cincinnati Reds when they won two straight pennants in 1939 and 1940, plus a championship (1940). He then moved up to become team president and in 1951 ran against Ford Frick, the National League president, for baseball commissioner. He conceded to Frick after 17 ballots, and then was appointed by the National League to succeed Frick as president where he served for 18 years. During his tenure, he oversaw the transfer of the National League to the West Coast and then the expansion of the league to New York, San Diego, Montreal, and Houston.

Warren Giles was very proud of his National League, especially when they dominated the American League in All-Star Game competition, just the opposite of what it is today. He would send a telegram to the winning National League team after each victory.

Hack Wilson was born Lewis Robert Wilson but was nicknamed "Hack" during his baseball career, possibly after a pro wrestler named Hackenschmidt. Physically, he had one of the most unusual bodies ever, standing 5′6″ tall and weighing 190 pounds. It didn't hinder him as a center fielder after he broke in with the Giants in 1923. Wilson played in the 1924 World Series, but didn't blossom until he played for Cubs manager Joe McCarthy. He led the league in homers four times and RBIs twice while leading them to the 1929 World Series, where he batted .471. He had a phenomenal season in 1930 when he batted .356, had 208 hits, set the league record for home runs with 56, and the major league record for RBIs with 191, which still stands today. He was never the same after McCarthy left and finished his 12-year career batting .307 lifetime.

Wilson was an alcoholic but Joe McCarthy handled him well and tried to show him the evils of alcohol with a demonstration. He put a worm in a glass of water and it moved freely, but in a glass of whiskey the worm died. McCarthy asked Wilson, "What does it prove?" Hack responded, "If you drink whiskey, you will never get worms."[34]

Induction

The 1979 Induction Ceremony was held on a warm August 6, before a crowd of 5,000, along with 28 Hall of Famers. It was held for the first time on the steps of the library rather than across from the library. This was a better backdrop for the dignitaries on the stage, making it easier to enter and exit.

This was also the first time that the ceremony and the Doubleday Game were scheduled over a two-day period rather than have both on the same day. This was done to give the older Hall of Famers the option of going home after the induction on Sunday and not having to deal with the heat and crowds at Doubleday Field for the Monday game.

The first honoree was Hack Wilson, who had died in 1948 at the age of 48. He was represented by his son, Robert Wilson. He spoke briefly, and told the audience how proud he was that his father's record (RBIs) had never been broken. He thanked the fans, especially those who "so thoughtfully called to congratulate me."

The next inductee was Warren Giles, who had died earlier in the year at the age of 82. Bowie Kuhn was proud to tell the audience that Giles had been wounded during World War I while fighting in France and was a very close friend. He introduced his son, Bill, the executive vice president of the Philadelphia Phillies. Bill Giles was happy to tell everyone that his father "would have been particularly proud today to be inducted with two other National Leaguers, Hack Wilson and a fellow named Willie." He called his father "a true giver." An example was when he withdrew from a long protracted election for commissioner of baseball in 1951 with Ford Frick being declared the winner. He did it because it was "in the best interest of baseball."

The final inductee was Willie Mays, 48, who gave a rambling speech that covered his long career as he paid tribute to many people who were good to him outside of baseball. He stressed to the young people in the audience the importance of a college education, something he regretted not having. He singled out his first manager, Leo Durocher, and praised the deceased Mets owner Joan Payson for bringing him back to New York. He was upset that the Giants, with whom he played most of his career, never sent the Hall of Fame his uniform while the Mets did.

It should be noted, unbeknownst to Mays, the Hall of Fame did have for some time several of his San Francisco Giants' articles, including a home uniform.

Mays only came back three times in 20 years, but since 2000, he has come every year.

CHAPTER 8

The Hall of Fame Celebrates
Its Golden Anniversary:
1980–1989

1980

The BBWAA had 385 ballots cast in 1980 and longtime Detroit Tigers' right fielder Al Kaline finished first with 88.3 percent (340 votes) in his first year of eligibility. Dodgers center fielder Duke Snider finished second with 86.5 percent (333 votes) in his eleventh year of eligibility. Snider received 1,831 votes during that time.

Snider told this story of the night after he heard of his induction. He was having dinner at a restaurant with friends in Brooklyn when several of the patrons recognized him, applauded, and sent a bottle of champagne to his table and toasted him. Then a young man about 30 approached his table and pulled out a baseball card that he had been carrying in his wallet since he was eight years old, and asked him to sign it. Snider said, "Take it from me, it does feel good to be remembered."[1]

The VC selected Boston Red Sox owner Tom Yawkey four years after his death.

Their other selection was Philadelphia Phillies right fielder Chuck Klein. Klein received 287 votes in thirteen BBWAA elections. Bill James states there was public pressure on the VC to elect him after they put in players like Chick Hafey and George Kelly because he had superior credentials to them (p. 169). Robert Cohen was very supportive of his induction, stating, "Klein was so dominant (1929 to 1933) that he rivaled Babe Ruth as the best rightfielder in baseball" (p. 187).

Inductees

Al Kaline overcame a congenital, deformed left foot to sign with the Detroit Tigers as a bonus baby in 1953. Despite being right out of high school, he became their regular right fielder in 1954. He then became the youngest player ever, at 20, to win a batting crown when he led the league in 1955 with a .340 average. He had a strong arm that helped him win ten Gold Glove awards, and he once went 242 straight games without an error. He finished with 3,007 hits, 399 home runs, and a lifetime batting average of .297.

Recovering from a broken arm in 1968, he helped the Tigers win the World Series, batting .379 with two home runs and eight RBIs. Manager Mayo Smith moved center fielder Mickey Stanley to shortstop so Kaline could get back in the lineup for the World Series, since there wasn't any designated hitter back then.

The new West Wing of the Hall of Fame was completed in 1980.

Duke Snider was born Edwin but his father nicknamed him "Duke" as a child. He helped the Dodgers make it to the World Series against the Yankees in 1949, the first of five post-seasons between the interborough rivals in eight years. He did well in the next four matchups when he hit more than .300 each time and twice hit four home runs each — including in 1955, Brooklyn's only championship. He batted .295 with 407 home runs lifetime. He was immortalized in the song "Talkin' Baseball," with its chorus of "Willie, Mickey, and the Duke," about Mays, Mantle, and him.

Snider swung at everything when he first came up, so Branch Rickey had him work with Hall of Famer George Sisler in spring training. He wasn't allowed to swing in the batting cage but had to give his opinion on each pitch after the umpire made the call. This helped him learn to swing at good pitches.

Chuck Klein broke in with the Phillies in 1928 as their right fielder, the start of a phenomenal six and a half years that was arguably as good a start for any player in the history of the major leagues. He hit .360 in his rookie year and .356 in 1929 while setting a National League home run record with 43. He hit .386 in 1930 with 250 hits, 40 home runs, 158 runs, and 170 RBIs while setting a league record with 59 doubles. He was the MVP in 1932 and a Triple Crown winner in 1933. He also had 44 assists in 1930. Klein was traded to the Cubs in 1934 where he played in his only World Series in 1935 and batted .333. He finished with 300 home runs and batted .320 lifetime.

The Phillies' pitchers helped Klein in 1929 when he won the home run title with 43. They walked Mel Ott of the New York Giants six times on the next-to-last day of the season, including one time with the bases loaded, which gave Klein the title over Ott, 43 to 42.

Tom Yawkey was born Thomas Austin, but his father died when he was very young and he was adopted by his mother's brother, William Yawkey, owner of the Detroit Tigers. He always had an interest in baseball and on his 30th birthday he bought the Boston Red Sox for 1.5 million dollars. He spent a lot of money on acquiring ballplayers, setting up a farm system, and refurbishing Fenway Park. This attitude helped to make the team competitive, winning pennants in three different decades, 1946, 1967, and 1975. Each time they extended the World Series to seven games before losing. They also missed a fourth pennant in 1948 after losing a one-game playoff to the Cleveland Indians.

Yawkey helped establish many charities and his philosophy was simple: "I was taught those born with material abundance should do what we can for those who aren't."[2]

The completion of a three-year expansion and renovation program took place on May 10, 1980, on the front steps of the museum. The new west wing more than doubled the size of the museum. Hall of Fame president Ed Stack presided over the dedication ceremony with Commissioner Bowie Kuhn being the featured speaker. The architect for the three million dollar project was the firm of Hutchins, Evans and Lefferts of New York City.

Induction

The 1980 Induction Ceremony was held on August 3 on a hot day when rain threatened but never happened as an occasional breeze helped to cool the day for the several thousand people in the crowd. There were 24 Hall of Famers present as the ceremony was televised live for the first time live on ESPN.

The person honored with the Ford Frick Award for broadcasting was the former New York Giants announcer, the late Russ Hodges. They played the tape of Hodges' description of Bobby Thomson's playoff home run in 1951 that helped the Giants win the game when he kept repeating, "The Giants win the pennant, the Giants win the pennant." Duke Snider, on the losing Dodgers team, uttered the funniest line of the day when he said, "I don't want to hear that."

The first inductee to be honored was Chuck Klein, who died in 1958 at the age of 53 and was represented by his grandnephew, Robert Klein. He thanked all the people of Philadelphia for their support and closed with, "And because of Cooperstown and the Hall of Fame, Chuck Klein will live on in many memories."

Tom Yawkey was the next inductee to be honored. He had died in 1976 at the age of 73. He was represented by his widow, Jean, as well as one of the greatest players of all time, Ted Williams, who spoke to the audience. Williams played 22 years for Yawkey's Red Sox and called him "the most considerate, kind, and respected man in all of baseball." He went on to tell how Yawkey helped establish the Baseball Players Fund, making every ballplayer "indebted to him." Williams also talked about his many charities including the Jimmy Fund for children's cancer research and establishing a Boys Town in Georgetown, South Carolina, called Tarra Hall.

Williams paid homage to Al Kaline and had special praise for Duke Snider when he said, "The baseball writers don't always get it right, because in your case they were ten years late in getting you here where you rightfully belong."

Al Kaline, 45, spoke next about the qualities of people who helped him — such as confidence, patience, care, loyalty, and love — and who took the time to share in achieving this "indescribable honor." He made a poignant comment about family, saying, "For all the fame and glory one derives from playing baseball, it isn't worth a thing without someone to share it with."

He has come back for 17 more inductions and his favorite Cooperstown memory is that both his parents were alive to share his induction with him.

Duke Snider, 53, had as one of his guests former boyhood friend Pete Rozelle, the National Football League commissioner. He thanked many people, including Dodgers team captain Pee Wee Reese for making all of the Dodgers "better players and better persons." He also expressed his feeling that Pee Wee should be in the Hall of Fame. He called teammate Jackie Robinson "the greatest competitor that I've ever seen." He spoke of other teammates as well, and also former and current general managers Branch Rickey and Buzzie Bavasi. He closed with, "I like to thank God for including me in his master plan for being in the Hall of Fame, and for being a Brooklyn and Los Angeles Dodger." He has returned some 16 times.

1981

The 1981 BBWAA election had 401 ballots cast and only Cardinals pitching great Bob Gibson was elected, receiving 84 percent (337 votes) in his first year of eligibility.

The VC elected Negro League pioneer Rube Foster and first baseman Johnny Mize. Sportswriter Norm Miller wrote "Behind Baseball's Hall of Shame" for *Family Weekly* magazine in 1981. He was upset that Mize received 1,099 votes in 11 BBWAA elections while Freddie Lindstrom received only 16 votes from the BBWAA and Earl Averill 35 votes, yet they were voted in by the VC in the 1970s.[3] *The Biographical Encyclopedia* called Mize "the rarest of hitters in that he was a genuine home run threat who hit for high average and didn't strike out much."[4]

Inductees

Bob Gibson overcame childhood illnesses to become not only a great pitcher, but a fierce competitor as well. Gibson also played basketball for the Harlem Globetrotters at the beginning of his baseball career. He had an outstanding slider that helped him win 20 or more games five times and strike out 200 or more batters nine times. Nineteen sixty-eight was a remarkable season for him because he won the MVP and the Cy Young Awards. That year he had 22 wins, an ERA of 1.12, and led the league in strikeouts (268) and shutouts (13). He won a second Cy Young in 1970 and was also an outstanding pitcher in three World Series, compiling a record of 7–2. "Gibbie" was the MVP in both the 1964 and 1967 Series won by the Cards. He pitched a no-hitter in 1971, won nine straight Gold Gloves, and hit 24 lifetime home runs. He finished with a record of 251–174 (.591).

He was one of several dominant pitchers in the 1960s who brought about a lowering of the pitching mound in order to get more offense back in baseball.

Rube Foster was born Andrew Foster but after he beat Rube Waddell and the Philadelphia A's in an exhibition game, he became known as the "Black Rube." He was the premier pitcher in black baseball in the first decade of the twentieth century and then managed the Chicago Leland Giants that supposedly won 123 of 129 games in 1910. He had disputes with Leland and formed the Chicago American Giants that won the East-West Colored Championships in 1914 and 1917, with future Hall of Famers Pop Lloyd and Pete Hill.

He was a successful player, manager, and owner, but the most important part of his legacy was when he formed the Negro National League in 1920 that consisted of eight midwestern teams. He brought stability and respectability to black baseball and became known as "The Father of Black Baseball."

Johnny Mize, Cardinals first baseman from 1936 through 1941, was called "Big Cat" because of his size, 6'2" and 215 pounds, yet he hit 43 triples in three years, leading the league with 16 in 1938. He also led the league in slugging percentage three times, home runs twice, as well as doubles and RBIs once during his six years with the Cards. He then spent five years with the Giants and again led the league in home runs twice, including 51 in 1947, and RBIs twice before being traded to the Yankees where he was a part of five straight championships from 1949 through 1953. He was the MVP of the 1952 Series when he hit a home run in three straight games. During his 15-year career he was a ten-time all-star, and finished with 359 home runs while batting .312.

The Big Cat was a tremendous pinch-hitter for the Yanks and led the league in pinch-hits from 1951 through 1953.

Induction

The 1981 Induction Ceremony was held at Cooper Park on a nice day with the temperature in the 80s as more than 3,000 fans and 23 Hall of Famers attended. The first inductee to be honored was Rube Foster, who suffered a nervous breakdown in 1926 and died in the Illinois Asylum in 1930 at the age of 51. He was represented by his son, Earl. He spoke briefly, expressing his gratitude to the Hall of Fame for their kindness as he opened and closed his remarks with several thank you's. He was unable to give his prepared speech because he was overcome with emotion.

Johnny Mize, 68, was introduced by Commissioner Kuhn, who quoted Yankees manager Casey Stengel who described the Big Cat perfectly when he said, "Mize was a slugger who hit like a leadoff man."

Mize began with a knock of the BBWAA when he said, "Years ago the writers told me I'd make the Hall of Fame, so I kind of prepared a speech. But somewhere in the 28 years it got lost." He continued by thanking the VC and responding to those who say that being selected by them is "going in by the back door." He said, "Look who's on the Veterans Committee, you see managers, general managers, ex-ballplayers, nearly all of them in the Hall of Fame. Now they're your peers, and you know in Hollywood, if you're picked by your peers, you receive an Oscar."

He talked about the coach at Piedmont College, Harry Forrester, who was so impressed with Mize that Forrester let Mize play three years for the college while Mize was still in high school. He closed by saying, "It's better when you're going into the Hall of Fame, and it's a lot better when you're able to smell the roses."

He came back for the next 11 years before passing away in his hometown of Demorest, Georgia, at the age of 80. Former director of research at the Hall of Fame Library Bill Deane remembers Mize driving to Cooperstown every year in his truck with the license plates that read "Big Cat."

Bob Gibson, 45, was the final inductee and he began by thanking the people of his hometown, Omaha, Nebraska, that drove to attend the induction. Gibson, whose father died before he was born, had rickets and asthma as a young child. He overcame it mainly because of his older brother Josh. He paid tribute to Josh, who taught him the fundamentals of not only baseball but basketball and track as well. He also paid homage to two of his managers, Johnny Keane and Red Schoendienst, for the confidence that they had in him.

He closed with, "I'm gonna get off of here before I do something I promised somebody I would never do." Gibson realized after his speech was over that he didn't mention owner Augie Busch and apologized. But it still didn't sit well with Busch because the Cards had given Gibson a $30,000 mobile home when they honored him with a day during his last season in 1975.

He didn't come back until 1992 and started coming on a regular basis in 1998. His favorite memory was in the fall of 2004 when he spent three days visiting the museum, and enjoying the town and its restaurants, which is hard to do on Induction Weekend.

1982

The 1982 BBWAA election had 415 ballots cast and home run king Hank Aaron and American and National League MVP Frank Robinson finished first and second respectively in their first year of eligibility. Aaron received 97.8 percent (406 votes) while Robinson received 89.2 percent (370 votes). We again ask the question: How could nine voters leave someone like Hank Aaron off their ballot?

The VC selected former commissioner Happy Chandler, who was ignored for many years after the owners didn't renew his contract in 1951. However, Joe Cronin, the American League president and chairman of the Veterans Committee, along with VC members, executive Gabe Paul and veteran sportswriter Joe Reichler, all helped to get him elected.

The other VC selection was Giants shortstop Travis Jackson, who tallied only 67 votes in 13 BBWAA elections. Bill James notes that many of Jackson's teammates on the Giants had been honored by the VC and asks facetiously, why shouldn't Jackson be honored? James feels that he is one of the worst selections made by the VC (p. 166). Robert Cohen calls Jackson a marginal Hall of Famer and views his selection with skepticism (p. 93). Joe Cronin, a Hall of Fame shortstop himself, said, "My only question about him being in the Hall of Fame is why it took him so long to get in."[5]

Inductees

Henry Aaron was a shortstop in the Negro Leagues before becoming an outfielder with the Milwaukee Braves in 1954. He became "Hammering Hank" after he began a streak of twenty straight seasons of hitting 20 or more home runs in 1955. He won the MVP in 1957 after leading the league in home runs and RBIs. He then batted .393 with three home runs to lead the Braves to the World Series title over the Yanks. He set the career home run record of 755 as well as the records for RBIs, total bases, and extra base hits. He finished his 23-year career with 3,771 hits while batting .305.

When Aaron broke Babe Ruth's career home run record of 714 on April 8, 1974, he said simply, "Thank God it's over." He received a lot of racially motivated death threats against him and his family requiring 24-hour police protection. Aaron was often forced to stay in different hotels from the team when they were on the road.

Frank Robinson played basketball with Bill Russell in high school, but baseball was his sport. He hit 38 home runs and was the Rookie of the Year for the Cincinnati Reds in 1956. He helped lead the Reds to the National League pennant in 1961 when he was the MVP. He was traded to the Baltimore Orioles in 1966 and won the Triple Crown and his second MVP, becoming the first player to win the award in both leagues. He capped off his season by being named the World Series MVP as the Orioles swept the Dodgers. Robinson helped manager Earl Weaver win three straight pennants and another title in 1970. He ended his 21-year career with 586 home runs and a batting average of .294. In 1975, he became the first black manager with the Cleveland Indians.

Reds general manager Bill DeWitt traded him to the Orioles because he thought that "he's an old 30." He went on to that phenomenal year in 1966 which cost DeWitt his job.

Albert Chandler was also known as Happy because of his jovial personality. He was the former governor of Kentucky and was serving as a U.S. senator when he was chosen by the owners to succeed Landis as commissioner after Landis died in 1944. He supported Branch Rickey and the integration of baseball in 1947 and helped the players' pension fund by negotiating the first television agreement. His suspension of manager Leo Durocher for a year and the suspension of 18 players for jumping to the Mexican League caused controversy. One of the players, Danny Gardella, sued baseball over the reserve clause and baseball settled with him before the case came to trial. Chandler wanted an extension of his contract and when the owners refused, he resigned a year early in 1951.

Happy Chandler invited Branch Rickey to his home and said to Rickey, "I'm going to have to meet my maker someday and if he asks me why I didn't let this boy play and I said it was because he was black, this wouldn't be a satisfactory answer."[6]

Travis Jackson became the regular shortstop for the New York Giants in 1924, held the job for the next 11 years and was named the captain in 1928. Jackson had an outstanding arm with good range so that he could play on the edge of the outfield grass. He led the league in fielding percentage twice, assists four times, and total chances three times. He was *The Sporting News* outstanding major league shortstop from 1927 through 1929. He played on four pennant winners with the Giants, including the World Series champion in 1933. He retired with a batting average of .291.

During his career he was given the nickname "Stonewall" after the Confederate general Stonewall Jackson because he was the anchor of the Giants defense.

Induction

The 1982 Induction Ceremony marked George Grande's inaugural performance as the master of ceremonies. You know he is doing a good job because he is still finding interesting things to say about each of the attendees all these years later.

Sunny skies greeted an estimated crowd of between 4,000 and 5,000 as a record 30 Hall of Famers were there for the ceremony.

This year also was also the inaugural annual golf and tennis tournament that is held Saturday morning of each Induction Weekend.

The first inductee to speak was Travis Jackson, 78, and he shared with the audience that his biggest thrill in baseball was being a member of the New York Giants for his whole career and playing in four World Series. He also mentioned the 13 Giants' teammates that are all in the Hall of Fame. He closed with, "I was voted into the Arkansas Hall of Fame with Bill Dickey and after that all of a sudden it was the National Hall of Fame."

He never came back and died five years later in the place that he was born and bred, Waldo, Arkansas, at the age of 83.

Commissioner Kuhn had many kind words to say about the next inductee, one of his predecessors as commissioner, Happy Chandler. He read a telegram from Ted Williams, who couldn't be there but stated, "Everyone is appreciative of your contribution to the game and your richly deserved recognition today."

Chandler, the career politician, probably gave the longest induction speech ever up until that time but his record didn't last long, because the next speech by Frank Robinson was even longer. Chandler, 84, expressed his glee by saying, "I feel a bit like a mosquito that flew over the fence into a nudist camp, I hardly know where to start."

He talked about Jackie Robinson, saying "For twenty-four years my predecessor [Judge Landis] would not let the black man play." Chandler went on, "I'm not going to be too harsh on him because he was doing what the owners wanted him to do and that was keep the game white and segregated." He said the owners anticipated Rickey's move to bring Robinson to Brooklyn so they had a meeting at the Waldorf Astoria in January 1947 and after a two-hour discussion, took a vote over which he presided, and the result was 15 no's and one yes. Later, when meeting with Branch Rickey, he discussed how it wasn't fair that these men could fight for their country in World War II and come home and not be allowed to play baseball. He then gave final approval of Robinson's contract from Montreal to Brooklyn. "I was doing what justice and mercy required me to do," he said.

He then talked about how when he got pension plans for all the state workers in Kentucky when he was governor and that spurred him to do the same for baseball players.

He came back the next six years and died in 1991 at the age of 92.

Frank Robinson, 47, joked about Chandler's speech being so long that he thought he would miss tomorrow night's game in Atlanta. (Robinson was the San Francisco Giants' manager.) Robinson's speech turned out to be longer — he spoke for thirty-two minutes. He then kidded Travis Jackson that he would give the 78 year old a tryout with his Giants after seeing 75-year-old Hall of Famer Luke Appling hit a home run off Warren Spahn in an Old-Timers game. He praised fellow inductee Hank Aaron as someone he always came up a little short by comparison, yet whom he admired not only for his athletic ability but "as a human being and an outstanding person." Robinson said he finally got even because he was going into the Hall of Fame before Aaron. He then paid tribute to all the people who helped him in baseball and closed by looking directly at Rachel Robinson, Jackie's widow, who was in the audience. He paid tribute to her husband "for opening doors and making it easier for all black players that followed."

Robinson only got back six times in the next twenty years, mainly because of his managerial duties which have now ended. As a result, he has been a regular since 2007. His favorite Cooperstown memory was his own induction because "you only get inducted once, showing how special and unique enshrinement can be." He is a member of the Hall of Fame's Board of Directors.

Bowie Kuhn introduced Henry "Hank" Aaron by saying that when he broke Babe Ruth's career home run record, it was voted by the media and baseball officials as the greatest moment in the history of baseball.

Aaron, 48, expressed his emotions in the beginning of his speech by saying, "I feel a great sense of humility, gratitude, and appreciation for this day." He went on to thank Jackie Robinson and Roy Campanella for paving the way for him and other black ballplayers. "They proved to the world that a man's ability is limited only by his lack of opportunity." He acknowledged that "the sheer majesty of this occasion and its significance overwhelms me." He finished by thanking all his friends who contributed to his success when he said, "I did not make this journey alone."

His attendance was only sporadic during the 1980s and 1990s but it has become more consistent the first decade of the new millennium. He was a member of the VC for two years before the whole format was revised in 2001.

A new exhibit entitled *Hank Aaron: Chasing the Dream* opened at the Hall of Fame in April 2009 in order to honor his historic career and his life after baseball.

1983

The 1983 BBWAA election had 374 ballots cast and the outstanding defensive third baseman of the Baltimore Orioles, Brooks Robinson, had the most votes in his first year of eligibility with 92 percent (344 votes).

The great Giants pitcher Juan Marichal finished second in his third year of eligibility with 83.7 percent (313 votes) for a total of 851 votes during his three years on the ballot.

The VC selected Dodgers manager Walter Alston seven years after he retired as their skipper. The VC also chose American League third baseman George Kell 26 years after he retired. Bill James and Robert Cohen are critical of his selection but their criticism has to be tempered with the fact that Kell received 1,111 votes in 13 BBWAA elections. James doesn't regard him as Hall of Fame material (p. 110). Cohen rates Kell the lowest of the 13 third basemen in the hall and states, "He is not productive enough for a player at his position to legitimize his presence in Cooperstown" (p. 79).

Inductees

Brooks Robinson took five seasons before establishing himself as the Orioles third baseman in 1960. He became known as the "Human Vacuum Cleaner" and went on to win 16 straight Gold Gloves. He finished his 23-year career with the all-time record for third basemen in games, putouts, assists, double plays, and fielding percentage. He was the MVP in 1964 when he batted .318 and led the league with 118 RBIs. He started 11 All-Star Games and was the MVP of the 1966 game. He helped lead the Orioles to four pennants and two World Series titles and batted .267 lifetime.

Robinson was the MVP of the 1970 World Series when he batted .429, but it was his fielding that set him apart. He made seven spectacular plays that earned him a car. This led Johnny Bench of the losing Reds to quip, "If he wanted a car that badly, we'd have given him one."[7] Ford Frick called it "the best World Series performance by an individual player."[8]

Juan Marichal came from the Dominican Republic and made an auspicious debut with the Giants in 1960, pitching a one-hit shutout over the Phillies and then four-hitting the Pirates. Six times he won 20 or more games, including a league-leading 25 victories in 1963 while pitching a no-hitter and 26 victories in 1968. Yet he never received a vote for the Cy Young Award because of Koufax in 1963 and Gibson in 1968 when both won the award unanimously. Yet Marichal won more games in the 1960s than Koufax and Gibson. The "Dominican Dandy" was a 10-time all-star and finished at 243–142 (.631).

Koufax and Marichal faced each other in 1965 at Candlestick Park. When Koufax didn't retaliate after Marichal knocked down two Dodgers batters, his catcher, Johnny Roseboro, whizzed the ball by Juan's ear as he threw the ball back during Marichal's at-bat. Marichal went berserk and hit Roseboro in the head with his bat. Ironically, in time Roseboro forgave him and even campaigned for Marichal's induction into the Hall.

George Kell distinguished himself as a good defensive third baseman. He is currently ranked fourth all-time with a fielding percentage of .969. Kell flourished with the Detroit Tigers for more than six seasons. He twice led the league in hits and doubles and also beat

One of the 43 bus groups that came to honor Brooks Robinson at his 1983 induction. This group came from York, Pennsylvania, where Brooks started his professional career.

out Ted Williams for the batting crown on the last day of the season in 1949 with a .343 average. He was selected for 10 All-Star Games and never struck out more than 37 times in a season. He finished with a batting average of .306 lifetime.

Kell had a very supportive partner in his wife, Charlene. She iced his chronic sore knees often when he was in the minors, convinced him not to quit when he was ready to take a job in construction, and encouraged him as he beat out Ted Williams for the batting title.

Walter Alston played in only one major league game and was a minor league manager in the Dodgers' organization for 10 years before becoming the surprise choice to lead Brooklyn in 1954. He won his first pennant and World Series over the Yankees a year later, and then lost to them in 1956. The Dodgers moved to Los Angeles in 1958 and a year later they again won the World Series. Alston went on to win four more pennants and two World Series titles. He was a low-key manager who adapted his managing style to his teams. He retired with a record of 2,040–1,613 (.558).

The Yankees played the Brooklyn Dodgers in five World Series from 1941 through 1953 and won each time. Yet when owner Walter O'Malley hired Alston, he predicted that his new manager would beat the Yankees. It took Alston a year to give Brooklyn its only championship (1955) and end once and for all the familiar Dodgers refrain, "Wait 'til next year."

Induction

The 1983 Induction Ceremony was held on July 31 in front of some 12,000 people, including 30 Hall of Famers. Local weather reports described it as a sweltering day, but that didn't deter some 43 chartered buses, 12 chartered airplanes and countless private cars coming to see Brooks Robinson inducted. Fans were there wearing the orange and black of the Baltimore Orioles.

The first inductee was manager Walter Alston, who was unable to attend after suffering a heart attack in April. He was represented by his grandson, Bob Ogle. Ogle told the crowd that his grandfather had asked him while in a Cincinnati hospital back in April to accept this award. Ogle admitted to the audience, "This is the most difficult thing I've ever had to do, but this is also the greatest honor of my life." The grandson said that the greatest thrill for Alston was winning the World Series championship in 1955 because it was not only his first but it was also Brooklyn's first as well. He closed by describing Walter Alston "as someone who manages as he lives, long and well, and he has done it without your noticing. It's obvious today that someone did notice and we thank you."

Si Burdick of the Dayton, Ohio, *Daily News* was the recipient of the J.G. Taylor Spink Award and during his acceptance speech he spoke of Walter Alston, whom he coincidentally had collaborated with to help write Alston's autobiography. Burdick spoke about the fact that most people weren't aware that after the Dodgers signed Jackie Robinson to play for Montreal in the International League in 1946, they also signed black ballplayers Roy Campanella and Don Newcombe to play for the Nashua, New Hampshire, minor league team where the manager was Walter Alston.

Alston died a year later from his heart ailment at the age of 72.

The next inductee was George Kell, 60, who congratulated the other winners, including his good friend Brooks Robinson. He and Robinson were both from the state of Arkansas, played together for one year with the Orioles (Kell's last and Robinson's first), and had been broadcast partners. Kell found it "unbelievable that we would wind up in Cooperstown together." He shared a nice note he received from Hall of Fame umpire Jocko Conlan, who said, "You never choked up on a baseball field, but I guarantee you'll choke up at the Induction Ceremonies." Kell agreed that it was very emotional, especially when he shared this honor with his 83-year-old father, who was watching the event on television in a nursing home back in Arkansas. He told how his father thought he and his two brothers would all be major league players, and one brother did make it, but his older brother was killed in World War II. He closed by telling how touched he was when his twelve-year-old neighbor, Ricky Roberts said, "Mr. Kell, we're proud of you and we'll be watching you on television."

His favorite Cooperstown memory is when Ted Williams, toward the end of his life and confined to a wheelchair, told everyone at the private dinner for the Hall of Famers, "I see guys in this room who come now and then, but coming back here every year is my goal and it should be yours." This helped to inspire some and when we interviewed George Kell by phone in 2005, he said that he looks forward to coming each year even after he was in a serious car accident a few years ago. His attendance record was almost perfect since 1991. He died in 2009 at the age of 86.

The third inductee was Juan Marichal, 45, who had the honor of being the first inductee from the Dominican Republic. The ceremony was televised in his native country. Commissioner Bowie Kuhn graciously greeted the people in the Dominican Republic by speaking to them in Spanish as he introduced Marichal. Kuhn mentioned his impressive All-Star record, which included pitching in eight games and giving up only one earned run in 18 innings. He was the MVP of the 1965 game.

Marichal first spoke in English saying that "I accept this honor on behalf of my family, my country, the Dominican Republic and all the people who assisted me in making this a reality." He went on to thank the San Francisco Giants, his teammates, and the fans, calling it a privilege to play for them. He then gave the same message in Spanish, acknowledging all the people who came from the Dominican Republic. He also paid tribute to those who couldn't make it but "are here with me in spirit."

He didn't come back the rest of the decade but has more than made up for it since, missing only two inductions since 1990.

The last inductee was the one that most in the crowd had been waiting to see, Brooks Robinson, 46. Bowie Kuhn introduced him as "one of the most successful and, need I tell you, most popular players in the history of the game." Robinson began by paying tribute to the city of Baltimore, having played his entire 23-year career there, and especially to the fans who supported him "on his good days and bad days." He also said, "This day is extra special for me because I am being inducted with my fellow Arkansasan, George Kell." Robinson continued, "He is a man who I admired both on and off the field." He also recalled his happiest moment in Cooperstown took place 22 years ago when, while playing in the annual exhibition game, it was announced during the fifth inning that his oldest son had been born.

He has come back some 19 times since, and is also a member of the Hall of Fame's Board of Directors.

1984

The 1984 BBWAA election saw 403 ballots cast and three players receiving the necessary 75 percent to earn induction. The great defensive shortstop Luis Aparicio finished first with 84.6 percent (341 votes) in his sixth year of eligibility. Aparicio received a total of 1,059 votes in his six BBWAA elections.

Minnesota Twins slugger Harmon Killebrew finished second with 83.1 percent (335 votes) in his fourth year of eligibility. Killebrew received 1,089 votes in four elections.

The final BBWAA selection was the right-handed pitching ace of the Los Angeles Dodgers, Don Drysdale, who finished with 78.4 percent (316 votes) in his tenth year of eligibility. Drysdale received 2,427 votes in 10 BBWAA elections.

Shortstop Pee Wee Reese was chosen by the VC in a unanimous vote his first year on the VC ballot, 26 years after he retired. His candidacy received support from sportswriters such as Leonard Koppett, Dave Anderson, Dick Young, and Will Grimsley. Previously, he received 1,718 votes during 14 BBWAA elections.

Catcher Rick Ferrell was the second inductee elected by the VC and this was his twelfth year on the VC ballot, after having retired as a player 37 years ago. His selection was also one of the most controversial picks ever made because he only received three votes in 15 BBWAA elections. The VC consisted of 18 members in 1984, which meant that he had to receive 14 votes in order to receive the necessary 75 percent. Therefore, Ferrell received more votes in the VC election than in all 15 BBWAA elections.

Bill Madden wrote that "there were many who thought the VC had elected the wrong Ferrell, that they had meant to name his brother Wes, who was a better hitter even though he was a pitcher."[9] Wes actually received 27 votes spread over six BBWAA elections. James Vail refers to Rick Ferrell as another of the 12 "more dubious selections ever" (p. 133). Vail believes his defensive skills as a catcher helped get him elected (pp. 167–168). Bill James compares his selection to Tom McCarthy, Roger Bresnahan, and Joe Tinker (p. 371). Finally, Robert Cohen calls him "the worst offensive catcher in the Hall of Fame who played after the Deadball Era" (p. 117).

Inductees

Luis Aparicio was born in Venezuela and was the son of his country's greatest shortstop but left to become the Rookie of the Year in 1956 with the Chicago White Sox. He led the league in stolen bases for the first of nine consecutive seasons. Defense and speed were his specialties and he would combine with second baseman Nellie Fox to lead the league in three defensive categories each as the "Go Go" Sox won the pennant in 1959. He was traded to the Baltimore Orioles in 1963 where he combined with Brooks Robinson to form an airtight left side of the infield that helped them win the World Series title in 1966. He was chosen to 10 all-star teams and set the record for games at shortstop.

Aparicio was chosen the Venezuelan Athlete of the Century in 1999. Tragically, in 2001, one of his daughters was shot by a carjacker and died in 2004.

Harmon Killebrew was recruited by a U.S. senator from Idaho, Herman Welker, and signed as a bonus baby with the Washington Senators in 1954. He became the regular third baseman in 1959 and led the league in home runs for the first of six times. "Killer" moved with the team to Minnesota (Twins) in 1961 and helped lead them to the World Series in 1965. He had his best season in 1969 when he was the MVP, with career highs in home runs (49) and RBIs (140). He was now a first baseman as well when the Twins lost to the Orioles in the first two League Championship Series (LCS) in 1969 and 1970. Killebrew finished his 22-year career as an 11-time all-star who hit 573 home runs.

"Killer" developed his enormous power and strength from lifting ten-gallon milk containers on his father's farm. During the Civil War, his grandfather was reputedly the strongest man in the Union Army.

Don Drysdale broke in with the Brooklyn Dodgers in 1956 as a 19-year-old rookie. He went on to lead the league in strikeouts three times and pitched 58 consecutive scoreless innings. Drysdale compiled a record of 3–3 in five World Series for the Los Angeles Dodgers that produced three titles. He won the Cy Young Award in 1962 when he led the league with 25 victories. "Big D" was an intimidating pitcher at 6'6" who hit 154 batsmen, but he also showed power as a hitter when he hit 29 lifetime home runs. He finished his career at 209–166 and prepared for his next career as a broadcaster by practicing in the bullpen between starts.

Drysdale and Sandy Koufax formed a tandem by holding out for a three-year contract at $500,000 each during the spring of 1966. This was before free agency and the Dodgers won out with Koufax signing for one year at $130,000 and Drysdale for $105,000.

Harold Reese, a.k.a. "Pee Wee," got his nickname after winning the Louisville marble championship at the age of 12. He broke in as the Brooklyn shortstop in 1940 with manager Leo Durocher sticking with him despite a lot of errors as the Dodgers went on to win the pennant in 1941. Reese's defense improved notably before he spent three years in the Navy during World War II. He was their captain as the Dodgers won six pennants and Brooklyn's only title in 1955. Reese was a 10-time all-star who batted .269 lifetime.

Once when the crowd taunted Jackie Robinson with racial insults, Reese went over to his second baseman and put his arm around him and spoke softly until the taunting stopped. Robinson would later say, "In my book there is none finer."[10] Reese is immortalized on his Hall of Fame plaque with the words, "Instrumental in easing acceptance of Jackie Robinson as baseball's first black performer."

Rick Ferrell became a catcher by default because he grew up with six brothers, all of whom were pitchers. He played 18 years and retired with the most games caught in the American League while batting .281 lifetime. It was on defense where he shined because of an accurate arm and the fact that he was a good handler of pitchers, including catching four knuckleball pitchers on the same Senators staff. He and his brother Wes were battery mates with both the Red Sox and the Senators. Ferrell was an eight-time all-star with his biggest thrill taking place in the inaugural All-Star game in 1933. He caught the whole game despite his team having Mickey Cochrane and Bill Dickey on the bench.

It's good that none of his critics wanted to box him because Ferrell won 17 of 18 professional fights in North Carolina to win the lightweight championship of the state.

Induction

The 1984 Induction Ceremony was held on August 11 with a half hour rain delay as a crowd of about 5,000 waited. MC George Grande, as is his custom, gave interesting tidbits about each of the 29 Hall of Famers present. Grande told how Bill Terry used only two bats in 1930 when he hit .401 and he still had one of them. He introduced the terrible-hitting pitcher Lefty Gomez with one of Lefty's funny one-liners when he said, "I had one weakness, a pitched ball."

This was also the last induction that Bowie Kuhn would be presiding over as the baseball commissioner and so Hall of Fame president Ed Stack thanked him for his 16 years and presented him with a gold lifetime pass, which took Kuhn completely by surprise. Kuhn genuinely enjoyed doing the Induction Ceremonies and said, "I thought then in 1969, and I still believe it, that this moment is the greatest time in the baseball calendar."

The first inductee to speak was Rick Ferrell, who at 78 was still an active scout with the Detroit Tigers. He began by humbly expressing how he felt: "There are so many great players that are not in the Hall of Fame so that this is an added honor to be elected by the Veterans Committee."

He talked about not being protected by the Detroit Tigers after three years in the minors, so Commissioner Landis declared him a free agent in 1928 when he signed with the St. Louis Browns. He also mentioned taking part in the first All-Star Game in 1933, his first night game in 1939, and the first airline flight as a member of the Red Sox, when he was one of only 17 players who volunteered to fly from St. Louis to Chicago in 1936. This was the first time it had been done and Ferrell, like most of the others, hadn't ever flown before. He closed with, "I've been to Cooperstown before, but this tops them all."

Ferrell came back seven more times before he passed away at the age of 89 in 1995.

Bowie Kuhn introduced Pee Wee Reese by stating that he was the only player to participate in the subway series between the Dodgers and the Yankees by playing every inning of every game of the seven World Series in the 1940s and 1950s. Kuhn also said, "The man from Kentucky was there for Jackie Robinson in 1947 with Robinson later saying, 'Pee Wee made me feel like I belonged.'"

Reese, 66, talked about his 18 wonderful years of playing in Brooklyn and playing at

Ebbets Field and all the wonderful fans including the Sym-Phony Band and Hilda Chester and her cow bell. He paid homage to the Dodgers' owners and the Hillerich and Bradsby Bat Company, where he was an executive. He commented on Bill Terry only using two bats in a season saying, "I used more than that in a week." He said, despite all his success with the Dodgers, he is more known today for when he was broadcasting the Game of the Week with Dizzy Dean. He paid tribute to his teammate Jackie Robinson, and "wished he could have been here today." He also paid tribute to Leo Durocher for all the patience he showed in him. "If it wouldn't have been for Leo I doubt seriously that I would be up here today." He closed with a tribute to his wife, stating, "I wore number one on my back for all the years that I played but she was number one in my heart."

Another example of fan loyalty happened at the 1983 induction and again in 1984. According to the local weekly newspaper, *The Freeman's Journal*, a Dodgers fan by the name of Harold Julius came all the way from California to honor both Walter Alston in 1983 and Pee Wee Reese in 1984. What made him a rather unusual fan is he billed himself as Tarzan and came dressed in a tiger-skin toga.

Reese never missed an induction for the next 14 years and died in 1999 at the age of 81.

The next inductee was Don Drysdale, 48, who followed his Dodgers teammate to the podium. He began by saying, "It's kind of like a day of Thanksgiving. To me, Thanksgiving comes early in 1984." He thanked the BBWAA "for making this fantasy come true." He paid tribute to the Dodgers organization and manager Walter Alston for his patience and then said, "If you could never play for Walter Alston, you may as well pack your suitcase and go home." His graciousness extended to a group that was probably never recognized by an inductee before and that was the Dodgers' trainers and medical staff. He acknowledged the various broadcasters he had worked with over the years and finished his speech by praising the fans. He said baseball would not survive without them "walking through turnstiles, turning on radios and televisions, and coming here to Cooperstown to witness these induction ceremonies."

Unfortunately, he never came back, and died in his sleep in 1993 in a hotel room where he was getting ready to broadcast a game from Montreal. He was only 56.

Bowie Kuhn introduced Luis Aparicio, 50, and spoke to the people briefly in Spanish as he sent greetings to the people of Venezuela and said that "Luis Aparicio was one of the greatest shortstops of all time and a credit to the people of Venezuela."

It should be noted that Jim Fanning, the director of player development for the Montreal Expos, was at the Pan Am Stadium in Caracas, Venezuela, to witness a Winter League game in January when the announcement was made that Luis Aparicio had been elected to the Hall of Fame. Fanning stated, "There were about 10,000 fans present when different groups started singing Venezuela's National Anthem. Play was stopped and then the crowd started singing it again, but this time in unison." Fanning continued, "It was the most impressive show of pride in a sports hero that I've ever seen."[11]

Aparicio began his brief induction speech with a little humor when he said the commissioner mentioned his different records but didn't say anything about all his errors. He paid tribute to his father and his father's American teammate in 1946, Roy Campanella, who was in the audience. He paid homage to his teammates and the different organizations that he played for "from the front office to the batboy." He himself was a batboy on his father's team. He closed with, "For me to be amongst the greatest players in baseball history will mean much more than I can say."

He didn't come back that decade but has missed only a couple of times since 1991, which is commendable since he is traveling all the way from Venezuela.

The fifth and final inductee of the day was Harmon Killebrew, 48 like Drysdale. He began his speech saying he was a cleanup hitter many times, "but this is the toughest cleanup hitting I've ever done." He told how devoted his father was to him and his siblings, especially about playing other sports besides baseball, like basketball, track, and football. His father had played college football for the great coach Greasy Neale and played a lot of ball with Killebrew and his brother on the front lawn. He recalled his mother saying, "You're tearing up the grass and digging holes in the front yard," to which his father responded, "We're not raising grass here, we're raising boys."

On a personal note, Killebrew was asked to speak at the 2004 Induction Ceremony and he told this same story, which happened to be my first induction that I attended with my wife, Pat. The next day while walking on Main Street, we saw him giving autographs and went over. Pat told him how touching that story was to her and he got up and hugged her.

He thanked everyone connected to his career including scouts, owners, teammates, and managers. He was especially gracious to Bowie Kuhn when he said, "I'm especially proud to take part in the last official act of our great commissioner, Bowie Kuhn." He finished with, "I consider this baseball's greatest honor."

Killebrew's favorite Cooperstown memory was his own induction. He said Jack Lang, the secretary of the BBWAA, said, "Your life will never be the same." "Jack was right," Killebrew acknowledged, "but it is still hard for me to believe that I belong to this elite group of men every time I put Hall of Famer behind my name." He has come back 16 times, including the last 12 in a row.

Ed Stack closed the ceremony by reading a telegram from President Ronald Reagan congratulating all five inductees.

1985

The 1985 election had 395 ballots cast and the top vote getter was relief pitcher Hoyt Wilhelm who received 83.8 percent (331 votes). Although he wasn't selected until his eighth year of eligibility, Wilhelm always did well on the BBWAA ballot, receiving 1,873 votes. He received support from prominent sportswriters Leonard Koppett, Tom Boswell, and Jim Murray.

Cardinals stolen base king Lou Brock finished second with 79.7 percent (315 votes) in his first year of eligibility. He became only the second player to be elected while finishing second with less than 80 percent of the vote during his first year of eligibility. The other player to do it was Jackie Robinson in 1962 when he finished second with 77.5 percent.

A controversy did develop as longtime White Sox second baseman Nellie Fox finished third in the BBWAA balloting with 74.7 percent. This meant that he missed induction by two votes. Chicago sportswriter Jerry Holtzman thought that was unfair and voiced his displeasure. Others thought that the vote should have been rounded off to 75 percent like they do with batting averages and ERA figures. Hall of Fame president Ed Stack disagreed, maintaining a pure 75 percent is needed and added that the board of directors is reluctant to change the system.

Hustling outfielder Enos Slaughter was chosen by the VC six years after his eligibility was up with the BBWAA. Two people on the VC who supported him were Cardinals teammate

Stan Musial and St. Louis sportswriter Bob Broeg. It bothered Slaughter that it took him 26 years after he retired to finally reach Cooperstown and he briefly addressed it during his induction speech. The results of the BBWAA voting show that he always had good support with 2,371 votes in 14 elections.

Shortstop Arky Vaughan was also chosen by the VC after receiving grassroots support, according to analyst Bill James. James, as we have pointed out regarding other candidates, can be very critical, but he can also be supportive. James chronicled two men who, although they worked separately, had the same goal, and that was to elect Arky Vaughan. Edward Kelly wrote an article in the November 1984 issue of *Baseball Digest* titled, "How about Ernie Lombardi and Arky Vaughan for the Hall?" (p. 348).

The other supporter was Dixie Tourangeau on behalf of the Committee to Elect Arky Vaughan to the Baseball Hall of Fame, who wrote persuasive letters to members of the Veterans Committee and enclosed a brief biography and clippings to prove his claim (p. 347). Later sportswriter Milt Richman wrote a pro–Vaughan story in 1985 (p. 348). This helped get him elected the same year because Richman was also a member of the VC.

Vaughan was quiet and shy and had little contact with reporters during his career. According to author David Fleitz, prominent *New York Times* columnist Arthur Daley put it best when he wrote, "He never said anything quotable or did anything worth mentioning."[12] Despite significant statistics, Vaughan received little support from the BBWAA as evident with only 219 votes in 12 elections.

Inductees

Hoyt Wilhelm was taught to throw the knuckleball in high school, and a year after beginning his professional career he was drafted during World War II. Wounded at the Battle of the Bulge, Wilhelm received a Purple Heart. In 1952, he finally made his debut with the New York Giants as a reliever when he was nearly 30. He went 15–3 and led the league in ERA and games pitched. He was 12–4 in 1954 when the Giants won the World Series. He pitched 21 years for nine teams as a reliever, starter, and then a reliever. He pitched a no-hitter at Yankee Stadium in 1958 and led the American League in ERA in 1959, one of only a few to lead both leagues in ERA. He retired at the age of 49 during the 1972 season.

Wilhelm's knuckleball was so erratic that five of his catchers set records for passed balls. A special enlarged mitt was designed for his catchers, leaving renowned sportswriter Jim Murray to exclaim, "The ball comes to the plate like a kid on the way to a bath."[13]

Lou Brock was traded from the Cubs to the Cards in 1964 for pitcher Ernie Broglio in one of the most lopsided deals ever, because the left fielder helped propel the Cards to the pennant and title in 1964. He led the league in stolen bases eight times, setting the single season record in 1974 with 118. He also set the career record of 938 stolen bases, both of which have been broken by Rickey Henderson. He was a clutch performer who hit .391 for three World Series and .375 for five All-Star Games. He retired batting .293 lifetime.

His greatest performance might have been his last year in 1979 when he came back from an injury-plagued 1978 and hit .304, reached the 3,000-hit plateau, and was *The Sporting News* Comeback Player of the Year. He did this all at the age of 40. What a way to exit!

Enos Slaughter was called "Country" because of his North Carolina rural background. He became the Cardinals' right fielder in 1938 and helped lead them to titles in 1942 and 1946. He was traded to the Yankees where he played on two more championship teams, including 1956 when he batted .350 in the series at the age of 40. Slaughter played in 10 straight All-Star Games and batted .300 lifetime.

While in the minors, Slaughter once got down on himself as he walked slowly in from the outfield. Manager Eddie Dyer responded, "Are you tired, kid? If so, I'll get some help for you."[14] This was a wake-up call for Enos as running and hustling became synonymous with him, as he showed against the Red Sox during the seventh game of the 1946 World Series. He scored the winning run by going from first all the way to home on a double.

Joseph "Arky" Vaughan got his nickname from a friend after his family moved from Arkansas to California when he was young. In 1932, he hit .318 as a Pirate rookie, but after 46 errors at shortstop, former Pirates great Honus Wagner tutored him. Vaughan improved and went on to lead the league in putouts and assists three times each. Offense was his forte, however, as he led the league in 16 categories during his 14-year career including runs, triples, and walks three times each. He also led the league in 1935 with a .385 batting average, and was a 9-time all-star. He helped the Dodgers win a pennant in 1947 and hit .318 lifetime.

Vaughan had a rift with Dodgers manager Leo Durocher in 1943 and left baseball. They patched things up in 1947 when he returned. The real reason he left was to help run his brother's ranch after his brother had been drafted into World War II.

Induction

The 1985 Induction Ceremony was held on the steps of the library with some 6,000 people and 25 Hall of Famers there to watch the proceedings in Cooper Park on a beautiful sunny day. Brent Musburger was the MC, substituting for George Grande. Hall of Fame president Ed Stack read a letter from President Ronald Reagan congratulating the inductees. He then introduced the new baseball commissioner, Peter Ueberroth.

The first inductee introduced was Arky Vaughan. Brent Musburger discussed Vaughan's background, including his tragic death in 1952 at the age of 40 in a boating accident. Musburger didn't mention the details: Vaughan was fishing in a dinghy with a friend when suddenly the friend stood up to cast his line and the boat capsized. They were only 200 feet from shore so they started swimming. Vaughan was a good swimmer but his friend wasn't. When the friend started to sink, Vaughan tried to rescue him and they both sank. Their bodies were discovered the next day.

Representing him at the ceremony was his daughter, Patricia Johnson. She said, "I'm very proud to be representing the Vaughan family in accepting this honor." She thanked the Hall of Fame and the VC and then singled out three men who were responsible for helping get him elected. The first was Wiley Thornton of Texas, who had passed away. She also mentioned two other men who had not seen her father play, but who became interested in him and researched his statistics. One was a Lieutenant Colonel Mike Stevenson, who came from her father's hometown of Fullerton, California, but was now stationed in Germany. The third man was the aforementioned Dixie Tourangeau, who she said had spent many hours researching her father's career and was there to honor him. She closed by saying, "The fame and glory that he never sought are now his forever."

The next honoree was Enos Slaughter, whom Musburger mentioned was the former baseball coach at Duke and finished with, "It came awfully late, but today we honor that 'old warhorse,' Country Slaughter."

Slaughter, 69, picked up on Musburger's words by beginning his speech with, "Of course it came a long time too late I thought, but that's life for us." He then thanked the

VC and all the fans who wrote him which "kept my spirit up." He then talked about the lesson manager Eddie Dyer taught him as mentioned in his bio, which he said helped to make running "his biggest asset." Later he did something unprecedented — he finished by calling Ted Williams up to the lectern. Slaughter then gave him the ball Williams had hit for a home run that won the 1941 All-Star game for the American League.

Slaughter, despite his disappointment at having to wait so long to be inducted, was appreciative of the honor and came back for the next 17 years. He even complained about the other Hall of Famers who haven't come back. He died in 2002 at the age of 86.

Hoyt Wilhelm, 62, began his induction speech by giving thanks to God and said, "I'm a little nervous and rightly so. I think I would be calmer pitching in Yankee Stadium before a full house; in fact, I know I would." Wilhelm admitted at the beginning of his career he was released while pitching in Class D and told to stop throwing the knuckleball by the manager. Luckily he didn't listen and made it back to the same team two weeks later. He told the audience that experience helps him now as a minor league pitching instructor for the Yankees when he has to tell a pitcher that he has been released. He tells them his story to give them encouragement. Wilhelm then told how his children were able to make the adjustment when he was pitching for so many clubs while they were in school. They would start school at the spring training site, next switch to a school system where he was pitching, and then finish up back home in North Carolina. He paid tribute to his first manager, Leo Durocher, and another manager, Paul Richards, whom he considered "one of the greatest pitching coaches that I ever had." He concluded by saying, "How fortunate I was to be on the winning team in a World Series, be an all-star in both leagues, pitch a no-hitter, and most importantly, fortunate enough to be elected to the Hall of Fame."

He came back five more times and died in 2002 at the age of 80.

Lou Brock, 46, spoke last and gave a profound speech, talking about his humble beginnings in the Jim Crow South of Louisiana in the late 1940s. He told how the radio broadcasts of Cardinals games by Jack Buck and Harry Caray transformed him. The first time he heard them broadcasting a game between the Cards and Dodgers, he declared, "I was so overwhelmed that I thought I had tuned into another world. A world in which life had no façade and that hurt and loneliness were not the natural price for being alive. Through these broadcasts, baseball fed my fantasies about what life offered. Baseball helped me follow my dreams of being a major league baseball player."

Once he made it to the majors, the three factors that helped him attain success were ability, determination, and the support of people. He then spoke about some of the people who have helped him including his high school baseball coach and the scout who signed him, the late ambassador of baseball, Buck O'Neil. His high school coach, Roosevelt Johnson, told him something that he has never forgotten, and something we could all use regarding our own self-esteem. Johnson said, "No one can make you feel inferior without first getting your permission." He closed with, "I feel proud to take my place among the greatest players ever to play major league baseball."

Brock didn't come back until 1993, but hasn't missed an induction since.

1986

Four hundred twenty-five ballots were cast in the 1986 BBWAA election with only slugging first baseman Willie McCovey qualifying. He received 81.4 percent (346 votes) in his first year of eligibility.

The VC chose Red Sox second baseman Bobby Doerr. Ted Williams was on the VC and undoubtedly was a major influence in his longtime friend and teammate being selected. Doerr received 407 votes in 11 BBWAA elections.

The VC also selected the good hitting and slow-footed catcher Ernie Lombardi. He had little support from the BBWAA, receiving 133 votes in 10 elections. Prior to his death, despite the poor showing with the BBWAA vote, Lombardi was bitter about not getting into the Hall of Fame and said that he would not accept it if the VC decided to admit him.

When he died in 1977, *The Sporting News* started a drive to get him in as part of his obituary. One reason it didn't happen was because Warren Giles, the president of the National League and a member of the VC, successfully lobbied against his candidacy. Giles' animosity against Lombardi stemmed from the time that he was the general manager of the Cincinnati Reds and had difficult negotiations with "Lom" over several contracts.[15] Robert Cohen felt he had too many liabilities stating, "When the VC elected Lombardi in 1986, it was not a very good decision" (p. 116). When all was said and done, Bill James called his election "a reasonably good selection by the Hall of Fame" (p. 303). Also, having former teammate Al Lopez on the VC probably helped Lombardi's cause as well.

Inductees

Willie McCovey, a.k.a. "Stretch," at 6'4", made an auspicious debut with San Francisco in 1959 with four hits off Robin Roberts, including two triples. He batted .354 in only 52 games and won the Rookie of the Year Award unanimously. He made the last out of the 1962 World Series against the Yankees when he lined out to second baseman Bobby Richardson. He was the 1969 MVP and was also the All-Star Game MVP that year with two home runs. Despite playing 22 years, McCovey missed a lot of playing time due to arthritic and surgically repaired knees and numerous other injuries. He finished with 521 home runs, including 18 grand slams.

McCovey came back to the Giants in 1977, following three years with the Padres and the A's. He hit 28 home runs and had 15 game-winning hits, including one on Willie McCovey Day, and was chosen the league's Comeback Player of the Year.

Bobby Doerr and Ted Williams were teammates in the Pacific Coast League when the Boston Red Sox acquired them. Doerr broke in with the Red Sox in 1937 and was their regular second baseman for the rest of his 14-year career. He batted .409 in the 1946 World Series, and handled 49 chances without an error. Doerr led the league in double plays five times, fielding percentage four times, and set an American League record in 1948 when he handled 414 chances without an error. He was a nine-time all-star, hit 223 home runs, drove in 1,247 runs, and batted .288 lifetime.

Despite being the second baseman for the arch rival Yankees, Joe Gordon and Doerr were the best of friends, so he had to be pleased when Gordon made the hall in 2009.

Ernie Lombardi had huge hands and he also had a prominent nose that earned him the nickname "Schnozz." The Schnozz swung a 46-ounce bat and used an interlocking grip on the bat which gave him good bat control. He won two batting titles and never struck out more than 25 times in a season. He blossomed for the Reds under Hall of Fame manager Bill McKechnie when he was the MVP in 1938. He was also Johnny Vander Meer's catcher when he threw two consecutive no-hitters. Lombardi was a feared hitter, but he was so slow that baseball historians John Thorn and Pete Palmer wrote, "He was the slowest of all of the Hall of Famers, including the exhibits."[16] He was an all-star eight times, won a second batting title, and batted .306 lifetime.

Lombardi suffered from depression and was put in a sanitarium after he attempted suicide following his playing days.

Induction

The 1986 Induction Ceremony was held on August 3 with 5,000 people in attendance. There were several light rain showers during the proceedings resulting in the inductees going on earlier in the ceremony. George Grande was back as MC and told an interesting anecdote about Jocko Conlan when introducing the 23 Hall of Famers who were there. Grande said, "We can thank Jocko Conlan for paper cups at the ballpark." The cups were introduced when fans at Ebbets Field started throwing beer bottles at him after they didn't like a call he made. He and concessionaire Harry Stevens got together and decided that beer would now be delivered in a paper cup.

The first inductee introduced was Bobby Doerr, 68. Commissioner Ueberroth mentioned his longtime rival with the Yankees, Tommy Henrich, who said, "Bobby Doerr is one of the very few men who have played the game and have no enemies."

During his speech, Doerr talked about his friend and teammate Ted Williams, who once made some suggestions on how he could improve his swing. Doerr wasn't comfortable doing it, which caused an exacerbated Williams to exclaim, "Okay you want to be a lousy .280 to .290 hitter, go ahead and hit that way." He closed by congratulating his fellow inductees and remembered a sign manager Sparky Anderson had over his office in the Detroit clubhouse that read, "Each 24 hours the world turns over and someone's sitting on top of it." Doerr continued, "I just hope I can sit up here on top just a little bit longer."

Doerr has come back more than 15 times since his own induction.

Commissioner Ueberroth then listed some of the accomplishments of the next inductee, Ernie Lombardi, which included two batting titles and an MVP award. Ueberroth stated these achievements were remarkable considering his legendary lack of speed. The commissioner continued, "Lombardi hit the ball so hard and with his lack of speed that the shortstop and the third baseman played well into the outfield grass when he came up to bat." The Schnozz joked about it at the time when he said, "It was four years before I found out that Pee Wee Reese was actually an infielder."[17]

Lombardi died in 1977 at the age of 69 so he was represented by his sister, Mrs. William Lenhardt. She spoke briefly and expressed her family's gratitude to the Veterans Committee as well as the sportswriters and the fans who supported him.

The final inductee was Willie McCovey, 48, who was praised by the commissioner for the time he spent in doing community work and visiting children in hospitals. He became a community relations specialist for the Giants, and beginning in 1980 the Giants started the Willie McCovey Award. This award is given annually to the San Francisco player who exhibits the spirit and leadership as exemplified by the award's namesake.

McCovey was very emotional during his speech and one time he broke down and took a minute before he was able to regain his composure. He began his speech by praising members of both his immediate family and then members of his baseball family. His baseball family included the scout who signed him, Alex Pompez, a former Negro Leagues entrepreneur who was inducted into Cooperstown in 2006. He talked about requesting the number 44 because that was his idol Henry Aaron's number. He showed his appreciation for the Giants' fans when he said, "The people of San Francisco have always welcomed me like the Golden Gate Bridge and cable cars, making me feel like a landmark, too." McCovey closed by thanking God and saying, "I have now become a player on the most distinguished team of all."

McCovey has come back more than 10 times since his induction. One problem he has is that he has to walk with canes because of his arthritic knees.

1987

The 1987 BBWAA election included 413 ballots that were cast and finishing first was sweet-swinging Cubs left fielder Billy Williams, who had 85.7 percent (354 votes). Williams was selected during his sixth year of eligibility. He received 1,373 votes in six BBWAA elections and just missed making it in 1986 by four votes with 74.1 percent of the vote. Soon after he got the good news, he said, "This is a crowning accomplishment like a scientist receiving a Nobel Prize, a writer a Pulitzer Prize, or an actor receiving an Oscar."[18]

Clutch pitcher Jim "Catfish" Hunter finished second with 76.3 percent (315 votes) in his third year of eligibility. Hunter had 816 votes in the three elections.

The final selection was made by the VC, and they picked the great-fielding third baseman of the Negro Leagues, Ray Dandridge. When hall president Ed Stack called to inform him of his selection, he didn't believe it and as it sank in, he grew quiet and began to cry.

Inductees

Billy Williams was the Rookie of the Year in 1961, when he hit 25 home runs and drove in 86 runs as the Cubs' left fielder. He was the *Sporting News* Player of the Year in 1972 when he led the league in batting (.333) and slugging average (.606) as he drove in 122 runs and hit 37 home runs. Williams played in 1,117 straight games that took a toll on him both mentally and physically. Finally Cubs manager Leo Durocher had him stay home so he couldn't use him. He was a six-time all-star and batted .290 lifetime.

Billy Williams' career almost didn't happen when he went AWOL from his minor league team at San Antonio because he was getting married and was homesick. Cubs coach Buck O'Neil visited him at his home and was able to convince him to come back.

Jim Hunter became "Catfish" after Kansas City A's owner Charlie Finley signed him and played up his country boy background. He pitched a perfect game in 1968, the year the A's moved to Oakland. He won 21 games or more five straight seasons and won the Cy Young Award in 1974, leading the league in victories (25) and ERA (2.49). He helped lead the A's to three straight world championships from 1972 through 1974. He then pitched for the Yankees and helped lead them to three straight pennants and two titles. Hunter was very consistent with an ERA of 3.25 in 10 LCS, 3.29 in 12 World Series games, and a lifetime ERA of 3.26. He retired with a record of 224–166 (.574).

Hunter became the first modern free agent in the major leagues after the 1974 season when Finley failed to pay a $50,000 insurance premium that was part of his contract. The reason he signed with the Yankees was because Clyde Kluttz, the same scout who signed him for the A's, was now a scout with the Bronx Bombers.

Ray Dandridge was a star third baseman in the Negro Leagues from 1933 through 1949. Although short and stocky, he was as good as Brooks Robinson in fielding his position, according to Monte Irvin, his teammate with the Newark Eagles. Teammates agreed, stating, "A train would have a better chance to go between his legs than a ground ball."[19] He was a part of the "million dollar infield" at Newark that included Hall of Famers Willie Wells and Mule Suttles. He once hit in 32 straight games in the Mexican League.

In 1950, he signed with the Giants Triple-A minor league team at Minneapolis. Dandridge was the first black player to be named Rookie of the Year and then MVP the following year in the American Association (AA). Ray never got the chance to play in the majors with the Giants, but he did help Willie Mays when he was at Minneapolis (AA).

Induction

The 1987 Induction Ceremony was held on July 26 on a day where the skies cleared after a morning rain and the temperature reached 85. There was a crowd of between four thousand and five thousand along with 28 Hall of Famers present.

Commissioner Ueberroth introduced the first inductee, Ray Dandridge, as "the greatest third baseman to never play in the major leagues." Ueberroth pointed out that Hall of Famer Roy Campanella said, "Dandridge was better than any third baseman I've ever seen." Inductee Dandridge, 78, began by saying, "This is probably the happiest day of my life." He went on to talk about his time at Minneapolis in the Giants' organization and his teammate, Willie Mays, and how when Mays got called up, he thought that he would also get the call, but it never happened. It should be noted Monte Irvin believes that possibly Giants owner Horace Stoneham was pressured to maintain a quota system in 1950, since they already had him, Hank Thompson, and later Willie Mays.[20] Dandridge closed with, "I want to thank each and every veteran on the committee for allowing me to smell the roses. I loved the game of baseball and today it looked like baseball loved me."

Dandridge came back the next two years before passing away in 1994 at the age of 80.

Ueberroth introduced the next inductee, Catfish Hunter, by announcing to the crowd, "Catfish earned the distinction of playing for both Charlie Finley and George Steinbrenner, which is enough in itself to put a player in the Hall of Fame."

Hunter, 41, the country boy from North Carolina, opened with an amusing story as he told about visiting some veterinarian friends just before he got to Cooperstown and spending some five hours working with them as they ministered to some farm animals. He then came to the Otesaga Hotel and said, "As I walked into the hotel, I smelt like a cow." The clerk at the desk questioned him, wanting to know who he was before sending him to his room.

He then told the story of how A's owner Charles Finley convinced him that since he liked to hunt and fish he had to have a nickname. So Finley concocted the story that Hunter ran away from home at the age of six and when his parents found him at a local pond, he was fishing and had just caught some catfish. Hunter thanked Finley for giving him the opportunity and also Steinbrenner for paying him enough money so that he could retire after five years with the Yankees. He closed with, "It's the greatest honor any guy could ever receive."

Hunter came back only twice, possibly because his wife, while attending the 1987 major league exhibition game at Doubleday Field, had one of the horses used for crowd control step on her foot and break it. He died of Lou Gehrig's disease in 1999 at the age of 53.

The commissioner introduced the last inductee, Billy Williams, 48, by pointing out that he had won the Rookie of the Year Award in 1961, and as a tribute to the first winner in 1947, the award would now be named after Jackie Robinson, forty years after his integration of Major League Baseball.

Billy Williams reflected on Robinson's legacy when he said that he might not be standing here today if it weren't for the courage of three men. He spoke naturally of Jackie but also of Dodgers executive Branch Rickey and former commissioner Happy Chandler. Williams praised both Rickey and Chandler for their joint decision to "bring Jackie Robinson to the major leagues." He personally thanked Chandler, who was at the induction. He also singled out Buck O'Neil for "counseling and guiding me from the minors to the majors." Williams then recalled his own difficulties with prejudice in 1959 when he was in the minors and wasn't allowed to eat at the lunch counter with the rest of the team in Corpus Christi, Texas. He also told of having to stay at a private home rather than the hotel with the rest of the team. He said, "These injustices weren't fixed by Major League Baseball, but by the government." He then reflected on the progress that still has to be made. He proclaimed, "We minorities have demonstrated over the past four decades our talent as players. Now we deserve the chance to demonstrate similar talents as coaches, managers, general managers, executives in the front office, and yes, as owners of major league clubs."

Williams spent many hours working on this speech with Stan Banash from a public relations firm in Chicago.[21]

His favorite Cooperstown memory was related to his induction. He remembered being picked up at the Albany Airport by a van with the Hall of Fame logo on it and then walking around the village with his family. He has been consistent in his attendance (just like when he was a player), having missed only four times since his own induction.

1988

A total of 427 ballots were cast in the 1988 BBWAA election and Pirates slugging outfielder Willie Stargell was the only player elected, receiving 82.4 percent (352 votes). He was the seventeenth player to be voted in during his first year of eligibility and easily the most controversial. Nine blank ballots were received, including two from the New York *Daily News* sportswriters, Phil Pepe and Bill Madden. Both felt that no one on the ballot was worthy of their vote for the Hall of Fame so they sent in blank ballots rather than not send in any ballot at all. This in itself was controversial because pitcher Jim Bunning finished second with 74.2 percent, and if the nine writers who sent in blank ballots had not sent in any ballot, then that would have meant nine fewer ballots giving Bunning the 75 percent needed for election.

Madden defended his move by saying, "To simply not return my ballot would be derelict in my duties as a voting member of the Baseball Writers Association."[22] Pepe was even more emphatic when he stated, "I felt the only way to dramatize my conviction was to return a blank ballot, thus making it necessary for an individual to get three votes to cancel my non-vote to meet the 75 percent qualification."[23]

The VC met in closed session to consider older major league players as well as managers, umpires, executives and Negro Leaguers, but selected no one.

Inductee

Willie Stargell began as a left fielder with the Pittsburgh Pirates and in 1965 had the first of five seasons where he drove in more than 100 runs. He led the league in home runs in 1971 (48) and 1973 (44). He switched to first base in 1975 and was the Comeback Player of the Year in 1978 before having a magical year in 1979. He tied with Keith Hernandez (Cardinals) as they became the first co-winners of the MVP award. He went on to be the MVP of the LCS when he batted .455 and won his third MVP of the season in the World Series, batting .400 and hitting the game-winning home run in the seventh game to beat the Orioles. He finished with 475 home runs and batted .282 lifetime.

At 39, Stargell was called "Pops," being the father figure of the team that won the title in 1979. He guided younger players as the team adopted the Sister Sledge disco hit, "We are Family." Pops also gave out gold stars to players for positive contributions.

Induction

The 1988 Induction Ceremony on July 31 began as a rainy, overcast, and humid day. It then became mainly a hot day for the ceremony. According to published reports, several thousand people came, including 20 Hall of Famers. Many fans came dressed in the black and yellow uniforms of the Pittsburgh Pirates in order to honor Stargell. The uniforms were complete with the embroidered stars similar to the ones Pops gave to teammates.

Willie Stargell, 47, began his speech humbly, by accepting the award on behalf of everyone associated with the Pirates' organization, and also paid special tribute to the city of Pittsburgh. He singled out a former teammate by saying, "He taught me the importance of being a man, to be able to command respect rather than demand it. I'm talking about a gentleman who has a special place in my heart and always will, Roberto Clemente." He then spoke of two former managers who brought titles to the Pirates. Danny Murtaugh "would sit back and tell Irish tales and chew his tobacco and then spit the juice on your shoes." Chuck Tanner "would stand right in front of you and smoke cigars." He then said, "Nevertheless, they were truly committed baseball men that helped me an awful lot." He closed by giving thanks to God and saying, "Baseball, I want to give something back to you because you've given me an awful lot."

Former director of research for the hall library, Bill Deane, said that Stargell added a nice touch to his Induction Weekend by giving gold stars to the Hall of Fame staff, just as he did to his teammates during the 1979 championship season.

He came back six more times before passing away in 2001 from a stroke at the age of 61.

1989

The 1989 BBWAA election had 447 ballots cast, and two players were elected in their first year of eligibility. Premier Reds catcher Johnny Bench finished first with 96.4 percent (431 votes), and the Red Sox outstanding left fielder Carl Yastrzemski finished second with 94.6 percent (423 votes).

The Veterans Committee chose longtime Cardinals second baseman, manager, and coach Red Schoendienst and veteran National League umpire Al Barlick.

Schoendienst was voted in by the VC six years after his BBWAA eligibility expired. He received 1,823 votes in 15 BBWAA elections. Barlick had been retired 18 years, and became the sixth umpire chosen by the VC for induction.

Three members of the Cooperstown Little League (*left to right:* Lucas Spencer, Dakin Campbell and Christian Connelly) carry the banner during the parade celebrating the 50th anniversary of the Hall of Fame on June 10, 1989.

Inductees

Johnny Bench became the first Rookie of the Year catcher in 1968, and then was the youngest MVP of the National League in 1970 at age 22, when he led the league in home runs (45) and RBIs (148). He was a repeat MVP in 1972, again leading the league in homers (40) and RBIs (125). Bench helped lead "The Big Red Machine" to the post season six times in ten years, including four World Series and two titles. He was the MVP of the 1976 Series and batted .357 in 12 All-Star Games. He retired with 10 straight Gold Gloves and 389 home runs.

Bench was the first to wear a batting helmet and use a hinged catching mitt when he was catching, which are standard equipment for catchers today. He had such a powerful arm he could catch one-handed and still pick off runners at first and throw out base stealers.

Carl Yastrzemski replaced legendary Ted Williams in left field for the Red Sox and came into his own with the first of three batting titles in 1963. He had a season for the ages in 1967 when he was the last player to win a Triple Crown. "Yaz" was also the MVP while leading the Sox to the pennant and then batted .400 in the World Series, with Boston losing to the Cards in seven games. Yaz hit .455 in the LCS in 1975 and .310 in the World Series as the Sox lost this time to Bench and the Reds in seven games. He retired in 1983 tying Brooks Robinson for playing the longest with one team (23 years) while playing the most games (3,308). He won seven Gold Gloves, had 452 homers, 3,419 hits, and batted .285.

The Red Sox' 1967 season was known as "The Impossible Dream" after they finished ninth in 1966. They were in a four-way pennant race right up until the last weekend of the season. Yaz carried his team, hitting .444 for his last 19 games and had 10 hits in his last 13 at-bats as Boston swept the Twins the last weekend to clinch the pennant.

Red Schoendienst was a sure-handed second baseman who handled 588 chances without an error during the 1949 and 1950 seasons. He helped lead the Cards to a World Series championship in 1946, and after being traded to the Milwaukee Braves he played in two World Series against the Yankees and won it all in 1957. He came down with TB after the 1958 World Series but recovered to play four more years. Red was a ten-time all-star and batted .289 lifetime. He managed the Cards to two pennants and one title in 1967.

He is another example of a player whose career almost ended before it got started. A staple flew in his left eye when he was a teenager and the doctors were able to save the eye, but he had double vision in the left eye, so he made himself into a switch-hitter.

Al Barlick was 25 when he made his 1940 debut as an umpire in the National League. His 28-year career was interrupted for two years in 1944 when he served in the Coast Guard during World War II. It was interrupted again for two years in 1956 when he suffered a heart attack. During his career, he umpired seven All-Star Games and seven World Series. He was known for his booming voice and flamboyant style on balls and strikes calls. Barlick took part in some memorable games. He was the first base ump when Jackie Robinson made his debut in 1947, and was also present when Willie Mays made his spectacular catch in the 1954 World Series.

Al Barlick led the union in their fight for better pay when the umpires refused to show up for the LCS in 1970. They returned for the next game after getting a four-year deal that increased their pay for the postseason.

The 50th anniversary of the National Baseball Hall of Fame and Museum was celebrated on June 10, 1989. Cooperstown had a huge parade in the morning and followed it up with the dedication of the new Fetzer-Yawkey wing. This was a $7 million project that added 18,000 square feet to the complex. This wing replaced the original Alfred Corning Clark Gymnasium that was adjacent to the museum building. John Fetzer, chairman of the board for the Detroit Tigers, and Jean Yawkey, chairwoman of the corporation that owned the Red Sox, were present to cut the ribbon, officially opening the new wing. Each owner made substantial contributions to make this addition possible.

The highlight of the new wing was a 200-seat movie theater where visitors would be entertained by a 13-minute multimedia presentation that utilized the latest state-of-the-art technology. The theater would also be used for seminars, guest lectures, etc. The new wing also contained considerable display and storage space as well as offices.

The final event of the day was the Equitable Old Timers Game and was played before 10,000 people at Doubleday Field. Retired players along with 10 Hall of Famers from the two leagues played each other. The Nationals beat the Americans 8–3. This same format was used again 20 years later when the Hall of Fame Classic was started in 2009 to replace the annual major league exhibition game.

Induction

The 1989 Induction Ceremony was held July 23 on a sun-drenched day with more than 20,000 people, making it the largest crowd ever for an induction ceremony. There were a record-tying 30 Hall of Famers present and red was the color of the day since the three players being inducted all played for teams with red uniforms. Each inductee was introduced by Bart Giamatti, the new commissioner. Unfortunately, this would be his only ceremony because he died of a heart attack the following September at the age of 51. The Hall of Fame Research Library is now named in honor of him.

He introduced the first inductee, Red Schoendienst, 66, who began by graciously recognizing the other inductees. He then told the audience how he hitchhiked a ride on a milk truck from his home in Germantown, Illinois, with two other buddies for a tryout with the Cards. "I never thought that truck ride would lead to Cooperstown and baseball's highest honor," he said. He then summarized his life story by making it analogous to a baseball infield. First base was growing up and playing baseball with his family in Germantown; and second base was his major league career and having some of the greatest players as teammates. They were close friend Stan Musial, Willie Mays, Hank Aaron, Warren Spahn, and Eddie Mathews. Third base was meeting his future wife on a streetcar 42 years ago. "She asked me for my autograph and two years later I signed her up." He closed with a favorite quotation from Albert Camus: "In the midst of winter, I finally learned that there was within me an invincible summer. Thank you, Veterans Committee," he added, "I'm humbly grateful."

During the weekend of his induction, members of his family wore red Little Orphan Annie wigs and red windbreakers with his number two on it around town and during the ceremony as well. He confessed later that he was more nervous about giving his speech than playing in a seventh game of a World Series, a sentiment we have seen shared by many of his fellow members.

His favorite Cooperstown memory was having his wife, children, and grandchildren with him for his induction. And, despite coming from a small town, he was also happy that two busloads and a full airplane of townspeople all came to his induction. He came back some 13 times, but he is now well into his eighties and hasn't been able to make it for the last several inductions.

Al Barlick, 74, spoke next and said, "I certainly never envisioned that one day I would have this honor that is being bestowed on me today." He closed with, "I hope my selection will serve as a motivation to all umpires of today and tomorrow to approach the game with the same degree of integrity, honesty, and sense of fair play that I hope will be attributed to me."

Baseball writer Mike Shannon witnessed the 1989 Induction and said, "Al Barlick delivered the most emotional speech of the day and had difficulty completing it."[24]

He had perfect attendance the next six years, then passed away in 1995 at the age of 80.

Johnny Bench, 41, was the next honoree and he began by saying, "It is a great privilege and honor to be with my idols." He told a delightful story about when his second-grade teacher asked her class what they wanted to be, he said, "I want to be a major league baseball player" and everyone laughed. He was asked the same question when he was in the eighth grade and he said the same thing and the class laughed again. He explained, "I was only 5' 2" and had size 11.5 feet so you might understand that Barnum and Bailey were the only people interested in scouting me." Finally, when the question was asked again in the eleventh grade, Bench said, "I had grown a full nine inches and now people didn't laugh quite so much."

After being introduced by their son Johnny during the 1989 Induction Ceremony, Ted and Katy Bench wave to "Ted's many fans."

Bench paid tribute to his former managers, including John McNamara, which elicited a number of boos from Red Sox fans, who remember him as Boston's manager when they lost the World Series to the Mets in 1986. Bench immediately responded, "Boo some other time, folks. This is a time for celebration." He concluded by quoting that famous catcher, Yogi Berra, "It's not over 'til it's over." Bench then thanked everyone.

Mike Shannon said later, "The confident Bench gave his speech extemporaneously."[25]

Bench has been a regular, returning many times, and is one Hall of Famer who really enjoys himself when he comes back. He has demonstrated this several times by putting on glasses and imitating the late broadcaster Harry Caray, when he sang "Take Me Out to the Ball Game." He has also shown his sense of humor during the inductions of Phil Rizzuto and Bruce Sutter, which will be mentioned later in the book.

His favorite Cooperstown memory was about his dad at his own induction. When Bench arrived at the Otesaga Hotel and came out of his room after putting away his suitcase, Enos Slaughter saw him in the hallway and said, "I just met your dad." At the elevator, and in the lobby, Pee Wee Reese and Ted Williams uttered the same refrain. Then he saw his father with his arm around Roy Campanella. During his speech, after he mentioned his father, he commented, "That's your cue, Dad." Bench went on, "I would be surprised if you all out there haven't met him yet. He has taken this town by storm."

The last inductee was Carl Yastrzemski, 49, and he began with a salute to Ted Williams. "I was a scared rookie hitting .220 after the first three months of the season and doubting my ability. Ted flew into Boston and worked with me for three days. He helped give me confidence that I could play in the big leagues." Yaz thanked Williams and said, "No man is an island. He must have a support system which without he cannot function."

He then gave a profound tribute to his dad. His father had the talent to have been a major leaguer, but lived in the time of the Depression and had to suppress his own desires to help his family survive. Yastrzemski then posed a question that he is often asked, "How do you stand up to the rigors of big league baseball and the pressure-packed situations?" He always answers, "Pressure, what pressure? Pressure is what faces millions and millions of fathers and mothers trying to earn a living every day to support a family, to give it comfort, devotion and love. That's what pressure is and that's what my mother and father gave me," as he introduced his father. (His mother had passed away.)

He then paid tribute to the late owner Tom Yawkey and his wife, Jean, who was there and had helped to dedicate the new Hall of Fame wing a month before. He closed with, "I'm so proud today to have played a role, however small, in a game which is America's pastime and a game which is a big part of my life."

He has returned only two times, including 2009, when Jim Rice, the man who followed him in left field for the Red Sox, was being inducted.

CHAPTER 9

50,000 People Come to See *"The Ryan Express," "Baby Bull," George and Robin Too: 1990–1999*

1990

The BBWAA cast 444 ballots in 1990 and elected two players, outstanding Orioles pitcher Jim Palmer and two-time National League MVP and second baseman Joe Morgan. Both were elected in their first year of eligibility with Palmer finishing first with 92.6 percent (411 votes), followed by Morgan with 81.8 percent (363 votes).

The Veterans Committee selected no one.

Inductees

Jim Palmer won 15 games for the Orioles in 1966 and then pitched a shutout at the age of 20 to help to defeat the Dodgers in the World Series. He overcame arm problems in 1967 and 1968 with successful surgery and went on to win 20 or more games eight times along with three Cy Young Awards. He also pitched a no-hitter and won four Gold Gloves. Palmer was 4–1 in six LCS and 4–2 in six World Series that included three titles. He pitched in five All-Star Games and finished with a record of 268–152 (.638).

Palmer had a love-hate relationship with manager Earl Weaver. Weaver complained about all the time Palmer missed because of injuries while Palmer retaliated, "The only thing Weaver knew about pitching is that he couldn't hit it." (Weaver was a career minor leaguer).[1] Despite their constant feuding, they did respect each other.

Joe Morgan became the Houston Astros' full-time second baseman in 1965, and worked hard to become a good defensive second baseman after leading the league in errors his rookie year. He went on to become a Gold Glover five straight times (1973 through 1977), and in 1977 he committed only five errors in 151 games. Morgan retired with the most putouts, assists, and total chances by a second baseman in National League history, and a final fielding percentage of .981. Offensively, he retired with 268 home runs and 689 stolen bases. He became the only second baseman to win back-to-back MVP Awards (1975 and 1976), leading the Cincinnati Reds' "Big Red Machine" to two world titles. Morgan was chosen for 10 all-star teams, batted .271 lifetime, and had an on base percentage of .392.

Future Hall of Fame second baseman Nellie Fox taught Morgan never to "take an error to the plate or a strikeout to the field" when they were teammates with Houston.[2]

Induction

The 1990 Induction Ceremony was scheduled for Cooper Park just like all the previous ones since 1966. The August 6 ceremony was cancelled at the last minute after the rains came down just as the event was about to begin. It was rescheduled for the next day with a backup plan in case it rained again. Sure enough, Monday's event was rained out and the backup plan was put in place. The event was moved to the Cooperstown High School auditorium, which held fewer than 1,000 people. This meant after invited guests and the print media were given their reserved seats, it left only a small number of seats for the fans, who had now waited two days to honor Palmer and Morgan. The hall worked it out so some fans were directed to the school cafeteria where they could watch by closed-circuit television. Those who were outside heard it over an audio system that was set up.

Hall chairman Ed Stack told the audience that due to the postponement, some 12 Hall of Famers left because of prior commitments, leaving 22 who were there for the ceremony.

Stack announced that Peggy and Frank Steele and Dick Perez of the Perez Steele Galleries would be making a contribution of $100,000 to create an endowment that would help to establish an internship program.

Stack then turned the program over to the new commissioner, Fay Vincent, who introduced the first inductee, Joe Morgan, 46. He began by telling the audience that due to the change in schedule he was able to get his ring and meet with many of the Hall of Famers at the Sunday Dinner, including one of his heroes, Ted Williams.

He spoke about the "Big Red Machine" in Cincinnati, where he learned all about winning from his Reds teammates. He credited manager Sparky Anderson as the "driving force" behind the success of those teams. Later in his speech he gave credit to Nellie Fox and Jackie Robinson for being role models for him as second basemen and "wished they could be here today." He was thankful that he was able to stay close to the game as an ESPN broadcaster. Morgan closed by paying tribute to the fans that were outside in the rain and expressed his gratitude to them for coming.

Morgan has returned often and is vice chairman of the board of directors.

Jim Palmer, 44, began by paying homage to his fellow inductee and also the fans "who were still out there on Sunday despite the five to six hours of rain."

He thanked his parents, who adopted him at birth. He paid tribute to former Orioles' owner Edward Bennett Williams, the famous trial lawyer, who compared trials to baseball stating, "It's all about winning. You have to be ready from a spiritual, intellectual, physical, and emotional level in order to succeed." Palmer thanked pitching coach George Bamberger for changing his windup, and orthopedic surgeon Dr. Robert Kerlan for saving his career when he had shoulder problems.

He then spoke about manager Earl Weaver and their differences. "I was 6' 4" and he was 5'6"." Every time he wanted to take me out, he would try and come to the highest point on the mound, and I wouldn't let him. But I learned a lot from Earl Weaver. One of the reasons I'm in the Hall of Fame," Palmer continued, "is that Earl had confidence in me. Any Oriole who played for Earl Weaver always went to spring training knowing that they would be on a contending club with a chance to win. I hope someday that he will be considered for the Hall of Fame because he certainly deserves it."

He closed by mentioning how everyone contributed to Baltimore's success, including a little-used sub named Lenny Sakata, who hit a three-run home run to help the Orioles win an important game on their way to the title in 1983.

Palmer has returned some 14 times since his induction.

1991

The 1991 BBWAA election had 443 ballots cast with three players achieving the 75 percent needed for immortality. Finishing with the most votes in his first year of eligibility was the magnificent hitter Rod Carew with 90.5 percent (401 votes).

Second was the successful and durable pitcher Gaylord Perry with 77.2 percent (342 votes). He was elected in his third year of eligibility and received a total of 966 votes. Despite being a 300-game winner, undoubtedly a number of electors didn't vote for him because of the constant accusations throughout his career that he threw the illegal spitter.

The third and final selection was the fine control pitcher Fergie Jenkins, who received 75.4 percent (334 votes—made it by one vote) in his third year of eligibility. Jenkins received 864 votes in three elections. His albatross, despite good statistical credentials, was an arrest for drug possession at the Toronto airport in 1980. The charge was thrown out but not before Commissioner Bowie Kuhn suspended him for 20 games and fined him $10,000. Later, Jenkins admitted occasional drug use and apologized for doing it.

Before the 1991 VC meeting, the Hall of Fame's Board of Directors passed a controversial new rule. A player who started his career in 1946, or after, in order to be considered by the VC in the future, had to have received at least 60 percent of the vote in at least one BBWAA election. According to James Vail, if this had been in effect with the VC, or one of its predecessors, only seven players who were chosen by the VC up through the year 2000 would have been eligible (p. 133). One reason it was done was to appease the writers. Many of the VC selections had minimal support when the players were eligible during the BBWAA elections as we have seen.

Several years prior to this rule, the VC had been limited to considering only those post–1945 players who had received 100 or more votes in any BBWAA election. When this new rule was enacted, all of the men who met the earlier requirement were grandfathered into the VC eligible group.

The Veterans Committee selected Yankees second baseman Tony Lazzeri. He received 455 votes during 14 BBWAA elections. Despite being a main cog in five Yankees championships, he was very quiet and didn't do interviews during his career. This apparently didn't help him with the BBWAA or the VC, because it took 52 years after he retired to finally be elected.

The final VC selection was maverick owner Bill Veeck. He was chosen 11 years after he had last owned a team and five years following his death.

Inductees

Rod Carew was the Rookie of the Year for the Minnesota Twins in 1967 and went on to lead the American League in batting seven times. Carew's best season was 1977 when he won the MVP by batting .388 while also leading the league in hits, triples, and runs. He was an excellent bunter and base stealer. One season he beat out 15 bunts for hits and stole home seven times another season. He started out as a second baseman, but had a weak arm, so he was moved to first base in 1976. He finished with the California Angels where he went to two LCS after going to two with the Twins. He was chosen for 18 all-star teams and retired with 3,053 hits, an OBP of .393, and batted .328 lifetime.

Noted sports columnist Jim Murray described Rod Carew in the following way: "Watching him hit is like watching Bulova make a watch or DeBeers cut a diamond. Rod Carew doesn't make hits, he composes them."[3]

Gaylord Perry began pitching for the San Francisco Giants in 1962. His older brother, Jim, also pitched in the majors and won 215 games. Gaylord won more than 20 games twice and pitched a no-hitter for the Giants. He was traded in 1972 to the Cleveland Indians, where he won his first Cy Young Award. He then became the only pitcher to win the award in both leagues when he did it again with the San Diego Padres in 1978. Perry finished his career as a five-time 20-game winner, a five-time all-star, and with a record of 314–265.

He wrote a book in 1974 in which he admitted using the illegal spitter that he had been accused of throwing most of his career. He confessed to using it on rare occasions but gained a psychological advantage due to his reputation. Dave Duncan caught him in Cleveland and said that he used the pitch only four times in two years.

Ferguson "Fergie" Jenkins went on to have 20 or more wins six straight seasons with the Cubs and won the Cy Young Award in 1971 when he led the league in wins (24), innings (325), and complete games (30). Jenkins was traded to the Texas Rangers in 1974 after he went 14–16 for the Cubs in 1973. He rebounded as he went 25–12 for his seventh 20-win season and was the American League's Comeback Player of the Year. Jenkins was a good fielding pitcher who rarely committed an error. He was also a premier control pitcher, striking out 3,192 while walking only 997. He finished with a record of 284–226.

Jenkins suffered several tragedies in his life. His mother was blind and died of cancer at 52. His second wife died in an auto accident, and later his fiancée committed suicide, but he overcame these personal losses with a positive outlook on life. He established his own foundation in 2000 which supports many charitable events in both Canada and the U.S.

Tony Lazzeri was a Yankees rookie second baseman who helped lead them to a pennant in 1926. He had 114 RBIs, the first of seven times he had more than 100 RBIs. He set a league record in 1936 when he drove in 11 runs in a game. He was called "Poosh 'em up Tony" by the Yankees' faithful, an accolade to his Italian heritage. Lazzeri was the anchor of the Yankees' infield that won five titles during his 12 years with them. He finished with 178 home runs while batting .292.

Lazzeri once hit a grand slam and also batted .400 in a World Series, yet he is most remembered for striking out with the bases loaded in the seventh inning of the seventh game of the 1926 Series against Grover Alexander. The Cardinals went on to win, yet most people forget the series ended as Babe Ruth was thrown out trying to steal second.

Bill Veeck lost a leg during World War II and was part of a syndicate that bought the Cleveland Indians in 1946. He signed the American League's first black player, Larry Doby, and then the oldest rookie, Negro League star Satchel Paige. His greatest moment came in 1948 when the Indians won the World Series. They also set an attendance record that stood for three decades. He bought the St. Louis Browns in 1951, then sold them in 1953. He became a majority owner of the Chicago White Sox in 1959, when they made it to their first World Series in 40 years. He sold them and then bought the Sox again before selling them for good in 1981.

Bill Veeck did many things to make baseball fun for the fan, but his most infamous stunt was putting a 3'7" midget into a game as a pinch-hitter with the Browns. He walked and then was taken out for a pinch-runner. American League president Will Harridge was outraged. He banned midgets and condemned Veeck for making a travesty of the game.

Induction

The 1991 Induction Ceremony had more than 5,000 people in attendance in sweltering 90-degree weather. There were 34 Hall of Famers present, matching last year's total before rain knocked out the first day. A canopy was used for the first time in order to keep them dry if it rained.

Hall chairman Ed Stack talked about the next expansion that would take place in the fall with the library building being enlarged to become a media center. The library would also be linked with the main building and the plaque gallery. The plaque gallery would be expanded to accommodate approximately 175 more plaques. The cost of this expansion would be an estimated $8.5 million.

Bill Veeck and Fergie Jenkins weren't the only 1991 inductees struck by tragedy. Misfortune also struck the other three inductees as you will see.

The inductees were called up in alphabetical order with Rod Carew, 45, being the first to receive his plaque. There was a large contingent of Panamanians who came to honor their countryman. Rod was touched when they played his country's national anthem before he received his plaque. He talked about growing up in Panama and coming to the United States to play baseball. It should be noted that he was given the first name of the American doctor who delivered him while his mother was on a train heading to the hospital. Carew spoke of several people from his past, including his former manager with the Minnesota Twins, Billy Martin. He thanked him "for taking a young kid and turning him into a man," and as a loud noise interrupted his talk, Carew continued, "I know that clap of thunder was Billy's message of saying he approves of what is happening today." He was very close to Martin, who served as a godfather to his second daughter. He acknowledged several other people, including the other honorees, and said in conclusion, "I'm in awe of being recognized alongside Ruth, Cobb, and Jackie Robinson, but the Hall of Fame is more. It's all the kids who ever played the game and all the fans who ever bought a ticket. It's the Say Hey Kid, The Duke, The Hammer, Big Train, Joe D, Teddy Ballgame, and many more." Carew continued, "Thanks to all of you for moving over and making a space for me in your shrine."

He didn't come back for ten years, but he has come for the last nine inductions. One reason he didn't come back was his youngest daughter died of leukemia in 1996.

The next honoree was Fergie Jenkins, 48, the first Hall of Famer from Canada, so it was very appropriate that as he strode to the podium, the high school band from his hometown of Chatham, Ontario, played "Canadian Sunset." He was very emotional in his speech as he talked about his late mother, who despite her blindness knew that baseball was the sport he should play. Jenkins was also a hockey player and was good enough in basketball to have played one season with the Harlem Globetrotters, a distinction he shares with another Hall of Famer, Bob Gibson. He acknowledged his father, who was there, as a former player in the Canadian Negro Leagues. Jenkins said, "His sacrifices have been rewarded by my achievements. So, I'm not being inducted alone on July 21, 1991, but with my father, Fergie Jenkins, Sr." He closed with, "It is with deepest humility that I accept this prestigious award. I will cherish it forever."

His favorite Cooperstown memory, like many others, is his own induction, but he is probably an exception to many other Hall of Famers in his honesty when he states that he "likes coming back to hear the other induction speeches." He has only missed two inductions since his own.

I have interviewed and spent time with Fergie Jenkins on several occasions during the induction weekends and I've found him to be very pleasant. He is forthright and informative, which will be discussed in the Afterword.

Tony Lazzeri died in 1946 of a heart attack at the age of 42. Fred Glueckstein authored an article that clarified his death. Lazzeri, who suffered from epilepsy, had fallen down and broken his neck after an epileptic attack. However, he died from a heart attack and not the broken neck.[4]

He was represented by his widow, Maye, at the ceremony. She spoke briefly and said, "I think this is the proudest moment in my life." She was there with her son and his wife and closed by praising the beautiful Cooperstown area and saying, "Everyone in the world should see it."

Gaylord Perry, 52, was next, and he also had been touched by tragedy. His wife had been killed in a car accident in 1987. Nevertheless, as he approached the podium to accept his plaque he showed his joy by pumping his fist several times. It should be noted that the spitball issue is addressed on his plaque, which contains the following phrase, "Playing mind games with hitters through array of rituals on mound was part of his arsenal." He made the audience laugh right after Commissioner Fay Vincent introduced him by saying, "It's about time to rain, isn't it?" He then spoke about his career and the Hall of Famers he played with on the San Francisco Giants, including Willie McCovey, Juan Marichal and "then the guy I learned more on how to play the game of baseball, how to pitch hitters, the greatest player that I ever saw, Willie Mays." He talked about the spitball issue and evoked laughter again from the audience when he said, "I really got to know the umpires by their first names. We seem to have a lot of business up there on the mound." It should be mentioned that, despite being the subject of many inspections by umpires over the years, he was thrown out of only one game during his career. He closed with, "I want to say a special thanks to everyone who made this possible."

Perry confessed in his book, *Me and the Spitter,* that he doctored the ball with a variety of substances including saliva, slippery elm, K-Y Jelly, baby oil and Vaseline. Although he rarely threw it, he would go through a herky-jerky pitching ritual where he would touch the back of his hair, the bill of his cap, belt buckle, shin, and sleeve before throwing a pitch. Gene Mauch, one of the opposing managers that he frustrated, said, "He should be in the Hall of Fame with a tube of K-Y Jelly attached to his plaque."[5]

Perry's favorite Cooperstown memory is his own induction, of which he says, "Over the years I look back on that day as one of the best days of my life. It's an honor and a privilege that I don't take lightly." He has missed just two inductions since 1991.

The last inductee was Bill Veeck, who died in 1986 at the age of 71. Accepting for him was his widow, Mary Frances, who began by thanking the 14 members of the Veterans Committee. She recalled how her husband was born into baseball and how he, more than any other owner, "had a better education from the ground up regarding running a baseball club." She described her husband as "curious, stubborn, creative, and obstinate, who had a great joy of living, and was fun to be around." She shared with the audience her husband's twelve commandments. Some of the more significant ones were, "Never, ever take yourself seriously. When hiring, be color blind, gender-blind, age- and experience-blind. You never worked for Bill Veeck, you worked with him. Answer all your mail, you might learn something. Also, be available to your fans, again you might learn something." She closed with, "Nobody understood better the importance of games and fun better than Bill Veeck."

Hall president Ed Stack recognized Hall of Fame second baseman Charlie Gehringer, who was retiring from the board of directors, and had also retired from the Veterans Committee the year before, after serving on it since 1953. He had also attended more inductions than any other Hall of Famer up until that time, and would attend his thirty-first and last in 1992, before passing away in 1993 at the age of 89.

1992

The 1992 BBWAA election had 430 ballots cast and finishing first was 300-game winner Tom Seaver. He finished first with 98.8 percent (425 votes) in his first year of eligibility. This was the highest percentage ever recorded in a BBWAA election, breaking Ty Cobb's old record of 98.2 percent set in 1936.

Finishing second was reliever Rollie Fingers, who had 81.2 percent (349 votes). This was his second year of eligibility and he also became the second reliever to be inducted into the Hall of Fame. He received a total of 640 votes in the two elections.

The VC selected the 1940s Detroit pitching ace Hal Newhouser. He received 846 votes in 12 BBWAA elections. He was chosen 37 years after he retired.

American League umpire Bill McGowan was selected by the VC as the seventh umpire. He was chosen 38 years after he retired and also 38 years after his death.

Inductees

Tom Seaver was the National League's Rookie of the Year in 1967 and helped turn around the Mets' losing ways in 1969 when he won the first of three Cy Young Awards. Seaver became "Tom Terrific" by going 25–7 as he led the "Miracle Mets" to the title. He won two more Cy Young Awards before a falling out with Mets general manager M. Donald Grant got him traded to Cincinnati in 1977. Highlights of his career include a 19-strikeout game, a no-hitter, 12 All-Star Games, and a 311–205 career record (.603).

Mets fans were outraged after his trade to the Reds, causing the venerable Red Smith to write, "Tom Seaver is his own man and unafraid to speak his mind. Grant traded him because he considered him a troublemaker. He mistakes dignity for arrogance."[6]

Rollie Fingers was a starter-reliever for the Oakland A's until manager Dick Williams made him a relief ace in 1971. He helped lead the A's to five straight postseasons and three straight world titles (1972 through 1974.) He was the MVP of the 1974 series when he won the first game with $4\frac{1}{3}$ innings of relief and then had two saves. He led the league in saves two years in a row with the San Diego Padres. Fingers was traded to the Milwaukee Brewers in 1981 and had his best year in the strike-shortened season. He won both the MVP and Cy Young Awards and led the league in saves (28) and had an ERA of 1.04. An arm injury caused him to miss the 1982 World Series and all of 1983. Fingers was a seven-time all-star and was the all-time saves leader (341) when he retired.

His trademark is his handlebar moustache. He grew it after A's owner Charlie Finley offered any player $300 to grow one.

Hal Newhouser was a nondescript 34–52 for the Tigers during the first five years of his career. He was able to turn it around in 1944 and 1945 when he had a combined record of 54–18 and became the only pitcher to win back-to-back MVPs. He was now "Prince Hal" because of his dominance, and he helped the Tigers defeat the Cubs in the 1945 World Series by winning two games. He silenced his critics that said he did well those two years because rosters were depleted during World War II when he led the league again in wins in 1946 and 1948 after everyone had returned. Hal was a relief pitcher for the 1954 Cleveland Indians pennant winners. He finished at 207–150 (.580) and with an ERA of 3.06.

A major reason for his turnaround was the Tigers' new catcher in 1943, Paul Richards. Richards was a master handler of pitchers. He taught Newhouser to calm down on the mound and showed him how to throw a slider to complement his fastball and curve.

Bill McGowan made his American League umpiring debut in 1925. He was colorful and one of the best at calling balls and strikes. He was chosen the top umpire in the league by a *Sporting News* poll in 1935, and from then on he was referred to as "Number One." He rarely threw people out but he had a temper and was twice suspended by the league. "Number One" started the second umpiring school in Florida, which went on to produce many major league umpires. He had a 30-year career, which included working the first All-Star Game and eight World Series. His proudest moment was being the crew chief for the first American League playoff game in 1948. McGowan worked the plate for the one-game playoff between the Indians and the Red Sox that decided the pennant.

Despite diabetes and heart problems, McGowan worked every inning of every game for sixteen and a half years, or 2,541 straight games. The "Cal Ripken of umpires" even has on his Hall of Fame plaque, "the most durable umpire in history."

Induction

The 1992 Induction Ceremony was held on August 2 on a warm day with more than 5,000 people, including a record 36 Hall of Famers. The ceremony was held for the first time at the new athletic facility, the Alfred Clark Gymnasium. This facility had replaced the original gym next to the museum that was now used for offices. It was opened to the whole community and was situated about a mile from the Hall of Fame complex on Susquehanna Avenue. The gym had an enormous field in back of the building, which would be able to accommodate many more people than Cooper Park, the site of the ceremony since 1966. Shuttle busses were now added to transport people from Doubleday Field to the gym. MC George Grande made reference to the new gym in his introductory remarks when he said, "We've got the cornfield, and we've got our own field of dreams today."

The first inductee to speak was Rollie Fingers, 45, who began his speech with humor as he said, "I'm a little nervous now because I'm not used to starting things." He continued, "As I look at this plaque with my likeness and the handlebar moustache, I know a hundred years from now there will be a ten-year-old boy who will go up to his dad and say, 'Hey Dad, they messed up on this. Shouldn't this say 1892 and not 1992?'"

He then got serious as he told a story about his father, who had passed away. At the age of eight, Fingers was careless with matches and started a fire in his bedroom that the fire department put out. When his father got home, he didn't spank him or get angry, but instead took him to the local sheriff's station. His father and the sheriff (a friend of the family) took him to a cell and put him in it and left him there. Finally after three hours ("and it seemed like three years," Fingers said) his father got him. Fingers said he never played with matches again and gained a lot of respect for his dad in how he handled the situation. Then he said, "It's kind of ironic that for seventeen years in the big leagues my job was putting out fires and not starting them." The rest of his speech was one of magnanimous gratitude as he thanked the respected Chicago sportswriter Jerry Holtzman for creating the save statistic, and also his former manager with the Oakland A's, Dick Williams, for salvaging his career and making him his ace reliever. He then paid tribute by naming nine former relief pitchers and seven contemporary relief pitchers, saying, "Each and every one of these pitchers had as much to do with the success and recognition of relief pitching as I did. It's just that I happen to be in the right place at the right time, and on the right ball club." He saluted his fellow inductees and closed graciously as he said, "I'd like to say to every relief pitcher before me, every guy who had to sit in a bullpen and wait for a phone call, and every guy who had to walk into a pressure situation, you all own a piece of this."

His two favorite Cooperstown memories are different from most because neither has to do with his own induction. The first was when he came to Cooperstown in 1965 to accept the American Legion Player of the Year Award at the age of 18. The second was when he rented a boat in 1996 and asked his fiancée to marry him while they were in the middle of Lake Otsego. He then said, "She had to say yes or I'd throw her overboard."

Fingers has had perfect attendance since his own induction.

Next up was umpire Bill McGowan, who died of heart problems in 1954, months after he retired from umpiring, at the age of 58. During the funeral in Silver Spring, Maryland, the four pallbearers were all major league umpires and graduates of his umpiring school.

Representing him at the induction was his son, Bill Jr. He spoke briefly, telling the audience that he was very proud of "Old Number One" for receiving this honor. He thanked everyone who was responsible, especially Ted Williams, who was a member of the VC in 1992 and worked very hard to get his father into the Hall of Fame.

Hal Newhouser, 71, was the next inductee and he began by honoring his 95-year-old mother who was there. He paid tribute to the city of Detroit, where he was born and raised and where he pitched most of his career. He thanked the school system "for teaching me the tool and die trade just in case I didn't make it in baseball." He then paid tribute to his catcher when he said, "If it wasn't for Paul Richards I doubt very much that I would be standing up here today." Prince Hal thanked the fans for their support that helped him make the Hall of Fame and the VC for looking at his record and saying, "Well this is Hal Newhouser's year." He thanked the Houston Astros organization for giving him a job as a scout for the state of Michigan. He closed with, "Everything that I have has been because of baseball, and may I say, baseball, I thank you."

It should be noted that Newhouser quit as an Astros scout right after they didn't take his advice and draft a shortstop from Michigan with the overall first pick in the 1992 Amateur Draft. They drafted Phil Nevin instead, and passed on Derek Jeter.

He came back for the next five years before passing away in 1998 at the age of 77.

Tom Seaver, 47, was the last to speak and he began with, "For me it's the last beautiful flower in the perfect bouquet because the twenty years that I had as a professional athlete and that twenty-year period before my professional career began all came together for me in this induction into the Hall of Fame." He then paid tribute to his good friends from the Mets, Bud Harrelson and Jerry Koosman, along with each pitching coach he had with the Mets, Reds, and White Sox. He gave credit for his 311 victories to his catchers, Jerry Grote with the Mets, Johnny Bench with the Reds, and Carlton Fisk with the White Sox. He closed with special praise for two people who had passed on, his mother and his manager with the 1969 Mets, Gil Hodges, the most important man in his professional life.

Seaver has never missed an induction and is a member of the Hall of Fame's Board of Directors. One reason he enjoys coming back is that he brings a special wine from his own vineyard in California to the special dinner that is held just for the Hall of Famers. Fellow pitchers Bob Gibson, Steve Carlton, Don Sutton, and Sandy Koufax share a table with Seaver in the Otesaga Ballroom the Sunday night following the Induction Ceremony. Recently, they have allowed catcher Carlton Fisk to join the select group as each of them brings a bottle of vintage wine that is sampled and shared.

1993

The 1993 BBWAA election had 423 ballots cast, and the only player to qualify was the slugging outfielder Reggie Jackson. He received 93.6 percent (396 votes) in his first year of eligibility.

No one was selected by the VC.

Inductee

Reggie Jackson helped lead the Oakland A's to three world titles from 1972 through 1974. He was the league's MVP in 1973 and then the MVP of the World Series. He was traded to the Orioles in 1976 where he played one year before becoming a free agent and signing with the Yankees. This was the beginning of a tumultuous but successful five seasons with them. He had issues with manager Billy Martin and captain Thurmond Munson but redeemed himself by hitting five home runs in the 1977 World Series victory over the Dodgers. He played in two more World Series with the Yankees before signing with the California Angels. He was a 14-time all-star, hit 563 home runs, and batted .262.

Jackson batted .357 with ten home runs in five World Series. He became "Mr. October" in 1977 when he hit four home runs in four at bats including three in Game Six.

Induction

The 1993 Induction Ceremony was again held at the Clark Gymnasium site on a pleasant day with the temperature in the low 80s. A record 38 Hall of Famers came along with an estimated crowd of between 15 and 20,000. Howard Talbot, the former director, was honored for his 43 years of service to the Hall of Fame by Chairman Ed Stack.

Jackson began by asking everyone in the audience to "stand up and relax" after they had been chanting "Reggie" for several minutes prior to his appearance at the podium. He paid homage to his father, a role model, who always corrected his speech so that he would use good English and not slur his words. Most importantly, his father especially stressed the importance of an education.

Jackson admitted to his controversial nature as a player and his tendency to be the center of attention. He mentioned teammate Mickey Rivers, an unforgettable character in his own right, who summed him up one day. "You know, Reggie, you got a white man's first name in Reginald, a Spanish middle name in Martinez, and a black man's last name." Rivers continued, "No wonder you're so fouled up."

Jackson then paid tribute to Jackie Robinson and Larry Doby for "being the trailblazers for all the black players who followed them." He praised Muhammad Ali and Martin Luther King, Jr., for having a positive influence on his life. Jackson spoke of the influence that several Hall of Famers unwittingly had on him. He spoke of former teammates, managers and owners and had kind words for his two Yankees adversaries, the late manager Billy Martin and the late catcher Thurman Munson. He acknowledged his best friend in baseball, reserve catcher turned broadcaster Fran Healy, who was there. Jackson went on to mention many people in baseball who were part of his experience, and called himself, "a small link in the chain of the wheel of baseball from the past greats to the modern stars that help keep baseball moving along for the benefit of the fans." He acknowledged Lou Gehrig with his closing words, "Today I consider myself the luckiest man on the face of the Earth."

During the 1993 Induction Weekend, Jackson showed his flair for the dramatic. He interrupted his golf game by hopping over a stone wall at the Farmers Museum to take part in a nineteenth-century town ball game that was being played by some local men. He proceeded to hit a 400-foot blast into the trees in his only at-bat. Later, he autographed the ball for the players and inscribed a note on a program for a wheelchair-bound fan who was watching the game. A participant wrote about the game, calling it "Mr. July."[7]

He has returned for most of the inductions since his own in 1993.

1994

The 1994 BBWAA election had 456 ballots cast and the outstanding left-handed pitcher Steve Carlton received 95.6 percent (436 votes). This was his first year of eligibility and the only question was would writers not vote for him because he spent most of his career not speaking to them. It appears only 20 writers felt that way.

The VC selected Yankees shortstop Phil Rizzuto. He received 1,128 votes in 13 BBWAA elections, which shows pretty good support. Although he was considered a better choice then some previous inductees, his selection still stirred a lot of controversy. Bill James thinks the main reason he is in is because he was a part of all those championship teams (p. 362). James Vail compares seven shortstops from the 1940s and feels many older fans would have said that Vern Stephens, Marty Marion, and Johnny Pesky were more deserving (p. 9). Robert Cohen felt that Rizzuto was funny, entertaining and unpretentious as a Yankees announcer, but looking at it objectively definitely feels he shouldn't be in the Hall of Fame (pp. 96–97). He also feels that Vern Stephens is more deserving of the honor than Rizzuto (pp. 99–100).

The things that helped Rizzuto were that he was in the public eye as a Yankees announcer and was a likable individual. He had the support of the New York newspapers as evidenced by a New York *Daily News* poll that produced more than 18,000 votes supporting him for the Hall of Fame. Also, influential baseball columnists such as Bill Madden, Leonard Koppett, Dave Anderson, and Dick Young all supported him for induction. Finally, the VC included close friend, teammate, and Hall of Famer Yogi Berra, fellow Yankees announcer and former National League president Bill White, and rival Dodgers shortstop and Hall of Famer Pee Wee Reese when Rizzuto was selected.

The final selection in 1994 by the VC was feisty manager Leo Durocher, who had been upset that he never received the honor when he was alive. Durocher received 57 votes in seven BBWAA elections.

Inductees

Steve Carlton helped the Cards win pennants in 1967 and 1968, including the title in 1967. "Lefty" had his first of six seasons with 20 or more wins in 1971 before being traded to the Phillies in 1972, where he was reunited with catcher Tim McCarver. There he became dominant, winning his first Cy Young Award unanimously in 1972. He also won pitching's Triple Crown, including 27 wins for a last-place team. The Phillies got better as he helped lead them to two World Series, including the one in 1980 when they won their first title with Carlton winning two games. He also was 4–2 in five LCS as he won three more Cy Young Awards. Carlton led the league in strikeouts five times, was named to 10 all-star teams, and finished 329–244 lifetime (.574).

He helped to revolutionize how players work out by becoming one of the first players to emphasize year-round conditioning. He also meditated with Eastern philosophy.

Phil Rizzuto was given the nickname "Scooter" because of the ground he covered. He became the Yankees' shortstop in 1941 and batted .307. He was an excellent bunter and was the league's MVP in 1950 when he had 200 hits and batted .324. He was very good defensively, with teammate Vic Raschi, summing it up best. "My best pitch," Raschi said, "is anything that the batter hits in the direction of Rizzuto."[8] He was a five-time all-star, played on nine pennant winners and seven world championship teams.

Rizzuto overcame a lot, beginning with the fact that he was only 5' 6" and had been turned away during a Dodgers tryout as "too small." He almost lost a leg to gangrene after an injury in the minors, overcame malaria that he contracted during World War II, and was beaned in 1946, causing dizzy spells the rest of his career.

Leo Durocher, as a shortstop, was part of the 1928 world champion Yankees and the 1934 Cardinals. He began managing in Brooklyn and led the Dodgers to the 1941 pennant. Always controversial, he was suspended in 1947 for one year by Commissioner Chandler for "conduct detrimental to baseball," due to his association with gamblers. He left the Dodgers in 1948 to go to the hated cross-town rivals, the New York Giants, and enjoyed his most success as he defeated the Dodgers for the pennant in a three-game playoff in 1951. The Giants repeated in 1954 and swept the favored Cleveland Indians in the World Series. He also managed the Cubs and Houston and compiled a record of 2,008–1,710.

Durocher was known as "Leo the Lip" because of his confrontational style. He argued once with umpire George Magerkurth when the ump threatened to bite off his head. Leo responded, "If you do, you'll have more brains in your stomach than in your head."[9]

Induction

The 1994 Induction Ceremony was held at the Alfred Clark Gymnasium where it would continue for all future inductions right up through 2009. The crowd was listed at 15,000 on a sun-drenched day with 36 Hall of Famers present.

The president of the Hall of Fame, Donald Marr, Jr., welcomed the crowd and was pleased to report that the expansion of the library connecting it to the Hall of Fame Gallery had now been completed. The architectural firm, Remick Associates of Cornwall, supervised the project as the library expanded from its original 7,500 square feet in 1968 to its present 30,000 square feet. The museum and the library were now connected by a walkway and additional space was allocated in the Hall of Fame Gallery for future inductees well into the twenty-first century. Outside an expanded library research area, a new exhibit, "Scribes and Mikemen," was opened to honor the recipients of the Ford Frick Award for broadcasters and the J.G. Taylor Spink Award for writers. Additionally, an exhibit entitled "Baseball at the Movies" also opened, featuring clips from noted baseball movies. Finally, the Bullpen Theater was constructed featuring a fifty-two seat video viewing area that would also be used as a lecture hall.

The first inductee to speak was Steve Carlton, 49, who said that he got his first break right there in Cooperstown in 1966 when he was recalled from the minors by the Cardinals to pitch in the annual exhibition game between major league teams at Doubleday Field. He struck out 10 Minnesota Twins and was back with the Cards to stay. He then showed a sense of humor as he thanked the baseball writers for voting for him despite the fact that he didn't speak to them for many years. "Actually being voted in by the writers is like Rush Limbaugh being voted in by the Clintons," he joked. Carlton also said not speaking to the writers for so long had its downside and gave an example. When he went to meet the president in 1987 as a member of the champion Minnesota Twins, pictures were taken on the White House lawn. The next day in one of the Minnesota newspapers he was listed as "an unnamed secret service agent."

He acknowledged people that were a part of his 24-year career, but he paid special tribute to two people. One was his longtime catcher, Tim McCarver, now an expert TV baseball commentator. Carlton said, "Behind every successful pitcher there had to be a very smart catcher, and Tim McCarver is that man." A lot of people don't know he was a great bridge player," Carlton added, "so he remembered everything about every situation so he made it easy for me." Their close relationship prompted McCarver to say, "When Steve and I die, we will be buried in the same cemetery, sixty feet, six inches apart."[10] He also spoke of Gus Heffling, his martial arts trainer, and stated, "I pitched until my mid–40s because Gus built up my strength and flexibility."

He recognized his fellow inductees and, in closing, said, "Memory is baseball's fourth dimension and I know the memory of this day will be with me and my family forever."

Carlton has had perfect attendance, never missing an induction since his own.

The next honoree was Leo Durocher, who died in 1991 at the age of 86, and was represented by his ex-wife, actress Laraine Day, and his son Chris. Ms. Day spoke first and told of her involvement with the BBWAA in 1951. Every year the New York Chapter of the baseball writers put on a skit and that year they were going to honor her husband with a roast. The writers' skit involved his wife, and rather then have one of their members play her, they recruited Ms. Day to play herself. Thus, she became the first female BBWAA member.

His son then said the last years of his father's life were spent waiting for a call from the Hall of Fame, and now that the honor had come, he accepted it on behalf of his mother and sister, Michele. He became very emotional, saying, "My father stands with us today."

According to Mike Shannon in *Tales from the Dugout*, Phil Rizzuto gave the best induction speech ever because "it was the funniest."[11] The humor began with the Hall's chairman, Ed Stack. He introduced the Scooter by stating, "Our final inductee brought us as much publicity over the last quarter of a century as anyone who has played the game." Stack continued, "I don't know how we are going to generate the same amount of interest now that the question, 'Don't you think Phil Rizzuto should be in the Hall of Fame?' has been settled." If you ever listened to Phil Rizzuto's 39 years as a beloved Yankees broadcaster, then you will identify with what Stack said next. "We know about Cora (wife), his children and their pets, his favorite snacks and favorite restaurants except the first name of his broadcast

Phil Rizzuto entertains the crowd with his 1994 induction speech.

partners." Stack concluded, "Scooter, before it gets too late and you have to beat the traffic, come join me."

Naturally, Phil Rizzuto, 76, began with his signature line, "Holy Cow!" He talked about growing up in Brooklyn, always wanting to be a ballplayer and wondering what else he could do because he wasn't good with his hands. He then began with his self-deprecating humor and said, "I almost took my fingers off trying to run my snow blower."

He talked about his time in the Navy during World War II, and how he would get seasick as a kid when he would ride on a ferry, and now here he was on a Navy ship, and he would get sick and other sailors would look at him and ask, "You're going to defend us?" Finally, he was put off the ship in New Guinea for his chronic seasickness, where "I thought I would see a lot of Italians," producing more laughter. Throughout his speech he would get sidetracked and he would tell everyone they could leave anytime they wanted. So he said it again while he was rambling, and as if on cue, Johnny Bench and Yogi Berra took him up on it and got up and left the stage. Fortunately, they did return. Adding to his performance while he was speaking was a household fly that kept bothering him as he tried to squat it away. He finished by saying, "God bless all of you, and God bless this wonderful game that they call baseball."

His favorite Cooperstown memory was his own induction, especially having had to wait so long for it to happen. He came back seven times and died in 2007 at the age of 89.

1995

The 1995 BBWAA election had 460 ballots cast, and the only player to achieve immortality was the Phillies' third baseman, considered by many to be the greatest of all time, Mike Schmidt. He was elected in his first year of eligibility with 96.5 percent (444 votes).

The VC normally elected a maximum of two candidates from either executives, managers, umpires and older major league players. This year they were to also consider candidates separately from the Negro Leagues and from the nineteenth century with the authority to select one from each category. The result was the VC selected the maximum number of four in their 1995 election.

They chose the stalwart center fielder of the Philadelphia Phillies, Richie Ashburn, who had been retired 33 years. He received 1,119 votes during 15 BBWAA elections. However, he wouldn't have been chosen under the 1991 BBWAA rule requiring a VC candidate to have achieved 60 percent in at least one BBWAA election since he never reached that percentage in any BBWAA election. However, one of his fans, Jim Donahue, was upset with the 60 percent rule so he started a petition campaign at Veterans Stadium in Philadelphia. Over the course of the 1992 and 1993 seasons Donohue got 165,000 signatures on a petition. This petition, along with some 55,000 postcards, was sent to the Hall of Fame's Board of Directors, protesting the rule. Despite this effort, nothing changed, but it must have helped because Ashburn was elected by the VC in 1995.[12] Bill James and Steve Carlton also supported Ashburn. James felt that he should be in the Hall (p. 325). Carlton spoke up for Ashburn during his 1994 induction speech.

The VC also selected an executive, the founder and later president of the National League, William Hulbert. His induction came 113 years after his death, the longest elapsed time from death to induction of any inductee.

Sportswriter Steve Wulf wrote an article in *Sports Illustrated* in 1990 stating that Hulbert deserves to be in the Hall of Fame "because he brought stability to the National League and helped rid the game of the influences of drinking and gambling."[13] Also Leonard Koppett, a member of the VC since 1994, showed his support for Hulbert in his book *The Thinking Fan's Guide to Baseball*, which helped to rectify this injustice.[14]

The VC also selected old-time pitcher Vic Willis 85 years after he retired as a player and 48 years after he died. Family members, noted sportswriter Furman Bisher, the Society for American Baseball Research (SABR), and even fellow inductee Richie Ashburn, as you will see in Willis's great-grandson's induction speech, were all involved in helping to get Willis into the Hall of Fame.

Willis's son, Vic Jr., started a vigorous letter writing campaign on behalf of his father back in the 1970s. Bisher wrote in 1971 that Willis belonged in, ahead of 300-game winner Early Wynn. Stephen Cunerd of SABR pointed out in an article in 1989 that Willis had a better ERA than 28 of the pitchers already in and more victories than 22 other Hall of Famers.[15]

Pitcher Leon Day became the twelfth member of the Negro Leagues selected for induction, and the first since 1987. He almost was voted in by the VC in 1993, but VC member Roy Campanella was dying and missed the meeting. Campy was ready to vote for his former Negro Leagues' opponent, causing Day to miss induction by one vote.

Inductees

Mike Schmidt led the league in home runs in 1974, the first of eight times leading the league, a National League record. He went on to lead the Phillies to the playoffs five times as well as to two pennants and the Phillies' first world title in 1980. He won the first of three MVPs in 1980 and was the MVP of the World Series, batting .381. Schmidt was also the MVP in the strike-shortened season of 1981 and again in 1986. Schmidt was excellent defensively as well with 10 Gold Glove Awards. He was chosen for 12 all-star teams and retired with 548 home runs and 1,595 RBIs, both records for third basemen.

Yet, as Bill James notes, "Schmidt had the worst rookie year of any Hall of Famer."[16] He batted .206 in 30 at-bats in 1972 and then .196 in his first full season (1973) with 367 at-bats. It all changed for him in 1973 when he developed his swing in winter ball.

Richie Ashburn was chosen *The Sporting News* Rookie of the Year in 1948 as he led the league in stolen bases and batted .333. This happened despite his missing the last six weeks of the season with a broken hand. "Whitey" was a premier leadoff hitter, twice leading the league in hitting, three times in hits, two times in triples, and four times in walks as he compiled a lifetime on base percentage of .396. Ashburn was a very adept center fielder as well with more than 500 putouts four times. He was a five-time all-star and finished with a lifetime batting average of .308.

During the last weekend of the season in 1950, the Phillies were playing the Dodgers when Cal Abrams tried to score from second on a single to center. Ashburn fired a strike as the catcher tagged out Abrams and the game remained tied until the Phillies won it in extra innings. Philadelphia's "Whiz Kids" had won their first pennant in 35 years!

Leon Day was called by Monte Irvin, "One of the most complete athletes I ever seen."[17] He was a 5'9" star pitcher who also played the infield and the outfield. He helped the Newark Eagles win the 1946 Negro World Series title. Day pitched an Opening Day no-hitter, struck out 18 batters in a game, and pitched in a record seven East West All-Star Games. He won the 1942 All-Star Game, striking out five of the seven batters he faced. He also played in the minors during the 1950s.

Day took part in D-Day (World War II) and played on integrated baseball teams in the armed forces. He once beat the Cincinnati Reds' future star pitcher Ewell Blackwell.

Vic Willis began with the Boston Beaneaters in 1898, and helped them finish first while he compiled a record of 25–13. He pitched a no-hitter in 1899 and during the 1902 season, he pitched the most complete games (45) in the National League since 1895. He also led the league in 1902 with 410 innings and 225 strikeouts while winning 27 games. He was traded to the Pittsburgh Pirates in 1906 and, in 1909, he won 22 games as they won a world title. He completed 82 percent of the games he started and was 244–207 lifetime.

Willis was present for possibly the worst tragedy that ever took place at a major league game. He had just pitched the Beaneaters to a victory in the first game of a doubleheader in Philadelphia on August 8, 1903. While changing in the locker room, he heard a loud crash and later discovered that an overhanging gallery in the left field bleachers had collapsed, carrying with it several hundred fans. Willis and other players from both teams helped pull victims from the wreckage where 12 people had been killed.

William Hulbert became part-owner of the Chicago White Stockings in 1871. They were one of the teams in baseball's first professional league, the National Association. Hulbert wasn't happy with the league's lax rules so, along with Albert Spalding, he wrote a new set of bylaws and formed the National League of Professional Base Ball Clubs in 1876. Hulbert supported Morgan Bulkeley, the owner of the Hartford, Connecticut, team, who became the league's first president. He did this because he needed the cooperation of the eastern owners, but after nine months Bulkeley was replaced by Hulbert at the urging of the other owners. He was president more than five years when he died at the age of 49.

Hulbert helped to stabilize professional baseball by having his league do the scheduling of all games, establish set ticket prices, form a system for choosing umpires, ban gambling at the ballparks and create a standard player contract. When he died Albert Spalding called him "the man who saved the game."[18]

Induction

The 1995 Induction Ceremony was held July 30 on a beautiful day with a record turnout of 40,000, the majority of them there to honor former Phillies Mike Schmidt and Richie Ashburn. It was reported that 200 buses brought Philadelphia fans to Cooperstown for the ceremony. There were 32 Hall of Famers present.

This was also the debut of the giant video screen that made it much easier for all the fans, especially the ones in the back, to see the ceremony.

Leon Day missed by one vote back in 1993 causing him to later lament, "I wish I could have done it when I could have enjoyed it."[19] Two years later Day heard of his induction while in a Baltimore hospital. He died six days later at the age of 78. Representing him was his widow, Geraldine, who told the audience that her husband had dreamed that morning Ed Stack had visited his hospital room and given him his ring. Later in the day he received the official word on his induction. His wife has been a regular at every induction since.

The next speaker was Susan Linder, the granddaughter of William Hulbert's grand-niece. Hulbert had died in 1882 from a heart attack at the age of 49. His gravesite marker at Graceland Cemetery in Chicago is in the shape of a baseball. Hulbert, by the way, is the only Hall of Famer who was born in the vicinity of baseball's home — 15 miles west of Cooperstown at Burlington Flats.

Ms. Linder began by stating that some of Mr. Hulbert's fans would say, "It's about time," especially his grandniece and her grandmother, Elizabeth Martin. Ms. Martin fought long and hard for her granduncle but was too ill to come. Ms. Linder then gave an enjoyable history lesson by comparing and contrasting the differences between the United States of Hulbert's time and today. America was in the midst of dealing with the period of Reconstruction following the Civil War while his hometown, Chicago, was recuperating from the tragic fire of 1871. She then explained how baseball was different by stating, "Fielders disdained the use of mitts, batters had the option of calling for high or low pitches, and players paid for their own uniforms and part of their expenses on the road." She said that Hulbert himself had problems with gambling and alcohol while a young man in Chicago, and after cleaning up his own act he set out to reform baseball. She declared, "He thought that a shot of virtue would be better for baseball than a shot of whiskey." She closed by expressing her gratitude to the hall for its hospitality.

The next inductee was Vic Willis, who had died in 1947 at the age of 71. He was represented by two people at the induction, his grandson, Ben Decker, and his great-grandson, Thomas Hunt, Jr.

Mr. Hunt spoke first and said 1995 marked the 100th anniversary of Vic Willis's entry into baseball. He thanked "all the people who have been supportive of Vic Willis for the Hall of Fame." He continued, "Coincidentally, one of those, who as a sportswriter wrote in support of Vic Willis's admission, was Richie Ashburn." Hunt addressed Ashburn and said, "It is a special honor to see Vic Willis admitted to the Hall of Fame with you."

Mr. Decker, as the representative for the 36 living members of the family, added, "Congratulations, Grandpa, you finally made it."

The fourth inductee and the first living one was Richie Ashburn, 68. He paid tribute to his first manager with the Phillies, Eddie Sawyer, for being "the greatest manager I ever played for," and fellow inductee Mike Schmidt. "I saw every game you ever played and it's a real treat to go in with you today." Ashburn also called for Vada Pinson, Ron Santo, Jim Bunning, and Nellie Fox to be admitted to the Hall of Fame. This might have helped because Bunning went in a year later and Fox two years later.

He closed with a funny Casey Stengel story, who was his last manager with the Mets. The Mets were playing the Cubs in 1962 in the last game of the season. After he and another Met had singled, the next batter hit a line drive that the second baseman caught, threw to second and then the relay went to first completing a triple play. The Mets lost the game, ending their season with the most losses ever (120) by a team since 1899. Later in the clubhouse Stengel said, "I don't want anybody to feel bad about this. This has been a real team effort," as the crowd responded in laughter. Ashburn then tied this effort into all the people who had helped him saying, "God bless you, especially the fans, you have made this the greatest day of my life."

Ashburn was a sportswriter who wrote a column twice a week for many years, and also was a Phillies' broadcaster since he retired as a player. He commented tongue-in-cheek about his long wait for induction. "I figured I'd be the one guy passed up for the Hall of Fame in all three areas as a player, writer, and broadcaster."[20]

He came one more time and died of a heart attack in his hotel room in 1997 at the age of 70. He was waiting to broadcast a Phillies game against the Mets, which made his death similar to Don Drysdale's.

Mike Schmidt, 45, began on a light note as he told the assembled Hall of Famers in an aside, "Wake up guys, I won't be long." He paid homage to his fellow inductees, especially Richie Ashburn, congratulating him on an honor "long overdue."

Early in his speech he said, "I could not approach it simply as an acceptance speech," and continued, "There isn't one man on this stage who would be here if it wasn't for the talent and sacrifices of other people along the way." He then spoke of the people back home in Dayton, Ohio, who helped him as well as his college coach at Ohio University.

Schmidt also gave his support to Pete Rose, his friend and teammate on the championship team of 1980, and called for his induction. He paid tribute to many others in the Phillies' organization, including four who supported him at various junctions of his career — Bob Boone, Richie Allen, Dave Cash, and the aforementioned Pete Rose.

Schmidt then made a poignant reflection on the uneasy relationship that he had with the Phillies' fans. He said, "If I had it to do all over again the only thing I would change is me. I'd be less sensitive, I'd be more outgoing, and I'd be more appreciative of what you expected of me." He called for an end to their uneasy relationship by stating, "Can we put that to rest today?" The fans responded with an outburst of applause. He then thanked them for their support and for being there for him today.

He closed with, "I like to thank God for this very special moment and for blessing my life in so many ways. Thank you for all coming and I'll cherish this honor forever."

He recalled that his favorite Cooperstown memory had nothing to do with baseball. "I shot a 64 on the Leatherstocking Golf Course on the Sunday morning of my induction. Just goes to show you how easy golf is when playing well is the farthest thing from your mind." Schmidt has returned some nine times since his own induction.

1996

The 1996 BBWAA election had 470 ballots cast but no one received the 75 percent needed for induction. This was the first time since 1971 that no one qualified in a BBWAA election.

The VC selected pitcher Jim Bunning for induction. He was selected the minimum five years after his last BBWAA ballot. He did very well in the BBWAA elections with a total of 3,213 votes over the course of 15 elections, missing induction by four votes in 1988.

The VC also selected Baltimore Orioles manager Earl Weaver ten years after he retired and coincidentally nineteenth-century Orioles manager Ned Hanlon, who was chosen nearly 90 years after he retired and some 60 years after he died. One reason it took so for Hanlon is probably because Hanlon was one of the architects of the ill-fated Players League that lasted only one year (1890). When his Pittsburgh team in the Players League outdrew the Pittsburgh team of the National League, he expected his team would be picked to join the National League, and when they weren't, he sued the league. The case went all the way to the Supreme Court where he lost.

Finally, they selected Negro Leagues left-handed pitcher Bill "Willie" Foster, the thirteenth player chosen from the Negro Leagues.

Inductees

Jim Bunning became a successful pitcher with the Tigers after developing a devastating slider. He went on to win 20 and led the league in victories for the only time in his career in 1957 while pitching his first no-hitter. He was traded to the Phillies in 1964 where he won 19 games. The season was topped off with a perfect game against the New York Mets, made extra special for the father of nine since it happened on Father's Day. Bunning won more than 100 games in each league, led each league in strikeouts, and was an all-star in each league as well. He was a seven-time all-star and was 224–184 lifetime.

Bunning used his degree in economics to help the Players Association establish an updated pension fund. He continued his service to others when he became a United States representative and then a United States senator from the state of Kentucky.

Earl Weaver became the Orioles' manager mid-season in 1968, after being a minor league manager for 12 years. Weaver won six divisional titles and four league titles. His teams won one title in four World Series appearances, achieved 100 victories or more five times, and finished first or second 12 out of 14 seasons. He was Manager of the Year two times and finished with a record of 1,480–1,060 for a winning percentage of .583.

Weaver was the "Earl of Baltimore" and worked individually with each of his players to get the most out of them. One example was pitcher Mike Cuellar, one of six Cy Young Award winners that Weaver developed. He realized Cuellar's problem was a language barrier so he had bilingual catcher Elrod Hendricks work with him and Cuellar bloomed.

Ned Hanlon was an outfielder in the major leagues for 13 years and became the manager of the Baltimore Orioles in 1892. They finished first three times and second twice. His Orioles teams were noted for the hit-and-run and covering for each other in the field. They were also noted for baiting umpires, tripping and holding players as they rounded third base, and perfecting the Baltimore Chop. They would make the ground around home plate hard so that when their players hit the ball down in front of the plate, it would bounce high and the batter would beat it out. He brought many of the Orioles' players with him when he took over the Brooklyn Superbas where he finished first in 1899 and 1900. He finished his 19-year managing career with a record of 1,312–1,164. (.530).

Hanlon is buried near three of his stars, Wilbert Robinson, John McGraw, and Joe Kelley, in a cemetery in Baltimore.

Bill "Willie" Foster had the most wins (143), and is considered by most the best left-handed pitcher in Negro Leagues history. He pitched for several teams, but he enjoyed most of his success with the Chicago American Giants. He led them to two straight titles over the Bacharach Giants in the 1926 and 1927 Negro World Series. He helped clinch the 1926 pennant by defeating "Bullet" Rogan and the Kansas City Monarchs in both games of a doubleheader on the last day of the season. He pitched a complete game victory for the west squad in the first East-West All-Star Game in 1933.

Rube Foster, Negro National League organizer, was his older half-brother. Foster pitched for Rube's Chicago American Giants but there was tension between them. Yet, future Giants' manager Dave Malarcher credited Rube with teaching Willie how to pitch.

Induction

The 1996 Induction Ceremony was held on August 4 with an estimated crowd of more than 5,000 people, including 35 Hall of Famers. It was a day marked by rain but the skies cleared up for the ceremony.

The first inductee to be honored was Willie Foster. The lefty pitcher was chosen 18 years after he died at the age of 74. His son, Bill Foster, Jr., was there to represent him. He talked about the pitching duels his father had with Satchel Paige, indicating that they faced each other "around 27 times." He described a doubleheader where they faced each other in both games and his son proudly said that his father won both games.

He went on to tell a story about when he was a Little League all-star and trying to win the batting title so he challenged his father to pitch to him. He badgered him for about a week until his father gave in and the first three times Junior got "good wood on them." Now his father told him what the pitch would be (fastball) and where it would be pitched and sure enough his father threw three straight strikes right by him without Junior being able to get the bat off his shoulder. Needless to say, that was the last time he ever challenged his dad.

He closed by saying, "I would love to see my father and tell him that he made it."

The next inductee was Ned Hanlon, who died in Baltimore in 1937 at the age of 79. Accepting for him was his grandson, Edward Hanlon. The grandson gave a brief history of the family, stating that Ned had five children, and that one of his sons was killed in World War I. He was the spokesman for 118 descendants who were present for the induction. He thanked the Hall of Fame for their hospitality and congratulated each of the other honorees, especially fellow Orioles manager Earl Weaver, calling it "a thrill that two great Baltimore managers from different eras could be inducted on the same day."

The grandson went on to talk about Hanlon's legacy and the connection between Hanlon and Weaver. Hanlon was on the Baltimore Parks Department Board in the 1930s when they constructed Memorial Stadium, home ballpark for Weaver's successful Baltimore teams. Ed Hanlon also said that his grandfather was responsible for the black and orange color scheme on the Orioles' uniform.

He thanked former baseball player and broadcaster Joe Garagiola and Baltimore sportswriters Steve Parks and John Steadman for their support of his grandfather and closed by thanking the VC for selecting his grandfather.

The next inductee was manager Earl Weaver, 59. He spoke of the many players he had on his Orioles teams that helped him achieve success, including current Hall of Famers Brooks Robinson, Frank Robinson, Reggie Jackson, and future Hall of Famers Eddie Murray and Cal Ripken, Jr. He also mentioned another Hall of Famer, Jim Palmer, with whom "I had more arguments with than my wife Marianna."

Weaver, halfway through his speech, paid tribute to his nemeses when he said, "And now it's time to recognize a group of baseball people that seldom receive credit for a job well done, the umpires. They accept the players' and managers' ire," he added, "and never let it affect their next call." He credited them with getting more than a million calls correct when he was managing with only 91 or 92 calls that he questioned. He went on to thank them for their good work.

He finished by declaring, "I'm proud of the fact that I was even considered for the Hall of Fame, let alone voted in. I'm proud of the fact that I spent my whole career in one city, and for that I would like to thank the wonderful fans of Baltimore for letting me stay."

His favorite Cooperstown memory is seeing his plaque hanging in the Gallery the first time. "As long as I live I'll never forget that feeling." He has only missed one induction since his own.

Jim Bunning, 64, was the last inductee, and began his speech by quoting from scripture. "Sunday is the day the Lord made for us to 'Rejoice and be glad.'" He continued, "If anyone has reason to rejoice and be glad, it's the Jim Bunning family." He congratulated his fellow inductees and paid tribute to his family like all inductees do, but in his case it included more than most as he had nine children. One of the persons he thanked was his baseball coach at Xavier University, Ned Wulk, who went on to become better known as the basketball coach at Arizona State University for 25 years.

Bunning did something unusual as he thanked every one of the VC by mentioning all 15 by name, with a special accolade to Allen Lewis, who covered him as a writer for the Philadelphia *Inquirer* and helped to convince the others of his worthiness for the Hall of Fame. He also thanked Frank Dolson, retired sports editor of the *Inquirer*, because Bunning was ready to withdraw his name from the BBWAA ballot after his first election but Dolson convinced him not to do it.

He called for the election of 300-game winners Don Sutton and Phil Niekro as well as Tony Perez, which all came to pass in the next few years. He went on to say how difficult it is to play baseball and used basketball great Michael Jordan as an example of someone who tried it and wasn't successful.

He finished up by comparing his then-current job as a congressman by saying that baseball prepared him for Congress. Baseball taught him self-confidence, teamwork, self-control and how to compete. Now the competition is about ideas and opinions rather than runs, hits, and strikeouts. He said, "The competition is as fierce as a pennant race. The people who succeed in the battle are the ones who have the most developed sense of competition and teamwork."

He concluded by saying, "Ladies and gentlemen, thank you very much. You've made this day the best day of my life."

Jim Bunning has only missed one induction since 1996.

1997

The 1997 BBWAA election had 473 ballots cast and knuckleball pitcher Phil Niekro was the only one elected with 80.3 percent (380 votes). Niekro was voted in during his fifth year of eligibility. The 300-game winner received 1,538 votes in five elections.

The VC chose second baseman Nellie Fox, 32 years after he retired and 22 years after he died at the age of 47. He had received 2,150 votes during 15 BBWAA elections. His last election in 1985 was when he missed by two votes as mentioned previously. This was the closest anyone ever came without achieving induction.

The VC also chose Dodgers manager Tommy Lasorda in his first year of eligibility, following his retirement as manager after the 1996 season. He heard about it at a spring training game at Dodgertown in Vero Beach, Florida. He was called to the press box and wept when it was announced. All 3,275 fans gave him a standing ovation.

This story is especially poignant given Lasorda's fierce loyalty to the Dodgers. He has worked with this team for more than 50 years as a player, minor league manager, coach, major league manager and now as an executive. His famous refrain is actually part of his Hall of Fame plaque, which reads, "Managed Dodgers with an impenetrable passion, claiming to 'bleed Dodger blue.'"

The final selection by the VC was shortstop Willie Wells, the fourteenth Negro Leagues member chosen. His friend and Negro Leagues Hall of Famer Cool Papa Bell was so upset that Wells hadn't gotten in prior to Bell's death in 1991 that he was willing to take himself out of the Hall of Fame and have them put Willie Wells in his place.

Inductees

Phil Niekro broke in with the Milwaukee Braves but didn't become a starter until his fourth season in 1967 when he went 11–9 and led the league with a 1.87 ERA. He went on to a 24-year career with most of those years spent with the Braves, for whom he was a three-time 20-game winner after they moved to Atlanta in 1966. He threw a no-hitter in 1973 and also garnered five Gold Gloves. He spent four years in the American League and ended his career with Atlanta at age 48 with a record of 318–274.

Niekro's father was a fastball pitcher in an industrial league when, one day while playing in the backyard, he showed his ten-year-old son how to throw the knuckleball. Phil never stopped perfecting the pitch and it became his ticket to the Hall of Fame. Niekro was affectionately called "Knucksie" by Braves fans for his mastery of the pitch.

Nellie Fox came into his own when he was traded from the Philadelphia A's to the White Sox in 1950, where he spent the next 14 years as their second baseman with the ever-present wad of chewing tobacco in his mouth. Fox led the league in 29 defensive categories and committed only 209 errors in his 19-year career that also included three Gold Gloves. He was a great bunter and slap hitter who led the league in hits four times, and singles a record eight times. He rarely struck out and played in 798 straight games. He retired as a Houston Astro and 12-time all-star with a batting average of .288 lifetime.

Fox and Aparicio were the catalysts for the 1959 "Go Go" Sox, with Fox winning the MVP. They won the pennant, and lost to the Dodgers in the World Series as Fox batted .375. Former manager Marty Marion said, "Playing without him is like trying to run a car without sparkplugs. He is the heart of the team."[21]

Tommy Lasorda started as a left-handed pitcher with the Brooklyn Dodgers and went

The Hall of Famers pose for a group picture at the Leatherstocking Golf Course during the 1997 Induction Weekend. *Left to right, standing:* Ralph Kiner, Lou Brock, Rollie Fingers, Robin Roberts, Fergie Jenkins, Duke Snider, Jim Bunning, Jim Palmer, Brooks Robinson, Billy Williams, Steve Carlton, Tom Seaver and Phil Niekro. *Seated:* Red Schoendienst, Johnny Bench, Joe Morgan, Enos Slaughter, Yogi Berra, Stan Musial, Whitey Ford, Earl Weaver, Pee Wee Reese and Phil Rizzuto.

on to become a Dodgers minor league manager and Walter Alston's third base coach before succeeding him at the end of the 1976 season. Lasorda went on to win eight division titles, four pennants and two World Series championships. His most satisfying title had to be in 1988 when he defeated the favored Oakland A's, highlighted by an injured Kirk Gibson hitting a walk-off home run in Game 1. His lifetime record was 1,599–1,439. Lasorda continued as a Dodgers executive after he retired, and then experienced a special moment in his life. He piloted the United States Olympic baseball team to the Gold Medal when they defeated Cuba in the 2000 Games in Sydney, Australia.

Willie Wells, as a shortstop, had good range, sure hands, and a quick release that compensated for a weak arm. He could also hit for average and power, although only 5'9". He led the Negro National League in batting twice, including .420 in 1930. He purportedly set the single-season record of 27 home runs in 1926 when he played for the St. Louis Stars. He also led the Stars to three league championships. He was a part of the Million Dollar Infield for the 1936 Newark Eagles that included Ray Dandridge and Mule Suttles.

Wells was called "El Diablo" (The Devil) because of his defensive prowess when he played in Mexico. He told noted sportswriter Wendell Smith why he played in Mexico: "I've found freedom and democracy here, something I never found in the U.S."[22]

On Saturday, August 2, 1997, a ceremony was held on the steps of the Hall of Fame honoring Jackie Robinson on the 50th anniversary of his breaking the color barrier in major league baseball. Hall chairman Ed Stack presided over the ceremony as New York governor

George Pataki announced the creation of New York's Freedom Medal in honor of Robinson. Rachel Robinson, Jackie's widow, and Hall of Famer Frank Robinson, baseball's first black manager, were present as well.

Induction

The 1997 Induction Ceremony was held on August 3 with 35 Hall of Famers present. Prior to the inductee speeches the president of the Hall of Fame, Donald Marr, spoke of a new permanent exhibit, *Pride and Passion: The African-American Baseball Experience.* It was in honor of Jackie Robinson's golden anniversary of the integration of major league baseball. The exhibit tells the story of African Americans in baseball from Civil War days up through the integration of the National and American leagues by Jackie Robinson and Larry Doby, respectively, and continues to the present day.

Ed Stack introduced the first inductee, Willie Wells, who was a fitting example to the new exhibit and the anniversary of the integration of baseball. Wells died in 1989 at age 82 in Austin, Texas, where he was born and bred. Accepting the award for him was his daughter, Stella Wells. Ms. Wells began by calling her father's induction beautiful. She said that her father always confided in her that he would get into the Hall of Fame by saying, "I might be dead, but I'll be in the Hall of Fame." She shared with the audience that baseball was a "way of life" for her dad and told how he pioneered the use of a batting helmet. He created one from a coal miner's helmet after returning to play following a beaning. She told of his two basic rules of life that he applied to everything including baseball. The first "was to get knowledge because knowledge is everything," and the second was to "do the best you can."

She talked about his friendship with Cool Papa Bell and how he called her after her father passed away in 1989 and how he was going "to take himself out of the Hall of Fame so that Willie would be admitted." She responded by telling him not to do that because her father wouldn't want him to do it. She closed by saying, "Cool Papa, we hope you and Dad are together and smiling down on us today because 'The Diablo' is in."

The next inductee was Nellie Fox, who died in 1975 at the age of 47. Representing him and his family was his widow, Joanne. She spoke lovingly of her husband in her opening remarks when she said, "As a beautiful bouquet of flowers can brighten our day, so can memories of time. Times we have shared with a very special person who we are honoring today." She said if he were alive now, he would have wondered, "Why all the fuss?" She acknowledged that "the fans kept his memory alive and are the reason we are here today." She paid tribute to three Hall of Famers who were there, his good friend Ted Williams, his protégé, Joe Morgan, and his double play partner, Luis Aparicio.

She closed with, "Every generation has its superstars, but Nellie Fox added another dimension to the game and that was he gave it his heart and soul."

A group of fans came from his hometown of Chambersburg, Pennsylvania, and many wore T-shirts honoring their hero. The impact that Nellie Fox had on fans is expressed in a recent book written by a former high school player about his memories of playing on a 1959 championship team in Mount Vernon, New York. The author, Bruce Fabricant, was a second baseman on the team and was nicknamed "Nellie." He attended the 1997 induction and writes, "I don't think anyone liked to play more than he did."[23]

The third inductee was Tommy Lasorda, 69. Ed Stack introduced him "as having given more after-dinner speeches than anyone else in the last quarter of a century." Stack went on, "He has charmed audiences by speaking warmly of his love for the game."

Lasorda didn't disappoint as he blended humility with humor during his speech. He began by saying that he was "scared to death" when he left home as a seventeen year old to start his baseball career and now, fifty-two years later, he came to Cooperstown "scared to death." He acknowledged his fellow honorees and recognized many people in the Dodgers' organization as well as three people of prominence who were there: actor Tony Danza and basketball coaches Rollie Massimino and Mike Fratello.

He then told a story about the importance of winning. He attended Sunday Mass in Cincinnati when the Dodgers were there to play the Reds. Who should sit next to him in church but the Reds' manager, John McNamara. As they were leaving church, McNamara quietly told him to wait for him outside and he would be right out. Lasorda looked in and saw him lighting a candle. Lasorda waited until he was finished and had left, then went in and blew out the candle that McNamara had lit. Later, during the game, Lasorda yelled over to his rival manager and said, "Hey Mac, it ain't going to work; I blew it out," as the Dodgers won 13–2.

He closed with another story about his dream as a youngster to pitch for his favorite team, the Yankees. Catcher Bill Dickey would be giving him signs while Gehrig and DiMaggio were on the field. Then his mother would come in, shake him and say, "Wake up, Tommy, it's time for school." He didn't want to leave because the dream was so real. He then went on and said, "I feel it won't be too long before my mother will be shaking me and saying, 'Wake up, Tommy, it's time to go to school.' I am living a dream."

He has returned for eight inductions.

The final inductee was Phil Niekro, 58, who began by recognizing the governor of Georgia, Zell Miller, who was there. He also acknowledged his childhood friend, the legendary basketball great, John Havlicek. He paid tribute to his fellow inductees and the fact that it was the golden anniversary of Jackie Robinson's integration of baseball. Niekro quipped that contrary to what some thought, he didn't play with Jackie Robinson.

He paid tribute to his younger brother Joe, who won more than 200 games as a major league pitcher and pitched nine times against Phil. Joe won five of those games and had one hit off Phil. It was a game-winning home run, and it was the only homer he ever hit.

He also recognized the Coors Silver Bullets women's baseball team that he managed.

He closed by acknowledging the fans when he said, "Whether you are sitting here in the first row or a way back on the hill, this game is owned and belongs to you, the fan. Cherish it and take care of it." Speaking of fans, four busloads of them had come all the way from Lansing, Ohio, to honor their hometown hero.

His favorite Cooperstown memory is, like most, his own induction and "seeing his plaque in the gallery, and having his family there to share it with him, made it a time that will never be forgotten." Also, Niekro, of Polish descent, told the story of his mother telling him about his late father, after the ceremony was over: "Dad is probably having a polka party in Heaven."

Niekro has returned to nine ceremonies, but also participates every year in the Fantasy Camp in the fall.

1998

The 1998 BBWAA election had 473 ballots cast, and 300-game-winner Don Sutton was elected in his fifth year of eligibility, receiving 81.6 percent (386 votes). Sutton received 1,555 votes in five elections.

The VC selected historic center fielder Larry Doby for induction 39 years after he retired as a player. He was chosen as a post–1945 player. James Vail questions the Doby selection because he received only 17 votes in two BBWAA elections in 1966 and 1967 and never received another vote, even though he was still eligible. Since he started his major league career after 1945 he doesn't meet the VC requirement of having received 100 votes or 60 percent in a BBWAA election (p. 142). Vail thinks the VC took into account the time he spent in the Negro Leagues prior to 1946 when considering him (p. 143). Nevertheless, Vail thinks Doby had good credentials but feels he was selected mainly as a player of "historical importance" since he was the first black player in the American League (p. 143).

Robert Cohen takes into account that Doby was a part of several historical firsts as he states, "All things considered while Larry Doby was not a truly great player, his selection by the Veterans Committee was a pretty good one" (p. 162).

The VC also picked executive Lee MacPhail. He had been retired from baseball for 13 years when he was selected. He became part of the first father-son tandem elected to Cooperstown because his father, Larry, had been elected in 1978.

The VC also selected shortstop George Davis in the category of a player before 1946. Davis had played half his career in the nineteenth century and had been retired almost 90 years and dead 58 years. He was considered a good choice and it happened because of the grassroots work of two men, Walt Lipka and Bill Lamb. Lipka was the historian for the city of Cohoes, New York, where Davis was born and raised. He was impressed with his baseball credentials but couldn't understand why no one knew anything about him. He contacted sportswriters but got nowhere until he read a biography in the *Baseball Research Journal* (published by SABR) by Lamb, an assistant prosecutor in Middlesex County in New Jersey. Together they worked to rectify this injustice and sent information about George Davis to the members of the VC. Also, respected *New York Times* columnist Dave Anderson wrote an article in support of Davis. The result was induction for the no-longer-obscure former Cohoes resident. Historian Lipka attended the Induction Ceremony along with a busload of equally proud Cohoes citizens.[24]

One reason given why Davis was not considered for the Hall of Fame for so many years was because he was forced to return to the Chicago White Sox after he lost his court case challenging the reserve clause in 1903. This came after peace was restored between the American and National leagues in 1902.

The final VC selection was pitcher Wilber "Bullet" Joe Rogan, the fifteenth former Negro Leaguer, who was chosen 31 years after he died.

Inductees

Don Sutton spent 16 seasons with the Dodgers and became their all-time leader in wins, strikeouts, innings, and shutouts. Sutton joined the Milwaukee Brewers in 1982 and beat Baltimore's Jim Palmer on the last day of the season to clinch the American League's East title. He pitched in five League Championships and had a record of 4–1 with an ERA of 2.06. Despite being on a pennant winner five times, he never won a title. Sutton took care of himself and was never on the disabled list until the end of his 23-year career. He was the MVP of the 1977 All-Star Game and was 324–256 lifetime (.559).

Sutton was accused of doctoring the ball like Gaylord Perry, so when they met, Sutton sarcastically said, "He gave me a jar of Vaseline and I gave him a piece of sandpaper."[25]

Larry Doby was a second baseman with Newark of the Negro National League before striking out on three pitches in his Indians' debut on July 5, 1947. Doby recovered and had an exceptional 13-year career. He switched to the outfield and became their center fielder after being tutored by former Indians great Tris Speaker. He batted .301 in 1948 and helped the Indians win the World Series as he batted .318. He led the league in home runs in 1954 (second time) and RBIs and was second in the MVP race as Cleveland won 111 games and the pennant. Doby was a seven-time all-star and batted .283 lifetime.

In some ways, Doby had a more difficult situation than Jackie Robinson because he was taken from the protective situation of the Negro Leagues without spending any time in the minors as Robinson had. Also, Robinson was brash and assertive while Doby was withdrawn and moody. Yet both helped pave the way for future black players.

George Davis came into his own after being traded to the New York Giants in 1893, where he became their full-time shortstop and had a productive nine years there as a player. He never batted less than .300 with them and also displayed power with 27 triples in 1893, 10 home runs twice, and had at least 100 RBIs three times. Off the field he helped rescue two women from a burning building on his way to a game.

He played seven years with the Chicago White Sox and hit .308 in the 1906 World Series as they upset the favored Cubs, their cross-town rivals. Davis also displayed speed with 619 lifetime stolen bases and wide range at short with an above-average arm. He retired after 20 years with a .297 batting average.

Davis jumped to the Sox and the American League in 1902 but didn't like it and went back to the Giants for four games. He never played for them again as he was forced to go back to the White Sox after he lost his court case in 1903.

Lee MacPhail, as director of the farm system, helped sustain the Yankees' dynasty with seven titles in 10 years. As the Baltimore Orioles' general manager, he traded for Frank Robinson, which helped them win a title in 1966. Finally, as president of the American League, he stepped in when negotiations stalled and helped end the 1981 strike.

As president of the American League, MacPhail helped resolve the pine tar incident of 1983. It happened after George Brett hit a home run against the Yankees and manager Billy Martin protested that he had too much pine tar on his bat and the umpires decided with Martin by disallowing the home run. MacPhail ruled that the Yankees should have protested before Brett's at-bat and not after it. The home run was allowed and, at a later date, the game was resumed from that point.

Wilber "Bullet" Joe Rogan didn't begin his Negro Leagues career until he was almost 30 after spending more than eight years in the United States Army. The 5'9" Rogan, known for his no-windup delivery, played only for the Kansas City Monarchs from 1920 through 1938. He was also a feared hitter who played everywhere except catcher. During 1924 he led the league in wins (16) and batting (.411). He then pitched three complete games and batted .325 as the Monarchs beat the Hilldale Daisies in the first Negro World Series. He got hurt and missed the World Series as the Daisies won in 1925. Rogan had the highest winning percentage in Negro League history with a record of 116–50 (.699).

We might have never known about Rogan if it weren't for Casey Stengel. Stengel barnstormed against Rogan's Army team and recommended him to the Monarchs' owner.

Induction

The 1998 Induction Ceremony was held on July 26 with a crowd that was below average according to local reports. It was a nice day, with a temperature in the 70s as 36 Hall of Famers were in attendance.

MC George Grande informed the crowd about a ceremony that was held in the morning on the steps of the library. It was renamed the Bart Giamatti Library and Research Center after the former commissioner who died in 1989, less than a year after he had taken the job. His widow, Toni, Hall of Fame president Donald Marr and Chairman Ed Stack, and the new commissioner, Bud Selig, were there for the dedication.

It should be noted that the 1998 induction would be the first time that a video presentation of the inductees would be shown prior to the presentation of the plaque.

The first inductee was George Davis. There was no one to represent the deceased Davis, so National League president Len Coleman accepted the plaque and gave a very short but compassionate speech. He cited Davis's accomplishments, telling the audience that after retiring he coached the baseball team at Amherst College and managed in the minor leagues. His life after that was unknown, except that he did leave a widow and no children, and that he was buried in an unmarked grave in a cemetery in Philadelphia. Coleman said the following, "Since no family members could be found, baseball in a way is George Davis's family. And as George sits, resting with the Father, he will hopefully feel a great sense of pride that his family has granted him its highest distinction, election to the Hall of Fame." Later, Cohoes historian Walt Lipka helped to raise $300 for a headstone for Davis's gravesite.

The next inductee to be honored was Wilber "Bullet" Joe Rogan, who died in 1967 at the age of 77. Commissioner Selig read from his plaque stating that he was a player-manager for the Monarchs, and then became an umpire for several years in the Negro Leagues. It should be noted that Rogan, always the instructor like he was when he was in the Army, was a unique umpire in that he went to the mound between innings and gave the pitcher tips. Representing the family was his son, Wilber Rogan, Jr. He began by thanking the VC and Larry Lester, his father's "number one supporter." He also thanked Buck O'Neil, former Monarch and member of the VC, plus Phil Dixon, author and Monarchs researcher. He closed by predicting six more for the Hall of Fame from the Negro Leagues. They were: Smokey Joe Williams, Mule Suttles, Turkey Stearnes, Biz Mackey, Hilton Smith and Willard Brown. Wilbert Rogan, Jr., was a perfect prognosticator because all six were eventually chosen.

The next inductee was Lee MacPhail, 80. He began, "I would like to thank the members of the Veterans Committee who felt that my career warranted this splendid honor." He was very humble, mentioning several of his contemporaries who could have been honored with the award.

MacPhail compared himself to his Hall of Fame father (Larry) by listing his attributes with words such as brilliant, colorful, creative, dynamic, and innovative and then said, "I was none of those things."

He then told a gratifying story about two members of the Hall of Fame whom he was associated with when he was the Baltimore Orioles' general manager. He was asked to participate when the Orioles were going to honor Brooks Robinson with a night at Memorial Stadium. MacPhail had been the general manager during the early years of Robinson's career, but now he was the president of the American League. A couple of nights before the ceremony, the Orioles were involved in a tight pennant race and were playing a game in Toronto where they were leading in the seventh inning when it started to rain. The Orioles' manager, Earl Weaver, was confident that the umpires would call the game, but it cleared up and the umpires wanted to resume the game. Weaver thought his players could get hurt on the wet field so he refused to let them go out and the Orioles ended up forfeiting the game. The Orioles protested but MacPhail upheld the ump's ruling. Naturally, the Baltimore fans were livid about this decision, so that when MacPhail was introduced to say a few words, the 50,000 fans that were there all started booing. All of a sudden Weaver came bounding out of the dugout and ran to MacPhail and put his arms around him and announced into the microphone, "Don't boo this man." The booing stopped and MacPhail said, "It was like Moses' parting of the Red Sea."

MacPhail, who was 91, missed the 2009 induction but had a perfect attendance record up until then. He also serves on the Hall of Fame's Board of Directors.

Larry Doby, 73, promised the other Hall of Famers that he would keep it short, saying, "I've been told that by my wife for 52 years." He expressed his gratitude toward Jackie Robinson, Branch Rickey, Happy Chandler, and Bill Veeck, saying, "If it wasn't for them, I might not be standing here today." He acknowledged Bill Veeck's widow by having her stand, and also praised the city of Cleveland for "treating my family with the greatest respect that any man could want." He closed with a tribute to another Hall of Famer who couldn't be there by saying, "I got a call today from one of the greatest people I know and had the privilege of playing against, Ted Williams."

It should be noted, that despite the many cruelties he had to endure as the first black to integrate the American League, he praised teammate Joe Gordon, a 2009 hall inductee. Gordon, the Indians' second baseman, was the only teammate who volunteered to have a catch with him in the pre-game routine during his first game after he joined the team on July 5, 1947. Nevertheless, his teammates did warm up to him, especially when the gregarious Satchel Paige joined the team in 1948. Doby and Paige went on to form an interracial barbershop quartet with white teammates Eddie Robinson and Jim Hegan.

Doby attended the next three inductions before passing away in 2003 at the age of 78.

The last inductee was Don Sutton, who began with a light-hearted comment, "If everything holds true to form with my career, Rollie Fingers will do the last two parts of my speech." He continued to display his sarcastic wit when he talked about being in the hall with all these great players. "If you don't feel an aura that's almost spiritual when you walk through the Hall of Fame with these people, then check tomorrow's obituary, you're in it."

Sutton spoke with pride when he talked about his sixth grade teacher, Henry Roper, a former professional baseball pitcher. Roper taught him so well that Sutton continued to pitch the way he taught him right up until his last major league pitch. He went on to praise a lot of his former teammates with special praise for his first manager, Walter Alston. He gave the most credit to a former pitching coach, Red Adams, who meant more to his career than anyone else. "Without him I wouldn't be standing here."

He talked with reverence about his father, who told him, "There are going to be a lot of people in baseball that are better than you, but don't let anyone out work you."

He saved his most emotional acknowledgment for his wife, Mary, and their baby daughter, Jackie, who survived tremendous odds after being born 16 weeks prematurely. She was now a healthy two year old. He addressed her by declaring, "You have helped remind me of how much more important life is than the things in life, even this."

He closed, "With apologies to Lou Gehrig, I'm the luckiest man on the face of the Earth."

Don Sutton has never missed an induction since.

1999

The 1999 election had the BBWAA cast 497 ballots and finishing first was flame thrower Nolan Ryan with 98.79 percent (491 votes). Ryan was selected in his first year of eligibility and finished with the second highest percentage ever, right behind former teammate and friend Tom Seaver, who had 98.83 percent.

Finishing second was Royals third baseman George Brett, who had 98.2 percent (488 votes). Brett was also elected in his first year of eligibility. This was the fourth highest percentage ever as Brett became the first Kansas City Royal to be elected to the hall.

Finishing third was Milwaukee Brewer shortstop Robin Yount with 77.5 percent (385 votes). He was elected in his first year of eligibility, making this the first class since the inaugural class of 1936 to have more than two players elected in their first year of eligibility.

The VC selected slugging first baseman Orlando Cepeda, who was elected to the Hall of Fame 25 years after he retired. He did well the 15 years that he was on the BBWAA ballot, as he finished with 2,406 votes. His best showing was his last year on the ballot in 1994, when he finished second with 73 percent, missing induction by seven votes.

The VC also selected National League manager Frank Selee, 94 years after he last managed in the major leagues and 90 years after he died. Selee had a winning percentage of .598 and won five pennants so there is no obvious reason why it took him so long. Nestor Chylak became the eighth umpire voted in by the VC. He was inducted 21 years after he retired and 17 years after he died.

Smokey Joe Williams was also selected by the VC, making him the seventh and final selection. He was the sixteenth former Negro Leaguer selected, some 67 years after he retired and 48 years after he died. It is a mystery why it took him so long, especially after a leading African American newspaper, the Pittsburgh *Courier*, conducted a poll in 1951 of knowledgeable baseball writers and Negro Leagues experts. They chose Williams over Satchel Paige as the outstanding Negro Leagues pitcher by a score of 20–19.[26]

Inductees

Nolan Ryan was part of the champion Miracle Mets in 1969, the only time he would make it to a World Series in his record 27-year career. He became a premier starting pitcher with the California Angels in 1972 where he had his best season in 1974 as he won 22 games, led the league in innings pitched and strikeouts, and threw a no-hitter while pitching for a last place team. Ryan spent the next 14 years in his home state of Texas with the Houston Astros and Texas Rangers. He was an eight-time all-star, pitched a record seven no-hitters, set the single season (383) and career (5,714) strikeout records, and finished with a record of 324–292.

"The Ryan Express" threw a 100-mph fastball that led Reggie Jackson to exclaim, "He puts fear in me because he could kill me."[27]

George Brett is the only player to win batting titles in three different decades, have six straight three-hit games, and retire with 3000 hits, 600 doubles, 100 triples and 200 stolen bases. He helped lead the Royals to three straight division crowns (1976 through 1978), only to lose to the Yankees all three times. He just played in 117 games because of a knee injury in 1980, yet was the MVP, winning his second batting crown (.390), and had 118 RBIs. This time they defeated the Yankees, but lost to the Phillies for the title. The Royals finally won their only title in 1985 when they defeated the Cardinals, and Brett won his only Gold Glove at third base. He was a consistent postseason hitter, batting .340 in six LCS and .373 in two World Series. He batted .305 lifetime.

He will always be remembered for the pine tar bat incident. The image of him storming out of the dugout at Yankee Stadium and going after umpire Tim McClelland is his most memorable moment despite all these accomplishments.

Robin Yount spent his entire career with the Milwaukee Brewers, where he broke in as an 18-year-old shortstop. He won his first MVP award in 1982 when he led the American League in four offensive categories and batted .331. He also won his only Gold Glove as he led the league in assists. Yount topped it all off by leading the Brewers to the World Series where they lost to the Cardinals as Yount batted .414. He became the first player to have two four-hit games in a Fall Classic and was named *The Sporting News* Player of the Year. He switched to center field in 1985 after suffering a shoulder injury and won his second MVP award in 1989. He finished with 3,142 hits and batted .285.

Yount left baseball in 1978 to become a pro golfer and returned to baseball after a few months. He later revealed he had hurt his foot in a motorcycle accident, and didn't tell anyone because he didn't think he would be able to play baseball at the same level.

Orlando Cepeda was a unanimous pick for Rookie of the Year with the San Francisco Giants in 1958 and helped lead them to the pennant in 1962. He was out most of 1965 following a knee operation, and was traded to the Cards in 1966, where he batted .301 and was the Comeback Player of the Year. He led the Cards to two pennants (1967 and 1968) and a world title in 1967 when he won the MVP award (unanimously again) in 1967. He was traded to the American League and won his fourth major award when he was chosen Designated Hitter of the Year in 1973 while with the Boston Red Sox. He batted .297 lifetime with 379 home runs.

Cepeda was the son of Perucho Cepeda, one of the greatest players to come out of Puerto Rico. He played basketball as a child rather than baseball because of the pressure of who he was but switched to baseball after he severely damaged his knee at the age of 15.

Frank Selee was the manager of the Boston Beaneaters in the 1890s when they won five pennants in eight years. He was fired when the team slipped but was hired by the Cubs in 1902 where he showed a knack for evaluating talent. He moved Frank Chance to first base, Joe Tinker to shortstop, and Johnny Evers to second base while acquiring pitcher "Three Finger" Brown. Sadly, Selee left after he came down with TB. Chance took over Selee's team and won four pennants and two titles. Selee finished at 1,284–862 (.598).

He had a deaf outfielder in the minors named "Dummy" Hoy. Selee came up with the idea of relaying the ump's ball-strike calls from the third base coaching box by raising fingers to the left-handed hitting Hoy. This may have been the first use of hand signals, and it helped Hoy as he went on to a 14-year major league career.

Nestor Chylak, as an American League umpire, established himself as a decisive, patient, consistent and unflappable arbiter. One of Chylak's proudest accomplishments is that he never threw the notorious umpire-baiter Earl Weaver out of a game. During his career, he worked six All-Star Games, three ALC Series, and five World Series, including the first series night game. He worked the 1960 classic when Bill Mazeroski hit the walk-off home run and the 1977 night game when Reggie Jackson hit three home runs.

His most memorable experience was at a Cleveland night game that was called Ten Cent Beer Night because a cup of beer cost only a dime. Chylak injured his wrist when fans ran out on the field earlier in the game. Then the Indians tied the game in the bottom of the ninth and had the winning run on third with two out when several hundred fans went berserk and stormed the field. Chylak immediately called the game and awarded a forfeit to the visiting Texas Rangers. Commissioner Kuhn lauded him for his decisiveness.

"Smokey" Joe Williams was given his nickname (supposedly after he shut out the New

York Giants in a 1919 exhibition game) by the Giants' Ross Youngs (Hall of Famer) when he said to Joe, "Hell of a game, Smokey."[28] Williams began with Rube Foster and the Leland Giants in 1910 and during his 23 years pitching for Negro teams he was considered by many as the fastest Negro pitcher ever — even faster than Satchel Paige. It was said that he was so fast that he needed two catchers to catch a game.

In 1930 Williams pitched a classic 12-inning game for the Homestead Grays against the Kansas City Monarchs, which he won 1–0 while striking out 27. He and his opposing pitcher scuffed up the ball making it difficult to see as the night game, played in poor lighting as well, ended when the third baseman "couldn't find the ball."

Induction

The 1999 Induction Ceremony was held on July 25, a hot day as the biggest crowd ever (more than 50,000), was there, including a record-tying 38 Hall of Famers. The national anthem was sung by Broadway star Patti LuPone, and the new president of the Hall of Fame, Dale Petroskey, was introduced.

Fans came from everywhere to honor their heroes. A transplanted Midwestern couple from Texas started planning their trip years ago in order to honor Robin Yount. A transplanted Texan came from Canada with his two-year-old son, who was named after his favorite player, Nolan Ryan. Many other Midwesterners drove and flew for their hero, George Brett. Fans came from Pennsylvania because they lived near umpire Nestor Chylak's home and they wanted to honor him even though he had passed away. A contingent of 500 fans that included the governor, Pedro Rosello, and Roberto Clemente's widow came from Puerto Rico to honor Orlando Cepeda. Finally, the owner of the Texas Rangers and future president of the United States, George W. Bush, was there for a former member of his team, Nolan Ryan.

The first inductee introduced by Commissioner Bud Selig was someone he was associated with for 20 years as the owner of the Milwaukee Brewers and that was Robin Yount. Selig said, "All I can say on behalf of myself and the fans of Milwaukee and Wisconsin, it has been an unbelievable privilege."

Yount, 43, began his speech by giving a personal anecdote about each of the three other living inductees that he was sharing the stage with today. First, when he was a rookie he spent a day in a rowboat fishing with Nolan Ryan and said, "There wasn't a lot of conversation that day." He added, "I never faced a pitcher with better stuff than Nolan Ryan." Next he spoke about being teammates with Orlando Cepeda, when he was 19 and playing winter ball in Puerto Rico. He told the crowd that "he went out of his way to make a young kid a long way from home feel comfortable." He then spoke about George Brett, his friend, and said simply, "Nobody played the game harder than George."

He later paid a special tribute to the late Harvey Kuenn, his first hitting coach and then his manager, when he said, "He taught me more about the game of baseball both on and off the field than anyone [else]." He also talked about Bud Selig, who he said really cared about his players. "Every time I left his office I always felt that something good was going to happen."

He closed like a number of others (the most recent being Don Sutton) when he said, "with all due respect, Mr. Gehrig, today I consider myself the luckiest man on the face of the Earth." He then asked everyone to remember the families of the men who lost their lives in the construction of the new stadium in Milwaukee.

Yount has returned infrequently because of coaching duties although he came in 2009.

Commissioner Selig, before introducing the next inductee, acknowledged Ted Williams, now confined to a wheelchair after a number of strokes, who was about to leave the stage for another commitment.

The next inductee was manager Frank Selee, who died of tuberculosis at the age of 49 in 1909. Since he had no representatives, Mr. Selig read from his plaque.

The third inductee was Smokey Joe Williams, who it should be mentioned was honored by the New York Giants before a game at the Polo Grounds in 1950. He died the next year at the age of 64. Since he also had no surviving family members, he was also recognized with Selig reading from his plaque.

The fourth inductee was Orlando Cepeda, 61. Cepeda was known as the "Baby Bull" since his father was called "The Bull." He continued the mutual admiration society started by Yount as he told the audience that he played with George Brett for two months in Kansas City in 1974 and said, "This kid is not going to make it." He then admitted "Sometimes you make mistakes." When he was with Yount in Puerto Rico, he knew "This kid is going to make it." Cepeda said hitting against Nolan Ryan "is like eating soup with a fork."

He singled out his first Giants manager, Bill Rigney, for the confidence he showed in him, and the Giants' organization that brought him back to baseball in 1996.

He thanked the Veterans Committee for selecting him, and closed by saying some words in Spanish for the large contingent of Spanish people in the audience, especially the many people waving Puerto Rican flags.

Besides his own induction, Cepeda's favorite Cooperstown memory is on his first visit for the annual Hall of Fame exhibition game in 1966 when he hit two home runs. He also enjoys coming back for each induction, and his perfect attendance attests to that.

The next honoree was umpire Nestor Chylak, who had passed away in 1982 at the age of 59. He was represented by his son, Bob, who gave a heartwarming speech about his dad. He told the crowd that his father heard about his son's birth when the message was shown on the scoreboard at Yankee Stadium while he was umpiring.

He thanked Ted Williams and Yogi Berra, who always spoke highly of Chylak when they played, and the rest of the VC for electing him. He also paid tribute to a special committee that was formed in Chylak's hometown of Scranton that helped "jump start his selection by the VC." He also thanked all the people who traveled from Scranton to attend this induction as well as former colleagues, umpires Richie Garcia and Don Denkinger, for being there as well.

He talked about his father's Ukrainian ancestry and how he had planned to be an engineer while attending Rutgers, but when World War II broke out, his father became a sergeant in one of the army's elite Ranger battalions assigned to the 106th Infantry Division. His unit was in the thick of the Battle of the Bulge and had a high casualty rate, but Chylak survived and received a Silver Star for bravery under fire and a Purple Heart after being wounded in the face by shrapnel.

Although his son didn't talk about it, his father was injured when a German shell exploded near his face, blinding him for a period of about 10 days. He ultimately recovered, but not before spending almost a year in military hospitals.

The thing that his father enjoyed the most was visiting a local veterans hospital on a weekly basis during the off-season in Wilkes-Barre, Pennsylvania, and spending hours there, leaving everybody "with a smile on their face." This is why his son was very forthright

Lou Brock signs at one of the free autograph sessions for kids at the Otesaga Hotel during the 1990s. Seated next to him in the white hat is Luis Aparicio.

when he called his father "my hero" and said, "I admired my father for the way he lived his life more so than for his career."

He concluded his speech with a story about his father when he was inducted into the Scranton Hall of Fame. Chylak had his 18-year-old son speak for him because he was delayed coming from a game in Cleveland. His son was nervous during his speech but before he was finished his father appeared with a big grin on his face. Bob Chylak then said, "Today as I look real hard, I can see him standing back there smiling."

The next inductee to speak was Nolan Ryan, 52, and he began by saying, "I am truly humbled by this honor." He thanked his wife and three children for their support as the main reason why he was able to play as long as he did. He mentioned people in each of the four organizations where he spent his major league career. He had special kudos for the Mets' scout who signed him, Red Murff, because "he wasn't discouraged by my build at

Stan Musial plays "Take Me Out to the Ballgame" on his harmonica during an induction in the 1990s.

6'2" and 140 pounds or the way I threw a baseball as many other scouts were." He also mentioned Tom Seaver for the influence he had on him, and owner Gene Autry of the Angels for the way he treated everyone.

He mentioned the Houston Astros conditioning coach, Gene Coleman, who helped him pitch as long as he did. Ryan also credited the pitching coach with the Texas Rangers, Tom House, for coming up with new training techniques that helped him get in the best shape of his life.

He singled out Marvin Miller, the first president of the Players Association, as having a significant effect on improving the financial situation of all players. Ryan illustrated his point by saying that when he first pitched in the majors he had to go back home and pump gas while his wife also had to work, which all changed for the better because of Miller. He saved his final accolade for the fans. "I was truly blessed by the support I received from the fans, and I appreciate all the times that you supported me over the 27 years I played."

Although Ryan has returned to the Hall of Fame on at least one occasion, he has never come back for another induction. Possibly it has to do with his philosophy of "never reminiscing or reflecting back, and instead being concerned with today and tomorrow."[29] He is now involved in ranching, banking, and is the president of the Texas Rangers.

George Brett, 46, was the last of the seven inductees, and he exclaimed, "God, Robin, you don't know how lucky you were to go first." He then complimented the Hall of Fame staff for making his family feel so welcome. "You are truly the game's caretakers."

Brett then continued by addressing his fellow inductees. He stated that good friend Robin Yount was his favorite opponent to play against and he was glad that Cepeda "wasn't a scout for Kansas City." He played against Nolan Ryan for 13 years and they hardly knew each other, but after being in New York City for the Hall of Fame press conference they "developed a little friendship and hopefully it will grow."

Brett paid tribute to many of his former teammates and managers including Whitey Herzog, with whom he had a special bond of hunting, fishing and playing golf together. He singled out former Royals owner Avron Fogelman for inspiring him to come into the 1985 season in the best shape of his career that helped the Royals win their only title. He had special praise for Charlie Lau, his first hitting instructor, who transformed him from a free swinger to a picture-perfect hitter by teaching him to shift his weight as he swung. Brett said, "Thank you for molding me and making today possible."

He acknowledged the people of Kansas City where he played for 21 years, met his wife, where his three boys were born (the youngest named after Robin Yount) and where he now lives. He also thanked the many people who made the long trip from KC to be with him in Cooperstown for the induction.

The most emotional part of his speech was when he talked about his three brothers, including Ken, a big league pitcher for 14 seasons. He said, "You know sometimes I wonder why all this happened to me and not you. All I ever wanted to be was as good as you," whereby he started to cry.

His favorite Cooperstown memory was the 2000 Induction because he was able to enjoy it and not be stressed out like he was for his own in 1999. He not only has come back for every induction, but he also participates in the Fantasy Camp every fall, which gives people a chance to play with Hall of Famers while raising money for the Hall of Fame.

CHAPTER 10

The Hall of Fame Welcomes Its First Woman Inductee and Cal and Tony Draw 75,000 People: 2000–2010

2000

Four hundred ninety-nine ballots were cast in the 2000 BBWAA election as longtime catcher Carlton Fisk finished first with 79.6 percent (397 votes). It was his second year of eligibility after having received 66 percent (330 votes) in 1999 when he finished fourth.

Finishing second was RBI producer Tony Perez, who had 77.2 percent (385 votes) in his ninth year of eligibility. He became the first Cuban major leaguer to be voted into the Hall of Fame. Perez received a total of 2,599 votes in the nine elections.

The VC selected Sparky Anderson as the 16th manager to be honored with induction. He was voted in by the VC five years after he had stopped managing.

The VC also selected nineteenth-century Cincinnati Reds second baseman Bid McPhee, whose career began before 1945. McPhee retired after the 1899 season and died in 1943 at the age of 83. He was so obscure that most Reds fans didn't know of him in 2000 and he wasn't chosen for the Cincinnati Reds Hall of Fame until 2002.

One reason everyone forgot about him was because he didn't have impressive batting statistics. According to David Fleitz sabermetrics made the VC aware of him. Statistical historians John Thorn and Pete Palmer developed their Total Player Rating that enabled them to attach meaning to fielding statistics, which helped them determine that McPhee was the greatest fielding second baseman of the nineteenth century.[1]

The VC selected center fielder Turkey Stearnes as the seventeenth Negro Leagues player.

Inductees

Carlton "Pudge" Fisk had an outstanding rookie season with the Red Sox in 1972. He won the Rookie of the Year (unanimously) and led the league in triples while winning his only Gold Glove as a catcher. He recovered from knee surgery in 1974 only to break his forearm in 1975. Fisk recovered from that as well, hitting .331 and helping to lead the Red Sox to the World Series by batting .417 in the LCS. He signed with the Chicago White Sox in 1981 and marked the occasion by reversing his uniform number from #27 to #72. Despite two broken hands in his 13 seasons with the White Sox, he set the record for games caught and home runs (since broken by Mike Piazza) by a catcher.

Fisk hit a most memorable home run at Fenway Park against the Cincinnati Reds in Game Six of the 1975 World Series. He began jumping and waving his arms when he was going down the first base line as his walk-off home run hit the netting attached to the foul pole in the twelfth inning. The left field foul pole is now called the Fisk Pole.

Tony Perez was nicknamed "Big Dog" by Reds manager Dave Bristol, who said, "If the game goes long enough, the Big Dog will bite."[2] The first baseman played in seven All-Star Games and was the hero in his first one in 1967 when he hit a home run in the 15th inning, winning it for the National League. Perez hit a decisive home run in the seventh game against the Red Sox in 1975 to help the Big Red Machine claim their first of two consecutive titles. He drove in the second-most runs, behind teammate Johnny Bench, in the National League in the 1970s.

He played in both leagues and for four teams (Reds twice) during his 23-year career. He enjoyed two distinctions: in 2,777 games he was never on the disabled list nor was he ever thrown out of a game.

George "Sparky" Anderson made an auspicious debut as a rookie manager with the Cincinnati Reds in 1970 when he won 102 games, beat the Pirates in the LCS, and lost to the Orioles in the World Series. He went on to win five division titles with the Reds, four pennants, and two World Series with the Big Red Machine (1975 and 1976). He then became manager of the Detroit Tigers in 1979 and in 17 years won two divisional titles, one pennant, and the 1984 World Series. He became the first manager to win World Series' titles in both leagues. He was named Manager of the Year in both leagues and finished with a record of 2,194–1,834 (.545), and 34–21 (.615) in postseason play.

Growing up in California, Anderson was the batboy for coach Rod Dedeaux and the USC Trojans for six years. He also won an American Legion championship as a player at Detroit's Briggs Stadium, where he would later win a title with the Tigers.

John McPhee became known as "Bid" while working as a young man in his uncle's hotel kitchen, where he did the bidding of anyone who needed him. He broke in with the Reds in 1882 when their team was in the American Association — they remained until joining the National League in 1890. McPhee holds both the single season and career record for putouts by a second baseman.. He also led the league 33 times in four different fielding categories. He wasn't a slouch as a lead-off hitter either, having 189 triples and 568 stolen bases lifetime. He played 18 years with the Reds and batted .272 lifetime.

Despite the fact that his father worked with leather as a saddle maker, he refused to wear a glove. He compensated by soaking his hands in brine each spring to toughen them for the season. Finally, he gave in after hurting his hand in 1896 and became the last infielder to start wearing a glove. It definitely helped as he fielded .978, the record for 29 years.

Norman Stearnes was called "Turkey" as a child because of the way he flapped his arms when he ran. He was a good center fielder with the speed to lead off or the power to bat cleanup. He batted more than .400 twice while leading the league in triples four times and home runs six times. He played for a number of teams from 1923 through 1941 while winning pennants with the Chicago American Giants and the Kansas City Monarchs. He played in four East-West all-star games and finished with 183 home runs and a career batting average of .345.

Stearnes had an idiosyncrasy and that was he would spend time talking to his bats. Negro Leagues' player and historian Buck O'Neil once visited his room at night and found him in his pajamas speaking to his bats. Stearnes told his 35-inch bat he would have hit the ball over the fence if he had used it instead of his 34-inch bat.

Induction

The 2000 Induction Ceremony was held July 23, on a partly cloudy day with 25,000 people in attendance, including a record 48 Hall of Famers. Many of the fans came from Cincinnati because not only were three Reds being inducted into the Hall of Fame, but Reds broadcaster Marty Brennaman was to receive the Ford Frick Award as well.

Also, Sparky Anderson as manager of the Reds, Tony Perez, the Reds' first baseman, and Red Sox catcher Carlton Fisk were all involved in the memorable 1975 World Series. The ceremony lasted about four hours with Carlton Fisk giving possibly the longest induction speech ever.

Yankee Stadium public address announcer Bob Sheppard was there celebrating 50 years as the Voice of the Yankees. He was also there to present the Hall of Fame with the microphone that he used for the past half century to introduce all the Yankees' Hall of Famers, and many of the other Hall of Famers as well, who were present on the stage.

Since Bid McPhee had no representative, Commissioner Bud Selig read from his plaque, which included, "he was the last second baseman to play without a glove."

Sparky Anderson, 66, spoke first and began with, "Please sit down because I learned a long time ago when the fans stand at a ballpark, they are getting ready to boo." He thanked everyone at the Hall of Fame for the way he was treated, having never experienced anything like that, leading him to say to his wife, "You know they're treating me so good, I feel like I'm important. Maybe I'll start acting like I'm important." She immediately burst his bubble when she said, "It wouldn't do any good, 'cause nobody would pay attention."

He stated that his coaches "worked with him and not for him," just as Al Lopez said in 1977. He also shared with the crowd simple words of advice that his father gave him: "Every person you meet, be nice to them and treat them like they are someone."

Nettie Stearnes represented her husband, Turkey Stearnes, who had died in 1979 at the age of 78. She was her husband's biggest booster because she stated in her opening remark, "I prayed for this to happen for 20 years and now that my prayers have been answered, I'm grateful." She then went on to thank many people as well as the VC for his induction. She was very gracious and proud to have her husband go into the Hall of Fame with the other four inductees. She said that her husband's induction "gives our family much needed closure."

Tony Perez, 58, began with, "It's hard to describe the emotion of happiness." Moments later he uttered, "I doubt that a king at his coronation feels better than me." He thanked the people of Cincinnati for "embracing me and refusing to boo me." He spoke of three special places, the United States (mainland), "where the best baseball is played," Puerto Rico, his adopted home, and Cuba, where he was born. He later quipped, "I think they made me wait so long because they wanted Sparky and me to go in together." He closed with a few lines in Spanish.

Before his induction, Dave Hyde wrote a column in the Florida *Sun Sentinel* entitled "Perez's Courage Unique in Hall of Fame." Hyde explained that Perez signed with the Reds in 1960 when Castro took over in Cuba. Perez started his minor league career in Geneva, New York; his four Cuban teammates all left because they were homesick, but he stayed in pursuit of his dream. On the advice of his father, Perez never returned to Cuba after 1962 because if he did, his parents were afraid he wouldn't be able to return to the United States. His parents never saw him play professional baseball, and he didn't see his father again until 1972 when his father was stricken with cancer. His dad died in 1979 but Perez wasn't able to return to Cuba until a year after his father was buried. Hyde exclaims, "No one else in the Hall gave more, lost more, sacrificed more in chasing their dreams than Tony Perez."[3]

He has only missed one induction since he was inducted.

The final inductee was Carlton Fisk, 52, nicknamed "Pudge" because he was chubby as a kid. He talked about growing up and going to the University of New Hampshire on a basketball scholarship and dreaming of "becoming a power forward for the Boston Celtics," but realizing it wouldn't happen because "power forwards don't usually stop growing at 6'1"."

Fisk paid homage to the Players Association and its leaders, Marvin Miller and Donald Fehr, as well as trailblazer Curt Flood "for his sacrifice," and the first successful free agents, Andy Messersmith and Dave McNally, "for their courage."

He talked about all his injuries, including his reconstructed left knee, figuring that he missed about five and a half years as a result of them. He was able to recover, thanks to strength and conditioning coach Phil Classen. Fisk also paid tribute to hitting coach Walt Hriniak as "the single most important person in my baseball life." He praised both by stating he would not have made it to the Hall of Fame without either of them.

He talked about many others who helped him and summed all of them up succinctly with an old Hopi Indian proverb, "You cannot pick up a pebble with one finger." He closed with, "It's not what you achieve in life that defines you, it's what you overcome."

The speech was reportedly 38 minutes and next year's inductees were kidded by some Hall of Famers not to "Fisk it."

Fisk's first visit to Cooperstown was a memorable one when he hit a home run at Doubleday Field in 1965 when he was 17 and a member of a Vermont American Legion team. He has come back for every induction since his own.

2001

The 2001 BBWAA election had 515 ballots cast and outfielder Dave Winfield finished first with 84.5 percent (435 votes). He was elected in his first year of eligibility. Winfield was originally from Minnesota and was friends with fellow inductee Kirby Puckett. They started the Winfield-Puckett Baseball League and, with the help of the Minnesota Twins, the league now has 2,000 kids playing baseball in Minnesota.

Finishing second was Twins center fielder Puckett who received 82.1 percent (423 votes). He was also elected in his first year of eligibility. Both he and Winfield were teammates on the Twins in 1994 and 1995. Puckett alluded to their friendship during his speech when he said, "I can't tell you what a joy it is to be inducted with a friend."

The VC elected slick-fielding Pittsburgh Pirates second baseman Bill Mazeroski 29 years after he retired. Maz received 1,324 votes after 15 years on the BBWAA ballot.

Despite this support from the BBWAA, his selection was controversial because he wasn't much of an offensive player. Bill James felt that although he was a below-average hitter for a second baseman, he was an outstanding defensive player, indicating that he was a Hall of Famer (p. 338). Robert Cohen rates him the worst second baseman in the hallowed shrine. Cohen calls Mazeroski below average offensively and believes he got in because former Pirates executive Joe Brown was on the VC (pp. 61–65).

Zev Chafets in his 2009 book, *Cooperstown Confidential*, credits John T. Bird as being the impetus behind Mazeroski's election. Bird was such a fan that he wrote a book, *The Bill Mazeroski Story*, and sent a copy to every member of the Veterans Committee. Bird then followed up with a four-minute campaign video, and traveled to where the VC met in Tampa, Florida, and lobbied for his man.[4]

The final selection by the VC was pitcher Hilton Smith, who was the eighteenth member of the Negro Leagues to be chosen for the hall. This was 18 years after the quiet and reserved Smith had passed away. David Fleitz reveals that Smith, contrary to his character, for many years after he retired sent press clippings and a short autobiography to Hall of Fame officials and various members of the VC along with clippings detailing the accomplishments of other prominent Negro Leaguers as well.[5] His hopes were raised when former teammate Buck O'Neil was appointed to the VC, who eventually helped get him elected.

Inductees

Dave Winfield joined a select group of players who went directly to the majors without playing in the minors. He played mainly right field during eight seasons with the San Diego Padres and then signed with the Yankees as their left fielder. He drove in more than 100 runs six seasons with them and played in one World Series while missing the 1989 season with a bad back. Despite being 6'6", Winfield was a five-tool player who won seven Gold Gloves and was an all-star 12 straight times. He finally won a title with Toronto in 1992 and finished with 3,110 hits, 465 home runs, and batted .283 lifetime.

Yankees owner George Steinbrenner feuded with Winfield, and tried to get dirt on his star, resulting in a three-year suspension for Steinbrenner. He also called Winfield "Mr. May" after he performed poorly in the 1981 World Series.

Kirby Puckett made a promising debut in 1984 with four singles and then batted .296 and led the league's outfielders with 16 assists for the season. Puckett went on to win six Gold Gloves but showed little power his first two seasons. Former Twins batting champ Tony Oliva rectified his lack of power by changing his batting stance. Puckett played in ten straight All-Star Games and was the 1993 All-Star MVP when he hit a home run and a double. He helped lead the Twins to titles in 1987 and 1991, hitting .357 in the 1987 World Series and .429 in the LCS in 1991. His defining moment came in the sixth game of the 1991 classic when he made an outstanding catch and then won the game in the eleventh inning with a home run. He retired with a .318 batting average.

The charismatic Puckett's life changed after he was hit by a Dennis Martinez pitch on September 28, 1995. His jaw was broken and the next season he was diagnosed with glaucoma, causing irreversible vision damage (right eye) and ending his 12-year career.

Bill Mazeroski had range, quickness, good hands, and an accurate arm and is arguably the best-fielding second baseman of all time. Charles Faber in his book, *Baseball Ratings*, awards points for fielding percentage, assists, chances, and range factor to all players with at least 10 years' experience, and Maz leads every player.[6] He won eight Gold Gloves and was so impressive in completing the double play that he was called "No Touch" because he never seemed to touch the ball when he was making the pivot. He holds both the season and career record for double plays by a second baseman.

Yet he is most known for the walk-off home run that he hit against the Yankees in the seventh game of the 1960 World Series. Every year on October 13, Pirates fans visit the place where Forbes Field was in order to honor his feat.

Hilton Smith pitched for the Kansas City Monarchs from 1936 through 1948. He had such an outstanding curveball that Stan Musial and Johnny Mize, after hitting against him in an exhibition game, said "they had never seen a curve ball like that."[7] Smith was 6–1 against major league barnstormers and helped the Monarchs win the Negro American League pennant four straight years. He won one game in the Negro World Series in 1942 when the Monarchs swept the Homestead Grays. Smith was the exact opposite of his flamboyant teammate Satchel Paige.

Smith served with Jackie Robinson in the army during World War II and recommended him to the Monarchs. Robinson played one year with them before his historic signing with the Brooklyn Dodgers prior to 1946.

Induction

The 2001 Induction Ceremony was held on a steamy afternoon on August 5 that was witnessed by 23,000 people with 43 Hall of Famers present.

The national anthem was sung by former Brooklyn Dodgers pitcher Ralph Branca. It was the 50th anniversary of his surrendering the home run to New York Giants Bobby Thomson that resulted in the Giants winning the pennant.

The invocation was given by former Pirates outfielder and Mazeroski teammate Al Oliver, who was now the deacon at Buela Baptist Church in Portsmouth, Ohio.

Dave Winfield, 49, led off and gave a long speech causing someone to joke, "It was that long because he thanked everyone he ever met." He began his speech with a bit of irony, stating he was born the day the Giants clinched the pennant on October 3, 1951.

He talked about the Negro Leagues Hall of Fame players such as Cool Papa Bell and Satchel Paige, saying, "Whatever bad things I experienced in Major League Baseball, it was better than anything they had to endure." He acknowledged that one of the nicest tributes he ever received was when they told him, "Man, you could have played with us."

Winfield said he had to decide what to do after he was drafted by the Minnesota Vikings as a tight end (he never played football at the University of Minnesota.) He was also drafted as a power forward by the Atlanta Hawks and Utah Stars (he played basketball in college). The Padres also drafted him after he starred for the University of Minnesota baseball team, which is what he chose because "baseball is the best game of all."

He talked about many people and had kind words for George Steinbrenner, thanking him for bringing him to the Yankees. "You know I'm glad that time and distance have brought about a respect and friendship that we didn't have early on and I'm glad we have it today." He also was gracious toward the five other teams that he played with.

Winfield spoke of overcoming adversity as one of the things that baseball has taught him, citing Abraham Lincoln as a perfect example. Lincoln overcame poverty, losing elections, and business failures but still rose above it all to become president. Winfield didn't mention this but he overcame his own adversity after he missed the entire 1989 season because of a slipped disc and a bad back to become the Comeback Player of the Year in 1990.

He talked about his foundation and some of the things that it has accomplished such as finding jobs for 25,000 kids in New York over a two-year period and providing scholarships for kids in Minnesota.

"Winnie" closed with, "I've given to baseball everything that I had and baseball has given its best back to me today."

His favorite Cooperstown memory was playing in the annual Doubleday Field exhibition game and getting to meet some of the Negro League Hall of Famers. He sat around laughing and joking with them. He has had perfect attendance since his own induction.

The next speaker was Bill Mazeroski, 64, and he began with a prelude of things to come when he said, "I've got twelve pages here. That's not like me. I'll probably skip half of it and get halfway through and quit anyhow. It's getting awfully hot out here so that's a good excuse to make it short." He then went on to tell the audience that he was being inducted because of his defensive abilities, stating, "Defense deserves as much credit as pitching and hitting." He thanked the Veterans Committee and thought the greatest thing that happened to him was when his number was retired by the Pirates, but then said, "it's hard to top this."

Maz started to lose it as he said, "I don't think I'm going to make it. I think you can kiss those twelve pages down the drain." He continued, "I want to thank all those friends who made this long trip to listen to me speak and hear this crap." He thanked everyone and said, "That's enough." Sobbing, he walked away from the microphone.

Later on, MC George Grande told the crowd that Mazeroski didn't get a chance to thank some people, including his wife and two sons, but then said, "Maybe it was one of the shortest speeches, but it was one of the most wonderful moments."

Mike Shannon, in his book *More Tales from the Dugout*, said, "It was the shortest but probably most memorable speech as everyone in the audience of 20,000 people rose to give him a thunderous ovation, including other Hall of Famers."[8]

Joe Morgan, Hall of Famer and a member of the board of directors, later told the crowd, "One of my duties is to talk to the inductees and kind of time their speeches. Until this year I have never been successful. So I want to thank Bill Mazeroski for helping me with that." The speech was actually two minutes and thirty seconds.

The late Gene Carney, SABR member, author, and longtime Pirates fan, was at the induction and adds that there were Pirates fans throughout the crowd who were wearing T-shirts that said, "Maz 2001—It's about time." Carney also said when Mazeroski was having a hard time continuing, many in the crowd were yelling, "You can do it, Maz."[9]

Bill Mazeroski is overwhelmed with emotion and can't finish his induction speech in 2001.

Mazeroski has had perfect attendance at every induction since.

It should also be noted that during his first All-Star Game in 1958, Maz was paid the ultimate compliment by his peers when both teams, during fielding practice, stopped to watch him work out around second base.

Finally, on a lighter note, Maz used only three or four gloves during his entire career. Once, while sitting in the dugout with the great Roberto Clemente, Clemente tried to give Mazeroski's glove away so that he would get a new one. This particular glove used to come apart and had leather patches all over it. Clemente picked it up and threw it to a kid in the stands. The kid took one look at it and threw it back.

The next inductee, Hilton Smith, had died in 1983 at the age of 76. He was represented by his son, DeMorris Smith. He picked up on Mazeroski's emotional speech by declaring, "Bill, you are a hard act to follow."

He reiterated that his father was a very humble and quiet individual. He mentioned places where his father played, beginning with the start of his career in Bismarck, North Dakota. This is the place where Smith participated with an integrated team that competed in the National Baseball Congress—it was where he impressed Monarchs owner J.L. Wilkinson, who signed him to a contract. Despite never playing in the major leagues, Smith once stated, "If I had my life to do over, I would live it the same way." He recalled that his father was a good and caring man who helped to find people jobs in the Kansas City area where the Smith family lived and even had some of them live in his home. He closed with, "The only regret I have is that he is not here today to see what is happening."

The last inductee of the day was Kirby Puckett, 41, who began by saluting the fans who came all the way from Minnesota for the induction saying, "You're the best." He also mentioned words of advice that his family had for him, which had to be music to the ears of the other Hall of Famers, and that was "to keep it short."

He acknowledged his fellow inductees and everyone connected to the Twins organization. He had special praise for Tom Kelly, the manager of the two world championship teams. Puckett also praised Tony Oliva, "who helped me become a better hitter." He expressed hope that someday Oliva would also be inducted.

Puckett addressed the young people in the audience by telling them the guiding principles of his life: believe in yourself and work hard because "anything is possible. It doesn't matter if you're 5'8" like me or 6'6" like my man Winnie, you can do it."

He admitted, "I didn't get to play all the years that I wanted to," but continued with his inspirational words by saying, "Don't feel sorry for yourself if obstacles get in your way. Our great Twins World Series teams faced odds and we beat them."

In closing, he said, "I faced odds when glaucoma took the bat out of my hands, but I didn't give in or feel sorry for myself. I've said it before and I'll say it again; it may be cloudy in my right eye, but the sun is shining very brightly in my left eye."

Puckett came to the next four inductions but died in 2006 of a stroke in Phoenix, Arizona, at the age of 45. His death was felt deeply by fans everywhere, especially in Minnesota, where he could have left as a free agent after the 1992 season but chose to stay, which endeared him to Twins fans even more. He also was involved in charities throughout the Minneapolis area and was given the Branch Rickey Award in 1993 for his extensive community service.

Although Puckett spoke lovingly of his wife and two kids during his induction speech, his marriage dissolved shortly thereafter. His wife and mistress each brought protective orders against him for physical abuse. A morals charge, filed by another woman, caused him to lose his job as a community ambassador with the Twins.

One obvious cause of his death at such a young age was the tremendous amount of weight he put on after his playing career was over. Many people think that his life deteriorated so quickly, contrary to the closing words of his induction speech, because he never really got over the fact that his career ended prematurely.

2002

Four hundred seventy-two ballots were cast in the 2002 BBWAA election, and only shortstop wizard, Ozzie Smith, was elected. He received 91.7 percent (433 votes) in his first year of eligibility. The day Smith received notification of his induction was also the same day that he carried the Olympic Torch in St. Louis for his leg of the journey on its way to the Winter Olympics in Salt Lake City in 2002.

The VC revised their voting procedures and wouldn't hold their next election until 2003.

Inductee

Ozzie Smith made his debut with the San Diego Padres in 1978 where he established himself as a great defensive shortstop with incredible range. He was traded to the Cardinals prior to the 1982 season where he helped them win four divisional titles, three pennants, and one World Series. Smith rarely struck out and stole 580 bases lifetime. He batted .303 in 1987, .556 in the 1982 LCS and .435 in the 1985 LCS. He won 13 Gold Gloves and retired with the shortstop record for total chances, assists, and double plays.

Smith was "The Wizard of Oz" for his defensive prowess, and was the idol of young fans as he performed his pre-game back flip. Sports columnist Tom Boswell paid Smith the ultimate compliment when he said, "His number should be #8 turned sideways because the possibilities that he brings to the position are infinite."[10]

Induction

The 2002 Induction Ceremony was held on July 28 before 19,000 people on a muggy day. There were 48 Hall of Famers present, tying the record that was set in 2000.

Ozzie Smith, 47, made it abundantly clear right from the outset that since he was the only inductee he was going to make the most of it. He gave a clever, innovative and probably the most thought-out induction speech ever given. He broke from tradition, just as he had when he played with his pre-game back flips, by coming out with a large Afro style wig on his head to lighten the mood and also remind people what he looked like when he broke in with the San Diego Padres. He then took the wig off and for his next innovation he had his 15-year-old son, Dustin, introduce him by reading from his plaque, something the commissioner normally does. Then he used props to make his speech more meaningful. He held in his right hand a copy of the book *The Wizard of Oz* by Frank Baum, which was appropriate since the title is his nickname. In his left hand Smith held a baseball cut in half.

Smith began by telling the audience this award was too special to "simply ad-lib a few random thoughts of appreciation and joy." Instead he used a thematic approach by metaphorically weaving the three main characters that Dorothy meets on the Yellow Brick Road with the inner layers of a baseball to tell his story.

Ozzie Smith's son, Dustin, reads from his fathers plaque during the 2002 Induction Ceremony.

First he told about his dream of becoming a baseball player and how he never let go of that dream which was equivalent to the cork that is the core of the baseball. This is the essence of what Dorothy's friend the Scarecrow wants and that is a brain so that he could think and dream.

The second character is the Tin Man and what he wants is a heart so that he can experience love and believe in himself. This is like the 200 yards of wool that surrounds the core of the baseball. This represents all the people who believed in him, including his high school baseball coach who wouldn't let him quit when he started to have doubts while playing in college. His college coach in turn taught him to develop his speed and pushed him to become a switch hitter. This is when Smith developed his personal credo, "That absolutely nothing is good enough if it can be made better, and better is never good enough if it can be made best."

He talked about the third and final character, the Cowardly Lion, who wanted courage so that he could face adversity and defeat it. Smith compares this to the outer covering of a baseball which is stitched 108 times. Smith compared the covering to the inner courage that he developed in order to "hang in there when times get tough." He then gave examples of many great things we would not have if those who were pursuing their dreams didn't have the courage to withstand rejection and disappointment. Some examples were the novel *Gone with the Wind*, Dr. Seuss, Jim Henson and the Muppets, and Thomas Edison and the light bulb. They were all rejected before winning acceptance.

He then talked about himself and how he couldn't run as fast or hit the ball as far as others, yet he was able to reach the "equivalent of Mt. Everest because it's all here in this ball, within this book, and within your hearts."

He closed with, "My glove has given me much, but more importantly it has given me the ability to give back."

Smith has given back by becoming very active with the Hall of Fame's Education Committee. He now has the title of educational ambassador and raises money for the Hall by taking part in the Ozzie Smith Turn Two Program. In it, he participates with donors who get the opportunity to play second base to his shortstop while they turn a double play. He also takes part in the Fantasy Camp in October and you can even hear his voice on the message machine when you call the Hall of Fame. Needless to say, he has had perfect attendance since his own induction.

Prior to this induction, author Mike Shannon wrote about an enterprising ten-year-old boy named Nicholas Voreyer who set up a refreshment stand along with four friends for fans to stop on their way to the ceremony. The young entrepreneur honored "The Wizard" with a display area called "Facts About Ozzie Smith." He made $32.50.[11]

Legendary Phillies broadcaster Harry Kalas was honored with the Ford Frick Award and during his acceptance speech he paid tribute to the events of 9-11-01. "We come here to Cooperstown to laud our baseball heroes each year. But all of us laud America's heroes from all walks of life, whose selflessness is on display daily. Those who lay their lives on the line for our safety, you are in our hearts."

2003

For the 2003 BBWAA election, 496 ballots were cast and switch-hitting first baseman Eddie Murray finished first with 85.3 percent (423 votes) in his first year of eligibility.

The time when inductees first get the phone call is usually the happiest of occasions, but unfortunately Eddie Murray's sister had just died so he could only say "Thank you" to secretary-treasurer of the BBWAA, Jack O'Connell.

Finishing second was catcher Gary Carter, who received 78 percent (387 votes) in his sixth year of eligibility. Carter received a total of 1,680 votes.

The Veterans Committee radically changed its composition and its election procedures in August 2001. The most significant change — it went from a 15-member committee in 2001 to encompassing all living Hall of Famers as well as all living recipients of the Ford Frick and J.G. Taylor Spink Awards. Also, two members of the previous VC Committee, whose terms had not expired, remained on the newly constituted VC. There were ten new procedures that began with the 2003 VC election. Some of them were:

Elections for players would be every two years, beginning in 2003. A player had to have played 10 or more years, not been active the last 20 years, and not on the ineligible list.

Managers, umpires, and executives would be elected from a single composite ballot every four years, beginning in 2003.

Special committees were appointed to select from an original list of 200 players to a final ballot of a minimum of 25 and a maximum of 30 players. The composite ballot of managers, etc., had 15 candidates.

Balloting would now be held by mail and not in a special meeting as was done before.

The players ballot and the composite ballot would be made public before voting. The results of the voting would also be made public.

A significant change was that every player on the final list did not have to have had a certain percentage of the votes on a BBWAA ballot in order to be eligible for the VC ballot as had been done in the past. This was important because it eliminated the 60 percent Rule. Despite the good intentions to make the process fairer, no one was elected from the players ballot nor the composite ballot of managers, umpires or executives in 2003.

Inductees

Eddie Murray was the Rookie of the Year with the Baltimore Orioles in 1977 and helped them make it to the World Series in 1979 and 1983. The Orioles won the world title in 1983 as Murray hit two home runs in the decisive Game 5. He played 12 seasons with the Orioles and then played for six more teams, including the Orioles again, during his 21-year career. The switch-hitting first baseman won three Gold Gloves and set the career record for assists by a first baseman. He would also play in another World Series with the Indians in 1995. Murray was chosen for eight all-star teams and finished with the most games played at first base. He was only the third player, along with Willie Mays and Hank Aaron, to have more than 500 home runs (504) and 3000 hits (3,255).

Eddie Murray didn't have a good relationship with the press, but he was, nevertheless, a leader in the locker room. Future Hall of Famer Cal Ripken said that he learned his legendary work ethic from Eddie Murray when they were teammates.

Gary Carter split his time between catching and the outfield as a rookie for the Montreal Expos in 1975 while also being named to the all-star team. After that, catcher became his primary position as he went on to win three Gold Gloves and retire with the most total chances. He was chosen for 11 all-star teams and was the game's MVP in 1981 and 1984. He did well in the postseason in 1981, batting .421 in the Divisional Series and .438 in the LCS. He was traded to the Mets and helped lead them to a World Series title in 1986 with two home runs and nine RBIs in the series win over Boston. Carter retired after 19 seasons with 324 home runs while batting .262 lifetime.

He won the National Punt, Pass, and Kick competition for seven year olds. He had considered going to UCLA as a quarterback before an injury ended his football career.

Induction

The 2003 Induction Ceremony on July 27 was witnessed by a crowd of 18,000, including 48 Hall of Famers, on a gray and overcast day. MC George Grande began by telling everyone that Gary Carter had a special guest who was there to honor him, and it was former president George H.W. Bush. Johnny Bench, who it seems could always be counted on to help out, sang the Canadian national anthem and later did his best Harry Caray imitation by donning thick glasses as he sang "Take Me Out to the Ball Game."

The winner of the Ford Frick Award was the funniest man in baseball, Bob Uecker. Uecker, a.k.a. "Uke," stole the show as the former catcher, known as "Mr. Baseball," was at his best with his self-deprecating humor. He had a lifetime batting average of .200 for six seasons yet insisted to the audience that "I should have gone in as a player." Some of his other memorable lines were, "I signed a $3,000 bonus with the hometown Milwaukee Braves," and noted, "My old man didn't have that kind of money to put out, but the Braves took it." He played for Phillies manager Gene Mauch who would call to him on the bench and bark, "Grab a bat and stop this rally." Uke said, "I'd take my kids to a game when I was playing and they would want to go home with another player." He made reference to Hall of Famer Lou Brock, who was there, and was his teammate on the 1964 world championship Cardinals. Uecker then said, "Bing Devine was the Cards' general manager, and as we got close to World Series time, Devine asked me to do him and the Cards a favor by letting the team inject me with hepatitis so that they could call up an infielder." His final line was, "I had a great shoe and glove contract with a company who paid me a lot of money never to be seen wearing their stuff."

Gary Carter, 49, was the first inductee to speak and he began, "I'm like a kid in a candy store today because Cooperstown is where all dreams come true." He then paid homage to the 12 years that he spent with the Montreal Expos and the fact that he is wearing an Expos' cap on his plaque by saying a few words in French.

He credited Karl Kuehl, his manager in both the minors and majors, for "always believing in me more than anyone else." Carter expressed his deep appreciation for former President Bush, who came with his grandson, Robert.

Carter then told an admirable story about fellow inductee Eddie Murray, his teammate on the Dodgers for one year. He told of a side of Murray that was completely different from the image of a cold and distant person as portrayed by the press. He told how Murray gave his bat to a six-year-old kid after he had just broken it during a spring training game. He then signed it and today that is one of D.J. Carter's (Gary's son) prized possessions.

His favorite Cooperstown memory is sitting in the rocking chairs on the veranda of the Otesaga Hotel with Eddie Murray and Johnny Bench right after his induction and taking in the view of beautiful Otsego Lake. He has not missed an induction since his own.

The last speaker was Eddie Murray, 47, who was serenaded by all the Orioles' fans in

Former president George H.W. Bush attends the 2003 induction with his grandson Robert.

the crowd with chants of "Ed-die, Ed-die, Ed-die" for a long time before he had to ask them to stop so he could begin.

He began by comparing himself to Ted Williams, and his induction in 1966. Williams said he must have earned it, considering he wasn't inducted because of his friendship with the writers. Murray said, "I guess I'm proud to be in his company." He continued by explaining his philosophy, "Baseball is a team game; you win as a team and you lose as a team, and it's not an 'I' or a 'me' thing." He continued, "And that's one reason I didn't have friendships with the media, maybe like I could have."

The thing he was most proud of was having played more games at first base than anyone else. He said, "I signed a contract to play 162 games." He talked about two of his managers, Hall of Famers Earl Weaver and Tommy Lasorda, both of whom were there. He said, "Earl didn't give me a day off; he didn't believe in it." One time Murray and Lasorda argued about giving him a day off, so he reluctantly sat. Then during the game Lasorda got him up to pinch hit twice, only to not use him, forcing Murray to sit down again. At last, he called him up a third time and this time Murray hit a game-winning home run. Murray then said gleefully, "And boy, did he look good."

He praised Jim Schaffer as the person who made him a switch hitter when Schaeffer coached him in the minors. He thanked many people, including teammate Cal Ripken, Jr.

Murray closed by saying that it took a while to get used to the "Ed-die" chant during his career, but now he loves it and told the crowd to resume the chant.

He has two favorite Cooperstown memories—the first being when he batted leadoff for the only time in his career during the Doubleday Game in 1983 and got a single. The second was worrying about whether he belonged after receiving notice of his election. Then, after a couple of nights during his Induction Weekend, realizing he did belong and could finally get some sleep. He has had perfect attendance since his own induction.

2004

The 2004 BBWAA election had 506 ballots cast. Finishing first was designated hitter (DH) and versatile fielder Paul Molitor. He received 85.1 percent (431 votes) in his first year of eligibility. He was the first player who played a significant part of his career as a designated hitter to be elected to the Hall of Fame.

Finishing second was former starter and ace closer Dennis Eckersley, who received 83.2 percent (421 votes). Eckersley was also elected in his first year of eligibility.

There was no Veterans Committee election, with the next one taking place in 2005.

Inductees

Paul Molitor showed his versatility by playing all infield and outfield positions for the Milwaukee Brewers during his 15 years with them. Called "The Ignitor" because he made things happen, he helped lead them to their first pennant in 1982, and batted .355 in the seven-game World Series loss to the Cardinals. "Molly" had a 39-game hitting streak in 1987 and led the league in runs and doubles while batting .353. Toronto signed him as a free agent before the 1993 season, and the Ignitor led them to their second straight world title. He was the MVP of the World Series while batting .500. The seven-time all-star was the third player (behind Ty Cobb and Honus Wagner) to have 3000 hits, 600 doubles, and 500 steals. He batted .306 lifetime.

Fans patiently wait for the 2004 Red Carpet Reception to begin.

During his career he had major injuries that limited him to 77 games in two seasons. It wasn't until he became a DH (designated hitter) that he became durable. He played in 161 games in 1996, led the league in hits with 225, and batted .341 for his hometown Twins at the age of 40.

Dennis Eckersley had an auspicious debut. As a starter with the Cleveland Indians in 1975, he had a three-hit shutout over the Oakland A's and didn't allow an earned run for his first 28⅔ innings. "Eck" pitched a no-hitter in 1977, when he also had a 21-inning hitless streak and made his first of six all-star appearances. He became a relief specialist in 1987 for the A's, and he excelled as they reached the World Series three straight times (1988 through 1990). He had his best year in 1992 with 51 saves and won both the Cy Young and MVP awards. Eckersley retired after 24 years with a record of 197–171 and 390 saves.

He gave up a home run to the hobbled Kirk Gibson of the Dodgers as the A's went on to lose the 1988 World Series. It was devastating, but he recovered and the A's went on to sweep the Giants in the 1989 World Series.

Induction

The 2004 Induction Ceremony on July 25 had a crowd of 15,000 with a record 50 Hall of Famers present on a day when the humidity was high. This was George Grande's 25th year serving as the master of ceremonies. Hall of Famer Fergie Jenkins sang the Canadian national anthem.

Paul Molitor, 47, was the first to speak and thanked the BBWAA "for not holding being a DH against me." He went on to pay tribute to Bill Peterson, who coached him when he played for the VFW, American Legion, and then in high school. Peterson also coached Dave

Winfield. "Not bad for two kids from St. Paul finding their way to Cooperstown and both coming through Coach Peterson's program," Molitor said.

He paid homage to Commissioner Selig for his friendship when he was the owner of the Brewers. "His door was always open and we talked about a lot of things or, as Bud would say, 'a plethora of things.'"

Molly then spoke of his two teammates that he played with for 15 years on the Brewers, Robin Yount and Jimmy Gantner. He was honored to follow Yount into the Hall as the second player from the Brewers. He then spoke fondly of Gantner. "Jimmy had a way with the English language that would make Yogi proud. Once he was caught in a rundown and made contact with the infielder and then looked at the umpire and said, 'That's construction, that's construction'" (obstruction).

Molly told a story about his late mother, who raised Paul and seven siblings and would always try to get to see her son play. She thought she would jinx him if she sat in the seat that was reserved for family members, so she would find an empty seat somewhere else. Then they would have to look for her and it was like "Where's Waldo?"

He proudly praised God for the gift he had given him, and then told of his friendship with his pastor, Greg Groh, with whom he took a trip to India, calling it "one of my life's greatest moments."

He spoke fondly of his time in Toronto where he finally got to be on a World Series winner and also for the Minnesota Twins, his hometown team, where he got his 3000th hit. He concluded by thanking the fans, especially a couple of hundred who had come from his old high school.

I can offer first hand evidence of Molitor's fans, having met a father and son at a minor league game the day before the induction at Doubleday Field who had come from Milwaukee to see their hero inducted.

Later, during the ceremony, Molitor was emotionally moved by Dennis Eckersley's induction speech, describing his battle to overcome alcoholism. During the post-induction press conference, Molitor spoke also of his abusing drugs early in his career.

His favorite Cooperstown memory is his induction when he reflected on the group photo taken back at the Otesaga Hotel. He remembers that "I felt overwhelmed by the fraternity that I had just joined as well as truly blessed." His attendance has been perfect ever since.

Dennis Eckersley began his induction speech by thanking the fans who came all the way from Oakland to join him, saying "it meant so much to me." (Again I can attest to that because I met a gentleman over the weekend who came by himself from Oakland to be there to honor Eck.) Later in his speech, Eckersley spoke about the Oakland A's fans again, thanking them for the ovation they gave him at the Oakland airport after the devastating loss to the Los Angeles Dodgers in the 1988 World Series. "I will never forget that moment," he said.

He praised his first manager, Frank Robinson, for his focus. "His intensely competitive style rubbed off on me." Eckersley saved his biggest accolades for A's manager Tony LaRussa and the pitching coach, Dave Duncan, for turning him into a closer. "Not only did they change how the late innings of a baseball game would be played, they carved out a role that was tailor-made for my personality. They created a platform for me to pitch another 12 years. And those 12 years were my ticket to Cooperstown."

The highlight of his talk was his openness in sharing with everyone how he overcame alcoholism. He realized his problem and put himself into a treatment center in Newport,

Rhode Island, after the 1986 season. "I knew I had come to a crossroads in my life. With the grace of God, I got sober, and I saved my life," he said. "It took a great deal of acceptance to come to terms with being an alcoholic, but the acceptance was the key to my sobriety. If I had not gained acceptance at that time in my life, I would not be standing here today."

Eckersley concluded by drawing an analogy to his job as a closer. "While retirement meant the end of my playing days, it didn't bring closure for me. Now I've come to the end, to Cooperstown, to close my career." He then added, "I'd like to leave a message of hope. With the grace of God you can change your life, whoever you are."

His favorite Cooperstown memory was his first private dinner with the other Hall of Famers. "They made me feel I was a part of the family." He hasn't missed any inductions since.

2005

The 2005 BBWAA election had 516 ballots cast. Finishing first was the good-hitting third baseman Wade Boggs, who earned 91.8 percent (474 votes) in his first year of eligibility. He was so excited when he was notified that he couldn't describe it. "Words like unbelievable and amazing don't work and I wish they would invent another word," he said. (Perhaps my six-year-old grandson could have helped him out with "awesome!")

Slick-fielding Cubs second baseman Ryne Sandberg finished second with 76.1 percent (393 votes) in his third year on the ballot. He received 946 votes in three elections.

This was the second attempt by the expanded Veterans Committee to elect a player but the result was the same — no one was elected.

Jane Clark, the chairman of the board of directors, responded by saying, "The results of the last two elections show that the writers by and large have done a great job of electing players to the Hall of Fame. The current process works by upholding the Hall of Fame's high standards for election and by providing a more open, more inclusive, and more understandable process."[12]

Some writers were critical of the results. Noted *New York Times* columnist Dave Anderson said, "It's time for Cooperstown to rethink this realigned committee's selection process, but also to question the responsibility of the committee. It's fair to wonder after two veterans committee shutouts how responsibly do the Hall of Famers take their duty as voters? Do they really study the two pages of statistics, rankings and highlights supplied to them for each of the 25 candidates — particularly those players from other eras whom they never competed against and probably know nothing about?"[13]

Inductees

Wade Boggs gave a preview of his batting prowess when he hit .349 in his first season with the Red Sox in 1982. During his 11 seasons with the Red Sox, Boggs led the league in batting five times during a six-year period while averaging .356 a season. He was an on-base machine as well, leading the league six times in on-base percentage and finishing his career with an average of .415. He played in the postseason six times but didn't win a World Series until he was with the Yankees in 1996. He also won his only two Gold Gloves with the Yankees, at the ages of 36 and 37. Boggs had at least 200 hits seven straight times, and led the league with 240 hits in 1985. The 12-time all-star finished with 3,015 hits while batting .328 lifetime.

Boggs had his quirks, such as always eating chicken before every night game. He kissed home plate after hitting a home run for his 3,000th hit with the Tampa Bay Devil Rays and rode on a New York City's policeman's horse after winning the 1996 World Series.

Ryne Sandberg, or "Ryno," was traded from the Phillies to the Cubs as a throw-in after his first season in 1981. Many believe that to be the best Cubs trade ever! He played both short and third before settling in at second base in 1983 where he displayed amazing range, winning his first of nine straight Gold Gloves. He won the MVP in 1984, leading the league in runs and triples while batting .314 and committing only six errors. He made his first of 10 straight all-star teams that season. He also helped lead the Cubs to the postseason where he batted .368 as they lost to the Padres in the LCS.

Sandberg retired in June of the 1994 season because he was unhappy with his performance. He came back in 1996 to play two more seasons and finished his 16-year career with 344 stolen bases, 282 home runs, and a batting average of .285.

Induction

The 2005 Induction Weekend began with a special event on Friday, July 29. Thirty-eight Hall of Famers were present on the steps of the hall to help cut a red, white, and blue ribbon that stretched all the way across the entrance to the museum. They were there, along with Chairman Jane Forbes Clark and President Dale Petroskey, to formally rededicate the Hall of Fame.

This was the grand opening of the three-year, $20 million renovation project that modernized the National Baseball Hall of Fame and Museum into a state-of-the-art experience for all visitors. Also present at the dedication were Cooperstown mayor Carol Waller, New York state senator James Seward, and New York assemblyman Bill Magee. The New York legislators had procured two grants worth $2.5 million that helped to fund the project.

The architect of the project, Hugh Hardy, rounded out the dignitaries who were present. The four objectives of the renovation project were:

1. Make the museum more accessible to the disabled.
2. Have a more logical flow to the museum by making more efficient use of space.
3. Improve temperature and humidity control to better protect all artifacts and documents.
4. Use more interactive technology to improve the visitors' overall experience.

There were several changes to the outside, beginning with the small courtyard that was between the museum and the office entrance. The exterior wall was moved outward toward the sidewalk. There would now be only one flagpole instead of two in order to improve handicap accessibility at the entrance to the building.

The enclosed ticket booth that was once in front of the doorway was gone and was replaced with a glass outside door and an inside door in order to create a weather seal to maintain the climate-controlled temperature inside the museum.

Once inside, visitors would find themselves standing in the grand foyer of the building with a glass partition directly in front of them. This allowed for a preview of the Hall of Fame Gallery that is on the other side of the glass wall. The ticket area would now consist of four marble ticket areas to the left side of the entrance.

Also, the Hall of Fame acquired additional storage space for their artifacts by expanding into the basement of the Cooperstown General Store, adjacent to the west wing of the building.

There would now be a spiral staircase and elevators that replaced the escalators to allow visitors to go to the second and third floors and explore the various galleries. The renovation helped to create 10,000 square feet of additional exhibit space that includes 14 new or improved exhibits, including interactive video terminals. All of this helps to create a traffic pattern that makes it easier for the visitor to trace the history of baseball in a natural progression, making for a better overall experience.

The 2005 Induction Ceremony took place on July 31 on a warm and partly cloudy day with 28,000 people in attendance, including many Cubs and Red Sox fans, naturally. There was a record 52 Hall of Famers present with Gary Thorne subbing for longtime MC George Grande, who missed for the first time in 26 years, due to family illness.

The crowd included former Buffalo Bills coach Marv Levy and funnyman Bill Murray. During the introductions, Father Robert Corral ended his invocation with, "One more request, God. Could you please remember the Cubs this year?"

Wade Boggs, 47, spoke first and began by telling everyone that he visited the Hall of Fame as an 18 year old playing in his first year of professional baseball, never thinking that some day his plaque would be hanging in Cooperstown.

Boggs singled out several coaches who were very helpful during his 11 years with the Red Sox: Walt Hriniak, hitting coach, who was "the biggest motivator I ever had," Johnny Pesky for all the time he spent with him to improve his fielding, and Bill Fischer, who spent countless hours pitching to him during batting practice, which helped him win five batting titles. He also praised Clete Boyer of the Yankees, who "took my fielding to a Gold Glove level."

He closed with a message to kids: "Our lives are not determined by what happens to us, but how we react to what happens, not by what life brings us, but the attitude that we bring to life." Continuing, he said, "A positive attitude causes a chain reaction of positive thoughts, events and outcomes. It is a catalyst and it sparks extraordinary results."

He also has had perfect attendance since his own induction.

Ryne Sandberg, 45, had a simple theme for his speech: respect. He used the word 17 times during his 25-minute speech. He talked about having to make a decision in his senior year of high school after being all-city in basketball for his team in Spokane, Washington. He had a chance to be the quarterback at Washington State University. (It should be pointed out that Sandberg never mentioned that he was good enough to be named to *Parade* magazine's All-American team.) Yet, after speaking with his older brother, he chose baseball after being chosen by the Phillies in the draft because "I had too much respect for the game to leave it behind."

Throughout his baseball career he was always taught, "never ever disrespect your opponent or your teammates or your organization or your manager, and never ever your uniform." Legendary broadcaster Harry Caray was a huge supporter and spoke about Ryno's power and speed but also the fact that he was the best bunter on the team. Sandberg's reply: "When did it become okay to hit home runs and forget how to play the rest of the game?" He emphasized, "These guys sitting here did not pave the way for the rest of us so that players could swing for the fences every time up, and forget how to move a runner over because it's disrespectful to the game."

He praised the Cubs' fans for all their support despite the frustration of no World

Series victory since 1908. He then told the story of a man finding a corked bottle on the beach and a genie pops out ready to grant the man one wish. The man wished for peace in the Middle East between the Palestinians and the Israelis and then gave the genie a map of the Middle East. The genie studied it for hours and then said, "This is impossible, is there anything else you want?" The man answers, "I always wanted to see the Cubs in the World Series." The genie looked at him and replied, "Let me see that map again."

Sandberg paid tribute to many in the Cubs' organization with a special wish for two of them. He called teammate and friend Andre Dawson "the best I've ever seen, and I hope that he will stand up here someday." He also mentioned Ron Santo, the Cubs' all-star third baseman, who keeps coming close in the VC voting for Cooperstown. "Ron Santo just gained one more vote for the Veterans Committee," he said.

Sandberg explained that he played the game the right way out of respect for baseball and not to validate his career with election to the hall. He closed with, "I hope others in the future will know this feeling for the same reason: respect for the game. When we played it was mandatory. It's something I hope we will one day see again."

David Haugh of the Chicago *Tribune* said that Sandberg rehearsed his speech for over two months and approached it "as my last hurrah." Haugh said, "Few words uttered by incoming Hall of Famers have been more pointed than Sandberg's."[14] Haugh stated Sandberg was taking a veiled shot at Sammy Sosa without naming him.[15]

Sandberg said that many of the Hall of Famers seated there congratulated him after it was finished. He said, "After a couple of guys came up to me and told me it was one of the best speeches they had ever heard, I knew I had nailed it."[16]

(I spoke with a buddy, Joe D'Amato, who has attended at least the last 15 inductions, and he thought it was the best speech he had heard.)

Sandberg's favorite Cooperstown memory was hitting a home run in his first at-bat in the 1988 Hall of Fame game at Doubleday Field. He also has had perfect attendance.

2006

The 2006 BBWAA election produced 520 ballots and the only player selected was split-fingered fastball relief specialist Bruce Sutter, who received 76.9 percent (400 votes). He made it on his thirteenth try, and received a total of 2,874 votes. Sutter became the fourth relief pitcher selected and the first player who had never appeared in a starting lineup and the only pitcher to have lost more games than he won.

Jeff Idelson, vice president of communications and education for the Hall of Fame at the time, told how Sutter found it so hard to believe he had been elected that any time the Hall of Fame called him after January following the original call, he would think the hall was calling to tell him it was a mistake and he wasn't chosen.

Realization definitely took place when Sutter received his replica plaque at the 2006 Induction Ceremony. The original plaque weighs 14.5 pounds, measures 15.5 inches tall, is mounted on a 1.5-inch marble frame and hangs permanently in the Plaque Gallery.

The Veterans Committee had no election in 2006.

A special group named the Committee on African-American Baseball conducted a five year study after Major League Baseball gave the Hall of Fame a $250,000 grant. The purpose of the grant was to do a comprehensive study of African Americans in baseball from 1860 through 1960. It was begun in 2001 and lasted until November 2005 when a committee of

12 voted on 39 final candidates for induction. The results were announced on February 27, 2006. Seventeen new members were elected, including the first woman, owner Effa Manley, making this the largest induction class ever. Also selected were pitchers Ray Brown, Andy Cooper, and Jose Mendez, first basemen Mule Suttles and Ben Taylor, second baseman Frank Grant and third baseman Jud Wilson. Also named were catchers Biz Mackey and Louis Santop and outfielders Willard Brown, Pete Hill, and Cristobal Torriente. Finally the committee picked pioneer Sol White and owners Alex Pompez, Cum Posey, and J.L. Wilkinson.

Inductees

Bruce Sutter was the third relief pitcher to win the Cy Young Award when he led the league with 37 saves for the Cubs in 1979. He was traded to the Cards in 1982 where he had even more success, becoming the highest-paid relief pitcher in baseball. He recorded the last six outs of the seventh game of the 1982 World Series as the Cards beat the Milwaukee Brewers. Sutter was the National League's dominant closer from 1977 through 1984. He led the league in saves five times and tied the existing record for saves in 1984 with 45. Opposing batters hit only .224 against him and he was named an all-star six times. He retired in 1988 at 35 after only 12 seasons due to shoulder problems.

Bruce Sutter owes his career to elbow surgery and pitching instructor Fred Martin. He couldn't throw his fastball after the surgery so Martin taught him the split-fingered fastball, which turned out to be his ticket to the majors and eventually the Hall of Fame.

Ray Brown pitched more than 15 seasons with the Homestead Grays. He was the ace of the staff that won nine straight pennants from 1937 through 1945. Brown helped the Grays win the Negro World Series in 1943, winning two games over the Birmingham Black Barons, including the decisive seventh game. The Grays defeated the Barons again in 1944 as Brown pitched one of his greatest games, shutting them out on one hit. Brown was a switch-hitting outfielder who also pinch-hit when he wasn't pitching.

The Pittsburgh *Courier* conducted a 1938 poll to pick five Negro League players that they thought could help the Pirates win the pennant. The first four were well known: Paige, Gibson, Leonard, and Bell, but the fifth was Ray Brown.

Willard Brown was a good defensive outfielder for the Kansas City Monarchs and helped lead them to six pennants, including a World Series title in 1942. Brown was considered the premier power hitter in the Negro Leagues during the 1940s and won several batting titles while playing in eight East-West all-star games. He was also known as "Ese Hombre" or "That Man" in the Puerto Rican Winter League, where he won two Triple Crowns.

Brown and Hank Thompson were signed by the St. Louis Browns in 1947 and became the first black teammates in that historic season as major league baseball became integrated. Brown became the first black to hit a home run in the American League but was released a month later after batting .167. He later played in the minors and finished fourth in home runs in the Texas League in 1954.

Andy Cooper was a left-handed pitcher and the ace of the Detroit Stars from 1920 through 1927. The Kansas City Monarchs considered him so valuable that they traded five players for him in 1928. The trade paid dividends a year later when they won the pennant. Cooper had an assortment of pitches that he threw at varying speeds along with a great pick-off move. He became the player-manager of the Monarchs in 1937 when they defeated the Chicago American Giants to win the pennant. At the age of 39, Cooper pitched seventeen innings in one of the playoff games that ended in a tie.

Monte Irvin revealed in his book, *Few and Chosen*, that Cooper was a left-handed relief specialist. Researchers went over old box scores and determined that he would hold the Negro Leagues record for saves, although it wasn't an official statistic then.

Frank Grant was an outstanding defensive second baseman during the nineteenth century who started his career by playing on integrated teams for six years in the minor leagues. He played with Buffalo in the International League for three years and batted more than .340 each season. Grant spent the rest of his career playing for Negro teams in Trenton, New York, and Philadelphia.

While in Buffalo, Grant had to contend with racial slurs, and had baseballs thrown at him while batting. He made his own shin guards to protect his legs from runners' spikes. In spite of these threats, Frank Grant became the best black ballplayer of the nineteenth century.

Joseph Preston "Pete" Hill was the premier black center fielder of the Dead Ball Era because of his exceptional speed, tremendous range, and deadly throwing arm. He played with the great shortstop Pop Lloyd and was recruited by the legendary Rube Foster for the Leland Giants and then the Chicago American Giants. He played more than 10 years for Foster and was his captain for nine of them. Later, when Hill became a manager, he patterned his style after his mentor. According to the records available, Hill batted .423 in 1910 and .400 in 1911. As player-manager of the Detroit Stars, he hit .391 at the age of 40 in 1921. His speed helped him steal a lot of bases and hit a lot of triples.

Fellow inductee Cum Posey called Hill "the most consistent hitter of his lifetime."[17]

Biz Mackey was a switch hitter who became a catcher after playing everywhere else. He helped the Hilldale Daisies win three straight pennants from 1923 through 1925 and helped lead them to victory in the 1925 Negro World Series. Mackey hit .375 to lead Hilldale to the title over Kansas City after the Monarchs had won in 1924. He led a group of black all-stars in 1927 that was one of the first American pro teams to tour Japan. Defensively is where Mackey excelled. He was quick and agile behind the plate and could throw runners out from the squat position. He was a player-manager half of his career and led the Newark Eagles to the Negro World Series title in 1946.

Hall of Famer Roy Campanella was his protégé. Campy said, "Mackey was a tough taskmaster and there were times he made me cry, but nobody was a better teacher."[18] Biz joined Campy at the L.A. Coliseum in 1959 before a record crowd after Campy was honored by the Dodgers following his terrible car accident.

Effa Manley was co-owner of the Newark Eagles with her husband, Abe, from 1935 through 1947. They worked well together as he took care of the field operations and she was in charge of the business end. She helped to arrange schedules, booked travel arrangements, managed payroll and negotiated contracts. Manley also encouraged all of her players to get involved in the community. Her purchase of a $15,000 air-conditioned bus in 1946 for the team's travel needs must have helped because they upset the heavily-favored Monarchs in the World Series that year.

When Jackie Robinson criticized the Negro Leagues in *Ebony* magazine she took umbrage by calling Robinson "ungrateful." "How could a child nurtured by its mother turn on her within a year after he leaves for success and good fortune? Jackie Robinson is where he is today because of Negro baseball."[19]

Jose Mendez pitched for his native Cuba and was called "El Diamante Negro" or "The Black Diamond" because of his outstanding success against visiting white major and minor leaguers. Mendez had a record of 44–2 against them, including beating Hall of Fame pitchers Eddie Plank and the great Christy Mathewson. John McGraw saw him pitch in Cuba and proclaimed, "If Mendez was white, I would pay $40,000 for him."[20] He came to the United States as part of the Cuban All-Stars and pitched a 10-inning perfect game in 1909. He managed the Monarchs to their first three pennants.

Mendez and the Monarchs played in the first Negro World Series in 1924 against the Hilldale Daisies. The series was all tied up at four games apiece. After a serious operation, Mendez was warned by his doctor that he could injure himself permanently by playing. He ignored the advice and pitched a three-hit shutout as the Monarchs won 5–0.

Alex Pompez was the owner of the Cuban Stars, one of the original eight teams when the Negro National League started in 1920. He brought Martin Dihigo to his Cuban Stars in 1926. His New York Cubans won their only World Series title in 1947 when they defeated the Cleveland Buckeyes. He was the vice president of the Negro National League for two years before he went to work for the New York Giants after the collapse of the Negro National League. Pompez helped persuade Monte Irvin to sign with the Giants in 1949. He became the Giants director of international scouting after they moved to San Francisco and signed Orlando Cepeda and Juan Marichal.

Pompez was a member of the Hall of Fame's Negro League Committee in 1971 that chose Satchel Paige as the first Negro Leaguer for induction.

Cum Posey had a 35-year run with the Homestead Grays as a player, business manager, manager, and eventual owner in 1920. They were a successful independent team during the 1920s, winning 80 percent of their games, mostly against semi-pro teams, but also holding their own against Negro Leagues teams and major leaguers. Finally, after joining two Negro Leagues that collapsed, they joined the Negro National League in 1935 and became the most successful team in Negro Leagues history. During their 14 years in the league they won ten titles, including nine straight and three World Series titles.

Posey's team was from just outside Pittsburgh, and was successful at the gate as well. They played many of their games at the Pirates' Forbes Field and the Senators' Griffith Stadium, drawing crowds of 20,000 to 30,000 for their games. Wendell Smith, respected black writer, said, "Cum Posey was the smartest man in Negro League baseball."[21]

Louis Santop was a 6' 4" left-handed hitting catcher who was known as "Top" and also "Big Bertha" for his prodigious home runs that he hit during the Dead Ball Era. He was a good defensive catcher who had a powerful arm and excelled at blocking the plate. It is said that he could throw a ball over the center field fence from home plate. Santop was the battery mate for Hall of Famer Smokey Joe Williams. He once hit a 485' home run for the Brooklyn Royal Giants and reportedly hit more than .400 several times.

Santop played on the Hilldale Daisies World Series title team in 1925, but unfortunately he is more known for an error that he made in the 1924 World Series. The error was critical as they lost to the Monarchs for the title.

George Suttles was called "Mule" after he worked in the coal mines of Birmingham, Alabama, as a young man. He was 6' 3" and 215 pounds and supposedly swung the heaviest bat ever at 50 ounces. Despite being beaned in 1927, Suttles played 27 years, spanning World Wars I and II as a first baseman and outfielder whose defense was, at best, adequate. He played for the Newark Eagles in 1936 and was part of the Million Dollar Infield that included Hall of Famers Ray Dandridge and Willie Wells. However, his best years were with the St. Louis Stars. He hit 133 homers, the third highest in Negro Leagues history. Suttles is one of seven Negro Leaguers to hit for the cycle.

When he came to the plate, fans shouted "Kick, Mule, Kick," hoping for a home run. He saved his most dramatic home runs for the East-West all-star games. He hit the first home run in the inaugural classic in Comiskey Park in 1933 and then the winning three-run homer in the 11th inning off Hall of Famer Martin Dihigo in the 1935 game.

Ben Taylor was considered the best-fielding first baseman in the Negro Leagues. He was called "Old Reliable" because he had sure hands and was a clutch hitter. As a defensive first baseman, Taylor was considered very adept at digging out throws in the dirt. He always hit well, but once the Dead Ball Era ended, he had averages of .407 in 1921, and .358 in 1922. He became a successful manager after retiring.

Ben was the youngest of the four Taylor brothers and, according to Monte Irvin, they were "the first family of Negro League baseball."[22] The oldest was C.I., who became the owner of the Indianapolis ABC's. "Candy" managed for 30 years and had 775 victories. John was a pitcher who won 14 games for the St. Louis Stars in 1926.

Cristobal Torriente was a Cuban five-tool center fielder who starred in Cuba before coming to the United States. He became the franchise player for Rube Foster's Chicago American Giants and helped lead them to three straight Negro National League pennants. He was the best player in the league in 1920 when he hit .432. "Torri" could also hit for power. Once he hit a legendary home run in Kansas City that cleared the center field fence and struck the face of a clock above the fence, causing its hands to spin wildly.

Torri's signature moment came when he played a series of exhibitions in 1920 in Cuba against the New York Giants and Babe Ruth. Torriente hit two home runs in his first two at-bats so Ruth, the former left-handed ace pitcher, came in from the outfield to pitch to him and he got a double. Ruth then struck out the next three batters and returned to the outfield. He hit a third home run and became known as "the Latin Babe Ruth."

Sol White started as an infielder in 1887 and spent 15 years playing for black and integrated teams. He finally found stability when he became player-manager of the Philadelphia Giants in 1902. White played shortstop while his second baseman was fellow inductee Frank Grant. When his team lost to pitcher Rube Foster and the Cuban Giants in 1903 for the "Colored Championship," White went out and recruited Foster and his team beat the Cuban Giants in 1904. He managed several more teams, including the powerhouse Philadelphia Giants, a team that he helped start.

In 1906, he wrote *Sol White's Official Baseball Guide*, a 129-page history of black baseball. White predicted blacks and whites would play together. When Jackie Robinson integrated major league baseball in 1947, White was still alive so he had to be overjoyed.

J.L. "Wilkie" Wilkinson had an integrated baseball team called the All Nations team in 1912 that disbanded and came back as the all-black Kansas City Monarchs. They joined the Negro National League (NNL) in 1920 and won the first Negro World Series in 1924. The Monarchs joined the Negro American League in 1937 and defeated the Homestead Grays (NNL) in the 1942 World Series and then lost in 1946 to the Newark Eagles (NNL). Wilkie built the Monarchs into a highly successful and longest-running franchise in Negro Leagues' history. Wendell Smith called Wilkie "a man who not only invested his money, but his heart and soul in the Negro Leagues."[23]

J.L. was an innovator who introduced night baseball to the Negro Leagues in 1930 by carrying a portable lighting system to the ballparks where the Monarchs played. The Monarchs played night baseball five years before the major leagues introduced lights!

Jud Wilson played third base for 24 years and although he wasn't much defensively, he was arguably the most prolific hitter in Negro Leagues' history. He had a lifetime batting average of .354 and helped lead the Homestead Grays to four straight World Series from 1942 through 1945. Satchel Paige gave him the nickname "Boojum" because that is the way the ball sounded as he hit line drives off the outfield wall.

Wilson was pugnacious and ill-tempered and during the last years of his career he suffered from seizures. Once after an all-star game, he was trying to get some sleep when his roommate came in drunk. He grabbed him by one ankle and hung him outside the window of the hotel several stories above the street. The roommate sobered up quickly as Wilson hauled him back into the room.

On May 14, 2006, a special event took place just outside the Hall of Fame Library with the unveiling of a statue honoring the All-American Girls Professional Baseball League (AAGPBL). This league was made famous by the movie *A League of Their Own.* On hand for the unveiling were 39 former members of the AAGPBL, along with Hall of Famers Phil Niekro, Robin Roberts, and Nolan Ryan. Ryan came partly because of his association with Don Sanders, his co-owner of two minor league franchises. Sanders helped to finance the Stanley Bleifield sculpture honoring the league.

A little more than two months later, on Friday, July 28, as part of the 2006 Induction Ceremony Weekend, a statue of Satchel Paige, also done by Bleifield, was unveiled. This was done to honor the 17 new inductees. Chairman Jane Forbes Clark spoke: "We are here to dedicate a statue of Satchel Paige, which will serve as a permanent tribute to everyone who worked or played in the Negro Leagues. He is the one individual who best exemplifies the excellence of play in the Negro Leagues."[24]

There were a number of Hall of Famers present, along with some relatives and friends of the 17 inductees. Linda Paige Shelby, a daughter of Paige's, representing her family, said, "It was something that these guys in their wildest dreams never thought would ever be happening. It's just fantastic."[25]

Induction

On July 30, more than 11,000 people, along with 41 Hall of Famers, were present on a clear day for the 2006 Induction Ceremony. The ceremony began with a short speech by Buck O'Neil, representing the 17 honorees, all of whom had passed away. The former Kansas City Monarch was everyone's favorite baseball ambassador ever since he stole the show during Ken Burns' epic television series on baseball. Many people were upset that he had not received the necessary 75 percent for induction but O'Neil gave the most magnanimous speech ever given at an induction.

He began by saying, "I have hit home runs, grand slam home runs, and I hit for the cycle. I've even hit a hole in one in golf. I've done a lot of things in my lifetime [age 94], including meeting President Clinton, but there is nothing I'd rather be doing than being right here and representing the people who helped build a bridge over the chasm of prejudice." He told of having no lasting feelings about the racism that he encountered as a player. He stated, "I hate cancer. My mother and wife died from it. I hate AIDS because a good friend died from it a few months ago." He continued, "I can't hate another human being." He finished by asking the crowd to join him in singing, "The greatest thing in all of my life, is loving you." O'Neil then asked the crowd to sit down. "I could talk to you ten minutes longer," he said, "but I've got to go to the bathroom."

I was saddened a few months later to learn of his death, but I felt privileged to have met the man several times and been present to hear his words on this Induction Sunday.

Fittingly, Jackie Robinson's widow, Rachel, and daughter, Sharon, were there, with Sharon expressing her feelings by stating, "It's an awesome responsibility to be up here and try to express how important this day is for us."

Ms. Robinson was also there that weekend for a signing of a book that she had written about her father. She was there with her mother, an icon in her own right, and I had the opportunity to say hello. I took a lighthearted approach, telling her that I wasn't sure if I could speak to her since I was a lifelong Yankees fan, and she went along, pretending to shoo me away. This helped to break the ice as I told her that I thought her husband did a good job portraying himself in his autobiographical movie, *The Jackie Robinson Story*. The movie was made around 1950, and I wondered why she didn't play herself in the movie. She said she was pregnant at the time with Sharon. Even though it was short, it was an experience that I wouldn't soon forget.

Commissioner Bud Selig, began reading from their plaques as each inductee was called.

Ray Brown was represented by his son, Truman Brown, and his nephew, Michael Flagg. He died in 1965 at the age of 57.

Brown married one of Cum Posey's five daughters. Posey, his fellow inductee, was his boss as the owner of the Homestead Grays. Brown married Posey's daughter at a ceremony at home plate. His son Truman's middle name was Posey.

Willard Brown was represented by his daughter-in-law, Mary Brown, and Brenda Raglin, his stepdaughter. He died in 1996 at the age of 81.

Following up on Brown's short stay with the St. Louis Browns, Bill James asserts that he wasn't accepted by most of his teammates. He used teammate Jeff Heath's bat to hit his historic home run. Heath then took the bat and shattered it against the dugout wall.[26]

Andy Cooper was represented by his son, Andy Cooper, Jr. His son spoke briefly and with pride about his father's accomplishment. Cooper died at the age of 43 in 1941.

He is one of 11 Kansas City Monarchs to be elected to the Hall of Fame. This list doesn't include Jackie Robinson and Ernie Banks, who also played for KC but made their mark in the major leagues.

Frank Grant was represented by his great-grandniece, Marion Grant Royston. When he died at the age of 72 in New York City, one of the pallbearers was Hall of Famer Smokey Joe Williams. Although he is buried in a potter's field in Clifton, New Jersey, Grant is honored with a plaque on a building near his birthplace in Williamstown, Massachusetts.

Pete Hill was not represented at the ceremony. Hill died in 1951 at the age of 71.

Fellow inductee Ben Taylor agreed with Cum Posey that Hill was the greatest hitter in the Negro Leagues from 1910 to 1920.

Biz Mackey was represented by Ray Mackey, his grandnephew. He spoke briefly and said, "When I heard of the committee, I felt that he was a shoo-in. He's here at the Hall of Fame where he'll rest with the great ones forever." Mackey died in 1965 at the age of 68.

He was considered such a great defensive catcher that in the Pittsburgh *Courier* poll, conducted in 1954, he was chosen over Josh Gibson as the top Negro Leagues' catcher.

Effa Manley was represented by her niece, Connie Brooks. Ms. Brooks thanked the Hall of Fame and read the inscription on her aunt's plaque. When she finished she added, "A glorious day for women." Manley died at the age of 84 in 1981.

Effa Brooks Manley was of German, Asian, and Indian descent. Her mother was white and her father black, but she was conceived when her mother had an affair with a white man. She grew up with black half-siblings and lived her life as a black woman.

She was outspoken and wasn't afraid to speak out against injustice. She was an early advocate of civil rights and, in 1934, helped organize a boycott of stores in Harlem when they wouldn't employ black salesclerks. The result was 300 black workers were hired.

She then arranged an Anti-Lynching Day in 1939 at the Eagles' Ruppert Stadium in Newark which helped to get federal legislation passed outlawing it. She eventually became treasurer of the Newark NAACP.

Manley's candidness upset her fellow male owners because she objected to their shoddy business practices. She wanted the league to have an independent commissioner and have penalties against players who jumped contracts and the owners who accepted them.

She also took on Branch Rickey, who wouldn't let her Newark Eagles player, Hall of Famer Monte Irvin, sign with the New York Giants. Rickey claimed his Dodgers still had rights to him from when he turned down their contract offer in 1945, saying he wasn't ready. Rickey had never given the Negro Leagues owners compensation when he signed Jackie Robinson, Roy Campanella, and Don Newcombe because he claimed they didn't have valid contracts with their Negro Leagues teams. Nevertheless, she forced Rickey to allow Irvin to sign with the Giants after she threatened to sue. Later she got $5,000 from Giants owner Horace Stoneham for Monte Irvin, and Indians owner Bill Veeck gave her $15,000 for signing Eagle Larry Doby.

Journalist Connie Woodward commented on Effa Manley in Larry Hogan's *Shades of Glory*: "She was a woman who was ahead of her time. Effa was an inspiration because she was successful at her male-oriented business. She was a role model for people like myself."[27]

Jose Mendez had no representative and died in 1928 of bronchopneumonia at 41.

Mendez had a blinding fastball and sadly once killed a teammate while pitching batting practice. Yet he was also an entertainer who played the cornet and guitar and later traveled the Caribbean playing his music and teaching baseball.

Alex Pompez also had no one there. He died in 1974 at the age of 83. He was born in Key West and married the sister of Massachusetts' first black U.S. senator, Edward Brooke.

Pompez, like a number of other Negro Leagues owners, made his money from the illegal numbers game. One prominent owner involved in the numbers game was Effa Manley's husband, Abe. Also, when Cum Posey almost went broke, he brought in a numbers man to help keep the Grays in business. Larry Hogan states, "Illegal enterprises provided much of the capital during the Depression for legitimate black businesses such as baseball."[28]

When Orlando Cepeda and Juan Marichal learned of the selection of Pompez to Cooperstown, they were very pleased. He helped them deal with harsh racial prejudice during spring training in Florida in the early part of their careers.

Cum Posey, Jr., was represented by his granddaughter, Nancy Boxill. Posey died in 1946 at the age of 55.

Posey's father was a wealthy shipping magnate in Pittsburgh and also part owner of the Pittsburgh *Courier*. His mother was the first black graduate of Ohio State. Cum was an outstanding basketball player who played at Duquesne and Penn State.

Louis Santop also had no representative. He died in 1942 at the age of 52.

Santop can be compared to Bill Buckner of the Boston Red Sox, who made a costly error in the 1986 World Series that eventually led to Boston's defeat. Buckner, like Santop, had a very good career, but probably will be remembered most for that error. Buckner was vindicated for his faux pas when he was invited back to Fenway Park in 2008. Santop, too, was vindicated by his selection to the Hall of Fame.

Mule Suttles was represented by his niece, Merrit Burley. She spoke briefly by thanking everyone for making her uncle a part of "this street of dreams." He died in 1966 at 66.

Suttles had 11 home runs in 77 at-bats against major leaguers in barnstorming games.

Ben Taylor had no representative and died in 1953 at the age of 64.

He was an excellent teacher and his prize pupil was the great Buck Leonard. Taylor taught him how to play first base when Leonard was starting out.

Cristobal Torriente was represented by his grandnephew, Orlando Gonzales, who read the inscription on the plaque in both English and Spanish.

Torriente was a colorful ballplayer who wore a red bandana around his neck and bracelets around his wrists that he would shake at the pitcher when he was batting.

Unfortunately, like many other ballplayers, he destroyed himself with alcohol. It got so bad that during Prohibition he would distill his own alcohol in his room. He died of cirrhosis of the liver in 1938 at the age of 44.

Sol White also had no representative and died in 1955 at the age of 87.

His *Official Baseball Guide of 1906* was almost lost when there were only three copies left in the 1980s. Fortunately, they were able to print more copies, thus preserving the only surviving photographs of early black stars and teams.

J.L. Wilkinson was represented by his son, Richard. J.L. died in 1964 at the age of 84.

Wilkinson was not only innovative in introducing night baseball; he also spent money to have a first-class organization. The Monarchs traveled to games in a specially designed Pullman railroad car. Buck O'Neil, who was his first baseman and manager for many years, told how he had all the players wear jackets and ties when traveling and always stayed in the best black hotels and ate in the best black restaurants.

Jud Wilson was represented by his grandniece, ShaRon Wilson. She spoke slowly as she read the inscription on his plaque. Prior to the induction, she found out about her grand- uncle's election while reading an issue of *Jet* magazine. She contacted the hall and later said, "I know he must have meant something as I read comments about him from Satchel Paige." She continued, "I get goose bumps and I feel privileged and like royalty."

Jud Wilson died in 1963 at the age of 69.

Wilson's terrible temper was well known if he didn't like an umpire's call. Once he erupted over a call by grabbing an umpire and lifting him off his feet. He finally calmed down when a teammate wielded a bat in defense of the ump.

Bruce Sutter had to wait as all the previous plaque inscriptions were read so it was understandable that he got tense waiting to speak. Former teammate Ozzie Smith and Johnny Bench sensed the situation and donned long gray beards to look like Sutter with his gray beard. He later said it worked because it made him relax.

Sutter promised the other Hall of Famers that he wouldn't take long and finished his speech in 12 minutes. He said he looked on this honor as the closure to his career because he was forced to retire prematurely due to shoulder problems. Sutter singled out several people, especially the late Fred Martin who taught him the split-fingered fastball when he was in the minors. He also had praise for major league pitching coach Mike Roarke and his manager with the Cards, Whitey Herzog, who "was like no manager I ever had."

Sutter talked admirably of his father, who told him a long time ago, "The game of baseball is perfect; the players are imperfect." He became very emotional at the end when he spoke of his wife, who was scheduled to have kidney surgery for cancer, never mentioning it except to say, "We've got some tough times ahead, but we'll go through it like we've gone through everything else — together." He then composed himself, closing with, "Father Time took away my arm and my hair and changed the color of my beard, but he can't take away my passion for the game."

"Greybeards" Ozzie Smith and Johnny Bench welcome Bruce Sutter to the 2006 Induction Ceremony.

His attendance at every subsequent induction has been perfect.

When something like an induction happens, there are many people who want to share in the joy. Sutter had relatives who came on their own and were outside the fenced-in area and were not a part of the people that each inductee is allowed to bring. Also celebrating were Sutter's high school baseball team dressed in specially designed T-shirts.

2007

The 2007 BBWAA election had a record 545 ballots cast. Cal Ripken, Jr., of the Baltimore Orioles, all-time consecutive games played record holder, finished first with 98.5 percent (537 votes). Ripken was voted in during his first year of eligibility and received the third highest voting percentage of all time.

Eight-time batting champ Tony Gwynn, right fielder of the San Diego Padres, finished second with 97.6 percent (532 votes). He also was elected in his first year of eligibility and received the sixth highest voting percentage of all time.

Despite Ripken's and Gwynn's tremendous results, there was controversy. Jayson Stark of ESPN was very critical of those eight voters who didn't vote for Ripken. It turns out that Paul Ladewski of the Chicago-area *Daily Southtown* revealed that he submitted a blank ballot because "he could not currently support any candidate who played between 1993 and 2004," a period he termed the "Steroids Era."[29]

Stark was even more upset about the Gwynn vote, stating, "For even 11 writers not to have cast a vote for Gwynn is an embarrassment to the BBWAA."[30]

Ladewski defended his position by stating, "Veteran players in the Steroids Era were aware of what went on around them, which made them accomplices to the worst scandal in baseball history." He goes on by making an interesting comparison to one of the eight players banned from baseball because of the Black Sox Scandal of 1919. He states,

"Lest we forget, that's the kind of thing that got Buck Weaver suspended for life without so much as a hearing."[31]

The VC for the third straight election (2003, 2005, 2007) elected no one from either the players ballot or the composite ballot for managers, umpires, and executives.

Inductees

Cal Ripken, Jr., was the Rookie of the Year in 1982 and then the league MVP twice, in 1983 and 1991. He also helped lead the Orioles to a World Series title in 1983. Despite being 6' 4", he distinguished himself defensively at shortstop by winning two Gold Glove Awards. He once went 95 games without an error and in 1990 made only three errors with 680 chances. He holds the American League record for double plays at shortstop (1,565). He played in six postseason series and batted .336. He appeared in 19 straight All-Star Games and finished his 21-year career with 3,184 hits and 431 home runs.

The highlight of his career was "The Streak." He broke Lou Gehrig's record in 1995 after he played in 2,131 straight games. He did it at Camden Yards and the game was stopped as he circled the perimeter of the field shaking the hands of fans who gave him a 22-minute standing ovation. Ripken ended the streak by choice in 1998 at 2,632 games.

Tony Gwynn won eight batting titles with the San Diego Padres, tying him for the most in the National League with Honus Wagner. He also had 160 lifetime assists and was a Gold Glove right fielder five times. He appeared in two World Series, and in his last one in 1998 he batted .500 as the Yanks swept the Padres. Gwynn batted more than .300 nineteen straight seasons, was chosen for 16 all-star teams, had 3,141 hits, and batted .338 lifetime. He also stole 319 bases and only struck out 434 times during his career.

Yet despite being one of the greatest hitters of all time, Gwynn almost quit baseball. He loved basketball and, in his senior year in high school, almost gave baseball up, but his mother convinced him to stick with it. When he got to San Diego State College, however, he played only basketball his freshman year. Future major leaguer and college teammate Bobby Meacham got him to play baseball his sophomore year and the rest is history.

Induction

The 2007 Induction Ceremony was held on July 29 and it turned out to be the biggest ever. There were 60,000 people expected but more than 75,000 showed up on a day that began with threatening clouds but gave way to clearing skies. There were also a record 55 Hall of Famers present. A big part of the record crowd came from San Diego for Tony Gwynn, but most came from Baltimore for Cal Ripken, Jr. People began making their reservations for rooms in the area as soon as Ripken retired in 2001.

The village has a population of 1,900, but for this day it became the eighth most populated community in the state. Despite this onslaught of humanity descending on the little village, everything went well. It was a testimony to Mayor Carol Waller and her village administration that everything went so smoothly. The mayor became so popular while helping direct a cleanup crew at Pioneer Park on Main Street that when people heard that

Part of the crowd of 75,000 people who await the 2007 induction to begin (*The Freeman's Journal*, Cooperstown, New York).

she was the mayor, they began asking for her autograph. She gladly obliged, making it the only free autograph that a fan could get on Main Street.

The Hall of Fame also was well prepared for Induction Sunday by recruiting 150 volunteers rather than the usual 50. They normally set out 1,200 chairs in the fenced-in area in front of the stage at the Clark Sports Center, but this year they set up 6,000 chairs.

The record crowd covered the entire field directly east of the Clark Sports Center along with the field across Susquehanna Avenue as well. Baseball writer Mark Newman aptly described the crowd as a "modern day Woodstock."[32] This record setting Induction Weekend also included a record 14,000 visitors at the museum on Saturday.

Tony Gwynn was the first to speak, but before he spoke, his daughter, Anisha, sang both the Canadian and the American national anthems.

He spoke about how he was struggling with the bat during his second year, so he had his wife, Alicia, videotape him and from then on for the rest of his career. The other major influence was one of his idols, Ted Williams. He told how after meeting Williams at the 1992 All-Star Game, Gwynn learned to focus on the art of hitting. He won the batting title four of the next five years.

He closed by telling how he loves being the baseball coach at his alma mater, San Diego State, because he loves teaching and it keeps him associated with the game. He thanked not only the fans who came all the way from San Diego, but also the fans who were watching the Induction back at PetCo Park (the Padres ballpark). He also made reference to the crowd by proudly declaring, "I can say in our first time here, our first Hall of Fame weekend, the people were lined up way back through the trees, so thank you."

Gwynn came back in 2008 but missed in 2009.

Cal Ripken, Jr., began his speech with a cute little story that put all of the adulation in perspective. It was about a ten-year-old boy that he was instructing who asked Cal, "So, did you play baseball?" Ripken said, "Yes, I played professionally." The boy went on, "Oh yeah, for what team?" Cal responded, "I played with the Baltimore Orioles for 21 years." And the boy asked, "What position?" Cal answered, "Mostly shortstop, but a little third base at the end." The boy then started to walk away and said, "Should I know you?"

He then mentioned that he got to a place like this because of all the people who supported him, but warned, "If I thank them individually, I'd keep you here longer than the streak." Speaking of the streak, he knows some look on it as a special accomplishment, which he appreciated, but he felt he was just doing his job. He then expressed his feelings when he said, "As I look out on this audience, I see thousands who do the same, teachers, police officers, mothers, fathers, business people, and many others." Ripken continued, "So I'd like to take the time to salute all of you for showing up, working hard, and making the world a better place."

He did acknowledge several people including his friend, former teammate, and now fellow Hall of Famer, Eddie Murray, who "inspired me with his play and his friendship."

He then spoke of his late father, Cal Ripken, Sr., when he said, "Imagine how lucky I am to call the man whose memory I revere to this day by so many important names such as teacher, coach, manager, and especially dad."

Just as he added a personal touch to the day he broke Lou Gehrig's consecutive game streak by shaking people's hands for 22 minutes, Ripken again added a personal touch this day when he acknowledged his wife, Kelly. He thanked her "for always being there for me," and pulled from his jacket pocket a white rose that was transported by his son Ryan, who was seated in the first row of seats next to his mother. Ryan pulled out of his pocket a white rose and handed it to her.

Ripken spent the rest of his speech stressing the most important thing in life — how we impact others, especially children. He learned this lesson the hard way as he cited several examples of immature behavior on his part at the beginning of his career. One pertinent story was about a family that had saved their money to come to Baltimore in order to see him play, but instead saw him thrown out of the game in the first inning. The result was that the family's young son cried the whole game. These lessons helped to change Ripken into a positive role model the rest of his career.

He realized that he could use baseball as a platform to "make this world a better place for the next generation." He talked about his program that teaches kids and their coaches all that he has learned to help them become the players of the future.

In closing, he said, "I experienced another new beginning with this induction, and I can only hope that all of us, whether we have played on the field or been fans in the stands, can reflect and see our lives as new beginnings that allow us to leave this world a bit better than when we came into it."

One of the most touching stories of the whole induction was Ernie Tyler, an umpire's attendant for the Orioles, who had a streak longer than Ripken's. Tyler had a streak of 3,760 games but ended it in order to be in Cooperstown to honor Cal Ripken, Jr.

Perhaps the most fitting sign of the day said, "Tony; Cal: A Class Act."

Ripken came back the next year, but missed 2009.

2008

The 2008 BBWAA election had 543 ballots cast. Only closer Rich "Goose" Gossage was chosen with 85.8 percent (466 votes). Gossage was elected in his ninth year of eligibility, accumulating 2,487 votes over that time. He is the fifth reliever and the first Hall of Famer from Colorado, where he still lives, to be inducted into the Hall of Fame.

The VC rules were changed after the 2007 election when no player had reached 75 percent in three elections. The change happened after Commissioner Selig had voiced frustration following the 2007 election and supported a revision in the process. There would now be two separate groups to vote on players. Voting for players whose career began after 1942 would be done by only the living Hall of Famers. (The living Frick and Spink award winners would be dropped from the process.) Their election would be every two years beginning in 2009.

Voting for players whose careers began before 1943 would be done by a composite committee of 12 Hall of Famers, writers and baseball historians. Their elections would be held every five years with the first one taking place in 2009.

This year there would be two composite ballots, one for managers and umpires, and the other for executives. A ballot of 10 managers and umpires was submitted to a 16- member panel consisting of 10 Hall of Famers (eight players and two managers), three executives, and three veteran media members for a final vote. This vote would take place every two years beginning in 2008.

Finally, after no one being voted in by the VC since 2001, five people were selected.

Tied for first was manager Billy Southworth with 81.3 percent (13 votes). Previously, Southworth received a total of 35 votes in seven BBWAA elections (1945 to 1952). After retiring as a manager 57 years before and 38 years after his death, he finally made it. Billy Southworth probably became the first inductee to make the Hall of Fame as a result of a grassroots campaign by way of the Internet. Ray Mileur, publisher of the fan-based St. Louis Web site "Birdhouse," started a campaign after Southworth wasn't included on the Veterans Committee ballot in 2003. Mileur thought that this was an injustice and had fans e-mail the Hall of Fame in support of Southworth. Carole Watson, Southworth's daughter, credits Mileur for promoting her father's overlooked credentials and was happy he was able to attend the induction.

Dick Williams also received 81.3 percent (13 votes). Williams told reporters after getting the good news that he didn't think it was going to happen. "When I die, if I didn't get in, I was planning on having my ashes spread around Doubleday Field."[33] He was inducted 20 years after he last managed with the Seattle Mariners.

The executive panel consisted of 12 members, including two former players in the Hall of Fame, along with seven executives, and three writers. They elected three executives.

Former Pittsburgh Pirates owner Barney Dreyfuss tied for first with 83.3 percent (10 votes). He received his final accolade 76 years after his death.

Former commissioner Bowie Kuhn also received 83.3 percent (10 votes). Kuhn received the honor less than a year after his death and 25 years after his contract was not renewed.

The election of Kuhn was controversial because his bargaining adversary, Marvin Miller, the longtime president of the players' union, received only three votes. It was noted that when all the former Hall of Famers were eligible to vote in 2007, Miller received 51 out of 81 votes compared to only 14 for Kuhn. Four years before that, in 2003, Miller had out-polled Kuhn 35–20.

The late Dodgers' owner Walter O'Malley received 80 percent (nine votes). He was honored 29 years after he died.

Inductees

Rich "Goose" Gossage relieved, started, and then went back to relieving where he became a dominating closer. He led the league in saves three times with the most important save coming in 1978 during the Yankees' one-game playoff against the Red Sox when he recorded the final eight outs. Gossage was picked for nine all-star teams and made it to three World Series. He pitched more than 100 innings as a closer four times, recording 52 saves where he had to get seven or more outs. Of today's premier relievers Trevor Hoffman did that only twice and Mariano Rivera once.

Gossage was part of a situation that had 55,000 people howling. Once after a couple of bad outings for the Yankees, he was called to relieve and got in the bullpen car to come into the game. All of a sudden, center fielder Mickey Rivers tried to prevent him from entering by throwing himself on the hood of the car. This lightened the tension, causing the umpire checking on it to laugh along with everyone in Yankee Stadium.

Dick Williams played 13 years and batted .260. He began managing in 1967, taking the Boston Red Sox from a ninth place finish in 1966 to the Impossible Dream team that won the pennant. He went to Oakland in 1971 and had his most success with the A's winning World Series titles in 1972 and 1973. The San Diego Padres, with fellow inductee Goose Gossage, became his third team to make the World Series in 1984. He had a record of 1,571–1,451 for five teams (.520) in 21 years.

He learned the following trick from watching fellow inductee Billy Southworth. Johnny Bench was up for the Reds in the 1972 World Series when the runner stole second. Williams went to the mound to talk to A's reliever Rollie Fingers. The count was 3–2 when the catcher positioned himself away from the plate, indicating an intentional walk. Bench was caught looking as Fingers got a called third strike on the outside corner.

Bowie Kuhn presided over baseball for 15 tumultuous years from 1969 until 1984. He fought with owners George Steinbrenner, Ted Turner, and Charlie Finley for not acting "in the best interest of baseball." He battled with Marvin Miller, director of the players' union, resulting in five work stoppages. He fought to uphold the reserve clause, but it was eventually dropped after negotiations with the players' union. He also dealt with players over illegal use of drugs and gambling, including the controversy over Mantle and Mays associating with Atlantic City casinos. Yet, he introduced night baseball to the World Series, helped institute bigger TV contracts, and started divisional play during his tenure.

Kuhn was most proud of his work on behalf of the Negro Leagues. He wanted to get former Negro Leaguers into the Hall of Fame but knew that he didn't have the support of the board of directors. So he proposed a separate display area for them in the building. The outcry from the BBWAA forced the hall to admit them on an equal basis in 1971.

Walter O'Malley became the Brooklyn Dodgers' owner in 1945. The Dodgers played in a small ballpark, Ebbets Field, where the neighborhood was deteriorating and attendance was down, so plans were made to build a new ballpark in another part of the borough. He didn't get the needed cooperation so he was allowed by the National League to consider Los Angeles, a city desperate for a major league team. The Dodgers moved there in 1958 and opened a new stadium in Chavez Ravine on April 10, 1962. O'Malley had led baseball's westward expansion and now had his privately owned ballpark.

O'Malley is still vilified for leaving Brooklyn. Sportswriter Dave Anderson maintains he was offered land where the Mets built Shea Stadium in 1964 but turned it down.[34]

Billy Southworth played 13 seasons as an outfielder and batted .297. He also played in two World Series and hit .345 in 1926 when the Cards won the world title. He was a player-manager for the Cards in 1929 and after finishing under .500 for half the season was demoted to the minors where he honed his managing skills and returned to the Cards in 1940. He was known as the "Little General" because he was a disciplinarian who stressed fundamentals. Southworth became the most successful manager of the decade. He won three pennants and two World Series with the Cards and then another pennant with the Boston Braves in 1948. He finished with a record of 1,044–704 (.597).

His son was a promising minor league ballplayer who enlisted in the Army Air Corps and flew 26 combat missions in World War II. He made it home alive only to be killed in 1945 while flying a training mission on Long Island.

Barney Dreyfuss emigrated from Germany at 18 to work in his cousins' distillery in Paducah, Kentucky, where he became a partner and eventually bought the Louisville Colonels' baseball team. They were eventually dropped from the National League, but Dreyfuss went on to become the owner of the Pittsburgh Pirates. During his 32 years as the owner, the Pirates won six pennants and two World Series titles. He accomplished many things, including being the owner most responsible for getting a commissioner after the Black Sox scandal. His great-grandson addressed the others in his induction speech.

He worked six days a week and went to school at night to learn English when he first arrived in the U.S. When he became sick, his doctor recommended he take up a sport and he chose baseball, becoming a player and a manager of semipro teams.

The 2008 Induction Weekend began on Friday, July 25, with the dedication of the Buck O'Neil statue. The lifesize statue, created by renowned sculptor William Behrends, stands inside the museum just before the hallway leading to the Hall of Fame Gallery.

The statue represents the Buck O'Neil Lifetime Achievement Award, which honors an individual whose extraordinary efforts to enhance baseball's positive impact on society have broadened the game's appeal, and whose character, integrity, and dignity are comparable to O'Neil's. He was the first recipient of the award. Chairman Jane Clark led the ribbon cutting ceremony that included 14 Hall of Famers and O'Neil family members.

I was fortunate to meet O'Neil's family outside of the museum the next day and share some experiences I had with Buck. Once, while waiting for his autograph, I saw how he warmed up to a young boy who was just ahead of me. He had him show Buck how he caught the ball when Buck threw him the ball that he had just autographed. I was also at a question and answer session with him inside the Bullpen Theater, where he talked about his experiences in the Negro Leagues. I took part in the discussion and when it was over, I was pleasantly surprised when he stopped me as I was leaving and wanted to know where I was from and where I had attended college.

These experiences were just a small sample of why he was known as Baseball's Ambassador.

Induction

The 2008 Induction Ceremony was held on a hot, sunny day on July 30 before a crowd of about 14,000 people. There were a record 56 Hall of Famers present.

Prior to the ceremony I interviewed several fans in the crowd outside the fence before the festivities began. I met a couple who were huge Goose Gossage fans. The husband had designed several goose pendants that his wife planned to give to Goose for his wife to wear. I spoke with a woman who came with her 87-year-old mother all the way from Seattle to be there to honor the Ford Frick Award winner, Dave Niehaus, the Seattle Mariners' broadcaster. And, after the ceremony, I met a member of Dick's Lunch Bunch, who get together for a weekly lunch with Dick Williams and had come all the way from Las Vegas, Nevada, to honor him.

Joe Morgan, the Hall of Famer and ESPN analyst, accepted the Lifetime Achievement Award for Buck O'Neil. "Some might say this lifetime achievement award is a bit overdue," he said. "However, for the award's first recipient and namesake, Buck O'Neil, the honor should be considered right on time. Being right on time has been both an irony and hallmark of Buck O'Neil's life."

The first speaker was Andrew Dreyfuss, the great-grandson of Barney Dreyfuss, who had passed away in 1932 at the age of 66. Slight like his great-grandfather, Andrew Dreyfuss quipped as he got ready to speak, "These plaques are pretty heavy. I only had about 20 more seconds in me." He was born 32 years after his great-grandfather had passed away, but he was very thorough in describing the many contributions made by him.

He began by telling everyone that his family was pleased that his great-grandfather would be reunited with the legendary Pirate Honus Wagner in the Hall of Fame and would join 12 other Pirates, including Bill Mazeroski and Ralph Kiner, who were there as well.

Some of the contributions that Dreyfuss made included helping to end the bitter battle between the American and National leagues when he helped to create the National Agreement in 1903. He is also referred to by many as the "Father of the World Series" because after the Pirates won the pennant in 1903, he proposed to the Boston Pilgrims (Red Sox), the American League winners, that they play a nine-game series to determine a champion. In 1909, Dreyfuss built Forbes Field, the first modern steel and concrete structure that had a double deck.

Andrew also described a very generous and benevolent owner whose losing team in the 1903 World Series actually earned more than the winning Pilgrims. Dreyfuss gave his share of the earnings to each Pirates player, but made the checks out to the players' wives in order to make sure they saved a portion of their earnings.

He closed his speech by telling how Dreyfuss had donated the funds to help rebuild the Columbia, South Carolina, wooden stadium (Pirates farm team) after it had burned down in 1926. He proclaimed, "Tonight at 7:00, 81 years after the new stadium opened in 1927, the Columbia Blowfish of the Coastal Plain League [summer league for college players] will play on the original Dreyfuss Field wearing 1927 replica jerseys to honor Barney Dreyfuss' induction into the Hall of Fame."

The daughter and the grandchildren of Billy Southworth were unable to attend so Bill DeWitt, Jr., principal owner of the St. Louis Cardinals (where Southworth achieved much success), was there instead. DeWitt said, "It's an honor and privilege to represent Billy Southworth's family." He died in 1969 at the age of 76.

DeWitt reviewed Southworth's career as a player but emphasized that "it was as a manager where he made his mark." Southworth led the Cards to 95 wins or more from 1941 through 1945 while winning three pennants and two world championships. He then went to the Boston Braves where, in three years' time, he took a losing franchise to the National League pennant. DeWitt also talked about how the Little General made use of relief pitchers in the middle innings and also platooned his position players when not too many managers were doing it in the 1940s.

DeWitt closed by describing Billy Southworth "as a humble and private man who taught his children 'humbleness is greatness.'"

Walter O'Malley died in 1979 at the age of 75. He was represented by his son, Peter, who had succeeded his father as president of the Dodgers. His son talked about his father's dream of "designing, building, and privately financing and maintaining the best baseball stadium." His dream started in Brooklyn in 1946 with replacing Ebbets Field, but after ten years of trying to no avail, he went to Los Angeles where Dodger Stadium eventually opened and was "the fulfillment of his dream."

Peter concluded that his father would have considered his own induction to be a tribute to all the men and women who were so loyal to the Dodgers' organization. He mentioned two former winners of the Ford Frick Award for broadcasting, the voice of the Dodgers, Vin Scully, and the Dodgers' Spanish broadcaster, Jaimie Jarrin. Scully was in his 59th year of broadcasting Dodgers' games and Jarrin was in his 50th year.

Bowie Kuhn died in Florida in 2007 at the age of 80, so his widow, Louisa, accepted his plaque. His son, Paul Degener, spoke eloquently for the family, defending his father during the speech. He began by explaining that his biological father was killed in a car accident six months before he was born. His mother, Louisa, later married a young lawyer, Bowie Kuhn, who now had a new family that included Paul's four-year-old brother, George. Later they were joined by his younger sister, Alix, and younger brother Stephen, all of whom were there with Paul.

Degener praised his father as a deeply religious man who always tried to be fair no matter how difficult the issue. He said his father was called racially insensitive because he wasn't there for Hank Aaron's record-tying 714th home run, yet he spent two years working to open the Hall of Fame to the Negro Leagues' stars.

Kuhn was called a prude because he wouldn't let a woman into the World Series clubhouse, yet he would spend night after night in a hospital AIDS ward reading to dying gay men.

Finally, he was called economically uninformed despite graduating from Princeton as an economics major and leading baseball to "new pinnacles of revenue from marketing, media, broadcast, and spectator attendance."

Degener spoke about some of the people his father truly admired such as Hall of Famer Monte Irvin, "a man of unexcelled decency," and Commissioner Happy Chandler, who supported the integration of baseball with Jackie Robinson. He also cited Rachel Robinson for her work with the Jackie Robinson Foundation.

He finished by acknowledging the fact that his father returned the all-star balloting to the fans. The 2008 classic had more than 30 million voters. Finally, his son said, "My father would be so happy to see today's departure from those dark days of animosity to a cooperative relationship between players and owners."

Goose Gossage, 57, smiled and raised his plaque over his head as Commissioner Selig read the words on it. One of the most intimidating pitchers of his era at 6'3", 235 pounds and a Fu Manchu moustache, Gossage was also a very emotional person off the field as he demonstrated in his 17-minute speech. He began with a startling revelation when he said, "Some of my greatest memories of Little League rival any of those I experienced as a big leaguer, believe it or not."

He told about losing his father when he was a teenager and when he signed his first contract with the Chicago White Sox organization right out of high school, he went back to his father's favorite hunting spot and cried. Later, he became very emotional as he spoke of some of the people whom he was close to in baseball and who had passed away — a former pitching coach, Norm Sherry, and several of his Yankees' teammates, Thurman Munson, Catfish Hunter and Bobby Murcer.

He paid tribute to Chuck Tanner, his former manager with the White Sox, and his first major league pitching coach, Johnny Sain. He gave special praise to former teammate Richie Allen, who taught him how to look at pitching from a hitter's perspective. Gossage called Allen "the greatest player I ever played with."

He called Yankees owner George Steinbrenner "the greatest owner of all time" because of his commitment to putting the best players on the field. He called for him to be enshrined in the Hall of Fame and "to be part of the great Yankees tradition."

Gossage acknowledged his fellow inductees, especially his former Padres manager, Dick Williams, conceding that during the 1984 World Series he should have listened to him and walked Kirk Gibson (gave up a three-run home run).

Gossage repeated something that he has said in the past. "I was like a kid getting on his favorite ride at Disney World and not getting off for 22 years."

"This experience has been overwhelming," he explained, "and I can't put it into words what it means. And I want to thank you from the bottom of my heart."

Gossage returned again for the 2009 induction.

Dick Williams, 79, was given some sage advice by his former Padres player, 2007 Hall of Famer Tony Gwynn. Gwynn warned him, "If you look at your family you're going to break down, so look out and pick a tree and talk to the tree." Williams then quipped, "I just hope it's not a weeping willow."

He began his 20-minute speech by saying, "I can't believe I'm standing before all these Hall of Famers. I'm not going to look behind me because I might start bawling."

He spoke briefly about his playing career saying that he learned a lot playing for the Dodgers' organization and was able to hang around because he could play many positions.

He managed in the minors for two years before getting his chance to manage the Impossible Dream team in Boston in 1967.

Williams admitted he "wasn't the easiest guy to work for" and talked about one of his former players in San Diego, Tim Flannery. He quoted Flannery as saying, "I loved Dick as a manager, but if I ever saw him after I stopped playing, I'd run him over with my car." Williams said he and Flannery laugh about it now, but then stated, "I still know what model car he drives and where he lives."

Williams talked about his two world titles with the Oakland A's in 1972 and 1973, and his three Hall of Famers, Reggie Jackson, Catfish Hunter, and Rollie Fingers as well as owner Charlie Finley. He also paid tribute to his last pennant winner with the San Diego Padres and their two Hall of Famers, Tony Gwynn and fellow inductee Goose Gossage.

He talked about his managerial career and shared his ten-year experience as a scout and advisor for the Yankees. He felt strongly that Yankees owner George Steinbrenner should be in the Hall of Fame, just as Goose Gossage had said before him.

He closed with, "My one big wish if I was ever elected to the Hall of Fame was that my wife, children, grandchildren along with my friends and lunch bunch crew would be here and watch this wonderful dream come true."

Williams came back for the 2009 induction.

2009

The 2009 BBWAA election had 539 ballots cast with left fielder Rickey Henderson finishing first with 94.8 percent (511 votes). He was voted in during his first year of eligibility.

Finishing second was Boston Red Sox left fielder Jim Rice, who had 76.4 percent (412 votes). His route to the Hall of Fame took a lot longer than Henderson's because this was his 15th and last year of eligibility with the BBWAA. He received a total of 3,974 votes, which gave him the distinction of the most votes in the history of the BBWAA elections.

My wife and I attended the Hall of Fame press conference held at the Waldorf Astoria Hotel in New York City on January 13, 2009. Rice and Henderson had been notified the day before, and had been flown to New York for the press conference, where they both put on their Hall of Fame shirts and caps.

Henderson told a memorable story about his breaking Ty Cobb's runs-scored record in 2001 in San Diego. He cherishes this record the most. He remembers coming back to the ballpark at night with the head groundskeeper for the Padres and spending four hours digging up home plate, which now occupies an important place in his home.

Later, when the joint press conference was over, each player conducted individual conferences. My wife remembered when Henderson played in New York for the Yankees, back in the 1980s. She started talking to his wife and then walked over to his individual conference. I was on the other side of the room when I heard his conference stop momentarily as some reporters started to laugh. This interruption was caused by my wife, Pat, shaking hands with Rickey.

The VC ballot for players whose career started after 1942 was reduced to ten names and each Hall of Famer received a ballot by mail in August 2008. Each was allowed to vote for four people. Again, no one reached 75 percent, with Cubs third baseman Ron Santo the closest with 60.9 percent. The next election will be in 2011.

The composite committee voting for players whose career began before 1943 did something that no VC had done since 2001—they elected someone! The honoree was second baseman Joe Gordon with 83.3 percent (10 votes). Gordon retired in 1950 and received 408 votes in 10 BBWAA elections from 1955 through 1970. Their next election is 2014.

Former Yankee Jerry Coleman, recent Ford Frick Award winner, said, "It's about time and 40 years too late. I voted and campaigned for him because he was a brilliant defensive second baseman. He made Rizzuto and Boudreau better."[35]

Inductees

Rickey Henderson began with the Oakland A's and the left fielder combined speed, power, and an ability to get on base to become the game's greatest leadoff hitter. Three times he stole 100 or more bases in a season and led the league 12 times in his 25-year career. He broke Lou Brock's single season and career stolen base records. Henderson scored at least 100 runs 13 seasons, and holds the career record for runs scored with 2,295. He was the 1990 MVP, won his only Gold Glove in 1981, and appeared in 10 All-Star Games. He made the postseason eight times and was a part of two world title teams. He played for nine teams and finished with 3,055 hits, 297 home runs, 1,406 stolen bases, the most unintentional walks at 2,129, and an on base average of .401 while batting .279.

Rickey Henderson received a $1 million bonus for signing with the A's and put the check up on his wall to remind himself that he was a millionaire. However, after a year of admiring it, he had to cash it because the A's wanted to balance their books.

Jim Rice spent 15 years as the Red Sox left fielder, following Ted Williams and Carl Yastrzemski. He had an outstanding rookie season in 1975 but missed the World Series because an errant pitch broke his hand at the end of the season. Rice won the MVP Award in 1978, leading the league in seven offensive categories, including total bases, 406, home runs, 46, and RBIs, 139, while batting .315. He played in the 1986 World Series and was chosen for eight all-star teams. He finished with 382 home runs, 1,451 RBIs, and batted .298 lifetime.

Rice helped save the life of a four-year-old boy in 1982 after he was hit in the head by a foul ball near the Red Sox dugout during a Game of the Week. He jumped in the stands and brought the boy to the clubhouse, from where he was then taken to a hospital.

Joe Gordon was an acrobatic fielding second baseman who helped lead the Yankees to five pennants in six years including four world titles. He batted .400 with six RBIs in the 1938 sweep of the Cubs and .500 with five RBIs in the victory over Brooklyn in 1941. Joe was chosen the league MVP in 1942 (batted .322, 18 home runs, and 103 RBIs). He was traded to Cleveland for pitcher Allie Reynolds where he would finish his career, but not before leading the Indians to their last World Series title in 1948. He finished his 11-year career with the most home runs (253) by a second baseman in the American League. As a manager he has the distinction of being involved in the only trade of managers. He was the Indians' manager when he was traded for Tigers manager Jimmy Dykes in 1960.

Being an accomplished gymnast at the University of Oregon helped Gordon with his acrobatic moves around second base.

During the 2009 Induction Weekend, I had the opportunity to meet two unique fans who demonstrate why this annual event is so special. The first individual is an entertainer from San Francisco. As I was walking along Main Street on Saturday night, I could hear a banjo playing and a crowd singing along. Upon closer observation I saw Stacy Samuels, better known as The Banjo Man. He wears a green cape and a yellow shirt, the colors of the Oakland A's. A helicopter hat is part of his attire, and I immediately recognized him from newspaper pictures that were taken during the 2004 Induction Ceremony. Five years ago, he had come for A's closer Dennis Eckersley, and now he was here for Rickey Henderson. He told me that he makes these helicopter hats and that he had made one for Henderson that included diamond studs. He is a fixture at most A's home games, and also performs at San Francisco Giants' games as well.

The Banjo Man then proceeded to the museum where he played and sang for the people. They were gathered for the traditional Saturday night Red Carpet event welcoming the Hall of Famers when they arrived for the reception. I saw him again on Sunday at the Induction where he sang "Hey Rickey" in honor of his guy.

The second gentleman was Willis "Buster" Gardner, a Babe Ruth impersonator from Oberlin, Ohio. He was dressed in a Yankees cap and shirt when our paths crossed at Pioneer Park on Main Street. He was with his wife, Cecile, and he told me he started being Babe in 1991. When Ruth's granddaughter, Linda Tosetti, saw him in Cooperstown for the first time several years ago, she exclaimed, "You are the grandfather I never met!"

Diehard Oakland A's fan Stacy Samuels entertains at his second induction in 2009 (*The Freeman's Journal*, Cooperstown, New York).

Gardner said that he and Cecile visited Ruth's gravesite at Gate of Heaven Cemetery in Valhalla, New York, about ten years ago. It was around October so he had a jacket over his Yankees outfit when he inquired at the Main Office as to the exact location of the Babe's plot. A woman was also there, inquiring about Ruth's plot, when she turned around, saw Buster, and screamed! Later, as he was walking around the back of the grave, a group of people did a double take and gasped when they laid eyes on him. He then answered questions and posed for many pictures. It is Buster's desire to return to the gravesite and "have a beer with the Babe."

Induction

The 2009 Induction Ceremony was held on July 26 before a crowd of 21,000, including 50 Hall of Famers. Due to the forecast, everything was moved up to beat the rain. As it turned out, it was a mixed bag of weather that included clouds, humidity, some light rain, sunshine, and finally a cool breeze coming at the end of the ceremony.

Lou Brock's wife, an ordained minister, gave the invocation.

Babe Ruth impersonator Willis Garner during the 2009 induction weekend (author's collection).

Joe Gordon, who had died in 1978 at the age of 63, was represented by his daughter, Judy, who wore a rubber band around her left wrist so that she could snap it in order to keep her emotions in check. She painted a picture of a very devoted father who was much more than a baseball player. At the beginning of her speech, she pointed out that her father's teammate, Larry Doby, the first black to integrate the American League, was also inducted on July 26, 11 years earlier. Her father was the only teammate who made an effort to have a catch with Doby before the game during his debut in 1947.

The main theme of her speech, however, was to celebrate Joe Gordon the man and not just the ballplayer. He was very humble and would always try to turn conversations away from baseball to some of his many other interests, including hunting and fishing. Gordon was also a classical violinist, a cowboy who would practice his calf-roping skills on Judy and her brother, and was such a good golfer that he shot an even-par 72 a week before he died. He was also an airplane pilot, ventriloquist, and a contortionist who made his kids laugh in restaurants by contorting his face, causing his wife to leave the table.

His daughter's rubber band wasn't working when she became very emotional at the end of her speech. She told the audience that her father never wanted a funeral when he died. "We consider Cooperstown and the National Hall of Fame his final resting place where he will be honored forever," she said.

Jim Rice, 56, began by mentioning Dick Bresciani, Red Sox historian, for "keeping my stats in the public eye."

He told how he received the news of his election from the president of the Hall of Fame, Jeff Idelson. He was surprised to be notified right after 12:30 because that's when he watches his favorite soap opera, *The Young and the Restless.*

Nevertheless, he put it all in context, stating simply, "I am a husband called Jim, I am a father called Dad, I am a brother called Ed, I am an uncle called Uncle Ed, and a grandfather called Papa. Finally, and I do mean finally, I am Jim Rice, called a Baseball Hall of Famer."

Rice talked about his early life, including his concern when he was forced in senior year to leave his all-black high school in Anderson, South Carolina, to attend another, mostly-white high school once the schools were integrated. It bothered him because he had to leave his future wife and friends but it turned out "to be a walk in the park," as he was received with open arms, and was even voted co-class president.

He thanked his family and coaches and gave a special tribute to Johnny Pesky, his personal hitting instructor, who was sick and couldn't be there. He also paid tribute to manager Don Zimmer, "who was a father figure to me," and his close friend, Cecil Cooper, the current manager of the Houston Astros.

He addressed the problems he had with the media by saying they would often ask him questions about other players, but he resisted, stating, "I refuse to be the media's mouthpiece." He then said, "Who would have guessed that I would be working at NESN, sitting across from Tom Caron, allowing all of you to see my winning smile."

He closed with: "I cannot think of anywhere I would rather be than to be here, right now, with you [looking at the fans] and you [turning to the Hall of Famers]."

Speaking of fans, I spent over an hour walking among them before the ceremony started. I was very impressed with the signs that Red Sox fans made to honor their hero. One said, "From the Wall to the Hall." Another was very clever with a takeoff on the MasterCard commercial, stating:

We watched Jim at spring training,	$1000
We watched Jim at Fenway,	$100
Finally, watching Jim in Cooperstown,	P "rice" less.

Even Jeff Idelson, who grew up in Massachusetts, admitted he collected all the baseball cards of Jim Rice because Rice was his favorite baseball player.

Rickey Henderson, 50, was the last of the inductees to be honored and he didn't disappoint, giving a 14-minute speech. He prepared for it by taking a speech class given by a friend at a community college.

He began by stating he loved the game so much, and that's why it was so difficult for him to give it up. He paid tribute to his family and his mother, who guided him to play baseball over football because she was afraid he would get hurt.

Yet the man who played for 25 years and still felt he could play for a major league team didn't take to baseball easily. It took a Babe Ruth League coach who induced him to play by feeding him doughnuts. And it took his guidance counselor in high school, who bribed him with quarters for hits and stolen bases, to finally convince him to stick with baseball.

Henderson talked about his baseball heroes, including Reggie Jackson, the hometown star when he played for the A's. Everyone laughed as he spoke about waiting after a game to get Jackson's autograph but all he got from him was a pen with Jackson's name on it.

He thanked minor league coach Tom Treblehorn, who helped him with his base stealing skills, and A's owner Charlie Finley for giving him the opportunity. "Charlie, wherever you and that donkey are, I want to say thank you."

He singled out his manager with the A's, Billy Martin, for being a good teacher and getting the most out of him. He lamented, "Billy, I miss you and I wish you were here."

Henderson called it his "good fortune" to play for nine teams because "it allowed me to meet fans all over the country. It's the fans that make the game fun. To all the fans, thank you for your wonderful support over the years."

He addressed the kids in the audience by imploring them "to follow their dreams because dreams do come true. Thanks to everyone for making my dream come true today."

Henderson closed as he thanked the BBWAA for voting him into the Hall of Fame and declared, "My journey as a player is now complete. I am now in the class of the greatest players of all time. And at this moment I am very, very humble."

Before his speech, people were worried that his tremendous ego might take away from the moment, especially since he stood out in his custom-made, cream-colored suit. They were also worried that he would speak in the third person by talking about himself by saying "Rickey," which he had done throughout his career. Everyone we spoke with was very pleased by his humility. I sat in the fenced-in area and the people on both sides of me were there for him. A father and son had come from Oakland and a young couple from the Midwest had flown and then driven to be here on their first visit to Cooperstown. Perhaps it was best put by his teammate and best friend in baseball, Dave Stewart. He was in the audience and raised his fist in triumph at the end of the speech. He called his friend's speech "entertaining and funny. I was proud to tears," he admitted. It was my proudest moment in the game listening to his speech."[36]

Another example of fan loyalty that I have seen during the five inductions I have attended was demonstrated by a woman holding a sign that read, "Rickey's Number One Fan." She was there with her husband and two-year-old son. Her name was Erin States and she had rooted for him since she was five years old. She would make signs that caught his attention while he was playing left field for the As. She continued to root for him no matter how many teams he played for and was even mentioned in his autobiography. She was so proud to come to his induction with her family all the way from California.

So we end our journey through all the years of induction ceremonies with a classic example of fan support that has been the essence of 70 years of adulation.

The 2010 Induction Class

As this book was readied for publication, the results of the Hall of Fame Veterans Committee and BBWAA elections were announced. The 16 member composite committee on baseball managers and umpires selected umpire Doug Harvey and manager Whitey Herzog. Harvey was named on 15 of the 16 ballots submitted and Herzog on 14.

Outfielder Andre Dawson was the only candidate to qualify in the BBWAA election. He had 77.9 percent (420 votes) out of 539 ballots cast. "The Hawk" made it on his ninth attempt and accumulated 2,750 votes during nine elections.

Andre Dawson was the Rookie of the Year for the Montreal Expos in 1976. He played center field but switched to right field because of knee problems that were aggravated by the artificial turf of Olympic Stadium. He became a free agent after 11 seasons and signed with the Chicago Cubs because it gave him the chance to play on the natural grass of Wrigley Field. Dawson won the league MVP in his first year with the last place Cubs in 1987. The Hawk had an exceptional arm and won eight Gold Gloves and also was an all-star eight times. He finished up his career with the Florida Marlins and retired in 1996 with 438 home runs and a .279 lifetime batting average. He became an executive with the Marlins and was part of the organization when they won the 2003 World Series.

The Hawk has the distinction of being one of three players to have his number (#19) retired with the Expos. He also has a street named after him in his native Miami.

Whitey Herzog was signed by the Yankees as an outfielder but never played for them during his eight year major-league career. Later he became a scout, coach, director of player development and farm system director, but it was as a manager that he found his niche. He led the Kansas City Royals to three divisional championships and the St. Louis Cardinals to three pennants and one World Series title. Contrary to Andre Dawson, Herzog found success with astro-turf. He developed his managing strategy to take advantage of the spacious AstroTurf stadiums in Kansas City and St. Louis. His managing style became known as "Whitey Ball" as his teams were known for speed, defense and relief pitching.

Doug Harvey umpired 4,670 games, the third highest of all time when he retired in 1992. He umpired for 31 years in the National League including four all-star games and five World Series. SABR named him the second greatest umpire behind Bill Klem in 1999. He was also chosen one of the 52 most influential figures in the history of sports officiating in 2007 by *Referee Magazine*. Harvey was known for his delayed and decisive calls, as he made sure he got it right before making the call. Harvey was so respected by the players and his fellow umpires that he was given the nickname "God." He was known for chewing a wad of tobacco when he umpired but was diagnosed with oral cancer in 1997 and today speaks to players and students about the dangers of tobacco.

Afterword

I would like to commend the Hall of Fame's Board of Directors for addressing the Veterans Committee problem in 2001. The VC has made a number of controversial choices over the years as we have documented throughout this book. The board made significant changes in the makeup of the committee along with the rules in order to make the process fairer. Since then, more changes have been made and the results have been discussed in Chapter 10. When the new process didn't produce any new inductees in three straight elections, they changed it again. The three smaller, composite groups worked and eight new inductees have been chosen in the last three elections.

The board has to decide if they should make changes regarding the 2011 election for players whose career started after 1942. The reason is that no one has been elected in four elections. First of all, I wouldn't change to a smaller composite group because the living Hall of Famers (64) have shown that they take their responsibility seriously. Each one voted on the 10 candidates that were on the 2009 ballot and they cast an average of 3.3 votes out of a possible 4 votes allowed.

However, there might be some ways to tweak the process that is in place now for a candidate to reach 75 percent. Every year during the Induction Weekend Sunday dinner, different Hall of Famers stand up and lobby for particular people. For example, Fergie Jenkins told us how he spoke up for former teammate Ron Santo; Sandy Koufax for former Dodger Maury Wills; and Tom Seaver for his former manager, Gil Hodges.

Why not have people at the Hall of Fame dinner or some other appropriate forum present arguments for and against all viable candidates? This would be in addition to all the information that is supplied about each candidate from the Elias Sports Bureau. Someone from the Historical Review Committee that helps to determine the final ballot could do it. Our democracy works this way when members of Congress debate the pros and cons of a piece of legislation. Why not use Hall of Famer, Senator Jim Bunning, an experienced lawmaker, to help with the process?

By the way, I wonder if there is a way for Hall of Famers like Bunning, Robin Roberts, Ralph Kiner, Nolan Ryan, Carlton Fisk, and anyone else to lobby the committee on executives for candidate Marvin Miller. These gentlemen were either active in the Players Union or spoke about Miller in their induction speeches. He missed by only two votes in the latest election (2010) so it might happen in the 2012 election.

Getting back to the other issue, another possible solution is to have a runoff election for the top vote getters like they had during several BBWAA elections. A proviso could be that two or more candidates have to reach a certain percentage, such as 60 percent, before there would be a runoff.

The biggest issue the BBWAA voters face is steroids. The Associated Press (AP) in November 2006 asked writers about their voting plans because home-run king and recently admitted (January 2010) steroid user Mark McGwire would be on the ballot for the first time in 2007. The AP received 125 responses and reported about three-fourths of those writers decided against voting for McGwire.[1] Bill Madden of the New York *Daily News* said he wouldn't vote for any player he suspects of using steroids, citing the five criteria set down for the voters in 1945. The criteria were playing ability, integrity, sportsmanship, character and contribution to the team for which they played. Madden said, "If the Hall of Fame doesn't want me or any other writer to take a stand, then take that clause out of the ballot. I plan to invoke that clause."[2] Taking an opposite view was ESPN sportswriter Jayson Stark. "I think I'm stuck with evaluating what the sport allowed to happen on the field. I think I feel more comfortable voting for players like McGwire than I do trying to pick and choose who did what and when and why."[3] The results for McGwire in four BBWAA elections (2007, 2008, 2009 and 2010) bear out the AP 2006 responses. He has never received more than 24 percent in each of these elections.

A possible solution to resolving the issue was presented to the BBWAA at a national meeting in July 2009. Rick Telander of the Chicago *Sun-Times* proposed forming a committee to develop guidelines on evaluating players from the steroid era. The proposal was voted down 30–25.[4]

Stay tuned because the issue will undoubtedly get more heated when accused steroid users Rafael Palmiero and superstars Barry Bonds and Roger Clemens come on the ballot in the next few years.

Here are some other ideas I have for the reader to ponder. Fergie Jenkins brought up an interesting idea when I interviewed him in 2005. He suggested that the Hall of Fame should consider recognizing the Japanese all-time home run leader Sadaharu Oh. It was brought up because of the upcoming World Baseball Classic at the time. This is the worldwide tournament that consists of teams representing countries from around the world. Japan has won both tournaments (2006 and 2009) with the United States finishing fourth in 2009. As baseball becomes more international, the idea of honoring a star such as Oh would become more realistic.

A group that definitely should be recognized by the Hall of Fame is baseball scouts. President Jeff Idelson told New York *Post* baseball writer Kevin Kernan that their work should be honored with an exhibit.[5]

Here are three other suggestions for recognition. The minor leagues were considered very important when the National Baseball Hall of Fame and Museum started. William Bramham, president of the minor leagues, participated with Landis, Frick and Harridge in the ribbon cutting ceremony during the dedication ceremony in 1939. Also, after the initial BBWAA election in 1936, the Centennial Commission was charged with picking five pioneers of baseball in December 1936. Two members of the six-man committee were Bramham and George Trautman, president of the American Association. The Hall of Fame could begin by giving recognition to the most significant minor league franchises in terms of history and success.

Also, Alexander Cleland and Lee Allen were two prominent individuals in the history of the National Baseball Hall of Fame and Museum as we have documented and should be recognized as such.

You can see by the increase in the number of ballots cast during the BBWAA elections that the group has become bigger. The group has added members from the electronic media such as ESPN and MLB.com. I believe they should also consider adding the television and radio broadcasters from each of the 30 major league teams. This would mean an additional 60 members although they could have the 10-year requirement as they do for the writers before they can become voters. These broadcasters see most, if not all, of their teams' games and would be more knowledgeable than some of the BBWAA members who have retired and don't see many games but still have a vote.

I will close with a final thought. If you are a baseball fan and have never attended a Hall of Fame Induction Ceremony then you definitely should consider doing it in the future. You will then see for yourself what all the adulation is about!

Appendix 1.
Hall of Fame Induction Roster

Ballplayer	Birth Date	Place of Birth	Death Date	Place of Death	Induction
Hank Aaron	2/5/34	Mobile, AL			1982
Pete Alexander	2/26/1886	Elba, NE	11/4/50	St. Paul, NE	1938
Walter Alston	12/11/11	Venice, OH	10/14/84	Oxford, OH	1983
Sparky Anderson	2/22/34	Bridgewater, SD			2000
Cap Anson	4/17/1852	Marshalltown, IA	4/14/22	Chicago, IL	1939
Luis Aparicio	4/29/34	Maracaibo, Venezuala			1984
Luke Appling	4/2/07	High Point, NC	1/3/91	Cumming, GA	1964
Richie Ashburn	3/19/27	Tilpen, NE	9/9/97	New York, NY	1995
Earl Averill	5/21/02	Snohomish, WA	8/16/83	Everett, WA	1975
Frank Baker	3/13/1886	Trappe, MD	6/28/63	Trappe, MD	1955
Dave Bancroft	4/20/1891	Sioux City, IA	10/9/72	Superior, WI	1971
Ernie Banks	1/31/31	Dallas, TX			1977
Al Barlick	4/2/15	Springfield, IL	12/27/95	Springfield, IL	1989
Ed Barrow	5/10/1868	Springfield, IL	12/15/53	Port Chester, NY	1953
Jake Beckley	8/4/1867	Hannibal, MO	6/25/18	Kansas City, MO	1971
Cool Papa Bell	5/17/03	Starkville, MS	3/7/91	St. Louis, MO	1974
Johnny Bench	12/7/47	Oklahoma City, OK			1989
Chief Bender	5/5/1884	Crow Wing County, MN	5/22/54	Philadelphia, PA	1953
Yogi Berra	5/12/25	St. Louis, MO			1972
Wade Boggs	6/15/58	Omaha, NE			2005
Jim Bottomly	4/23/00	Oglesby, IL	12/11/59	St. Louis, MO	1974
Louis Boudreau	7/17/17	Harvey, IL	8/10/01	Frankfort, IL	1970
Roger Bresnahan	6/11/1879	Toledo, OH	12/4/44	Toledo, OH	1945
George Brett	5/15/53	Glen Dale, WV			1999
Louis Brock	6/18/39	El Dorado, AR			1985
Dan Brouthers	5/8/1858	Sylvan Lake, NY	8/2/32	East Orange, NJ	1945
Mordecai Brown	10/19/1876	Nyesville, IN	2/14/48	Terre Haute, IN	1949
Raymond Brown	2/23/08	Alger, OH	2/8/65	Dayton, OH	2006
Willard Brown	6/26/15	Shreveport, LA	8/4/96	Houston, TX	2006
Morgan Bulkeley	12/26/1837	East Haddam, CT	11/6/22	Hartford, CT	1937
Jim Bunning	10/23/31	Southgate, KY			1996
Jesse Burkett	12/4/1868	Wheeling, WV	5/27/53	Worcester, MA	1946
Roy Campanella	11/19/21	Philadelphia, PA	6/26/93	Woodland Hills, CA	1969
Rod Carew	10/1/45	Gatun, Panama			1991
Max Carey	1/11/1890	Terre Haute, IN	5/30/76	Miama, FL	1961
Steve Carlton	12/22/44	Miami, FL			1994
Gary Carter	4/8/54	Culver City, CA			2003
Alexander Cartwright	4/17/1820	New York, NY	7/12/1892	Honolulu, HI	1938
Orlando Cepeda	9/17/37	Ponce, PR			1999
Henry Chadwick	10/5/1824	Exeter, England	4/20/08	Brooklyn, NY	1938
Frank Chance	9/9/1877	Fresno, CA	9/15/24	Los Angeles, CA	1946
Happy Chandler	7/14/1898	Corydon, KY	6/15/91	Versailles, KY	1982

Ballplayer	Birth Date	Place of Birth	Death Date	Place of Death	Induction
Oscar Charleston	10/14/1896	Indianapolis, IN	10/5/54	Philadelphia, PA	1976
Jack Chesbro	6/5/1874	North Adams, MA	11/6/31	Conway, MA	1946
Nestor Chylak	5/11/22	Olyphant, PA	2/17/82	Dunmore, PA	1999
Fred Clarke	10/3/1872	Winterset, IA	8/14/60	Winfield, KS	1945
John Clarkson	7/1/1861	Cambridge, MA	2/4/09	Belmont, MA	1963
Roberto Clemente	8/18/34	Carolina, PR	12/31/72	San Juan, PR	1973
Ty Cobb	12/18/1886	Narrows, GA	7/17/61	Atlanta, GA	1936
Mickey Cochrane	4/6/03	Bridgewater, MA	6/28/62	Lake Forest, IL	1947
Eddie Collins	5/2/1887	Millerton, NY	3/25/51	Boston, MA	1939
Jimmy Collins	1/16/1870	Buffalo, NY	3/6/43	Buffalo, NY	1945
Earle Combs	5/14/1899	Pebworth, KY	7/21/76	Richmond, KY	1970
Charles Comiskey	8/15/1859	Chicago, IL	10/26/31	Eagle River, WI	1939
Jocko Conlan	12/6/1899	Chicago, IL	4/16/89	Scottsdale, AZ	1974
Tom Connolly	12/31/1870	Manchester, England	4/28/61	Natick, MA	1953
Roger Connor	7/1/1857	Waterbury, CT	1/4/31	Waterbury, CT	1976
Andy Cooper	4/24/1898	Waco, TX	6/3/41	Waco, TX	2006
Stan Coveleski	7/13/1889	Shamokin, PA	3/20/84	South Bend, IN	1969
Sam Crawford	4/18/1880	Wahoo, NE	6/15/68	Hollywood, CA	1957
Joe Cronin	10/12/06	San Francisco, CA	9/7/84	Osterville, MA	1956
Candy Cummings	10/18/1848	Ware, MA	5/16/25	Toledo, OH	1939
Kiki Cuyler	8/30/1898	Harrisville, MI	2/11/50	Ann Arbor, MI	1968
Ray Dandridge	8/31/13	Richmond, VA	2/12/94	Palm Bay, FL	1987
George Davis	8/23/1870	Cohoes, NY	10/17/40	Philadelphia, PA	1998
Leon Day	10/30/16	Alexandria, VA	3/13/95	Baltimore, MD	1995
Dizzy Dean	1/16/10	Lucas, AR	7/17/74	Reno, Nevada	1953
Ed Delahanty	10/30/1867	Cleveland, OH	7/2/03	Niagara Falls, Ontario	1945
Bill Dickey	6/6/07	Bastrop, LA	11/12/93	Little Rock, AR	1954
Martin Dihigo	5/25/05	Matanzas, Cuba	5/20/71	Cienfuegos, Cuba	1977
Joe DiMaggio	11/25/14	Martinez, CA	3/8/99	Hollywood, FL	1955
Larry Doby	12/13/24	Camden, SC	6/28/03	Monclair, NJ	1998
Bobby Doerr	4/7/18	Los Angeles, CA			1986
Barney Dreyfus	2/23/1865	Freiburg, Germany	5/5/32	Pittsburgh, PA	2008
Don Drysdale	7/23/36	Van Nuys, CA	7/3/93	Montreal, Quebec	1984
Hugh Duffy	11/26/1866	Cranston, RI	10/19/54	Boston, MA	1945
Leo Durocher	7/27/05	West Springfield, MA	10/7/91	Palm Springs, CA	1994
Dennis Eckersley	10/3/54	Oakland, CA			2004
Billy Evans	2/10/1884	Chicago, IL	1/23/56	Miami, FL	1973
Johnny Evers	7/21/1881	Troy, NY	3/28/47	Albany, NY	1946
Buck Ewing	10/17/1859	Hoagland, OH	10/20/06	Cincinnati, OH	1939
Red Faber	9/6/1888	Cascade, IN	9/25/76	Chicago, IL	1964
Bob Feller	11/3/18	Van Meter, IA			1962
Rick Ferrell	10/12/05	Durham, NC	7/27/95	Bloomfield Hills, MI	1984
Rollie Fingers	8/25/46	Steubenville, OH			1992
Carlton Fisk	12/26/47	Bellow Falls, VT			2000
Elmer Flick	1/11/1876	Bedford, OH	1/9/71	Bedford, OH	1963
Whitey Ford	10/21/28	New York, NY			1974
Rube Foster	9/17/1879	Calvert, TX	12/9/30	Kankakee, IL	1981
Bill Foster	6/12/04	Rodney, MS	9/16/78	Lorman, MS	1996
Nellie Fox	12/25/27	St. Thomas, PA	12/1/75	Baltimore, MD	1997
Jimmie Foxx	10/22/07	Sudlersville, MD	7/21/67	Miami, FL	1951
Ford Frick	12/19/1894	Wawaka, IN	4/8/78	Bronxville, NY	1970
Frankie Frisch	9/9/1898	Bronx, NY	3/12/73	Wilmington, DE	1947
Pud Galvin	12/25/1856	St. Louis, MO	3/7/02	Pittsburgh, PA	1965
Lou Gehrig	6/19/03	New York, NY	6/2/41	Riverdale, NY	1939
Charlie Gehringer	5/11/03	Fowlerville, MI	1/21/93	Bloomfield Hills, MI	1949
Bob Gibson	11/9/35	Omaha, NE			1981
Josh Gibson	12/21/11	Buena Vista, GA	1/20/47	Pittsburgh, PA	1972
Warren Giles	5/28/1896	Tiskilwa, IL	1/7/79	Cincinnati, OH	1979
Lefty Gomez	11/26/08	Rodeo, CA	2/17/89	Greenbrae, CA	1972
Joe Gordon	2/18/15	Los Angeles, CA	4/14/78	Sacramento, CA	2009

Ballplayer	Birth Date	Place of Birth	Death Date	Place of Death	Induction
Goose Goslin	10/16/00	Salem, NJ	5/15/71	Bridgeton, NJ	1968
Goose Gossage	7/5/51	Colorado Springs, CO			2008
Frank Grant	8/1/1865	Pittsfield, MA	5/27/37	New York, NY	2006
Hank Greenberg	1/1/11	New York, NY	9/4/86	Beverly Hills, CA	1956
Clark Griffith	11/20/1869	Clear Creek, MD	10/27/55	Washington, DC	1946
Burleigh Grimes	8/18/1893	Emerald, WI	12/6/85	Clear Lake, WI	1964
Lefty Grove	3/6/00	Lonaconing, MD	5/22/75	Norwalk, OH	1947
Tony Gwynn	5/9/60	Los Angeles, CA			2007
Chick Hafey	2/12/03	Berkeley, CA	7/2/73	Calistoga, CA	1971
Jesse Haines	7/22/1893	Clayton, OH	8/5/78	Dayton, OH	1970
Billy Hamilton	2/16/1866	Newark, NJ	12/16/40	Worcester, MA	1961
Ned Hanlon	8/22/1857	Montville, CT	4/14/37	Baltimore, MD	1996
Will Harridge	10/16/1883	Chicago, IL	4/9/71	Evanston, IL	1972
Bucky Harris	11/8/1896	Port Jervis, NY	11/8/77	Bethesda, MD	1975
Gabby Hartnett	12/20/00	Woonsocket, RI	12/20/72	Park Ridge, IL	1955
Harry Heilmann	8/3/1894	San Francisco, CA	7/9/51	Southfield, MI	1952
Rickey Henderson	12/25/58	Chicago, IL			2009
Billy Herman	7/7/09	New Albany, IN	9/5/92	West Palm Beach, FL	1975
Pete Hill	10/12/1880	Pittsburgh, PA	11/26/51	Buffalo, NY	2006
Harry Hooper	8/24/1887	Bell Station, CA	12/18/74	Santa Cruz, CA	1971
Rogers Hornsby	2/27/1896	Winters, TX	1/5/63	Chicago, IL	1942
Waite Hoyt	9/9/1899	Brooklyn, NY	8/25/84	Cincinnati, OH	1969
Cal Hubbard	10/31/00	Keytesville, MD	10/17/77	St. Petersburg, FL	1976
Carl Hubbell	6/22/03	Carthage, MD	11/21/88	Scottsdale, AZ	1947
Miller Huggins	3/27/1879	Cincinnati, OH	9/25/29	New York, NY	1964
William Hulbert	10/23/1832	Burlington Flats, NY	4/10/1882	Chicago, IL	1995
Catfish Hunter	4/8/46	Hertford, NC	9/9/99	Hertford, NC	1987
Monte Irwin	2/25/19	Columbia, AL			1973
Reggie Jackson	5/18/46	Wyncote, PA			1993
Travis Jackson	11/2/03	Waldo, AR	7/27/87	Waldo, AR	1982
Ferguson Jenkins	12/13/43	Chatham, Ontario			1991
Hughie Jennings	4/2/1869	Pittston, PA	2/1/28	Scranton, PA	1945
Ban Johnson	1/5/1864	Norwalk, OH	3/28/31	St. Louis, MO	1937
Judy Johnson	10/26/1899	Snow Hill, MD	6/15/89	Wilmington, DE	1975
Walter Johnson	11/6/1887	Humboldt, KS	12/10/46	Washington, DC	1936
Addie Joss	4/12/1880	Woodland, WI	4/14/11	Toledo, OH	1978
Al Kaline	12/19/34	Baltimore, MD			1980
Tim Keefe	1/1/1857	Cambridge, MA	4/23/33	Cambridge, MA	1964
Willie Keeler	3/3/1872	Brooklyn, NY	1/1/23	Brooklyn, NY	1939
George Kell	8/23/22	Swifton, AR	3/24/09	Swifton, AR	1983
Joe Kelley	12/9/1871	Cambridge, MA	8/14/43	Baltimore, MD	1971
George Kelly	9/10/1895	San Francisco, CA	10/13/84	Burlingame, CA	1973
King Kelly	12/31/1857	Troy, NY	11/8/1894	Boston, MA	1945
Harmon Killebrew	6/29/36	Payette, Idaho			1984
Ralph Kiner	10/27/22	Santa Rita, NM			1975
Chuck Klein	10/7/04	Indianapolis, IN	3/28/58	Indianapolis, IN	1980
Bill Klem	2/22/1874	Rochester, NY	9/1/51	Miami, FL	1953
Sandy Koufax	12/30/35	Brooklyn, NY			1972
Bowie Kuhn	10/28/26	Takoma Park, MD	3/15/07	Jacksonville, FL	2008
Nap Lajoie	9/5/1874	Woonsocket, RI	2/7/59	Daytona Beach, FL	1937
Kenesaw Landis	11/20/1866	Millville, OH	11/25/44	Chicago, IL	1944
Tommy Lasorda	9/22/27	Norristown, PA			1997
Tony Lazzeri	12/6/03	San Francisco, CA	8/6/46	San Francisco, CA	1991
Bob Lemon	9/22/20	San Bernardino, CA	1/11/00	Long Beach, CA	1976
Buck Leonard	9/8/07	Rocky Mount, NC	11/27/97	Rocky Mount, NC	1972
Fred Lindstrom	11/21/05	Chicago, IL	10/4/81	Chicago, IL	1976
Pop Lloyd	4/25/1884	Palatka, FL	3/19/65	Atlantic City, NJ	1977
Ernie Lombardi	4/6/08	Oakland, CA	9/26/77	Santa Cruz, CA	1986
Al Lopez	10/20/08	Tampa, FL	10/30/05	Tampa, FL	1977
Ted Lyons	12/28/00	Lake Charles, LA	7/25/86	Sulphur, LA	1955

Ballplayer	Birth Date	Place of Birth	Death Date	Place of Death	Induction
Connie Mack	12/22/1862	East Brookfield, MA	2/8/56	Philadelphia, PA	1937
Biz Mackey	7/27/1897	Eagle Pass, TX	9/22/65	Los Angeles, CA	2006
Larry MacPhail	2/3/1890	Cass City, MI	10/1/75	Miami, FL	1978
Lee MacPhail	10/25/17	Nashville, TN			1998
Effa Manley	3/27/1897	Philadelphia, PA	4/6/81	Los Angeles, CA	2006
Mickey Mantle	10/20/31	Spavinaw, OK	10/13/95	Dallas, TX	1974
Heinie Manush	7/20/01	Tuscumbia, AL	5/12/71	Sarasota, FL	1964
Rabbit Maranville	11/11/1891	Springfield, MA	1/5/54	New York, NY	1954
Juan Marichal	10/20/37	Laguna Verde, Dom. Rep.			1983
Rube Marquard	10/9/1886	Cleveland, OH	6/1/80	Baltimore, MD	1971
Eddie Mathews	10/13/31	Texarkana, TX	2/18/01	La Jolla, CA	1978
Christy Mathewson	8/12/1880	Factoryville, PA	10/7/25	Saranac Lake, NY	1936
Willie Mays	5/6/31	Westfield, AL			1979
Bill Mazeroski	9/5/36	Wheeling, WV			2001
Joe McCarthy	4/21/1887	Philadelphia, PA	1/13/78	Buffalo, NY	1957
Tommy McCarthy	7/24/1863	Boston, MA	8/5/22	Boston, MA	1946
Willie McCovey	1/10/38	Mobile, AL			1986
Joe McGinnity	3/19/1871	Rock Island, IL	11/14/29	Brooklyn, NY	1946
Bill McGowan	1/18/1896	Wilmington, DE	12/9/54	Silver Spring, MD	1992
John McGraw	4/7/1873	Truxton, NY	2/25/34	New Rochelle, NY	1937
Bill McKechnie	8/7/1886	Wilkinsburg, PA	10/29/65	Bradenton, FL	1962
Bid McPhee	11/1/1859	Massena, NY	1/3/43	San Diego, CA	2000
Joe Medwick	11/24/11	Carteret, NJ	3/21/75	St. Petersburg, FL	1968
Jose Mendez	3/19/1887	Cardenas, Cuba	10/31/28	Havana, Cuba	2006
Johnny Mize	1/7/13	Demorest, GA	6/2/93	Demorest, GA	1981
Paul Molitor	8/22/56	St Paul, MN			2004
Joe Morgan	9/19/43	Bonham, TX			1990
Eddie Murray	2/24/56	Los Angeles, CA			2003
Stan Musial	11/21/20	Donora, PA			1969
Hal Newhouser	5/20/21	Detroit, MI	11/10/98	Bloomfield Hills, MI	1992
Kid Nichols	9/14/1869	Madison, WI	4/11/53	Kansas City, MO	1949
Phil Niekro	4/1/39	Blaine, OH			1997
Walter O'Malley	10/9/03	New York, NY	8/9/79	Rochester, MN	2008
Jim O'Rourke	9/1/1850	East Bridgeport, CT	1/8/19	Bridgeport, CT	1945
Mel Ott	3/2/09	Gretna, LA	11/21/58	New Orleans, LA	1951
Satchel Paige	7/7/06	Mobile, AL	6/8/82	Kansas City, MO	1971
Jim Palmer	10/15/45	New York, NY			1990
Herb Pennock	2/10/1894	Kennett Square, PA	1/30/48	New York, NY	1948
Tony Perez	5/14/42	Ciego De Avila, Cuba			2000
Gaylord Perry	9/15/38	Williamston, NC			1991
Eddie Plank	8/31/1875	Gettysburg, PA	2/24/26	Gettysburg, PA	1946
Alex Pompez	5/14/1890	Key West, FL	3/14/74	New York, NY	2006
Cumberland Posey, Jr.	6/20/1890	Homestead, PA	3/28/46	Pittsburgh, PA	2006
Kirby Puckett	3/14/60	Chicago, IL	3/6/06	Phoenix, AZ	2001
Charlie Radbourn	12/11/1863	Rochester, NY	2/5/1897	Bloomington, IL	1939
Pee Wee Reese	7/23/18	Ekron, KY	8/14/99	Louisville, KY	1984
Jim Rice	3/8/53	Anderson, SC			2009
Sam Rice	2/20/1890	Morocco, IN	10/13/74	Rossmoor, MD	1963
Branch Rickey	12/20/1881	Flat, OH	12/9/65	Colombia, MO	1967
Cal Ripken, Jr.	8/24/60	Havre de Grace, MD			2007
Eppa Rixey	5/3/1891	Culpepper, VA	2/28/63	Cincinnati, OH	1963
Phil Rizzuto	9/25/17	Brooklyn, NY	8/13/07	West Orange, NJ	1994
Robin Roberts	9/30/26	Springfield, IL			1976
Brooks Robinson	5/18/37	Little Rock, AR			1983
Frank Robinson	8/31/35	Beaumont, TX			1982
Jackie Robinson	1/31/19	Cairo, GA	10/24/72	Stamford, CT	1962
Wilbert Robinson	6/29/1863	Bolton, MA	8/8/34	Atlanta, GA	1945
Bullet Rogan	7/28/1889	Oklahoma City, OK	3/4/67	Kansas City, MO	1998
Edd Roush	5/8/1893	Oakland City, IN	3/21/88	Bradenton, FL	1962
Red Ruffing	5/3/05	Granville, IL	2/17/86	Mayfield Heights, OH	1967

Ballplayer	Birth Date	Place of Birth	Death Date	Place of Death	Induction
Amos Rusie	5/30/1871	Mooresville, IN	12/6/42	Seattle, WA	1977
Babe Ruth	2/6/1895	Baltimore, MD	8/16/48	New York, NY	1936
Nolan Ryan	1/31/47	Refugio, TX			1999
Ryne Sandberg	9/18/59	Spokane, WA			2005
Louis Santop	1/17/1890	Tyler, TX	1/22/42	Philadelphia, PA	2006
Ray Schalk	8/12/1892	Harvel, IL	5/19/70	Chicago, IL	1955
Mike Schmidt	9/27/49	Dayton, OH			1995
Red Schoendienst	2/2/23	Germantown, IL			1989
Tom Seaver	11/17/44	Fresno, CA			1992
Frank Selee	10/26/1859	Amherst, NH	7/5/09	Denver, CO	1999
Joe Sewell	10/9/1898	Titus, AL	3/6/90	Mobile, AL	1977
Al Simmons	5/22/02	Milwaukee, WI	5/26/56	Milwaukee, WI	1953
George Sisler	3/24/1893	Manchester, OH	3/26/73	Richmond Heights, MO	1939
Enos Slaughter	4/27/16	Roxboro, NC	8/12/02	Durham, NC	1985
Hilton Smith	2/27/07	Giddings, TX	11/18/83	Kansas City, MO	2001
Ozzie Smith	12/26/54	Mobile, AL			2002
Duke Snider	9/19/26	Los Angeles, CA			1980
Billy Southworth	3/9/1893	Harvard, NE	11/15/69	Columbus, OH	2008
Warren Spahn	4/23/21	Buffalo, NY	11/24/03	Broken Arrow, OK	1973
A.G. Spalding	9/2/1850	Byron, IL	9/9/15	Point Loma, CA	1939
Tris Speaker	4/4/1888	Hubbard, TX	12/8/58	Lake Whitney, TX	1937
Willie Stargell	3/6/40	Earlsboro, OK	4/9/01	Wilmington, NC	1988
Turkey Stearnes	5/8/01	Nashville, TN	9/4/79	Detroit, MI	2000
Casey Stengel	7/30/1890	Kansas City, MO	9/29/75	Glendale, CA	1966
Bruce Sutter	1/8/53	Lancaster, PA			2006
Mule Suttles	3/31/00	Blocton, AL	7/9/66	Newark, NJ	2006
Don Sutton	4/2/45	Clio, AL			1998
Ben Taylor	7/1/1888	Anderson, SC	1/24/53	Baltimore, MD	2006
Bill Terry	10/30/1898	Atlanta, GA	1/9/89	Jacksonville, FL	1954
Sam Thompson	3/5/1860	Danville, IL	11/7/22	Detroit, MI	1974
Joe Tinker	7/27/1880	Muscotah, KS	7/27/48	Orlando, FL	1946
Cristobal Torriente	11/16/1893	Cienfuegos, Cuba	4/11/38	New York, NY	2006
Pie Traynor	11/11/1899	Framingham, MA	3/16/72	Pittsburgh, PA	1948
Dazzy Vance	3/4/1891	Orient, IA	2/16/61	Homosassa Springs, FL	1955
Arky Vaughan	3/9/12	Clifty, AZ	8/30/52	Eaglesville, CA	1985
Bill Veeck	2/9/14	Chicago, IL	1/2/86	Chicago, IL	1991
Rube Waddell	10/13/1876	Bradford, PA	4/1/14	San Antonio, TX	1946
Honus Wagner	2/24/1874	Chartiers, PA	12/6/55	Carnegie, PA	1936
Bobby Wallace	11/4/1873	Pittsburgh, PA	11/3/60	Torrance, CA	1953
Ed Walsh	5/14/1881	Plains, PA	5/26/59	Pompano Beach, FL	1946
Lloyd Waner	3/16/06	Harrah, OK	7/22/82	Oklahoma City, OK	1967
Paul Waner	4/16/03	Harrah, OK	8/29/65	Sarasota, FL	1952
John Ward	3/3/1860	Bellefonte, PA	3/4/25	Augusta, GA	1964
Earl Weaver	8/14/30	St. Louis, MO			1996
George Weiss	6/23/1895	New Haven, CT	8/13/72	Greenwich, CT	1971
Mickey Welch	7/4/1859	Brooklyn, NY	7/30/41	Concord, NH	1973
Willie Wells	8/10/06	Austin, TX	1/22/89	Austin, TX	1997
Zack Wheat	5/23/1888	Hamilton, MO	3/11/72	Sedalia, MO	1959
Sol White	6/12/1868	Bellaire, OH	8/26/55	Central Islip, NY	2006
Hoyt Wilhelm	7/26/23	Huntersville, NC	8/23/02	Sarasota, FL	1985
J.L. Wilkinson	5/14/1878	Algona, IA	8/21/64	Kansas City, MO	2006
Billy Williams	6/15/38	Whistler, AL			1987
Dick Williams	5/7/29	St. Louis, MO			2008
Joe Williams	4/6/1886	Seguin, TX	2/25/51	New York, NY	1999
Ted Williams	8/30/19	San Diego, CA	7/5/02	Inverness, FL	1966
Vic Willis	4/12/1876	Cecil County, MD	8/3/47	Elkton, MD	1985
Hack Wilson	4/26/1900	Ellwood City, PA	11/23/48	Baltimore, MD	1979
Jud Wilson	2/28/1894	Remington, VA	6/24/63	Washington, DC	2006
Dave Winfield	10/3/51	St. Paul, MN			2001
George Wright	1/18/1847	New York, NY	8/21/37	Boston, MA	1937

Ballplayer	Birth Date	Place of Birth	Death Date	Place of Death	Induction
Harry Wright	1/10/1835	Sheffield, England	10/3/1895	Atlantic City, NJ	1953
Early Wynn	1/6/20	Hartford, AL	4/4/99	Venice, FL	1972
Carl Yastrzemski	8/22/39	Southampton, NY			1989
Tom Yawkey	2/21/03	Detroit, MI	7/9/76	Boston, MA	1980
Cy Young	3/29/1867	Gilmore, OH	11/4/55	Newcomerstown, OH	1937
Ross Youngs	4/10/1897	Shiner, TX	10/22/27	San Antonio, TX	1972
Robin Yount	9/16/55	Danville, IL			1999

Appendix 2.
Award Recipients

Ford C. Frick Award

1978 Mel Allen, Red Barber
1979 Bob Elson
1980 Russ Hodges
1981 Ernie Harwell
1982 Vin Scully
1983 Jack Brickhouse
1984 Curt Gowdy
1985 Buck Canel
1986 Bob Prince
1987 Jack Buck
1988 Lindsey Nelson
1989 Harry Caray
1990 By Saam
1991 Joe Garagiola
1992 Milo Hamilton
1993 Chuck Thompson
1994 Bob Murphy
1995 Bob Wolf
1996 Herb Carneal
1997 Jimmy Dudley
1998 Jaime Jarrin
1999 Arch McDonald
2000 Marty Brennaman
2001 Felo Ramirez
2002 Harry Kalas
2003 Bob Uecker
2004 Lon Simmons
2005 Jerry Coleman
2006 Gene Elston
2007 Denny Matthews
2008 Dave Niehaus
2009 Tony Kubek

J.G. Taylor Spink Award

1962 J.G. Taylor Spink
1963 Ring Lardner
1964 Hugh Fullerton
1965 Charles Dryden

1966 Grantland Rice
1967 Damon Runyon
1968 H.G. Salsinger
1969 Sid Mercer
1970 Heywood Broun
1971 Frank Graham
1972 Dan Daniel, Fred Lieb, J. Roy Stockton
1973 Warren Brown, John Drebinger, John F. Kieran
1974 John Carmichael, James Isaminger
1975 Tom Meany, Shirley Povich
1976 Harold Kaese, Red Smith
1977 Gordon Cobbledick, Edgar Munzel
1978 Tim Murnane, Dick Young
1979 Bob Broeg, Tommy Holmes
1980 Joe Reichler, Milton Richman
1981 Bob Addie, Allen Lewis
1982 Si Burick
1983 Ken Smith
1984 Joe McGuff
1985 Earl Lawson
1986 Jack Lang
1987 Jim Murray
1988 Bob Hunter, Ray Kelly
1989 Jerome Holtzman
1990 Phil Collier
1991 Ritter Collett
1992 Leonard Koppett, Bus Saidt
1993 Wendell Smith
1995 Joseph Durso
1996 Charley Feeney
1997 Sam Lacy
1998 Bob Stevens
1999 Hal Lebovitz
2000 Ross Newhan
2001 Joe Falls
2002 Hal McCoy
2003 Murray Chass
2004 Peter Gammons
2005 Tracy Ringolsby
2006 Rick Hummel
2008 Larry Whiteside
2009 Nick Peters

Appendix 3. Official Score of Baseball Centennial Game

OFFICIAL SCORE

OF BASEBALL CENTENNIAL GAME

CAVALCADE OF BASEBALL

Cooperstown, N. Y., June 12, 1939

MAJOR LEAGUES

Between

the Hans Wagner Team and the Eddie Collins Team

	THE WAGNERS	Pos.	AB	Runs	Hits	T.B.	2B	3B	H.R.	Sac. Hits	Bases on Balls	Hit by Pitcher	Runs Batted in	Stolen Bases	Strike outs	P.O.	A	E	D.P.
1	Wally Moses (Phila.-A)	rf	2	0	0	0	0	0	0	0	0	0	0	0	0	0	0	0	0
2	Terry Moore (St. Louis-N)	cf	1	0	0	0	0	0	0	0	0	0	0	1	1	0	0	0	
3	Arky Vaughn (Pitts.-N)	ss	2	1	1	2	1	0	0	0	1	0	0	0	0	3	3	1	1
4	Charley Gehringer (Det.-A)	2b	2	0	0	0	0	0	0	0	1	0	0	0	0	2	4	0	1
5	Joe Medwick (St. Louis-N)	lf	3	0	0	0	0	0	0	0	0	0	0	0	1	0	0	0	
6	Moe Berg (Bost.-A)	c														1	0	0	0
7	Frankie Hayes (Phila.-A)	c	2	1	1	2	1	0	0	0	0	1	0	0	2	0	0	0	
8	Herold Ruel (Chi.-A)	c	0	0	0	0	0	0	0	0	0	0	0	0	1	0	0	0	
9	Morrie Arnovich (Phila.-N)	cf	3	0	1	1	0	0	0	0	0	0	1	0	1	3	0	0	0
10	Jimmie Wilson (Cinn.-N)	1b	1	1	0	0	0	0	0	0	0	0	0	0	6	0	0	0	
11	Harry Lavagetto (Brook.-N)	1b	1	0	0	0	0	0	0	0	1	0	0	0	2	1	0	1	
12	Marvin Owen (Chi.-A)	3b	3	1	1	2	1	0	0	0	0	0	0	0	0	0	0	0	
13	Billy Jurges (N.Y.-N)	3b	2	0	0	0	0	0	0	0	0	0	0	0	0	0	0	0	
14	Bob Grove (Bost.-A)	P	0	0	0	0	0	0	0	0	0	0	0	0	0	0	0	0	
15	Vanny MacFayden (Bost.-N)	P	1	0	1	2	1	0	0	0	0	0	2	0	0	0	0	0	
16	Johnny Allen (Cleve.-A)	P	0	0	0	0	0	0	0	0	0	0	0	0	0	0	0	0	
17	s Babe Ruth		1	0	0	0	0	0	0	0	0	0	0	0	0	0	0	0	
18																			
19			23	4	5	9	4	0	0	0	3	0	4	0	3	21	8	1	

Passed Balls: No. left on Bases: 4 Number out when Winning run was scored:

s Batted for MacFayden in 5th inning. *t* Batted for in inning. *u* Batted for in inning.

v Batted for in inning. *y* Ran for in inning. *z* Ran for in inning.

Double Plays (Names) Vaughn, Gehringer to Lavagetto

Hit into Infield Double Plays (Names)

	THE COLLINS	Pos.	AB	Runs	Hits	T.B.	2B	3B	H.R.	Sac. Hits	Bases on Balls	Hit by Pitcher	Runs Batted in	Stolen Bases	Strike outs	P.O.	A	E	D.P.
1	Lloyd Waner (Pitts.-N)	cf	2	0	0	0	0	0	0	0	0	0	0	0	0	0	0	0	0
2	Rupert Thompson (St. Louis-A)	cf	1	0	0	0	0	0	0	0	1	0	0	0	0	0	0	0	
3	Billy Herman (Chi.-N)	2b	4	0	0	0	0	0	0	0	0	0	0	0	0	0	2	0	0
4	Mel Ott (N.Y.-N)	rf	4	0	1	1	0	0	0	0	0	0	0	2	0	0	0	0	
5	Hank Greenberg (Det.-A)	1b	2	1	2	2	0	0	0	0	1	0	0	0	9	2	0	1	
6	Geo. Selkirk (N.Y.-A)	rf	1	0	0	0	0	0	0	0	0	0	0	0	0	0	0	0	
7	Taft Wright (Wash.-A)	rf	2	1	1	1	0	0	0	0	0	0	0	1	1	0	0	0	
8	Arndt Jorgens (N.Y.-A)	c	3	0	1	1	0	0	0	0	0	0	1	0	0	5	1	0	1
9	Stanley Hack (Chi.-N)	3b	3	0	0	0	0	0	0	0	0	0	1	0	0	1	4	0	0
10	Cecil Travis (Wash.-A)	ss	1	0	0	0	0	0	0	0	0	0	0	0	0	0	0	0	
11	Eddie Miller (Bost.-N)	ss	2	0	1	2	1	0	0	0	0	0	0	1	1	0	0	0'	
12	Jerome "Dizzy" Dean (Chi.-N)	P	1	0	0	0	0	0	0	0	0	0	0	0	1	1	0	0	
13	Johnny VanderMeer (Cinn.-N)	P	0	0	0	0	0	0	0	0	0	0	0	0	0	0	1	1	
14	Sylvester Johnson (Phila.-N)	P	1	0	0	0	0	0	0	0	0	0	0	0	0	0	0	0	
15	s Jim Shilling (Cleve.-A)		1	0	1	1	0	0	0	0	0	0	0	0	0	0	0	0	
16																			

17																					
18																					
19				28	2	7	8	1	0	0	0	2	0	2	0	3	18	11	1		

Passed Balls:

No. left on Bases: 7

Number out when Winning run was scored:

1 Batted for JOHNSON in 7th inning. 2 Batted for ___ in ___ inning. x Batted for ___ in ___ inning.

v Batted for ___ in ___ inning. 1. Ran for ___ in ___ inning. 2. Ran for ___ in ___ inning.

Double Plays (Names) VANDERMEER, JORGENS, GREENBERG to JORGENS

Hit into Infield Double Plays (Names)

Score by Innings	1	2	3	4	5	6	7	8	9	10	11	12	13	14	15	16	17	18	19	Totals
WAGNERS	0	0	2	0	0	2	x													4
COLLINSES	0	0	0	0	0	2	0													2

PITCHER'S SUMMARY

Won	Pitcher	Club	Lost	Innings Pitched	Total Batters Facing Pitcher	Runs	Hits	Earned Runs	Sac. Hits	Bases on Balls	Hit Batsmen	Struck Out	Wild Pitches	Balls	Started	Finished
	DEAN	COLLINS		2	6	0	0	0	0	0	0	2	0	0	1	0
	VANDER MEER	"		1	7	2	2	1	0	2	0	0	0	0	0	0
	JOHNSON	"	1	3	13	2	3	2	0	1	0	1	2	0	0	1
	GROVE	WAGNERS		2	8	0	1	0	0	0	0	0	0	0	1	0
	MACFAYDEN	"		3	12	0	2	0	0	1	0	1	0	0	0	0
1	ALLEN	"		2	10	2	4	2	0	1	0	2	0	0	0	1

ALWAYS FILL IN

Men on Bases when ___ was relieved in ___ inning. No. Men Out

" " " ___ " " " ___ " " " " "

" " " ___ " " " ___ " " " " "

Weather Conditions: CLEAR - WARM   Ground Conditions: GOOD   Time: 1:40

Umpires: KLEM (N.L.), PLATE; ROMMEL (A.L.), BASES

Harold R. Hollis   Official Scorer

Hit Home Run with Bases Full

REMARKS

NOTE: "Total Batsmen Facing Pitcher" in the summary means the actual number of men who went up to bat, regardless of how they were put out or reached first. In order to check, add the Sacrifice Hits, Bases on Balls and Hit Batsmen to total of "At Bat" in the Box Score, which then should equal the "Total Batsmen Facing Pitcher."

Chapter Notes

Introduction

1. National Baseball Hal of Fame and Museum, Inc.: 1936–2009.
2. Jeff Idelson, "My Favorite Cooperstown Memory," *2005 Hall of Fame Yearbook*.
3. James, *Whatever Happened to the Hall of Fame?* pp. 65–69.
4. Vail, *Road to Cooperstown*, pp. 56, 107.
5. Cohen, *Hall of Fame or Hall of Shame?* pp. 23–24.
6. Koppett, *The Thinking Fan's Guide to Baseball*, p. 348.

Chapter 1

1. Block, *Baseball Before We Knew It*, p. 256.
2. Jeff Idelson, *Cooperstown Crier*, July 22, 2004.

Chapter 2

1. Vlasich, *Legend for the Legendary*, p. 31.
2. Ibid., pp. 34–35.
3. Lenny DiFranza, "The First Artifacts Donated to the Museum," *Memories and Dreams*, December 2006.
4. Holtzman, ed., *No Cheering in the Press Box*, p. 201.
5. Vlasich, *Legend for the Legendary*, p. 100.
6. Ibid., pp. 140–142.
7. Ibid., p. 225.
8. Nucciarone, *Alexander Cartwright: The Life Behind the Baseball Legend*, pp. 226–227.
9. Boston, *1939: Baseball's Tipping Point*, p. 199.
10. Vlasich, *Legend for the Legendary*, pp. 171–173.
11. Ibid. p. 175.
12. Reisler, *A Great Day in Cooperstown*, p. xiii.
13. Vlasich, *Legend for the Legendary*, p. 199.
14. Ibid. p. 167.
15. Boston, *1939: Baseball's Tipping Point*, pp. 240–241.

Chapter 3

1. Daniel Ginsburg, SABR Bio Project on Ty Cobb.
2. Pietrusza, Silverman, and Gershman, eds., *Baseball: Biographical Encyclopedia*, p. 569.

3. Fleitz, *More Ghosts in the Gallery*, pp. 3–4.
4. Jones, ed., *Deadball Stars of the American League*, p. 435.
5. Ibid., p. 390.
6. Light, *The Cultural Encyclopedia of Baseball*, p. 551.
7. Huhn, Provenzale, Goss, *SABR 2008 Baseball Research Journal*, pp. 19–20.
8. Pietrusza, Silverman, and Gershman, eds., *Baseball: Biographical Encyclopedia*, p. 590.
9. Herman, *Hall of Fame Players: Cooperstown*, p. 31.
10. Pietrusza, Silverman, and Gershman, eds. *Baseball: Biographical Encyclopedia*, p. 1064.
11. Candy Cummings, *1908 Baseball Magazine*.
12. Pietrusza, Silverman, and Gershman, eds., *Baseball: Biographical Encyclopedia*, p. 404.
13. Smith, *Baseball Hall of Fame*, p. 6.
14. Reisler, *A Great Day in Cooperstown*, p. 25.
15. Smith, *Baseball Hall of Fame*, p. 20.
16. Reisler, *A Great Day in Cooperstown*, p. 200.
17. Vlasich, *Legend for the Legendary*, p. 202.

Chapter 4

1. D'Amore, *Rogers Hornsby: A Biography*, p 125.
2. Simon, ed., *Deadball Stars of the National League*, p. 364.
3. Fleitz, *Ghosts in the Gallery*, p. 45.
4. Frommer, *Old-Time Baseball: America's Pastime in the Gilded Age*, p. 132.
5. Pietrusza, Silverman, and Gershman, eds., *Baseball: Biographical Encyclopedia*, p. 597.
6. Reidenbaugh and Hoppel, eds., *Cooperstown: Where the Legends Live Forever*, p. 245.
7. Fleitz, *More Ghosts in the Gallery*, p. 63.
8. *Hall of Fame Players— Cooperstown*, p. 167.
9. James Forr, *SABR Bio Project on Pie Traynor*.
10. Pietrusza, Silverman, and Gershman , eds., *Baseball: The Biographical Encyclopedia*, p. 404.
11. Ibid., p. 405.
12. Shirley Povich, "'Business Pressure' Kept Gehringer Away," *Sporting News*, June 22, 1949.

Chapter 5

1. *The Sporting News Presents Heroes of the Hall*, p. 359.

2. John Bennett, SABR Bio Project on Jimmie Foxx.

3. Pietrusza, Silverman, and Gershman, eds., *Baseball: The Biographical Encyclopedia*, p. 1197.

4. Light, *The Cultural Encyclopedia of Baseball*, p. 13.

5. *The Sporting News Presents Heroes of the Hall*, p. 421.

6. Pietrusza, Silverman, and Gershman, eds., *Baseball: the Biographical Encyclopedia*, p. 1256.

7. Smith, *Baseball Hall of Fame*, p. 88.

8. *The Sporting News Presents Heroes of the Hall*, p. 50.

9. Boston, *1939: The Tipping Point*, p. 184.

10. Christopher Devine, SABR Bio Project on Harry Wright.

11. *The Sporting News Heroes*, p. 447.

12. Ibid., p. 43.

13. Pietrusza, Silverman, and Gershman, eds., *Baseball: The Biographical Encyclopedia*, p. 688.

14. James, *The New Bill James Historical Baseball Abstract*, p. 374.

15. Engelberg, *DiMaggio: Setting the Record Straight*, p. 305.

16. Ibid.

17. Pietrusza, Silverman, and Gershman, eds., *Baseball: The Biographical Encyclopedia*, p. 249.

18. James, *The Bill James Guide to Baseball Managers from 1870 to Today*, p. 97.

19. Boston, *1939: The Tipping Point*, p. 121.

Chapter 6

1. James, *Whatever Happened to the Hall of Fame?*, p. 156.

2. James, *The New Bill James Historical Baseball Abstract*, p. 728.

3. Jeff Idelson, "An American Original: From Farm to Fame, He's a Legendary Feller," *2007 Hall of Fame Yearbook*.

4. Pietrusza, Silverman, and Gershman, eds., *Baseball: The Biographical Encyclopedia*, p. 759.

5. Interview with Dr. Susan Dellinger.

6. Robinson, *Promises to Keep*, p. 54.

7. Rampersad, *Jackie Robinson: A Biography*, p. 6.

8. Ibid., p. 7.

9. Fleitz, *Ghosts in the Gallery*, p. 136.

10. Ibid., p. 138.

11. Fleitz, *More Ghosts in the Gallery*, p. 90.

12. Simon, ed., *Deadball Stars of the National League*, p. 218.

13. Frommer, *Old-Time Baseball: America's Pastime in the Gilded Age*, p. 125.

14. James, *Whatever Happened to the Hall of Fame?*, p. 325.

15. *The Sporting News Presents Heroes of the Hall*, p. 472.

16. Light, *The Cultural Encyclopedia of Baseball*, p. 38.

17. Vincent, *The Last Commissioner: A Baseball Valentine*, pp. 14–15.

18. "Stengel, Williams Are Inducted," *The Freeman's Journal*, July 27, 1966.

19. Pietrusza, Silverman, and Gershman, eds., *Baseball: The Biographical Encyclopedia*, p. 938.

20. James, *The New Bill James Historical Baseball Abstract*, p. 754.

21. Light, *The Cultural Encyclopedia of Baseball*, p. 573.

22. Larry Ritter, *Baseball Quarterly*, Winter, 1977.

Chapter 7

1. Ralph Berger, SABR Bio Project on Earle Combs.

2. Hogan, *Shades of Glory*, p. xviii.

3. Fleitz, *Ghosts in the Gallery*, p. 152.

4. Bob Broeg, "Of Bad Days—For Chick and Others," *St. Louis Post-Dispatch*, January 30, 1968.

5. Mansch, *Life and Times of Rube Marquard*, p. 209.

6. Reidenbaugh and Hoppel, eds., *Cooperstown: Where the Legends Live Forever*, p. 249.

7. Connor, *Voices from Cooperstown*, p. 280.

8. Ibid., p. 281.

9. James, *The New Bill James Historical Baseball Abstract*, p. 891.

10. Ibid.

11. *The Sporting News Presents Heroes of the Hall*, p. 506.

12. Reidenbaugh and Hoppel, eds., *Cooperstown: Where the Legends Live Forever*, p. 354.

13. Barra, *Yogi Berra: Eternal Yankee*, p. 396.

14. Hogan, *Shades of Glory*, p. 278.

15. Reidenbaugh and Hoppel, eds., *Cooperstown: Where the Legends Live Forever*, p. 128.

16. Ibid.

17. Pietrusza, Silverman, and Gershman, eds., *Baseball: The Biographical Encyclopedia*, p. 212.

18. Ibid., p. 595.

19. Ibid., p. 74.

20. Irvin with Pepe, *Few and Chosen: Defining Negro Leagues Greatness*, p. 104.

21. Pietrusza, Silverman, and Gershman, eds., *Baseball: The Biographical Encyclopedia*, p. 567.

22. Ibid., p. 608.

23. James, *The New Bill James Historical Baseball Abstract*, p. 732.

24. Fleitz, *Ghosts in the Gallery*, p. 164.

25. Reidenbaugh and Hoppel, eds., *Cooperstown: Where the Legends Live Forever*, p. 198.v

26. Fleitz, *Ghosts in the Gallery*, p. 168.

27. Pietrusza, Silverman, and Gershman, eds., *Baseball: The Biographical Encyclopedia*, p. 528.

28. Ralph Berger, SABR Bio Project on Amos Rusie.

29. *The Sporting News Presents Heroes of the Hall*, p. 47.

30. Skipper, *Biographical Dictionary of the Baseball Hall of Fame*, p. 84.

31. Appel and Goldblatt, *Baseball's Best: The Hall of Fame Gallery*, p. 413.

32. Interviews with Peter Clarke and Catherine Walker.

33. John Saccoman, SABR Bio Project on Willie Mays.

34. Reidenbaugh and Hoppel, eds., *Cooperstown: Where the Legends Live Forever*, pp. 341–342.

Chapter 8

1. Connor, *Voices from Cooperstown*, p. 284.
2. *2008 Hall of Fame Yearbook*, p. 55.
3. Norm Miller, "Behind Baseball's Hall of Shame," *Family Weekly*, August 2, 1981.
4. Pietrusza, Silverman, and Gershman, eds., *Baseball: Biographical Encyclopedia*, p. 789.
5. Fred Down, "Quips and Quotes on Hall of Famers," *Ventura County* (Calif.) *Star Free Press*, August 1, 1982.
6. Vascellaro, *Hank Aaron, a Biography*, p. 142.
7. Pietrusza, Silverman, and Gershman, eds., *Baseball: Biographical Encyclopedia*, p. 954.
8. Frick, *Games, Asterisks and People*, p. 225.
9. Bill Madden, "Hall of Shame," New York *Daily News*, January 3, 1988.
10. Reidenbaugh and Hoppel, eds., *Cooperstown: Where the Legends Live Forever*, p. 259.
11. Stan Isle, "Venezuelans Sing for National Hero," *The Sporting News*, January 1984.
12. Fleitz, *More Ghosts in the Gallery*, p. 184.
13. Mark Armour, SABR Bio Project for Hoyt Wilhelm.
14. Reidenbaugh and Hoppel, eds., *Cooperstown: Where the Legends Live Forever*, p. 295.
15. Pietrusza, Silverman: Gershman, eds., *Baseball: Biographical Encyclopedia*, p. 672.
16. Skipper, *Biographical Dictionary for the Baseball Hall of Fame*, p. 186.
17. Reidenbaugh and Hoppel, eds., *Cooperstown: Where the Legends Live Forever*, p. 200.
18. Pietrusza, Silverman, and Gershman, eds., *Baseball: Biographical Encyclopedia*, p. 1229.
19. Irvin with Pepe, *Few and Chosen: Defining Negro Leagues Greatness*, p. 65.
20. Ibid., p. 67.
21. Joe Donnelly, "Joy, Sadness and an Appeal," *Newsday*, July 27, 1987.
22. Bill Madden, "Only the Truly 'Great' Players Belong," New York *Daily News*, January 14, 1988.
23. Phil Pepe, "Standards Have Eroded," New York *Daily News*, January 14, 1988.
24. Mike Shannon, *Spitball Magazine*, Fall 1989.
25. Ibid.

Chapter 9

1. *The Sporting News Presents Heroes of the Hall*, p. 363.
2. Reidenbaugh and Hoppel, eds., *Cooperstown: Where the Legends Live Forever*, p. 237.
3. Light, *Cultural Encyclopedia of Baseball*, p. 166.
4. Fred Glueckstein, SABR Bio Project on Tony Lazzeri.
5. Light, *Cultural Encyclopedia of Baseball*, p. 699.
6. Pietrusza, Silverman, and Gershman, eds., *Baseball: Biographical Encyclopedia*, p. 1015.
7. Charles Fruehling Springwood, "Mr. July," *Baseball Hall of Fame's Memories and Dreams*, October 1993.

8. Pietrusza, Silverman, and Gershman, eds., *Baseball: Biographical Encyclopedia*, p. 947.
9. Ibid., p. 318.
10. Light, *The Cultural Encyclopedia of Baseball*, p. 167.
11. Shannon, *Tales from the Dugout*, p. 162.
12. Zimniuch, *Richie Ashburn Remembered*, pp. 64–74.
13. Reidenbaugh and Hoppel, eds., *Cooperstown: Where the Legends Live Forever*, p. 155.
14. Koppett, *The Thinking Fan's Guide to Baseball*, pp. 350–352.
15. Jim Wojtanik, "Willis Takes His Place Amongst Greats," Oneonta *Daily Star*, July 28, 1995.
16. James, *The New Bill James Historical Baseball Abstract*, p. 538.
17. Irvin with Pepe, *Few and Chosen: Defining Negro Leagues Greatness*, p. 132.
18. *2009 Hall of Fame Yearbook*, p. 73.
19. Herman, *Hall of Fame Players: Cooperstown*, p. 189.
20. Jeff Mills, "Ashburn Was a Whiz at Leading Off," Oneonta *Daily Star*, July 28, 1995.
21. *The Sporting News Presents Heroes of the Hall*, p. 180.
22. Hogan, *Shades of Glory*, p. 296.
23. Rick Carpiniello, "Book Recalls Championship Season," *The Journal News*, May 24, 2009.
24. Owen S. Good, "It Doesn't Hurt to Have a Fan Cheering for You," Oneonta *Daily Star*, March 4, 1998.
25. Herman, *Hall of Fame Players: Cooperstown*, p. 290.
26. Hogan, *Shades of Glory*, p. 118.
27. Light, *The Cultural Encyclopedia of Baseball*, p. 803.
28. Fleitz, *More Ghosts in the Gallery*, p. 204.
29. Reidenbaugh and Hoppel, eds., *Cooperstown: Where the Legends Live Forever*, p. 281.

Chapter 10

1. Fleitz, *Ghosts in the Gallery*, p. 227.
2. James, *The New Bill James Historical Baseball Abstract*, p. 437.
3. Dave Hyde, "Perez's Courage Unique in Hall of Fame," South Florida *Sun-Sentinel*, July 21, 2000.
4. Chafets, *Cooperstown Confidential*, pp. 91–94.
5. Fleitz, *More Ghosts in the Gallery*, p. 222.
6. Pietrusza, Silverman, and Gershman, eds., *Baseball: The Biographical Encyclopedia*, p. 733.
7. Ralph Berger, SABR Bio Project on Hilton Smith.
8. Shannon, *More Tales from the Dugout*, pp. 101–104.
9. Gene Carney, *Shadows of Cooperstown: Observations from Outside the Line*, Note 243, August 7, 2001.
10. Pietrusza, Silverman, and Gershman, eds., *Baseball: The Biographical Encyclopedia*, p. 1051.
11. Shannon, *More Tales from the Dugout*, pp. 83–84.
12. "Baseball Hall of Fame Balloting, 2005," Wikipedia, p. 4.

13. Ibid., p. 5.
14. David Haugh, "A Place to Preach? Sandberg Uses Hall Speech to Make a Point," Chicago *Tribune*, July 29, 2006.
15. Ibid.
16. Ibid.
17. Irvin with Pepe, *Few and Chosen: Defining Negro Leagues Greatness*, p. 152.
18. James, *The New Bill James Historical Baseball Abstract*, p. 371.
19. Hogan, *Shades of Glory*, p. 355.
20. Ibid., p.144.
21. Ibid., p. 320.
22. Irvin with Pepe, *Few and Chosen: Defining Negro Leagues Greatness*, p. 24.
23. Hogan, *Shades of Glory*, p. xxxi.
24. Justice B. Hall, "Statue of Paige a Moving Tribute," MLB.com, July 28, 2006.
25. Ibid.
26. James, *The New Bill James Historical Baseball Abstract*, p. 683.
27. Hogan, *Shades of Glory*, p. 356.
28. Ibid., p. 262.
29. "Baseball Hall of Fame Balloting, 2007," Wikipedia, p. 4.
30. Ibid., p. 5.
31. Ibid.
32. Mark Newman, "Hall of Fame Welcomes Two Class Acts," MLB.com, July 29, 2007.
33. Barry Bloom, "The Impossible Dream: Williams Finds Place Among Elite," *2008 Hall of Fame Yearbook*.
34. Dave Anderson, "Time Doesn't Relieve the Pain, or Change the Facts," *New York Times*, September 30, 2007.
35. Barry Bloom, "Veterans Elect '40s Star Gordon to Hall," MLB.com, December 8, 2008.
36. Bob Nightengale, "Henderson Steals Show," *USA Today*, July 27, 2009.

Afterword

1. "Baseball Hall of Fame balloting, 2007," Wikipedia, p. 3.
2. Ibid.
3. Ibid.
4. Associated Press, "Writers Discuss Steroids," July 15, 2009.
5. Kevin Kernan, "Baseball Shrine a Hall Lot Better," *New York Post*, May 4, 2008.

Bibliography

Books

Adomites, Paul, et al. *Cooperstown: Baseball's Hall of Famers*. Lincolnwood, IL: Publications International, 1999.

Appel, Martin, and Burt Goldblatt. *Baseball's Best: The Hall of Fame Gallery*. New York: McGraw-Hill, 1977.

Barra, Allen. *Yogi Berra: Eternal Yankee*. New York: Norton, 2009.

Block, David. *Baseball Before We Knew It: A Search for the Roots of the Game*. Lincoln: University of Nebraska Press, 2005.

Boston, Talmadge. *1939: Baseball's Tipping Point*. Albany, TX: Bright Sky Press, 2005.

Chafets, Zev. *Cooperstown Confidential: Heroes, Rogues and the Inside Story of the Baseball Hall of Fame*. New York: Bloomsburg, 2009.

Cohen, Robert. *Baseball's Hall of Fame or Hall of Shame?* Las Vegas: Cardoza, 2009.

Connor, Anthony J. *Voices from Cooperstown: Baseball's Hall of Famers Tell It Like It Was*. New York: Galahad Books, 1982.

D'Amore, Jonathan. *Rogers Hornsby: A Biography*. Westport, CT: Greenwood Press, 2004.

Engelberg, Morris, and Marv Schneider. *DiMaggio: Setting the Record Straight*. St. Paul: MBI, 2003.

Fleitz, David L. *Ghosts in the Gallery at Cooperstown: Sixteen Little-Known Members of the Hall of Fame*. Jefferson, NC: McFarland, 2004.

_____. *More Ghosts in the Gallery: Another Sixteen Little-Known Greats at Cooperstown*. Jefferson, NC: McFarland, 2007.

Frick, Ford. *Games, Asterisks and People: Memoirs of a Lucky Fan*. New York: Crown, 1973.

Frommer, Harvey. *Old-Time Baseball: America's Pastime in the Gilded Age*. Lanham, MD: Taylor, 2006.

Gafur, Rudy. *Cooperstown Is My Mecca*. Delhi, Ontario: NCC, 1995.

Gillette, Gary, and Pete Palmer, eds. *The ESPN Encyclopedia*. 5th ed. New York: Sterling, 2008.

Herman, Bruce. *Hall of Fame Players: Cooperstown*. Lincolnwood, IL: Publications International, 2005.

Hogan, Lawrence. *Shades of Glory: The Negro Leagues and the Story of African-American Baseball*. Washington, DC: National Geographic Society, 2006.

Holtzman, Jerome, ed. *No Cheering in the Press Box*. New York: Holt, Rinehart and Winston, 1973.

Irvin, Monte, with Phil Pepe. *Few and Chosen: Defining Negro Leagues Greatness*. Chicago: Triumph Books, 2007.

James, Bill. *The Bill James Guide to Baseball Managers from 1870 to Today*. New York: Scribner's, 1997.

_____. *The New Bill James Historical Baseball Abstract*. New York: Free Press, 2001.

_____. *Whatever Happened to the Hall of Fame? Baseball, Cooperstown and the Politics of Glory*. New York: Fireside Press, 1995.

Jones, David, ed., and the Deadball Era Committee of The Society for American Baseball Research. *Deadball Stars of the American League*. Washington, DC: Potomac Books, 2006.

Kellogg, David. *True Stories of Baseball's Hall of Famers*. San Mateo, CA: Bluewood Books, 2000.

Koppett, Leonard. *The Thinking Fan's Guide to Baseball*. Wilmington, DE: Sports Media, 2004.

Kuhn, Bowie. *Hardball: The Education of a Baseball Commissioner*. Lincoln: University of Nebraska Press, 1987.

Light, Jonathan Fraser. *The Cultural Encyclopedia of Baseball*. 2nd ed. Jefferson, NC: McFarland, 2005.

Mansch, Larry D. *Rube Marquard: The Life and Time of a Baseball Hall of Famer*. Jefferson, NC: McFarland, 1998.

Nucciarone, Monica. *Alexander Cartwright: The Life Behind the Baseball Legend*. Lincoln: University of Nebraska Press, 2009.

Okrent, Daniel, and Steve Wulf. *Baseball Anecdotes*. New York: Oxford University Press, 1989.

Olney, Buster. *The Last Night of the Yankee Dynasty*. New York: HarperCollins, 2004.

Pietrusza, David, Matthew Silverman, and Michael Gershman, eds. *Baseball: The Biographical Encyclopedia*. Kingston, NY: Total/Sports Illustrated, 2000.

Purdy, Dennis. *The Team by Team Encyclopedia of Major League Baseball*. New York: Workman, 2006.

Rampersad, Arnold. *Jackie Robinson: A Biography*. New York: Knopf, 1997.

Reidenbaugh, Lowell, Joe Hoppel, and the editors of *The Sporting News. Baseball's Hall of Fame — Cooperstown: When the Legends Live Forever.* New York: Gramercy Press, 2001.

Reisler, Jim. *A Great Day in Cooperstown: The Improbable Birth of Baseball's Hall of Fame.* New York: Carroll and Graf, 2006.

Ritter, Lawrence S. *The Glory of Their Times: The Story of the Early Days of Baseball Told by the Men Who Played It.* Enlarged ed. New York: Perennial Books, 2002.

Robinson, Sharon. *Promises to Keep: How Jackie Robinson Changed America.* New York: Scholastic Press, 2004.

Shannon, Mike. *More Tales from the Dugout.* New York: McGraw-Hill, 2004.

_____. *Tales from the Dugout.* Lincolnwood, IL: Contemporary Books, 1997.

Simon, Tom, ed., and the Deadball Era Committee of the Society for American Baseball Research. *Deadball Stars of the National League.* Washington, DC: Brassey's, 2004.

Skipper, John. *A Biographical Dictionary of the Baseball Hall of Fame.* Jefferson, NC: McFarland, 2000.

Smith, Ken. *Baseball's Hall of Fame.* Rev. ed. New York: Grosset and Dunlap, 1970.

Spatz, Lyle, ed. *The SABR Baseball List and Record Book: Baseball's Most Fascinating Records and Unusual Statistics.* New York: Scribner's, 2007.

Sporting News. *Official Major League Baseball Fact Book.* 2004 ed. St. Louis: Sporting News Books, 2004.

_____. *Sporting News Presents Heroes of the Hall: Baseball's All Time Best.* St. Louis: Sporting News Books, 2002.

Sugar, Bert Randolph, with Bruce Curtis. *Bert Sugar's Baseball Hall of Fame: A Living History of America's Greatest Game.* Philadelphia: Running Press, 2009.

Vail, James. *The Road to Cooperstown: A Critical History of Baseball's Hall of Fame Selection Process.* Jefferson, NC: McFarland, 2001.

Valenti, Dan. *Baseball Comes Home: A History of the Baseball Hall of Fame Game — 1940–2008.* Richfield Springs, NY: CR, 2008.

Vascellaro, Charlie. *Hank Aaron: A Biography.* Westport, CT: Greenwood Press, 2005.

Vecsey, George. *Baseball: A History of America's Favorite Game.* New York: Modern Library, 2006.

Vincent, Fay. *The Last Commissioner: A Baseball Valentine.* New York: Simon & Schuster, 2002.

Vlasich, James A. *A Legend for the Legendary: The Origin of the Baseball Hall of Fame.* Bowling Green, OH: Bowling Green State University Popular Press, 1990.

Zimniuch, Fran. *Richie Ashburn Remembered.* Champaign, IL: Sports Publishing, 2005.

Newspapers

Albany Times Union
Chicago Tribune
Cooperstown Crier
Freeman's Journal
Hartford Courant
Journal News
New York Daily News
New York Post
New York Times
Newsday
Oneonta Daily Star
Pittsburgh Courier
Richmond Times-Dispatch
St. Louis Post Dispatch
San Diego Union
Schenectady Gazette
Sports Weekly
Sun Sentinel
Syracuse Post Standard
USA Today
Utica Observer Dispatch
Ventura County Star and Free Press

Magazines

Baseball Magazine
Baseball Quarterly
Baseball Today
Ebony
Family Weekly
SABR Baseball Research Journal
Saturday Evening Post
Spitball
The Sporting News
Sports Collectors Digest
Sports Illustrated
Hall of Fame Publications
Hall of Fame Newsletter
Hall of Fame Yearbook
Memories and Dreams Magazine

Internet Sites

Major League Baseball.com (MLB.com)
National Baseball Hall of Fame and Museum (http://www.baseballhalloffame.org)
Notes from the Shadows of Cooperstown and Observations from Outside the Lines (http://www.baseballlibrary.com)
Society for American Baseball Research (SABR) (http://www.SABR.org)
The Sporting News (http://www.sportingnews.com)
Wikipedia Encyclopedia (http://en.wikipedia.org/wiki)

Index

Numbers in **bold italics** indicate pages with photographs.